INFORMATION SYSTEMS

a BUSINESS APPROACH

3RD EDITION

INFORMATION SYSTEMS

SYSTEMS

a BUSINESS APPROACH

3RD EDITION

steve BENSON
Edith Cowan University

craig STANDING
Edith Cowan University

WILEY

John Wiley & Sons Australia, Ltd

Third edition published 2008 by
John Wiley & Sons Australia, Ltd
42 McDougall Street, Milton Qld 4064

First edition published 2002
Second edition published 2005

Typeset in 10.5/12.5 pt Times

National Library of Australia
Cataloguing-in-Publication data

Benson, Steve.
Information systems: a business approach.

   3rd ed.
   Bibliography.
   Includes index.
   ISBN 978 0 470 81344 7 (pbk.).

   1. Management information systems. 2. Information
   resources management. I. Standing, Craig. II. Title.

658.40380285

Typeset in India by Aptara
Layout by Wiley Composition Services

Printed in China by
Printplus Limited

10 9 8 7 6 5 4 3 2 1

Contents

Preface   xi

About the authors   xiv

Acknowledgements   xiv

▶ Chapter 1

Setting the scene   1

Introduction   2
Three waves of knowledge   2
Data, information and knowledge   3
What is a system?   5
What is an information system?   6
   The history of information systems   6
What is an information system for?   8
The relationship of information systems to
other disciplines   9
   Information systems or information
   technology?   9
   Is information systems management a subset
   of management?   10
Technology and business trends   11
   Reducing market entry costs   13
   Tactical and strategic links   14
   Changing the way people work   14
   Business process re-engineering (BPR)   14
Aspects of competition: competitive
forces   15
   Technology convergence   17
   E-commerce   18
   Proliferation of technology and
   communication   19
   Moving to a knowledge economy   19
Business pressures and responses   20
Direct and indirect benefits of information
systems   21
Why study information systems?   23
   Information systems and the marketing
   major   23
   Information systems and the accounting and
   finance majors   23
   Information systems and management   24
   Enterprise resource planning (ERP)   24
Making technology manageable   25
Keeping up to date   26
Summary   26
Questions   26
Exercises   27
CASE STUDY: Parking
is such sweet sorrow   28
References   29

▶ Chapter 2

Business software   31

Introduction   32
The history and nature of software   32
   Vaucanson   32
   Jacquard   33
   Babbage   33
   Hollerith   33
   Summary of computing's historical
   progression   34
Generations of software   34
   First-generation languages   35
   Second-generation languages   35
   Third-generation languages   35
   The software crisis   36
   Fourth-generation languages   36
   Fifth-generation languages   37
Contrasting hardware and software   37
An introduction to contemporary
software   39
   Applications software   40
   Systems software   44
   Communications software   47
The nature of competition in the software
industry   47
   The step–lock cycle   47
   The graphical user interface   47
   Apple and Microsoft   49
   Linux   50
   How communications software can break the
   step–lock cycle   50
Common horizontal applications
software   51
   Email and browser software   52

Document management   52
Project management and scheduling   52
Evaluating horizontal software   52
**Packaged, customised and custom built:
strategic and tactical implications   53**
Packaged software   54
Customised software   54
Custom software   54
**The relationship among systems software,
applications software and hardware   56**
Intelligent agents   56
Intelligent agent applications   58
The future of intelligent agents   59
Open source vs proprietary software   59

Summary   61
Questions   62
Exercises   63
CASE STUDY: Mervyn's garden
centres   63
References   65

> **Chapter 3**

Business information
systems   67

Introduction   68
Transaction-processing systems   69
Batch and real-time systems   70
Transaction-processing systems
summary   72
Databases   73
Methods of data organisation   75
Management information systems   79
Management reporting system   80
Decision support system   81
Decision support and data warehouses   82
Expert systems   83
Executive information system   85
Groupware   87
Putting things into context   92

Summary   93
Questions   94
Exercises   94
CASE STUDY: Boomer's
Fitness   95
References   97

> **Chapter 4**

Communication and
networks   98

Introduction   99
Digital and analog information   99
Digital and analog signalling   100
Digital and analog communication   101
Asynchronous and synchronous
communication   103
Communication modes   104
Circuit and packet switching   104
Communications media   105
More on optical fibres   106
Communications networks   107
WANs and LANs   108
Cellular and wireless communications   109
Differences between LANs and WANs   112
Metropolitan area networks   112
Other reasons for networking   113
Basic local area networking technology   114
PC network interface card   114
Cabling   114
Interconnection devices   115
Network operating system   115
Ethernet   116
Satellites   116
Advantages of satellites   116
Disadvantages of satellites   117
The Internet   117
Internet access   119
Intranets   120
Extranets   121
Client–server issues   121
TCP/IP and DNS explained   122
Threats to networks   123
Firewalls   123
Proxy servers   124
Firewalls, intelligent switches and virtual
networks   126
Future developments   127
Discussion   128

Summary   129
Questions   129
Exercises   130
CASE STUDY: You ain't seen
nothing yet   131
References   134

▶ Chapter 5

Systems integration: information systems at work   135

Introduction   136
Information systems management — centralised or distributed?   136
  Centralised information systems organisation   136
  Distributed information systems organisation   137
  Hybrid information systems organisation   138
Funding the information systems function   138
  Unallocated cost centre   138
  Allocated cost centre   139
  Profit centre   139
Some information systems job descriptions   139
  Chief information officer (CIO)   140
  Systems manager/operations manager   141
  Database administrator   141
  Network administrator/manager   141
  Solutions architect   141
  Project architect/applications development manager   142
  Project manager   142
  Web manager/administrator   142
  Systems analyst/business analyst   142
  Programmer   143
  Chief technology officer   143
  Training officer   144
Outsourcing   144
  Advantages of outsourcing   145
  Disadvantages of outsourcing   145
  What to consider when outsourcing   146
  Outsourcing: the current picture   148
Islands of information and proprietary systems   148
  Open systems   149
Systems integration   150
Enterprisewide client–server architecture   151
Extended ERP systems   152

ERP and small-to-medium entities (SMEs)   154
Application service providers   154
Problems with introducing ERP or other changes   157
Summary   158
Questions   159
Exercises   159
CASE STUDY: Toy Time   160
References   162

▶ Chapter 6

Introduction to systems development   163

Introduction   164
The systems development environment   164
The systems development lifecycle (SDLC)   164
The skills required by systems analysts   168
  Communication and interpersonal skills   168
  Analytical and problem-solving skills   168
  Technical skills   169
The tasks involved in each stage of systems development   169
  Information systems planning   169
  Feasibility phase   170
  Analysis phase   171
  Requirements phase   172
  The role of CASE   173
  Alternative solutions phase   173
  Design phase   174
  Hardware and software acquisition   176
  Implementation   177
  Testing   178
  Systems conversion   178
  Maintenance   179
  The lifecycle for small systems   179
Information gathering   180
Systems modelling   181
  Data modelling   182
  Entity relationship diagrams (ERDs)   182
  Data analysis   185
  Process modelling   188
  Data dictionary entries   192
  Decision tables   193
  Structured English   193

Systems development methodologies 194
  Behavioural methodologies 195
**Examples of information systems
methodologies 195**
  Information engineering 195
  Object-oriented methodology 195
  Prototyping 198
  Feasibility prototyping 199
  Requirements prototyping 199
  Design prototyping 199
  Implementation prototyping 199
  Rapid application development (RAD) 199
  Agile software development 200
  Soft systems methodology (SSM) 200

Summary 202
Questions 202
Exercises 202
CASE STUDY: Content
management systems at
Kromann Reumert 203
References 204

Exercises 226
CASE STUDY: AP Consulting
Group 226
References 227

Chapter 7

Strategic information systems management 205

Introduction 206
The importance of strategy 206
**Information systems and IT as a strategic
driver of the business 208**
**Information systems management in
organisations 208**
The role of strategic planning 209
Strategic analysis approaches 212
  Competitive analysis 213
  Information architecture 216
  Alignment of information systems with
  business goals 217
  Business process re-engineering (BPR) 218
  Using value-chain analysis for strategic
  analysis 219
  Outsourcing as an information systems
  strategy 220
Resource-based strategies 222

Summary 225
Questions 225

Chapter 8

Managing the information systems function 228

Introduction 229
**Managing people and relationships in the
information systems function 229**
  Managing information systems
  professionals 231
  Managing internal and external
  relationships 231
**The role of power, politics and culture in
information systems 231**
Innovation and creativity 233
**Managing information systems
operations 233**
**Information systems continuity planning and
security management 236**
  Security risk analysis 237
  Physical security 237
  Software security 238
Data privacy 240
**Managing projects and development
teams 240**
  Senior executive support 240
  Assessing the organisation's
  requirements 241
  Defining the scope of the project 241
  Assessing the most worthwhile projects 241
  Being wary of changing requirements 241
  Blending team-member skills 241
  Setting realistic targets 241
Assessing project risks 242
  Risk identification 242
  Risk assessment 242
  Risk response 243
  Risk reassessment 243
Monitoring project progress 243
  Corrective action 245
Using charts in project management 245
**The capability maturity model for
software 248**

Summary 249

Questions 250

Exercises 250

CASE STUDY: A nightmare project 250

References 252

Chapter 9

E-business 253

Introduction 254
E-business opportunities 254
Types of systems 256
Business-to-consumer e-business 256
Consumer-to-consumer e-business 257
Business-to-business e-business 257
Intranets 259
E-business as a strategic driver 259
E-business models 261
Website functionality 261
Organisational structure 262
Organisational management 262
Other business model components 262
Effective e-business models 262
E-business strategies 262
Marketing and advertising on the Internet 262
Retailing on the Web 264
Customer service and support on the Web 266
Environmental scanning 267
B2B e-business 267
E-marketplaces 268
Intra-organisational systems 272
Virtual organisations 272
E-government 273
Strategic concepts related to e-business 273
Creative destruction 274
Channel conflict 274
Disintermediation 274
Global strategy 275
Summary 276
Questions 276

Exercises 276

CASE STUDY: Westsea Airport's Web strategy 277

Reference 279

Chapter 10

Web commerce development 280

Introduction 281
Characteristics of web applications 281
History of the Internet 282
Web technologies 282
Browsers 283
Search engines 283
Hypertext and hyperlinks 283
HTTP 283
Websites 284
Web addresses 284
Mobile commerce 284
Web authoring tools 285
Assessing the feasibility of adopting web commerce 287
Project complexity and scope 287
Defining the users 289
Working with different cultures and languages 290
Design issues for web commerce 291
Web accessibility issues 292
Evolution of website designs 293
Techniques for marketing and attracting visitors to sites 299
Online communities 299
Online customer interaction and involvement 300
Building trust online 301
Measuring the effectiveness of the website 303
Summary 304
Questions 304
Exercises 305
CASE STUDY: Colours of Spain 305
References 308

Chapter 11

Information systems infrastructure 309

Introduction **310**
What is infrastructure? **310**
A brief history of the computer **311**
   Generation one: valves (1946–59) — transforming business processes **311**
   Generation two: transistors (1959–64) — transforming organisations **311**
   Generation three: integrated circuits (1965–71) — transforming markets **313**
   Generation four: very large-scale integration (1971–present) — transforming society **313**
Types of computers in current use **313**
   Supercomputers **314**
   Mainframes **314**
   Minicomputers **314**
   Workstations **314**
   Microcomputers or PCs **314**
   Handheld and wearable computers **315**
   Blade servers **316**
The architecture of the modern computer **317**
   Measuring memory capacity and processor speeds **317**
   An overview of the system unit **319**
   How programs run **320**
   Problems with the von Neumann architecture **321**
More on PC system components **321**
   Input devices **321**
   Processors **322**
   Faster computers **322**
   Output devices **323**
   Primary storage **325**
   Secondary storage devices and media **325**
Moore's law **328**
How to buy a PC **328**
Buying hardware for business systems **330**
   Expression of interest **331**
   Offloading problems **332**
The importance of hardware standards **333**

Information systems and IT governance **333**
   Information systems and IT governance and help desks **334**
Summary **335**
Questions **335**
Exercises **336**
CASE STUDY: Westralian Insurance Brokers **337**
References **339**

Chapter 12

Personal productivity with information systems 340

Introduction **341**
Skills needed in the knowledge economy **341**
   Research and information gathering **341**
   Planning **342**
   Processing information **342**
   Creativity and problem solving **343**
   Communication **343**
Using personal information systems and IT **343**
Information overload and personal information systems **346**
   Developing a personal information system **349**
Email **350**
   Speed **350**
   Cost **351**
   Accountability **351**
   Conferencing **351**
   Security **351**
Personal and professional ethics **352**
Ergonomics **355**
   Physical issues **355**
   Psychological issues **355**
Summary **356**
Questions **357**
Exercises **357**
CASE STUDY: Mandy's information overload **357**
References **359**

Glossary **361**
Index **373**

Information Systems: A Business Approach third edition has been developed and organised for:

> students, professionals, managers, accountants and other professional groups who require a foundation in information systems with a business emphasis

> undergraduate courses in which there is an information systems component of study

> undergraduate courses in computer science in which a business approach to information systems is required

> postgraduate courses in which there is a foundation-level unit in information systems

> master of business administration (MBA) courses in which there is an information systems component

> professional-level courses in information systems and information technology (IT).

This text forms the basis for lecture, seminar and tutorial materials and can be used in standard, online and flexible delivery modes.

Why we wrote the book

There are many foundation-level textbooks on information systems and IT, so why have we written another? We argue that our book is different. It provides a business perspective on information systems and emphasises how information systems can be used to improve the strategic, tactical and operational performance of business.

It is important to realise that information systems are not merely supporting technology for business operations, but are major competitive forces in their own right and drivers for organisational change. These themes recur throughout the text and are examined in depth in our coverage of e-commerce.

Another major difference is our emphasis on principles. Our text highlights core principles of business and information systems and illustrates them using regional and global examples. In a world in which technology and business environments change rapidly, it is important to focus on developing transferable skills that can be applied to new problems and situations as they arise. In all our dealings with information systems consultants and employers, we found this to be a constant theme: a sound knowledge of business and information systems principles, adaptability and flexibility, and good communication skills are prerequisites for success.

We have updated many of the examples and case studies for the third edition of the book. We have also expanded coverage of information systems ethics, information systems governance, data modelling and analysis, wireless networks and object-oriented development. A new chapter called 'Information systems infrastructure' has been added that includes information on hardware.

Our target audience has not changed since we wrote the first edition. However, we have been pleased to note that the book has found its way into businesses and consulting houses in different parts of the world, confirming its relevance to professional practice.

Key features of the book

Before writing this book, we undertook an extensive review of information systems curricula in universities and colleges in Australia, Europe and the United States. Each of the resulting

12 chapters was developed and modified in close consultation with academics and students. Our intention was to produce a book that was applicable and adaptable to a wide variety of course structures. The book incorporates the following useful features:

> *Principles:* The key principles of the information systems discipline are highlighted throughout. These provide a solid foundation for new students so that they can gain an understanding of the concept and the principle behind it, as well as examples of it in practice; that is, teach through principles — support by examples.

> *Reflection questions:* In accordance with the principles of good cognitive design, each chapter includes questions closely associated with their related concepts. These often relate to the reader's personal observations or extra options not covered in the text. These questions can form the basis of research exercises or be used as rhetorical questions to stimulate the reader's thought processes for a few seconds. Accordingly, the book actively engages readers in learning.

> *IS in action:* The 'IS in Action' boxes provide up-to-date illustrations of how real-world organisations are using information systems to increase productivity, reduce costs or gain competitive advantage. They serve as a mechanism to show the concepts in practice in the business environment, and allow students to look through a window to the professional world of information systems. The companies and situations chosen reflect the global nature of information systems and information technology and highlight best practice on a world scale. Once information systems skills and knowledge have been gained, those same skills are in demand internationally.

> *Infobytes:* Each chapter includes 'Infobytes': concise, up-to-date examples of the latest technologies and developments related to the information systems profession.

> *Key concepts:* These short statements are embedded into each chapter and provide insight and advice from a practitioner's perspective.

> *Case studies:* At the end of each chapter, a case study focuses on the concepts and principles emphasised in that chapter. The case studies can be used as individual exercises or as the basis of tutorial sessions using group work to discuss the various issues that arise from the material. Each case has key questions that can be used to start the analysis. The case studies encourage the development of metacognition and communication skills in students.

> *Questions:* Each chapter has questions designed to help revise the chapter's material. These can be used to test students' knowledge and understanding of each chapter.

> *Exercises:* These provide tasks to be completed by students to consolidate understanding of the principles or to gather and analyse additional information. The exercises can form the basis of a tutorial or laboratory session.

Organisation of the book

The text divides into two sections. The first five chapters introduce students to the various components of information systems within a business context, including software, networking, systems integration, enterprise resource planning and knowledge management.

The second part of the text covers the development and management issues related to information systems and e-business. A major feature of the book is its coverage of e-business strategy and development. These are given considerable emphasis because they are such an important part of the many organisational transformations that are taking place.

The last chapter examines the topic of personal information management, which is relevant to students and practitioners alike. Although organisational information systems have made great progress, the individuals in organisations are often drowning in a sea of information. This chapter examines the tools, methods and techniques that can be used to operate effectively on a personal level in business.

We are confident that you will find this text readable and relevant.

Steve Benson and Craig Standing
August 2007

About the authors

Steve Benson

Dr Steve Benson is currently a senior lecturer in management information systems at Edith Cowan University in Western Australia. He holds a first-class honours degree in computer science and geology and a master of science in systems design from the University of Manchester. He completed a doctorate of philosophy at Curtin University in Western Australia, where he researched teaching excellence in information systems.

Steve has worked as an analyst and software developer in real-time and business systems and has more than 20 years' experience in tertiary education, including periods as head of department and school. His background also includes motor vehicle engineering, management, geology and computer science. He has published at international conferences and in international journals. Steve maintains a small but active consultancy, providing specialist services to education and industry in Australia and Canada, and is a member of both the Internet Society and the IEEE.

Craig Standing

Craig Standing is currently professor in strategic information systems in the School of Management and Information Systems at Edith Cowan University in Western Australia. He completed a master of science in computation at the University of Manchester Institute of Science and Technology, and a doctor of philosophy at the University of Western Australia. He is a member of the British Computer Society and the Australian Computer Society.

Craig has an international reputation in the field of management information systems, has published widely in leading journals and has presented his work at conferences worldwide. He is a consultant to local and international companies in the private and public sectors, specialising in information systems strategy and knowledge management.

Acknowledgements

The authors and publisher would like to thank the following copyright holders, organisations and individuals for permission to reproduce copyright material in this book.

Images
• fig. 1.1: Watson, Richard T 2006, 'Data management', *Databases and organizations*, John Wiley & Sons, Inc., p. 25 • fig. 1.4: Haag, Stephen 2005, *Management information systems for the information age*, McGraw-Hill, p. 242 • fig. 1.5: © Chris Anderson. www.thelongtail.com • fig. 2.1: Screen shots reprinted by permission from Microsoft Corporation • fig. 2.3: Bootstrap Alliance/Douglas Engelbart • fig. 4.3: © Bryan Christie Design • fig. 6.3, fig. 6.4, fig. 6.9: © Knowledge Base • fig. 8.5: Special permission to reproduce 'Capability Maturity Model', © 2000 by Carnegie Mellon University, is granted by the Software Engineering Institute • fig. 9.5: Screenshot reproduced with the permission of eBay Inc. © EBAY INC. All rights reserved • fig. 10.2: © IBM • fig. 10.5: © Optus • fig. 12.2: © John Wiley & Sons Australia/ Taken by Kari-Ann Tapp.

Text

• p. 244: © iStart Publishing. www.istart.co.nz • pp. 305–7: © Crown copyright 2007 • p. 354: © Hong Kong Computer Society www.hkcs.org.hk • p. 234: 'Harnessing brainwaves', by Ian Grayson, *The Australian*, 24 October 2006 • pp. 298–9: Matt Mickiewicz, www.sitepoint.com • p. 258: This case is reproduced with permission of Nortel Networks www.nortel.com. 'Supporting healthcare to make telemedicine a reality', Copyright © 2005 Nortel Networks. All rights reserved • p. 302: Barnes, SJ and Vidgen, R 2002, 'An integrative approach to the assessment of e-commerce quality', *Journal of Electronic Commerce Research*, vol. 3, no. 3 • pp. 215–16: US Patent and Trademark Office, Department of Commerce. http://www.uspto.gov/go/cio/sitp/OCIO_SITP_FY05.pdf, p. 1 • p. 209: Woodside Energy Ltd.

Every effort has been made to trace ownership of copyright material. Information that will help to rectify any error or omission in subsequent editions will be welcome. In such cases, please contact the Permissions Section of John Wiley & Sons Australia, Ltd who will arrange for the payment of the usual fee.

CHAPTER 1
Setting the scene

LEARNING OBJECTIVES

After reading this chapter, you should be able to:

» recall Drucker's three waves of knowledge

» explain the distinctions among data, information and knowledge

» define what is meant by the term 'system'

» describe what an information system is, how information systems are developed and the nature of the discipline

» appreciate the relationship between information systems and other disciplines such as computer science, information technology (IT) and management

» list and briefly explain the three main functions that information systems serve

» understand the broad relationship between information systems, business and technological trends

» explain the value of Porter's five competitive forces model as a strategic analysis tool

» list some of the benefits of information systems from a business perspective

» understand the terms business process re-engineering (BPR) and enterprise resource planning (ERP), and the role that information systems have in those fields.

Introduction

There have been huge advances in technology and communication since the publication of the first edition of this book. These are best regarded as 'enabling mechanisms' or opportunities to transform and improve how businesses operate and compete. The principles for effective business operations have not changed significantly in the past hundred years or so. Economic, social and technical trends do shape how businesses organise and operate though. Information systems as a discipline has an intimate relationship with business. Businesses define their own information systems, and information systems constantly redefine business. In seeking to define information systems for the purposes of this text, we found two visions that seem to prevail in academia and industry. The first is that information systems is about 'developing a business philosophy of technology', and the second is that information systems is about 'using technology to gain tactical and strategic advantages in business'. The second view comes closest to what we believe: information systems is so much more than 'business computing'.

The aim of this chapter is to define a context for the study of information systems as a business discipline. It will help you to realise that it does not exist in a vacuum — it relates to every other business discipline. These disciplines in their turn operate in broader social and economic contexts. To be effective in the workplace, you will need to appreciate these contexts because they will dictate what you do, how you do it and why you do it. Information systems are social systems (at the very least they are systems with social implications). Although information systems make extensive use of technology, most consultants will tell you that they work in a 'people business' and that human factors are often more important than technical ones in successful systems. Understanding this will give a much better chance of success with information systems projects than those who take a narrower, technical view. Remember, 'Everything is connected to everything else' (attributed to Lenin; see Lyn & Jay 1989).

Three waves of knowledge

To understand where information systems are taking us, the nature of competition and the trends that influence business need to be understood. To understand trends, the past needs to be examined. The Industrial Revolution transformed how societies were structured and operated. It tends to be taught in schools as matter of factual history, that is, as something that happened at some time in the past and is now over. The truth is that the Industrial Revolution is still on a roll; however, its major effects can be examined. First, population centres developed around areas that had the right sort of resources (iron, coal, clay) and were fairly easily accessible by water or road. Other transport issues would be considered later. This led to the development of areas of expertise or 'clusters'. The economies were those of scale because transport costs were relatively low compared with manufacturing costs. With maturity, the centres of expertise were so well established that it was cheaper to take raw materials to manufacturing centres than to move people to the source of the raw material. Peter Drucker, in his book *Post-capitalist society*, describes this period as the first wave of knowledge creation: the application of knowledge to industrial tools and technologies.

Drucker describes the second wave as the application of knowledge to human endeavour. This culminated in the development of scientific management by Frederick Taylor and

Henry Ford, but the foundations had been laid more than a century earlier by Eli Whitney, whose manufacturing systems allowed unskilled labour to mass-produce goods and armaments. The development of the production line, attributed to Ford, was merely an extension of the worker specialisation seen in the Chicago meat-packing factories in the 1860s. This second wave still represents the state of the art for most of the world. However, this wave peaked in the 1960s, when computer technology began to be applied to engineering and business in a truly commercial sense. Again, the economies are those of scale, being mass manufacture and, by implication, mass standardisation (the importance of standards is something this text returns to again and again).

Drucker's third wave concerns the application of knowledge to knowledge and consequently the creation of wealth. Here is where businesses will differentiate themselves in the 'knowledge economy'. Here change is constant, and organisations must learn, adapt and manage their knowledge resources to survive. The fundamentals of competition (innovation, quality, speed to market and price) will still be significant spurs for business, but the environments we operate in are in a state of flux. As an example, consider the establishment of large economic trading blocs such as the European Union and negotiations for free trade zones. This wave represents a real challenge for information systems professionals, but it also offers wonderful career and consulting opportunities. This text is intended to help you position yourself to take advantage of those opportunities.

Understanding information systems involves considering the key concepts and components, the nature of the information systems paradigm (discipline) and its relationship to other business disciplines. The aim is to help you to develop a useful understanding of a vital business sector and the context in which it operates by presenting different but complementary perspectives of information systems with an emphasis on principles and information systems in practice. You should keep that goal in mind as you read through this book.

Data, information and knowledge

To understand what information systems are, some terms need to be introduced and a context for study established. Different kinds of information systems and how they process data are considered in chapter 3, but for now it is enough to distinguish among data, information and knowledge.

> Data (singular form *datum*) are the raw inputs of information systems. For example, data might be the customer, order and payment details that are gathered in day-to-day business activities.

> Information is processed or value-added data. From an input/output perspective, data are put in, processed in some way and then put out. This view is rooted in the data-processing thinking of the 1950s and 1960s, which tends to focus on processes rather than on outcomes. Information comprises data that have been manipulated or summarised to highlight trends or features.

> Knowledge is understanding what the information means or implies. Knowledge is a human thing — it is based on experience and is subjective in nature.

As an example of the differences among data, information and knowledge, think about a spreadsheet that gives the raw sales figures for each product line for each financial quarter over a full year. These raw figures are data that require a great deal of processing: producing a graph or chart summarising the data would yield information. Managers request information and apply their knowledge to make decisions or plans. Figure 1.1 shows the relationships among data, information and knowledge.

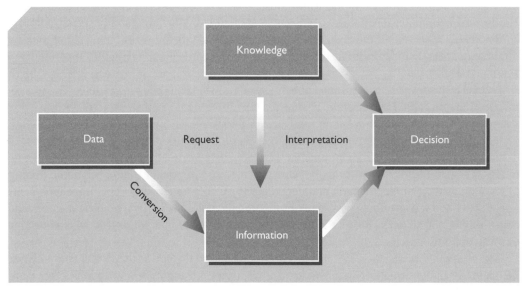

Figure 1.1 The relationships among data, information and knowledge
Source: Watson, RT 2006, 'Data management', *Databases & organizations*, 5th edn, John Wiley & Sons, New York, p. 25.

Information systems is about generating and managing information. Think of information as an asset or strategic resource. The more up to date and accurate your information is, the greater the advantage you possess. The business environment is now far more volatile than in the past. Being quick can make the difference between profit and loss on the stock market. Knowing the assets and share value of your business can enable decisions to be made regarding takeovers. Chief information officers (CIOs) manage corporate information. They see information in several different ways: as a resource or raw material for the business, as a commodity that they can buy and sell and as an asset that has intrinsic value — and those views are not mutually exclusive.

> **Reflection question 1:** How would you go about classifying information for business
> purposes?

IS in action

Pass the parcel

Logistics is the management of supply lines, including acquisition, storage, transport and delivery. Many businesses have diverse operations, forcing them to use several logistics providers, which makes management more complicated and causes the businesses to lose sight of the bigger (integrated) picture. Parcelhouse is a specialist business that provides a web-based interface for disparate logistics systems. Although a relatively small company,

Parcelhouse is a true multinational, headquartered in Stockholm with branches in Sydney, London, Munich and Gothenburg. It was founded by executives from DHL and Tetrapak, with the aim to 'eliminate the inefficiencies caused by the lack of logistics information management and integration'.

As the company grew, it became clear that its existing systems were constraining it. Any company in startup phase is usually very vulnerable unless care is taken to preserve capital. Put simply, the company needed to expand its customer base and develop its information systems infrastructure to support existing and new customers. Given the time-critical nature of the logistics business, corporate customers will not tolerate systems outages and poor performance. Parcelhouse needed to find the upfront investment, which could have diverted it from its strategic priorities and exposed it to risk.

It became apparent that the best solution was to outsource the problem, with IBM Global Services emerging as the partner of choice. The new system allowed Parcelhouse to pay for servers, bandwidth and storage capacity on a usage basis, removing the need for high capital expenditure. The technical solution was based on internationally recognised standards, providing both flexibility and scalability. If Parcelhouse needs to grow quickly then the systems can grow with it in an incremental fashion. But the real test of any business system is the bottom line. The new system has three times the customers with no increase in IT costs, and improved technology has reduced downtime to zero. As the business grows, the saving will increase proportionally. Moral: when the price of self sufficiency is too high, think outside the square.

Source: Information from www.parcelhouse.com and http://www-306.ibm.com.

It is more difficult to define knowledge than to define data or information. Indeed, its definition is controversial. Data and information can be measured in bytes, but what are the units of knowledge? Although some people contend that knowledge is meta-information, that is, information about information, a more constructive perspective is taken here. Knowledge is understanding the meaning and importance of information. Given that people interpret information on the basis of their own experience, knowledge must be subjective and internally (and personally) constructed. There is a naive realist assumption among many managers that information and knowledge are the same thing (Benson & Standing 2000). As the 'knowledge economy' grows in importance, managers need to shift their focus from information to knowledge. Because information and knowledge are different, trying to manage them in the same way is a recipe for failure. Drucker (1993) equates knowledge with power; so the challenge faced by most businesses is how to encourage employees to share knowledge rather than keep it to themselves.

What is a system?

A system is 'a collection of parts that work together to achieve some purpose', according to Alfred Howarth, a retired British computing academic. Given that it comes from a person with two degrees in mathematics and many years' experience in using computers to model real-world phenomena, this is a surprisingly accessible answer. However, how people define things largely depends on their life experiences, so there is an element of subjectivity. To reach a more widely applicable definition, a few more viewpoints must be examined. Howarth's view was influenced by his work: the word 'parts' implies a physical nature to the systems he was modelling. Others regard a system as a set of related ideas or constructs that are organised in some way. In this context, the system is purely abstract, perhaps a set of defined terms or an entire philosophical paradigm.

A distinction can be made between natural and human-made systems: the solar system is natural, the social security system is human-made. Some systems might be a combination of physical, abstract, natural and human-made subsystems. Here are some generalisations about systems.

> A system has a purpose or function.
> A system has a context or environment in which it has applicability.
> A system has a boundary that marks the limits of its environment.
> The removal of a single component of a system will cause that system to fail.
> A system usually has inputs and outputs.
> Complex systems usually consist of subsystems, which in turn may have subsystems.
> A component may belong to more than one system.

Looking at this list, you can now understand the quotation 'Everything is connected to everything else'. The interconnectedness of systems, subsystems and components is what makes life so difficult for system developers. Where to draw the boundary of a system is one of the most difficult questions that has to be considered in designing any system. Fortunately, there are methods, tools, techniques and even systems for thinking about systems, as chapter 6 describes.

What is an information system?

Over the years, the reliability of the underlying technology improved and it was realised that information systems had a social dimension, because many of the problems were identified as being people related. The definition of an information system became broader, and the components of an information system were generally accepted as:

> people
> data and information
> procedures
> software
> hardware
> communications.

These components and their interactions are explained in some detail throughout this book and provide a basic structure not only for developing information systems but also for the discipline as a whole.

The history of information systems

Information systems have been around for at least 6000 years. Early information systems gave rise to the development of written language, accountancy, taxation and banking (Davies 1996).

The application of computing technology to information processing occurred at the end of the 1950s. In the 1960s, computer systems began to be used for truly commercial purposes. Before then, they had been used in science and engineering in the first phase of the information revolution. Just as the Industrial Revolution extended physical capabilities, so the information revolution extended mental capabilities, initially in the area of calculation, problems that would take a human a lifetime to solve could be handled by a computer on a time scale that was almost immediate (e.g. finite element analysis calculations for the design of a modern skyscraper). From there, it was a short step to using computers to gain access to, process and filter huge quantities of data. This did not produce knowledge or give insight, but simply allowed mundane tasks to be automated and interesting questions to be raised and (potentially) answered. Many of the scientists and engineers who had worked in computer science fields moved into information-related activities, bringing with them a mindset that was rigorous, logical and grounded in mathematical notation. This exerted a huge influence over the development of the discipline for many years to come.

By the early 1970s, 'information systems' was appearing in the curricula of American universities. A question that needs to be asked is whether the mere inclusion of a subject in university curricula qualifies it as a discipline. The prevailing view seems to be that information systems as a field was then insufficiently mature to be considered a discipline in its own right. It seemed to be dependent on computer science and management for its existence.

Two kinds of disciplines are relevant in this context: scientific and engineering. People who work in scientific disciplines are concerned with classifying phenomena and developing and testing theories. In contrast, those who work in engineering disciplines are concerned with constructing and testing artefacts. Weber (1997) notes that both scientific and engineering disciplines were represented in the emerging information systems field. This led to the somewhat schizophrenic nature of information systems, as practitioners wondered whether they belonged to a scientific or engineering discipline.

A discipline has a paradigm (system of working) and an infrastructure (journals, committees and so on) that provide coherence. The more mature the paradigm, the higher the level of coherence and the better defined the discipline; that is, an orthodoxy of terminology, philosophy and methodology emerges.

For pure sciences, the paradigms are well established and reasonably easy to articulate. For social sciences (education, psychology and so on), the paradigms are not well defined — indeed part of the paradigm is to seek to define the paradigm. Such a high level of self-reference actively prevents a high degree of coherence, resulting in divergence and differentiation, that is, schools of thought within the discipline.

In the mid-1970s, another school of information systems thinking emerged, which considered information systems to be a social system. Management had also been involved in the information systems area, because it was business related. With four main constituents, the emerging information systems discipline was lacking coherence. Additionally, the academic publishing system encouraged authors to produce highly specialised papers, focusing on the differences among authors rather than on searching for common ground. When one considers the range of jobs within the industry and the huge number of specialist journals on information systems, it would seem that the discipline is fragmented. However, talking to practitioners and academics elicits broad agreement on the core concepts.

During the formative period of information systems as a subject, however, there was little agreement about what constituted information systems. In 1972, John Dearden of the Harvard Business School wrote, 'Management Information Systems is embedded in a mish-mash of fuzzy thinking and incomprehensible jargon' (Weber 1997, p. 2). Dearden's comments provoked an outcry from academia and industry. The most notable reaction was a sudden quest for respectability, as journals, professional bodies and conferences promoted credible research and scholarship began to emerge. At the first International Conference on Information Systems, Keen (1980) argued that information systems researchers should borrow from other (more developed) disciplines, such as economics and behavioural sciences. It is possible that research methods became more important than research subjects for a time. However, this tended to emphasise the multidisciplinary nature of information systems.

Any discipline that is rapidly evolving and growing and is partly based on rapidly developing technology is unlikely to be stable. With increasing maturity, higher-level (and less divisive) views of the nature of information systems have emerged. Unlike for other philosophies, there is no great search for eternal truths or answers to the big questions. Real-world constraints mean that the perfect system will never be built; instead, the search is directed towards finding the best compromise.

What is an information system for?

According to McKeown (2003), an information system exists to fulfil three basic functions:

> remembering the past
> handling the present
> preparing for the future.

Consider a motorcycle dealership. The level of stock on hand is variable. The owners do not want to tie up too much capital in components; equally, they do not want to lose business and let their customers down. They know purchasing behaviour has seasonal variations: many customers put their motorcycles off the road in winter and go into maintenance mode, but when summer comes, those customers take to the road, and demand for service items such as air filters and brake pads increases.

Table 1.1 shows the three basic information systems functions and associated tasks. The information needs of businesses will vary, as will the technology deployed to fulfil the tasks. However, the three basic functions apply to any information system.

TABLE 1.1 Three information systems functions with example tasks

Information systems function	Information systems task
Remembering the past	Analysing past transaction and purchasing patterns
Handling the present	Recording current transaction patterns, automating payment and ordering mechanisms, effecting stock control
Preparing for the future	Planning future inventory on the basis of statistical forecasts

The relationship of information systems to other disciplines

This chapter has alluded to the multidisciplinary nature of information systems. Given that 'everything is connected to everything else', it would be useful to see exactly where the field of information systems sits in relation to other disciplines.

Information systems or information technology?

Some managers tend to regard information technology (IT) and information systems as being the same thing. This is not the case: information systems rely on technology and on other things such as people and procedures. Put simply, IT is about the 'what' questions of systems (e.g. what provides the processing power?). Information systems are about the 'how' and 'why' of systems (e.g. how do we manage the system? Why are we doing this?).

IT consists of the hardware, software and communications that support information systems. There is a degree of overlap between the two. A person who wants to be effective in information systems needs an understanding of the principles of IT, but access to technical expertise when it is needed is important. To establish a context for how the different technical disciplines relate, refer to figure 1.2, which shows a framework for relating business and computing disciplines. Progressing from left to right in the figure, the trend is to move away from detailed, concrete, machine-oriented areas to more abstract, human-oriented areas, that is, from technical skills to transferable skills. Note that working in a technical discipline requires a considerable amount of effort to keep up to date with the changes in technology. Although this makes for an interesting life, it makes it harder to develop a career path (therefore the popularity of MBA courses). Information systems depends on technology but places a much greater emphasis on transferable skills; in short, it is easier to maintain skills

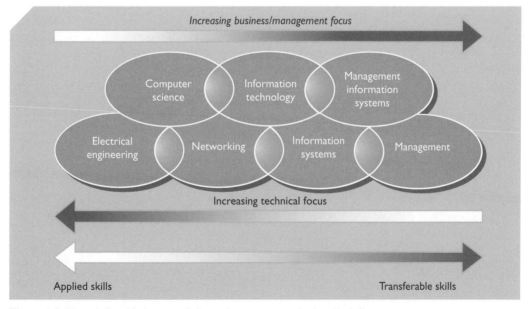

Figure 1.2 The relationship between information systems and other disciplines

in the information systems area than it is in the computer science area. Moving from electrical engineering to management, the trend is from highly to loosely structured activities.

Is information systems management a subset of management?

The information systems area has always had a need for high capital expenditure and a greater degree of complexity than other management functions. Additionally, problems are associated with security and ethics. Being effective in this area requires an unusual blend of attributes. Information systems management draws on financial, human resources, operations and strategic management disciplines but could not easily be classified as any one of these. There is a reluctance on the part of many organisations to accept information systems management as a school of management in its own right. In many cases, there is a prevailing culture that says 'if you are a manager, you can manage anything'. This is somewhat contentious. Many projects fail because of overconfidence on the part of management. Some managers fail to realise the limitations of their staff and the supporting technology. Yourdon (1997) refers to these as 'death march' projects, in which management pursues mission-critical systems with insufficient funds, staff and time. System development and project management are examined in chapters 5 and 6. If anything needs to be emphasised, it is that the human aspects of information systems management are vital. After all, any technical problem has a technical solution, so long as staff have sufficient motivation. Motivating staff is the real problem.

The multidisciplinary nature of information systems means that their management cannot be regarded as a proper subset of any other school of management. For at least a quarter of a century, there have been professional journals, conferences and associations for information systems management. It could therefore be argued that information systems management is sufficiently distinct to be regarded as a discipline in its own right. It affects every other business discipline, as discussed in the following sections. Figure 1.3 shows that an information system

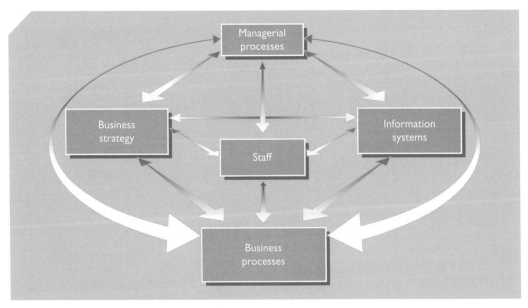

Figure 1.3 Five components of a business system

is usually part of a business system, which in turn may be regarded as the interaction of five main constituents: staff, managerial processes, business processes, business strategy and information systems. Each component actively helps to define every other component. Note that the entire business system revolves around the staff.

Technology and business trends

Any work of art, building or artefact is a product of its time and culture and is best appreciated when something is known of its time and culture. Information systems, technology and management philosophies are also products of their time and culture. To appreciate them, the trends that have led to their creation and shaped their development must be examined. Overwhelmingly, these trends have been economic.

In 1994, John Naisbit wrote one of a series of books on megatrends (Naisbit 1994). His insightful analysis was wide ranging, but only a few of his themes will be covered here. First, Naisbit argues that economic trading blocks are getting bigger. Next he suggests that companies are getting smaller on average, which comes about from the application of intelligence and technology. The evidence for this may be found by examining the decline in the contribution of the *Fortune* 500 to the gross domestic product (GDP) of the United States over 20 years, during which time it virtually halved. (The *Fortune* 500 is an annual list of the 500 largest industrial corporations in the United States, published by *Fortune* magazine; the corporations are ranked on such things as revenue, profits and market value.) At the time Naisbit was writing, a little more than 55 per cent of the GDP of the United States came from small-to-medium entities (SMEs), many of them true multinationals. These trends continue (Audretsch et al. 2000): personal wealth is increasing, and downsizing continues as a corporate phenomenon. Naturally, there are exceptions. Some mega-corporations — most notably those in the communications and media sectors — continue to grow, but on average companies are getting smaller.

What circumstances brought about this state of affairs? Advances in manufacturing technology account for some of this shift. A traditional large corporation relies on economies of scale, reducing the unit cost of manufacture by bulk purchases, mass manufacture and substantial investment in infrastructure. This massive investment requirement was the barrier to market entry for manufacturing 'wannabes'. The advent of microprocessors and flexible manufacturing systems (FMS) has allowed many smaller companies to enter the market, since the entry costs have been reduced by the new technology.

FMS are computer-operated manufacturing tools that can carry out a wide range of processes. The new machinery is capable of performing many tasks rather than a few highly specialised tasks. This allows production lines to be much smaller and makes it economical to set up for small production runs because FMS do not need to retool when switching between production runs. Additionally, manufacturing instructions and designs can now be accepted in electronic form, eliminating several steps in the old-fashioned process. This technology-driven shift means that geographic proximity is a more important advantage than sheer size, FMS technology allows factories to be small and easily relocatable. Because only 5 per cent of manufacturing time is spent in adding value to the product, purchasing materials in bulk to obtain discounts does not yield a significant advantage. Bulk handling requires storage facilities and often leads to overcapitalisation in stock. Small companies are able to accept and make small deliveries frequently and quickly, allowing just-in-time (JIT) delivery and manufacturing strategies to be used. Coupled with fast payment mechanisms, this shortens timelines and speeds cash flow, improving the competitive edge. Some areas of the UK car industry make use of many small suppliers, not only giving greater flexibility and reducing stock-on-hand levels but also spreading risk. A strike from a major supplier would have crippled production previously, but now a car manufacturer can simply increase orders to other suppliers. Some manufacturers have taken the concept a little further. In some of the Volkswagen factories, the people who make the doors actually fit the doors; so Volkswagen is able to reduce labour costs and stock on hand. This suggests two things: first, that the car manufacturing industry is in a process of transition to becoming a car manufacturing community; second, that intellectual capital is of increasing importance in the new industrial paradigm

IS in action

Keep on trucking, keep on tracking

The concept of JIT delivery is familiar to most logistics managers. Offloading inventory problems onto suppliers and reducing inventory to free investment capital are fundamental to effective competition in the manufacturing sector. Keeping track of inventory from many diverse suppliers becomes critical as stock levels are reduced. Ford's approach at its truck-building facility in Michigan is to use radio frequency identity (RFID) tags to create a real-time location system. Ford's major logistics supplier, TNT Logistics NA is deploying technology from WhereNet Corp that tracks inbound and outbound parts, using the information gained to provide real-time updates to its information systems for stock control and transactional processing. The Dearborn TNT facility aggregates parts from many suppliers and then ships them to Ford's manufacturing centre as they are needed. Ford's logistics operations are much simplified because it deals with what amounts to a single supplier. The system is capable of detecting parts as they leave the storage facility and provides the factory with advance notice of delivery to improve the efficiency of the operation. The system takes JIT to a new level. JIT requires more individual shipments and increasing fuel prices may force many companies to re-examine their logistics operations and consider increasing their inventory levels, but it is unlikely that stock levels will ever return to the excesses of the 1970s.

Source: Information from Sullivan, L 2005, 'Ford Motor enlists RFID just-in-time delivery system', *InformationWeek*, 2 November, www.informationweek.com.

[**Key concept:** The secret of success is to work smarter — not harder.]

The prevalence of microprinting shops also emphasises the advantage of geography over size; here the costs of distribution become the most significant factor in competition. Printing technology has improved so that it is now economic to set up very short production runs, in that regard it has some of the advantages that we normally associate with FMS. Another factor to consider is the volatility of the business environment: things change quickly. The critical elements of competition are innovation, quality and speed to market. It is usually easier for small organisations to achieve in these areas than it is for large organisations. Many larger companies are restructuring along clustered lines to try to obtain the benefits of both large and small business organisational management.

Reducing market entry costs

The major barrier costs to market entry are usually advertising and business promotion. Many new companies have a very high dollar-turnover-to-staff ratio compared with those of traditional manufacturing concerns. One reason is that they tend to make products that have a high level of intellectual content, such as software. Once the initial design and concepts are verified, the major costs are advertising and shipping, because few raw materials are involved in the process.

In a traditional mass-marketing operation, businesses make use of broadcast advertising. The cost of TV advertising for an SME in startup phase is usually prohibitive. However, depending on the nature of the business, Internet operations may be ideal. Here, the consumer has taken on the bulk of the costs: a computer, Internet service provider (ISP) fees and communications costs. A large corporation can have only one website in a meaningful sense; that is, the name www.largecorp.com is unique, just as www.smallbiz.com is. In one sense, as far as the consumer is concerned, both large and small companies are on the same footing when it comes to searching the World Wide Web. Unless a company pays to register with an intermediary such as a search engine, then a user search will find both large and small companies competing to provide similar products and services. This competition can be global in nature.

infobyte

Cheats never prosper?

It is well known that there is an underground market for student assignments. All Jens Schriver did in 1995 was develop a low-cost website called cheathouse.com, which put the market onto the Internet and brought it out into the open. Students could pay $14.95 or submit an essay for a full year of access. With membership in excess of 60 000 and more than 6000 visitors a day, business is good. Schriver does not have an ethical problem with what he does and takes care to remove plagiarised material from the site. 'I provide a service not too different from that of a library. It can be used legitimately, to do research and get inspired, or it can be used to outright plagiarise. I don't try to parent my users, it's completely up to them what they do with the essays.

Source: Information from www.cheathouse.com.

The shift in costs from business to customer has been accompanied by a corresponding shift in power. Note that the World Wide Web is not a broadcast system. It is not a one-on-one communication. The user-to-web site relationship is in the nature of $1:n$; that is, the consumer has a greater choice of companies and websites. This means more competition and, consequently, reduced prices. This theme is elaborated on later in the text. The proliferation of media such as TV channels has made advertising a hit-and-miss affair. Consumers 'channel hop' to avoid advertisements, so much advertising expenditure is wasted. However, it is obvious that traditional marketing models do not lend themselves to new styles of operation.

❯ **Reflection question 2:** Is it now possible for mass advertising to hit its target market effectively? What would you suggest to make sure that advertising is effective?

Tactical and strategic links

Improvements in technology and communication allow companies to make their suppliers and dealerships partners in their own enterprise. For example, Harley-Davidson uses an extranet (a private network that allows companies to interconnect their systems in selected areas) to facilitate the distribution of product information to and from its dealers. This allows the turnaround time on warranty claims to be shortened. The system also lets parts be supplied worldwide in a short time, which means that dealers can spend less on inventory and more on customer service and marketing. Cash flow is improved for Harley-Davidson and its dealer network: a win–win scenario.

[**Key concept:** Use technology to create umbilical cords — make your suppliers and resellers full partners in your enterprise.]

Changing the way people work

Currently, smaller organisations are able to enjoy the benefits of technology previously enjoyed only by large companies. All these business transformations were made possible by providing information for business operations and decision making.

> **Reflection question 3:** In times past, a company would specialise in certain areas and product lines. Is specialisation still a viable business strategy? Or do the economies of scope now outweigh economies of scale?

Often (but not always), a database is at the heart of the business. Information is only one part of the equation. Communication systems allow business to reduce the effects of distance. There is a trend in information systems to create systems that are modular in nature: communications may be thought of as the 'glue' that binds systems. The bland statement that 'geography is history' is contentious, but it is worth noting that many people now telecommute, that is, use a computer and modem to work from home. It may be that these people are marginally less efficient, but the company does not need to provide an office. Telecommuters also provide their own heat and light, so company infrastructure costs may be offloaded to the employee. Thus businesses can become smaller in a physical sense while continuing to grow. Direct and indirect overheads can be reduced and cost savings can be high.

Business process re-engineering (BPR)

Many of the computer systems in current use date from a time when the technology was relatively primitive. Staff had to change their work patterns to suit the computer. Contemporary technology is much more capable and gives users greater freedom and more control over their day-to-day work. Improvements in technology allow businesses to examine their core processes and see how they can be improved, such as shortening timelines, speeding cash flow and eliminating intermediaries where possible, with the object of achieving greater effectiveness (doing the right thing) and efficiency (doing it well and economically). This analysis and improvement of operations is termed business process re-engineering (BPR). It is often undertaken as part of an enterprisewide planning exercise; it should be considered continuous.

[**Key concept:** New technology creates new opportunities — be prepared to take advantage of them.]

Aspects of competition: competitive forces

Three major elements of competition in business are implicit in the preceding discussion: innovation, quality and speed to market. Many luminaries would argue that only innovation is necessary. In the strict sense, 'innovation' is not the right term because it implies a totally new thing; most innovation in business is creative change, building on what was already there. The real trick is to make innovation a core business process and for e-businesses this is a real necessity.

To consider competition, an integrating theoretic framework is needed. Some of these are considered in chapter 7. This section looks at the five forces model proposed by Michael Porter of the Harvard Business School in 1979, as shown in figure 1.4 (Haag, Cummings & Phillips 2007).

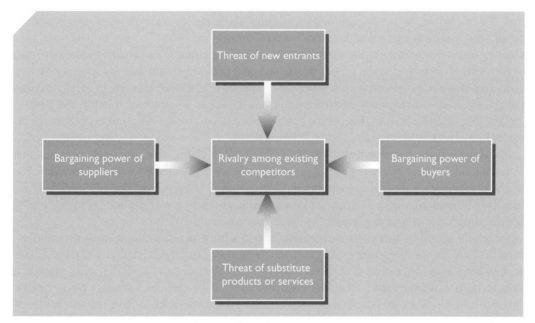

Figure 1.4 Porter's five competitive forces
Source: Haag, S, Cummings, M & Phillips, A 2007, *Management information systems for the information age*, 6th edn, McGraw-Hill Irwin, New York, p. 242.

This model has been widely used to help businesses think about strategy and the impact of IT and information systems. For this reason alone, it has featured in most information systems textbooks for more than 20 years. It would be useful to examine each force in turn and then think how information systems could change the competitive dynamic.

> *Supplier power:* The question here is how easy is it for suppliers to push up prices? How dependent is a business on its suppliers? (Information systems make it easier to find and do business with alternative suppliers.)

> *Buyer power:* How easy is it for buyers to drive prices down? Businesses that deal with a few powerful suppliers are not in a position to dictate terms. (Information systems can make it easier to find and penetrate new markets.)

> *Competitive rivalry:* This relates to how many competitors a business has and their capability. A business operating in the 'me too' market has little power, but one operating in a specialist or niche market has few rivals and is therefore powerful. (A company using custom software may have a distinct advantage over one that does not.)

> *Threat of substitution:* Can customers switch their business to alternative products and services easily? (Using information systems to create 'umbilical cords', e.g. automating an ordering process, can make switching harder.)

> *Threat of new entrants:* The easier and cheaper it is for competitors to enter the market, the less powerful a business is. (If a company has made a large investment in strategic information systems, a potential entrant does not have the same benefits of the economies of scale, so entering the market would be difficult and expensive.)

The temptation is to take a naive approach and treat the model as though it is some magical formula that will yield meaningful answers if we just plug in the right data. It must be appreciated that Porter's model is a powerful analytical tool, which can provide insights. Inexperienced people can (and do) misapply the model with interesting results. The development of most theoretical models is heavily influenced by the prevailing cultural and business environments. When Porter framed his model, it was predicated on a perfect market, as envisaged in an era of economic rationalism. E-commerce was almost unheard of and markets were generally reasonably stable. The contemporary environment is very different. Markets are volatile and governments create legislation that affects how businesses operate, constraining and distorting market forces. Some researchers have suggested that a sixth force is now needed to complete the model: public opinion (which can be a major influence on business behaviour). It is not suggested that Porter's model should be abandoned, merely that it be used judiciously with full consideration of the contemporary business environment. See chapter 7 for more on Porter's model. There are many other frameworks and methods for strategic analysis, and it is often useful to employ several simultaneously to gain a more complete understanding of the situation.

Generally speaking, larger businesses tend to be much better at strategic analysis and planning than are smaller companies. This is in part a product of corporate culture. Big businesses tend to be much more mature and capable in regard to planning and have the capacity to do it very well. After all, the stakes are relatively high and the consequences of failure can be severe. Smaller businesses are constrained by staff numbers and time, and so have less capacity and capability. The simple truth is that small businesses need to do these things well if they are to succeed, and if they can not do them in house then they need to bring in consultants who have the required expertise. Good analysis and planning are necessary (but not of themselves sufficient!) conditions for success in business.

infobyte

The long tail in retail

Chris Anderson, editor in chief of *Wired* magazine has put forward a theory that our culture and economy are moving away from mainstream products and services (at the head of the demand curve in figure 1.5) and towards a large number of niches in the 'long tail'. Whereas businesses used to operate by the 80:20 rule, in which 80 per cent of business came from 20 per cent of one's trading partners, the modern paradigm is that 98 per cent of your inventory is in demand somewhere. Anderson also makes the point that if you offer your customers ten things, they are likely to buy one; if you offer them 1000 things, demand is less concentrated. The tendency of large business and entertainment networks to focus on bestsellers means that the demand in the long tail goes unsatisfied. Therefore, niche marketing and mass customisation offer the best opportunities for business growth. Information systems makes it easier to exploit niches and the Internet allows international customers to be reached. Every tune in Apple's iTunes portfolio, including relatively obscure titles, has been sold at least once.

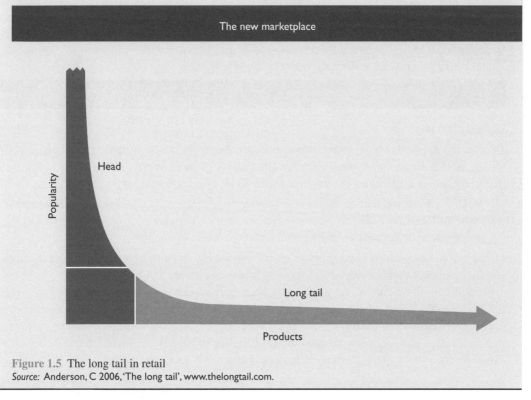

Figure 1.5 The long tail in retail
Source: Anderson, C 2006, 'The long tail', www.thelongtail.com.

Technology convergence

As touched on in the discussion of manufacturing, technology has tended to be developed in specialised areas. Integrating various incompatible technologies into a cohesive whole is very difficult and usually not possible. Current trends show various, previously separate, technologies are now melding, for example, cable TV can be used to deliver Internet services and telephone communications.

Mobile phones provide photo and video service, send and receive email and faxes and allow web browsing. Mobile phones can be used instead of credit cards. They can be used to control 'smart' household devices. The development of personal media players offers further potential for technology convergence. The trend seems to be one of fewer devices but with greater functionality, mirroring the trend seen in the emergence of FMS. On a larger scale, this seems to promise powerful new synergies with profound implications for business.

What's the score?

For anyone learning to play a musical instrument, the learning curve can be very steep. Struggling with musical notation, finding melodies that cannot be played on your favourite instrument and being unable to find other people to practice with are common frustrations. Smartscore is a system that can convert sheet music into midi files and vice versa. Users can compose, edit, transpose and arrange music before creating midi files or sheet music output. A karaoke view allows singers and players to follow music on screen for rehearsal purposes. Musitek, the company that developed Smartscore, was established in 1991 and has been responsive to customer feedback. The development of the software has been a long process of continual improvement and demonstrates the importance of niche markets to e-businesses and the importance of imbuing products with intelligence.

Source: Information from www.smartscore.com.

E-commerce

Despite the enormous hype that surrounds e-commerce, it is not suitable for all retail operations. Bob Seeman, state sales manager for Frasers (a large Western Australian motorcycle importer), which specialises in road bikes such as Harley-Davidson, says:

> Buying a Harley-Davidson bike is a complete experience; it is emotional, and although some customers will purchase a motorcycle online, most prefer to do business personally, and trying to do it on the Internet goes against the nature of our business.

Frasers promotes products and services on its website but most customers do business personally. In contrast, other businesses are moving into e-commerce at a high rate.

Some see e-commerce as supplementing their current business operations; others see their business models being totally transformed. A third category encompasses those companies that have never operated in traditional modes. The nature of the relationships between customers and businesses and between businesses is changing drastically. Information systems allow every aspect of the supply chain to be managed efficiently and effectively.

Turnitin.com or turnitoff?

Turnitin.com allows academics and students to ensure that their work is plagiarism free. The subscription-based service is used by several thousand universities worldwide. Work submitted for analysis becomes part of Turnitin's vast database. Some universities are abandoning the service though because of student protests for reasons such as 'presumption of guilt', 'breach of intellectual copyright' and Turnitin's US ownership. There is little doubt that most students are honest but some are cheating and not getting caught, as universities balance student rights against academic standards. Currently, Turnitin is one of the best tools in the fight against plagiarism.

Source: Information from an article that appeared in *McGill Daily*.

Proliferation of technology and communication

Most information systems were fairly centralised 30 years ago. The technical knowledge required to use them was restricted to an educated elite. Now the technology is widespread, and there is an entire generation who cannot remember life without the PC. The development of the Internet enabled new relationships and patterns of business to be formed. The impact is said to be akin to that of the printing press in Gutenberg's day. Although the Internet is no longer in its infancy, its full impact has yet to be realised. However, the true value of the Internet is not vested in what can be owned and controlled but in what can be shared and extended.

Moving to a knowledge economy

Many newer businesses do not manufacture anything; they make a profit by leveraging intellectual capital. They operate in a 3S model: synergise, synthesise, specialise. For example, consider the establishment of a web-based business that arranges romantic weekends. The proprietor would need to know about airlines, hotels and suppliers of limousines, champagne, flowers and chocolates. Getting all these people to work together yields the synergy, which gives a marketable service that no single company could supply individually. Deciding which services and products to include in the package is synthesis. Finally, tailoring the promotional marketing to sell the same product to different groups is where the specialisation comes in. The collected fees are returned to the suppliers less the proprietor's percentage. Startup fees would be quite low and the Internet would enable a global market to be reached. Obviously, better promotional marketing would improve profits, but enough should be made to be going on with and to prove the concept before a business development loan is sought. The main input would have been the idea.

Modern information systems allow many ideas that were previously impracticable to be realised. They also allow older business models to be revisited and improved. The knowledge economy relies on the application of knowledge-to-knowledge-related activities to produce wealth. Information systems are an integral part of this

IS in action

A new life

The three-dimensional virtual world that is Second Life (www.secondlife.com) is now mature. The underlying concept is simple, a computer-simulated world with slick graphics. Businesses have created virtual presences and millions of people have created virtual communities. IBM has spent millions of dollars a year consolidating its presence and each day vast sums move around in Second Life's booming (if virtual) economy. What started out as an imaginative idea has become a multimillion-dollar industry, with the boundaries between reality and the 'metaverse' becoming blurred. The technology has the potential to displace web-based approaches to e-business. Specialist companies have evolved to help businesses market themselves in the new environment. One such company is Hong Kong's Asia Solution Connect, which provides a total metaverse marketing service, including content production and account management. Second Life has news services, TV and radio channels, and provides lecture and meeting spaces to industry and academia. Users interact with the site through an 'avatar' (a user-defined animated character), which can fly, jump and teleport.

(continued)

In the early 1990s, all a company needed to do to establish an online presence was to put up a web page, now it must create three-dimensional objects such as buildings and landscapes in the metaverse and populate them. Given the level of difficulty associated with development, it is not hard to understand why some of this virtual real estate sells for very large amounts. Asia Solution Connect's clients include Sony, Logitech and Nokia, which gives some idea of how seriously business is taking metaverse marketing.

Business pressures and responses

The business environment is in a constant state of flux; that is, the only constant is change. When an environmental pressure increases, a business must respond if it is to survive and maintain its competitive position. Figure 1.6 shows the major business pressures.

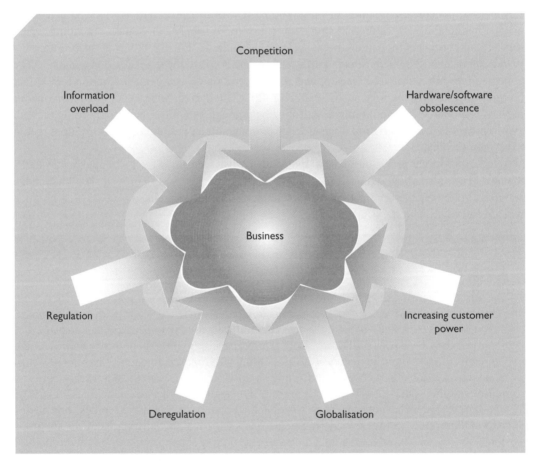

Figure 1.6 Seven major business pressures

Responses to pressures may take many forms, but almost all reduce to three main aspects: quality, innovation and speed. Figure 1.7 shows seven major responses to business pressures.

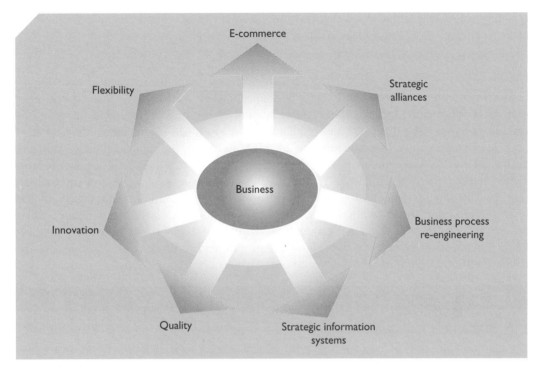

Figure 1.7 Seven major responses to business pressures

As may be imagined, the behaviour of a business over time is marked by the dynamic interaction of pressures and responses. The difficulty most businesses have is in anticipating the pressures and taking evasive action.

Direct and indirect benefits of information systems

Part of your job as an information systems professional will be to present solutions to clients. As with any other form of marketing, you should never sell the product; you should sell the benefits. This requires you to do some research and engage in careful thought and prediction. Benefits may be direct (tangible) or indirect (intangible). Indirect benefits can only be estimated, but direct benefits can be predicted with a high degree of certainty.

For example, consider the introduction of computerised stock control to a motor vehicle dealership. The direct benefit is to improve response times to queries and, as a consequence, make more sales, which can be quantified. Staff in the parts department now have more time to devote to relationship marketing of parts and service, which is an indirect benefit, as is the improved image the company enjoys as a result of using new technology. Indirect benefits are harder to quantify but are no less real. The real benefits accrue by changing the nature of competition. When Volkswagen discovered that many of its dealers were failing to retain post-warranty service work on Volkswagen cars, it developed automated engine analysers and fitted each new car with a diagnostic plug. This new technology allowed Volkswagen dealers to complete engine tuning and diagnosis in a matter of moments and reduce their service charges to retain customers. Non-Volkswagen workshops were still able to carry out work on Volkswagen cars but were no longer able to compete on time and cost. This is a classic example of a business using technology as a barrier to stifle competition.

[**Key concept:** Technology can be used to create barriers to competition.]

If obvious benefits are discernible within a single organisation, then greater benefits should accrue when computer networking and communication are added. Being able to use other sources of information increases the overall amount of information available for decision-making purposes. The difficulty now is that there is too much information. Much of it is not relevant and may be contradictory, but establishing that it is requires detailed sifting and analysis. Diversity and complexity are the enemies of managers. Careful assessment of information needs is required, followed by a restriction on the types and number of information sources. This should ensure cost-effective information management. Information needs should be reviewed frequently. In addition to the direct costs of storage of information, indirect costs are associated with acquisition and manipulation of that information. For most organisations, the indirect costs of systems far outweigh the hardware and software costs. For most sizable organisations, the communications costs far outweigh data-processing costs.

IS in action

A whole new ball game

Australia's elimination from the 2006 World Cup was controversial. For many fans, the entire tournament was rife with controversy and the performance of referees was described as 'dismal' in polite circles. Quite apart from player theatrics and professional fouls, the simple question whether a goal was scored or not proved very hard to answer. Could technology help? Several companies have made claims to have developed a hi-tech soccer ball that can be tracked accurately. RFIDs can be embedded in a soccer ball so that there should be no doubt whether a ball crossed the line. To date, there has been no agreement regarding the deployment of the technology. However, the 2006 World Cup organisers did make use of RFID tags in more than three million tickets. The main problems that accompany major sporting events are ticket 'scalping' (in which tickets are sold on at inflated prices) and conflict among different groups of fans. Crowd control and segregation are major problems for stadium management.

To purchase one of the hi-tech tickets, fans were obliged to provide a lot of personal information, which could then be crosschecked against databases of known soccer hooligans. The RFID tags were read on entry to the stadium and the details checked against passports and other identity documents so that only genuine ticketholders would be admitted. The tags were also used to make sure that opposing groups of fans were kept apart. In the event of a disturbance, every security staff member had equipment capable of reading the RFID tag and consequently identifying offenders. Civil libertarians were concerned about the ticketholder information being held and misused but authorities ensured that all information held was deleted after the event. Disputes over goals and fouls remain part of the game but there is little doubt that RFID technology helped to make the 2006 World Cup one of the best organised and peaceful in sporting history.

Source: Information from Borland, J 2006, 'World Cup soccer loves to hate high-tech', 19 June, http://news.com.com; Chhabra, G 2006, 'Act sober with RFID World Cup tickets', 15 June, RFID World, www.rfid-weblog.com.

Why study information systems?

There is an apocryphal story about a bank robber. On sentencing, the judge asked the man why he had taken to robbing banks. The man replied, 'Because that's where the money is'. The job opportunities in information systems are wide ranging, international and well paid. Best of all, the work is usually interesting, varied and satisfying. A useful thing about information systems is that the skills one develops are transferable, having broad applicability. The skills also have a long shelf life, which makes it easier to pursue a career.

This text is written for students who are pursuing a business qualification. Although some students may go on to major in information systems, for many, this text may be all the study that they ever undertake in the area. In either case, it is important to realise the context in which we work.

Information systems exist to serve business. As information systems practitioners, it is important to speak the same language as the client, and invariably this is the language of business couched in such terms as cash flow and return on investment. Equally, there is an onus on businesspeople to be able to converse with information systems specialists on an equal footing. So it would be useful to examine the relationship of information systems to other business disciplines that are studied as part of a business degree.

Information systems and the marketing major

Traditional 4P models of marketing (product, promotion, place and price) still have relevance in a world in which relationship marketing is in the ascendancy. In fairness, more sophisticated models have been developed. As an example a tourism marketing mix might also include partnership, people, packaging and programming — giving eight Ps. Market research is about collecting information on customers, prospects, sales patterns and so on. Promotional marketing includes advertising, distribution and delivery. It is hard to imagine any sizable company not using software for analysis, budgeting and forecasting. Information systems can affect all of these areas but is especially useful in identifying and creating relationships and in-depth analysis.

Marketing also makes use of temporary information systems. Think about organising a large convention or trade fair over two weeks. In addition to all the usual behind-the-scenes management that takes place, networked multimedia displays to guide visitors around the display centres are needed. Competitions and other promotions are used to gather potential customer information for later analysis. At the end of the two weeks, the entire system is dismantled and much of the equipment returned to the leasing company.

Hospitality and tourism are often considered to be a subset of marketing. Hotel management systems include complex food inventory systems, accounting systems and modelling software intended to improve occupancy rates and profit.

Information systems and the accounting and finance majors

Much of basic accounting is repetitious in nature. The automation of those mundane processes has produced a shift in the nature of accounting from bookkeeping to managerial decision-making. Data must be captured, manipulated, stored and audited. Increasingly, accountants are involved in policy formulation and system security. Much of accounting is about reducing complexity and diversity by standardising and automating procedures.

Many accountants rise to become senior managers. They understand the business as a series of cash flows. Information systems is complementary to this because it enables the business to be considered as a series of information flows. Accountancy is about recording the past for legal and planning purposes.

Finance concerns itself with the present and the future, answering such questions as 'What is our profit this year to date?' and 'What is our predicted return on this investment?' Most business decisions are based on financial considerations — it is hard to imagine any business being able to reach a decision quickly without the aid of information systems to retrieve, analyse and model data. Information systems security is vital for most organisations, and it is increasingly important to the accounting profession. In many SMEs, the accountant becomes the de facto information systems manager, overseeing the implementation of business processes and controls through the system. Because much of computer security relates to internal controls, accountants frequently take a leadership role in systems security and audit. For e-businesses that need to meet certain criteria to obtain a web seal (this is issued by a third party and tells potential customers that the business can be trusted and has quality processes in place), accountants are heavily involved in ensuring compliance (see also information systems governance in chapter 11). The professional accounting bodies (e.g. CPA Australia) usually insist that their members have knowledge and proficiency in information systems and IT.

Information systems and management

Human resources managers are beset by large amounts of legislation that must be strictly adhered to. Additionally, attracting, retaining and developing staff are major tasks. The real challenge is to match the staffing capability to the current and future needs of the business cost effectively. This entails salary forecasting and skills requirement analysis, because there is a fine line between under- and overstaffing. Each employee must have his or her own set of records. The most mundane part of the operation is payroll. Information systems are an integral part of human resources management and, properly used, they can allow a manager to spend more time out of the office networking with staff and focusing on strategic issues. As a simple example, consider the advantages of a web-based system that would allow employees to update their own details, such as pay disbursements, leave and superannuation. These routine tasks are usually handled by clerical staff, so there is considerable potential for cost savings.

Operations managers are concerned with balancing inventory against cash flow. All manufacturing requires processes and products to be monitored for quality and waste reduction. Reordering can be automated using materials requirements planning systems. Information systems allow several perspectives of manufacturing to be obtained, so that individual processes and overall pictures may both be examined.

Generally, the more structured and better understood processes are, the easier it is to automate and support them using information systems, so human resources managers and operations managers are extensive users of information systems.

Enterprise resource planning (ERP)

As the modelling and forecasting capabilities of information systems applied to manufacturing became apparent, the question arose whether these techniques and thinking styles could be applied to other areas of business. The answer was 'yes'. The techniques used in production management were extended to total supply chain management, human resources management, accounting, finance and marketing. Integrating all these functions into a single enterprisewide system to shorten timelines and yield inherent synergies became known as **enterprise resource planning (ERP)**.

The best-known ERP software, comprising large modular integrated subsystems, is the German product SAP (the company name is System Anwedung Produkte). The modular approach means that businesses simply buy what they need. Because the modules are intended to be used by many businesses, they provide everything that a business needs, but not necessarily everything that it wants. For the few percentage that 'want' deficit, a business can pay to customise the package or more commonly adapt its processes to suit the requirements of the system. Once this has been done, the business has an information systems infrastructure that supports multisite, concurrent business processes and is easier to update and maintain.

Converting from a traditional style of operation to ERP is not without risk, since the transition process usually has teething problems, and if the analysis and planning have not been thorough, the systems will not function as required. ERP tends to be the province of large, wealthy organisations because of the costs involved and the scale of the conversion. Most analysts would recommend undertaking BPR at the same time as implementing ERP.

Making technology manageable

Technology is wonderfully seductive, and it is easy to become too involved. Technical problems are very satisfying to deal with because there is usually a single problem and results are almost always forthcoming. Business and management problems are not so easy to deal with, because there is a degree of uncertainty and several problems tend to be handled concurrently. Some management and business problems are insoluble, so the best that can be hoped for is to improve the situation. Although technology can create opportunities, the business plan should be business driven, not technology driven. You need to balance being ignorant of technical issues and being too knowledgeable. As a guideline, consider your personal video recorder or MP3 player — you do not need to have detailed technical knowledge to use the device effectively. The same applies to information systems technology — you need to focus on what you can do with the technology rather than the details of how it works.

[**Key concept:** Business drives technology — technology creates new opportunities for business.]

infobyte: Net consumers or net consumed?

The average British person with broadband spends 50 days per year online, with about 23–24 hours per week online. When other media usage is considered, the Broadband Brit spends almost 50 hours per week consuming media — and this does not include cinema, mobile phones and SMS. Allowing 40 hours per week for work, 10 hours for transport and an hour a day for sundry items, the average week must have less than 30 hours' sleep time. The social and health impacts of technology on lifestyle are truly 'staggering'. Curious as this is, it does indicate where future business opportunities lie.

Source: Information from Johnson, B 2006, 'British Internet users spend 50 days a year surfing Web', *The Guardian*, 8 August, http://technology.guardian.co.uk.

Keeping up to date

The natural environment for information systems is business. By reviewing the changes and trends that are taking place in business and society, the effects that information systems are having may be seen and it is possible to estimate the effects that they might have in the future. Information systems professionals need to be good at understanding the big picture. A substantial portion of this chapter is devoted to a review of the nature and history of information systems. The onus is now on you to make the connections between academic coverage of business and information systems and the real world. As you work through this text, this task should become easier. However, it is strongly suggested that you make use of the World Wide Web and some of the more popular journals and magazines to keep your awareness up to date. Should you eventually work in information systems, membership of professional bodies and attendance at meetings and seminars provide a cost-effective way to keep up to date.

Summary

This chapter introduced you to the background and nature of information systems and the issues surrounding the discipline. Most important is the relationship between information systems and other business disciplines. The key points in this chapter are:

> Data, information and knowledge are different things but they need to be considered holistically.

> Information systems is a business discipline in its own right but it relates to and supports every other business discipline.

> To be effective in information systems, it is necessary to know something of other business disciplines to develop a shared understanding with clients.

> Information systems is not about technology; rather, it is a framework for thinking about and managing technology.

> Information systems and communications have been instrumental in the huge growth of the SME sector by lowering market entry and operating costs.

> As the mundane aspects of business have been automated, there has been a tendency to move towards a knowledge economy in which intellectual capital is vital.

> Information systems permit business processes to be transformed and integrated, allowing new forms of management and competition.

Questions

1. It has been said that in Australia, WWW stands for the World Wide Wait. Use the Internet to examine download speeds for different countries and say whether you think the point is justified. Give reasons for your answer.

2. If you shop at any of the major supermarket chains in Australian, then the concept of a loyalty card should be very familiar to you. What are the advantages of the loyalty card from the customer's point of view? What does the supermarket chain get from the exercise? Now consider the loyalty card concept using Porter's model. Which of the five forces are affected and how?

3. Over the past 30 years, huge sums of money have been invested in information systems and IT. Somehow, improvements in staff productivity have failed to keep pace with this investment. Do you think that the relationship between the amount of money spent on technology and the increase in productivity is direct or is it more complicated? How do you account for the lack of increase of knowledge worker productivity?

4. Apple's iTunes has had a significant effect on the recorded music industry. Apple has been careful to make sure that its download tracks have the same wholesale price as tracks bought in music stores. Some people argue that this phenomenon has returned the industry to the 1950s, before albums existed, when customers just bought the singles that they wanted. Does the increased choice have to mean a reduction in profitability? How do you view consumer power in the light of this?

5. Just as the industrial revolution destroyed the extended family, the information revolution is destroying the nuclear family. Does this statement have any validity? Consider personal media players, mobile phones, time spent online and so on before answering.

6. Consider the phenomena of outsourcing and flexible manufacturing systems. What are the implications for manufacturing if these trends are pursued to their logical extreme? Is this likely to happen?

7. The Internet has made it much easier to access information for student assignments and term papers, but how can you be sure that the information you are using is accurate, current and unbiased? Do the same issues have relevance for businesses? What would you suggest to improve the situation?

8. Think about a supermarket chain operating a computerised checkout system (point of sale system). What advantages (immediate and potential) does the business obtain from its system? (*Hint:* think about integrating different aspects of business operation.)

9. Think about your web surfing and online purchasing experiences (if any) and suggest assessment criteria for judging the quality of websites and web-based systems. What do you think are the three most important aspects and why?

10. It is apparent that the World Wide Web may have levelled the playing field between large and small companies in terms of establishing a Web presence by lowering barrier costs to entry, but do larger companies make better use of their websites than small ones?

Exercises

1. Imagine that you have been retained to produce a list of the function requirements for the next-generation Rolex watch. What features should it include? Should it be electronic or mechanical? Justify your suggestions.

2. In our daily lives, we disclose information to many different businesses. While the information is fragmented, there is little real threat to personal privacy but as soon as information from different sources can be assembled in one place to form a more complete picture, it becomes more useful to businesses and more threatening to individuals. Identify the types of information that businesses would want to have available to them and why. Identify potential areas of concern for consumers. Now outline a simple code of practice that would help businesses and consumers.

3. If you have not visited eBay already, then take the time to do so and research a little of the company history. In particular, pay attention to the importance of PayPal. Can you apply

Porter's five competitive forces model to explain the rise of eBay and how it keeps the competition at bay?

4. As president of the student guild, part of your brief is to generate income for the organisation. Most students on campus have wireless networked laptop computers and the university has a well-developed wireless networking infrastructure. You have a brilliant idea, a wireless-enabled, campuswide 'eBay' facility, which will allow staff and students to buy and sell goods to each other, as well as being able to purchase selected consumer goods, music downloads and concert tickets. Your mother (who is about to retire from her work as a nurse) is so enthusiastic about the project that she wants to invest a significant portion of her superannuation payout in the new business. What issues do you need to resolve to develop a cogent business plan? What potential risks do you envisage? What do you think about the ethics of using your mother's superannuation to fund the business?

CASE STUDY: Parking is such sweet sorrow

Hoboken in New Jersey, the United States, has long been a leader in the deployment of technology. It was the site of the first brewery in the United States, Thomas Edison drove an early electric train to Montclair from its terminal and it is argued that soft ice-cream was invented there. As in many American cities, parking is something of a problem in the central business district and traditional multistorey car parks do not make the most efficient use of storage space.

The solution Hoboken decided to adopt was to buy into a fully automatic parking facility. These are quite rare. They make very effective use of space by eliminating access ramps and laneways. Each car parked in the facility is lifted and shuffled into one of many densely packed parking bays. Because humans do not need access to the parking bays, cars can be very closely parked horizontally and vertically. The system can retrieve a car in 30 seconds. The lift systems work independently, with each entry and exit station handling 40 cars per hour. Each space is an individual machine, which acts in a cooperative way. Over time, the facility 'learns' about customer and car movements and rearranges its load to minimise collection time. The entire facility can be managed remotely.

The city of Hoboken owns the parking facility, and Robotic Parking (based in Clearwater, Florida) owns the software that controls its operation.

Any automatic facility has the potential for problems, such as hardware failures or software glitches. So when customers found that their cars were trapped inside the parking facility, they were quick to blame the technology. However, the technology had not malfunctioned. The system had been disabled because of a dispute over the licensing terms of the software.

The city of Hoboken, in the days before the contract was due to expire, had its police force remove all Robotic Parking staff from its premises, not realising that the company had intellectual copyright of the software that made the large-scale parking facility work, as well as physical ownership of the technical manuals. The parking facility simply ceased to function.

A court battle ensued. The city accused Robotic Parking of sabotaging its own code; the software developer accused the city of allowing competitors into the garage and consequently damaging its business. During the dispute, the cars that had been trapped inside the garage remained trapped.

The terms of the agreement reached in the case stipulated that Robotic Parking is obliged to provide technical support for the duration of a three-year software licence and that the city must pay US$5500 for each month it continues to use the software.

Although this case has been settled, it has provoked a lot of discussion on the ethics of including 'time bombs' in software systems to enforce the terms of their licence. Specialised software systems are increasingly sophisticated and complex, and many vendors are able to exploit this. It has been argued that a change to the law is needed but other people take the view that legislative changes are pointless because vendors will find a way around the new laws by carefully worded contracts. The consensus is that the old maxim '*caveat emptor*' (let the buyer beware) is now more relevant than ever.

Source: Information from Quinn, N 2006, 'Giant robot imprisons parked cars', *Wired News*, 8 August, http://www.wired.com.

Questions

1. Why do you think that so much software is licensed to users rather than purchased outright?

2. Could the city of Hoboken have handled the situation better so that cars were not held hostage? What factors do you think led to the situation escalating to breaking point?

3. Should vendors be able to enforce the terms of the software license by placing logic bombs (pieces of software that can render the system useless) in their systems? Explain why.

4. If you were about to embark on a similar project, what precautions would you take to avoid the problems that Hoboken experienced?

5. Should vendors have exclusive rights over their software or are there circumstances under which the purchaser should be able to use the software when the license has expired or to alter the computer programming in some way?

6. Do you think that politicians could create laws to prevent this sort of thing? Realistically, do you think that they have sufficient knowledge and expertise? If not, then who should do it?

7. Can you think of any clauses you would add to Hoboken/Robotic Parking contract to make dispute resolution easier? You do not need to phrase this in strict legal terms, just think about the processes that would need to be followed in the event of a dispute.

References

Audretsch, DB, Carrie, MA, van Stel, AJ & Thurik, AR 2000, 'Impeded industrial restructuring: the growth penalty', Tinbergen Institute discussion paper, www.tinbergen.nl/discussionpapers/00095.pdf.

Benson, S & Standing C 2000, 'Synergising the personal–corporate knowledge nexus', in Benyon-Davies, P, Williams, MD & Beeson, I, *Proceedings of the 5th UK Academy of Information Systems*, McGraw-Hill, Maidenhead, pp. 139–47.

Davies, G 1996, *A history of money from ancient times to the present day*, rev. edn, University of Wales Press, Cardiff.

Drucker, PF 1993, *Post-capitalist society*, Harper Business, New York.

Haag, S, Cummings, M & Phillips, A 2007, *Management information systems for the information age*, 6th edn, McGraw-Hill Irwin, New York.

Keen, P 1980, 'Reference disciplines and a cumulative tradition', in McLean, ER, *Proceedings of the First International Conference on Information Systems*, Philadelphia, pp. 9–18.

Lyn, J & Jay, A 1989, *The complete Yes Minister*, BBC Books, London, p. 457.

McKeown, PG 2003, *Information technology and the networked economy*, Harcourt College Publishers, Orlando.

Naisbit, J 1994, *Global paradox: the bigger the world economy, the more powerful its smallest players*, William Morrow & Co., New York.

Porter, M 1979, 'How competitive forces shape strategy', in *Harvard Business Review*, vol. 57, March–April, pp. 86–93.

Weber, R 1997, *The ontological foundations of information systems*, Accounting Research Methodology Monograph no. 4, Coopers & Lybrand, Melbourne.

Yourdon, E 1997, *Death march: the complete software developer's guide to surviving 'mission impossible' projects,* Yourdon Computing Series, Prentice Hall, New York.

CHAPTER 2
Business software

LEARNING OBJECTIVES

After reading this chapter, you should be able to:

» understand the nature, broad history and five generations of software and relate them to hardware generations

» contrast hardware and software

» describe the types of software in current use

» understand the step–lock cycle and how communications can alter the pattern of competition in the software industry

» distinguish between horizontal and vertical software

» distinguish among packaged, customisable and custom software, and explain their relative merits

» describe the relationships among systems software, applications software and hardware

» explain what is meant by the term 'intelligent agents' and give examples of their use

» understand the nature and importance of open source software.

Introduction

A detailed understanding of the underlying technology is not necessary to be an effective and visionary manager. However, you do need to understand the nature of what you manage. The process of producing software is covered in chapter 6, but for now it is sufficient to examine the major categories of software in common use and the major trends in the software industry. As with hardware, reducing diversity and complexity simplifies management and reduces risk and cost in the process.

Consider the material in this chapter from the perspective of someone who is managing the information systems function for a sizable organisation. Even though it has been clearly stated that business economics now favour smaller organisations, considering larger organisations will encourage you to develop a 'big picture' perspective, which will be useful to you when managing the development of systems. The departments of many larger organisations operate as quasi-independent business units — they are almost small–medium businesses in their own right. This allows a high degree of autonomy for the business units, which, in turn, allows senior management to focus on outcomes rather than processes. Software plays a vital role in this.

This chapter gives a brief selective coverage of the history of software, covering the main issues from a business perspective. Specific types of software application are discussed later in the book, but it is assumed that you are reasonably familiar with products that are available for desktop computers. Some background knowledge of developmental trends in software, together with an understanding of the different kinds of software in use and their tactical and strategic aspects, is very useful for anyone who needs to be involved with information systems project development or management.

The history and nature of software

The development of software has closely paralleled that of hardware. Each generation of hardware has had its own generation of associated software. From earliest times, the tools and the intelligence that uses them have been clearly distinguished. As technology has grown in complexity, it has become possible to automate some of the more routine tasks. It is now common to have tools that control other tools, as well as specialist tools and multipurpose tools. It may be seen that the same sort of distinctions have emerged in software. But when did software actually appear?

Vaucanson

Jacques de Vaucanson was (arguably) the earliest developer of software. Appointed as inspector of silk factories in France in 1741, he turned his attention to the problems of mechanising the industry (Britannica 2001). Celebrated as an inventor of mechanical automata, Vaucanson had produced a lifelike flute player in 1738 and a remarkable mechanical duck the year after. In developing his automata, he designed the programmed behaviour into the device. The mechanical duck's movements would eventually show repetition. Changing the behaviour of the duck required changing its design and internal workings. In 1745, he developed a fully automatic weaving loom, which allowed intricate patterns to be produced, and chose to use punched cards as the medium of control. Punched cards had been used before but only for generic settings; a human operator was still required to provide the skilled input. Vaucanson's loom needed no skilled operator. The skill came in designing fabrics and transcribing those designs to punched cards. Once produced, the cards could be duplicated and reused on another Vaucanson loom. What prevented the take-up of the technology was that Vaucanson's cards could not be used on anything other than one of his looms. It would be comparable with someone nowadays producing a desktop software package that was not PC-compatible. The Vaucanson loom was largely ignored for the remainder of the eighteenth century.

Jacquard

Joseph Marie Jacquard discovered Vaucanson's loom and modified it in concept. Instead of a specialised loom, he produced a general-purpose attachment that could be fitted to any loom. The Jacquard attachment became available in 1804–05. By 1812, there were more than 11 000 in use in France alone. An entire industry evolved to make and sell the cards ('software') that operated the looms.

Babbage

Charles Babbage first described his idea to make a 'computer' (actually a general-purpose analytical engine) in 1834 and had completed his first prototypes of elemental devices within two years. In 1822, he had designed a difference engine, a sophisticated mechanical calculator. Although the difference engine did work, the British government decided not to continue funding the project. Babbage improved the design and Georg Scheutz and his son, Edvard, successfully constructed a device based upon Babbage's design in 1853–54 (Babbage Institute 2007). The driving force behind its development was the need to improve military effectiveness, which entailed detailed calculations for accurate navigation and ballistics.

Sadly, Babbage was working in an area in which few people were interested. Babbage's thinking was surprisingly modern: his engine was divided into four units, each with its own function: input, processing ('mill' in Babbage's terminology), storage and output. Three types of punched card were used: constant cards for inputting a constant value; variable cards for variables and transporting values between the functional units; and control cards to control how the mill operated (some information systems professionals still use the term 'mill time').

Babbage spent his entire fortune in a fruitless quest to build his analytical engine (Bromley 1987). His reasons for failure were twofold: first, most Victorian engineering was insufficiently accurate for his needs (although it was theoretically possible to build the device with Victorian technology); second, he was a born tinkerer and kept trying to improve the design with new ideas in the course of production. Little of Babbage's machinery remains, but in 1991, the Science Museum in South Kensington, London, constructed a portion of his difference engine no. 2 using his design and Victorian technology. It functioned perfectly. Both Babbage and his assistant, Countess (Ada) Lovelace, had programming languages named after them.

Hollerith

Herman Hollerith applied Babbage's punched card concept to data collection and processing in the US census in 1890. His technology allowed data capture over a wide range, enabling detailed demographic information to be obtained. Although his machinery carried out integration, its main function was counting and totalising. Nonetheless, it revolutionised the process, saving more than US$5 million — the census takers compiled their results in just six weeks (Meyers 1999; Russo 2001). Hollerith founded the company that would later become IBM. His methods were in use until the 1960s over several generations of hardware.

GaAs works

It is the sort of announcement that can go unnoticed. Freescale Semiconductors had found a way to apply traditional microchip methods to new, higher-speed chips based on Gallium Arsenide (GaAs). So why is such a technical press release of any significance to mainstream business? We are almost at the limits of conventional chip technologies in terms of miniaturisation, if we need more speed, then we need new architectures or new materials or both. GaAs chips will be up to 20 times faster than silicon chips, which offers new applications and business opportunities. Imagine a mobile phone, organiser, wireless Internet device, media player and a blisteringly fast games machine all on the same microchip. One of the major constraints on effective mobile commerce is that restricted processing power in mobile phones prevents the use of demanding multimedia and strong security methods, so GaAs chips could fuel new entertainment, communication and marketing models. While technology can create opportunities, imagination and vision are vital ingredients of business competition and development.

Source: Information from Freescale Semiconductors 2006, 'Gallium Arsenide (GaAs) MOSFET', www.Freescale.com.

Summary of computing's historical progression

With Vaucanson, it may be seen that the information and data required to control a process are separate from the machinery that carries out that process. With Jacquard, the element of portability is added, increasing the applicability of the technology. Babbage provided the clear distinction between data and control codes (although he reverted to machine dependency). Finally, Hollerith showed that information has an existence independent of control codes and hardware. All these ideas are still in evidence today.

[**Key concept:** One generation of software outlives several generations of hardware.]

Generations of software

The previous section explains the division of hardware and software; now there is a need to refine the discussion of software. An understanding of the development of software over several generations will serve to emphasise the importance of standards and of software portability. In particular, the development of modular, well-designed software marks the beginning of the modern software industry. As the demand for applications software grew exponentially, it could not be met by contemporary methods; software needed to be reusable and portable or very easy to develop. The first three generations of software were driven by the technological development of computer hardware; the next generations (see the section on 'The software crisis') would seem to be responses to market forces. It should be noted that the three generations overlap to some extent. Second- and third-generation languages are still widely used today alongside more modern fourth-generation products.

First-generation languages

In the early days of modern computing (the mid-1940s to the mid-1950s), the data and control codes were input as a set of binary digits or machine code. Each machine was different, and the task of programming required intimate knowledge of the machine architecture. Although the task of programming was labour intensive, the cost of manufacturing and maintaining the hardware was enormous by comparison. The number of programmers greatly exceeded the number of computers. Each machine had so many unique features that programs and even programming techniques were not portable from one machine to another. This period of software development was triggered by the advent of first-generation electronic computers. These used vacuum tubes in their construction and were very limited in their processing capability.

Second-generation languages

With improvements in technology and an increased demand for programs, assembly languages began to emerge. These made use of mnemonic codes such as ADD and other instructions that could be recognised by the processor. Although these simplified the task of programming somewhat, they could not be described as user friendly. They offered little in the way of portable software. Assembly codes emerged towards the end of the first generation of computers, and were made possible by the invention of transistors, which formed the basis for the second generation of computers (in the mid- to late-1950s). Although people still program in assembly languages, their use is restricted to specialist applications, such as industrial process control, and embedded systems, such as traffic light controls. Most serious business software is developed using third- or fourth-generation languages.

Third-generation languages

Towards the end of the 1950s, the demand for computer technology for business applications increased dramatically. Obviously, without software, hardware is useless. Two distinct needs emerged: to simplify the task of programming so that the number of programmers could be increased; and to make the software that they produced portable so that it could be used on different computers irrespective of processor architecture. First- and second-generation programs were unsuited to these needs. New kinds of programming language were required: languages that were higher level, that is, as close as possible to natural human languages. These languages had to be as portable as possible so that programs could be used on many different computers and that duplication of programming effort was reduced.

Three major high-level languages emerged at the end of the 1950s: FORTRAN (IBM's FORmula TRANslator), COBOL (COmmon Business Oriented Language) and LISP (LISt Processing language). These were remarkable for several reasons. All three languages incorporated the concept of substructures within programs, which allowed portions of programs to be reused. COBOL had separate descriptions for data and procedural code.

Each language relied on compiler technology for its implementation. A compiler is a program that translates all of a high-level language program into a form that the processor can handle; that is, it translates high-level language into executable code for the processor. The high-level language is now independent of the underlying hardware (the compiler is, of course, still machine dependent). A compiler translates all of a program at one and the same time. An alternative approach is to perform translation as required using an interpreter. Generally, interpreters are more flexible but slower than compilers. In the 1950s and early 1960s, punched cards and tape were still the preferred medium for inputting code and data. In this way, one generation of software was able to outlive several generations of hardware, and a program could be duplicated and run on many computers. The basis of the modern software industry had been established. In the early stages of this generation of software, computers were constructed using integrated circuit boards with transistors and so on mounted on them. As microprocessors replaced circuit boards, third-generation languages continued (and continue!) to be used, a testament to the portability of the programs. In the early part of this software generation, designers began to consider data and processes as separate things. For many people, this marks the beginning of information systems in the true sense of the term.

> **Reflection question 1:** Software piracy was never an issue in the early days of modern computing. Why do you think this was?

The software crisis

The success of third-generation languages transformed computing and led to the establishment of information systems as a practice in its own right. However, while the demand for software increased exponentially, the supply of computer programmers increased linearly. Improvements in technology had led to the mass production of computers, and the cost of labour began to exceed hardware costs. The resulting shortfall was obvious in that companies could not build the systems they wanted because of lack of software. This shortfall was termed the software crisis. Several solutions were proposed.

Simplifying programming

Sets of tools designed to help the developer produce good-quality code more quickly were developed but failed to produce the expected increase in programmer productivity. Although the task of programming was much easier, the relative complexity of the programs was much greater, so the two tended to cancel each other out. Object-oriented programming (OOP) is covered in chapter 6 but note that OOP favours rapid development and prototyping and facilitates code reuse at a component rather than module level.

Reusing software

Instead of having each program tailored to a particular application, there was movement to produce code that was more modular in structure, enabling it to be reused in other systems. This in turn required the development of sophisticated design and management methodologies to ensure reusability and the adoption of internationally recognised language standards.

Developing new paradigms

If traditional programming methods were impeding progress, then moving to another method of working seemed logical. The development of large, customisable software packages that provided general solutions to business problems was one approach. The development of more specialised packages, such as databases with their own inbuilt languages, was another.

Fourth-generation languages

The first three generations of programming language were procedural languages. In other words, the software developer had to know what was required and how it should be performed.

There were many users who knew exactly what they wanted from the system but who had no idea about how to write a program to perform the task. **Fourth-generation languages** (or **nonprocedural languages**) are query oriented in that a user need only specify what is required and the underlying software will sort out the business of how it is to be obtained. Because databases were at the heart of most corporate information systems, they were where the languages tended to evolve. SQL (Structured Query Language, a high-level database-oriented language for nonprogrammers) is the best known example of a fourth-generation language. It is very high level and closer to natural language than third-generation languages. It was developed as a database language in 1969 and first published in 1970. Whereas previous generations of software have been linked to and driven by technical developments, SQL was developed to simplify the process of information retrieval from very large databases. The conceptual breakthrough was that users no longer needed to know how to program, merely how to formulate a query. This made the business of 'programming' simpler and allowed more systems to be developed more quickly.

It is not uncommon to see third-generation programming embedded into fourth-generation programs. The huge development effort expended in producing transaction-processing systems has yielded fast and efficient (if primitive) programs that operate on files. Rather than redevelop everything, it is easier to embed the new database query language statements into the older third-generation code. This also gives much greater sophistication in terms of control.

>**Reflection question 2:** Is there still a software crisis?

Fifth-generation languages

With each generation of language, software developers have moved further away from the underlying hardware; in other words, the degree of abstraction has increased. There has been a distinct progression from machine level to human level, from syntax to semantics. The fifth generation, if it ever arrives, will use natural language. Although speech recognition systems and elementary dictation systems exist, they remain at a fairly primitive level. Dictation software usually has high correction requirements. There are systems that accept voice input, but these are restricted to single words or short phrases of known format. Parsing entire sentences and interpreting their meaning requires a high degree of intelligence. This problem is compounded by the diversity of sentence construction. It is very likely that these difficulties will be overcome in the near future.

Contrasting hardware and software

Think about the nature of costs in the hardware industry. To a great extent, it relies on a large market to justify its existence. Substantial effort is devoted to design, and the expense of putting together an assembly line is huge. In addition, components, labour, packaging, shipping and warranty have costs.

Software also requires a substantial effort in design, simply because of the nature of the market. Whereas the cost of fixing a design flaw in a microcomputer requires resetting the assembly line and recalling all affected units, often the only thing faulty software requires is the amendment or addition of a few lines of code. The additional information can be downloaded from a website instantly. With the exception of intelligence, no raw materials are required for the production of software and it can be sent anywhere in the world on a DVD for a few dollars. This is not the case for hardware, which can be expensive to pack and ship. The software industry has much higher turnover per employee than traditional manufacturing. But in an industry in which innovation is a major competitive factor, much of the income may be spent on research and development. This may hinder the growth of smaller companies. However, it is possible that a software futures market will emerge. If so, it will provide a means of funding software development.

The software industry has grown so much that it now exerts considerable influence on the direction that hardware development takes. Many computer manufacturers optimise their hardware so that it runs the most popular software more efficiently. This in turn causes market distortion and makes it hard for new and potentially better software to enter the market.

As are audio and video recordings, software is not usually purchased, but licensed. This imposes restrictions on users regarding unauthorised duplication and use. Licences may be for a single machine or an entire site. Usually, licences are restricted to a particular version of the software. To date, no software producer has promoted a licence that operates on a charge-for-use basis.

It is possible to change the entire look, feel and behaviour of software with relatively few additions to or modifications of the code. Because of this, software packages contain fossil relics of previous systems. The economics of the situation mean that a lot of software has grown beyond its original specification. This, in turn, imposes technical and operational constraints on companies. The sheer development effort may mean that the software system can never be replaced, only modified or maintained. Many large corporate databases could represent more than 400 person years in development costs. It is easier to build a financial case for replacing a small system that is obsolete. Much of the software was designed and produced at a time when RAM was scarce and processors were slow; this limits the performance of many systems. Finally, the nature of software means that it is relatively easy to steal and smuggle. Software piracy is a major problem for most developers, especially in nations that do not recognise copyright laws. It is argued that piracy deprives the industry of the funds it needs to produce better products. Software pirates argue that the industry overcharges for its products anyway. Often, the only way a company can promote a software product is to offer a cut-down version as shareware or freeware in the hope that the demand for extra functionality and services will make the product commercially viable. These companies may turn a blind eye to a little piracy.

IS in action

The $100 laptop

In 2005, Nicholas Negroponte, the chairman of MIT's media laboratory, announced a non-profit initiative that would produce more than 100 million laptops, each costing US$100. These would then be sold to governments of developing nations for distribution to their children. Brazil, Argentina, Egypt, Nigeria, Thailand, India and China have been selected as target nations. The initial cost is about US$135 but this will reduce as production is scaled up. The computer is frugal in terms of power, and several human power options are being investigated. These will be separate from the laptop, to avoid placing a strain on the device. Wireless networking is built into the computer, which has no hard drive. Instead, 500 MB of flash memory is used to store software and data. Designed by Quanta Computer Inc. in Taiwan, the laptop project is truly international and its sponsors include Google, AMD, Red Hat, Brightstar Corporation, News Corporation, Nortel Networks and Canonical Ltd.

With affordability being a major driving force behind development, it was obvious that commercial, proprietary software was not an option. Not only would it have been too expensive, it would have been too demanding in terms of processing power and storage space. Accordingly, Linux is the operating system of choice and developers are working on open source software for educational purposes. Despite its budget price, the laptop features some sophisticated technology: 'better definition than 95% of the laptop displays on the market today; approximately 1/7th the power consumption; 1/3rd the price; sunlight readability; and room-light readability with the backlight off' (SPIE 2006).

The main challenges are not technical but educational, revolving around building a learning culture using the laptops. To establish the viability of the concept, 50 000 of the computers have been used in Maine. Teachers involved with the experiment have been described as 'euphoric'. Negroponte's ambitions do not end with the US$100 laptop, he has issued a challenge to the information technology community to produce an SVGA projector the size of a beer can for less than US$30.

Source: Information from SPIE — The International Society for Optical Engineering 2006, '$100 laptop nears launch', www. Newsroom.spie.org.

> **Reflection question 3:** Are there any circumstances under which you would find software piracy ethical?

An introduction to contemporary software

Modern software comes in three main flavours: applications, systems and communications. A clear division of functionality simplifies software development and means that each can be independent, so long as the interfaces among them are preserved. This allows companies to specialise in developing different kinds of software.

> *Applications software.* This is software that does something of direct benefit to users. This might be something as mundane as word processing, or as complicated as answering a detailed market analysis query. When using applications software, a user is restricted to the features the application offers (some organisations may restrict user access to applications only as a security measure; granting access to file systems and systems software would make hacking much easier and consequently more likely).

> *Systems software.* This is software that performs two basic functions. It manages the underlying resources of the computer so that users and applications software do not need to become embroiled in heavy-duty technical issues. It manages the computer's memory, hard drive and shares processor time among the different programs that need to be run (see the discussion of the operating system in 'Systems software', page 44). It also provides a measure of transparency in doing this. As an example, the command to print should be independent of the make and model of printer. Its second major function is to provide a friendly interface to allow users to carry out basic tasks such as file management or installing new equipment.

> *Communications software.* As the name implies, this is software that handles all communications to and from the computer. This is usually invisible to the user as computers cooperate on a common task or handle printing.

The relationship between users and the different kinds of software is simple: users run applications and access system utilities through systems software. Applications programs use systems software and communications software to do their jobs.

Applications software

Applications software may be specialised for some particular function in a company (vertical software), for example, an in-house financial modelling package, or the software may be general-purpose software (horizontal software), which has been bought 'off the shelf' ready to use. The term 'horizontal' implies that the software package has the potential to be used right across the organisation. Word processing and spreadsheet packages are good examples. Why reinvent the wheel? It makes far more sense in economic terms to buy general-purpose software off the shelf. The economies of scale ensure that horizontal software is very competitively priced because it is intended for the mass market. The development effort and costs of custom software (home-grown vertical software) are huge and are unlikely to be recovered because by definition there is little or no potential for resale. The only time that software should be developed is when there is no alternative for highly specialised but strategically important applications. A category of software falls between these two extremes: applications software environments that can be customised to meet the needs of a particular organisation (customisable software). Here, the software developer produces a very flexible high-quality package. Technical staff can then adapt the product to the needs of the organisation so that it is convenient for all users to work with.

In buying off-the-shelf products, companies are taking advantage of the developer's economies of scale: they do not need to maintain a large technical staff with diverse skills, they have access to user support and they can get the product quickly. Many large software projects may require more than 100 people years of development effort. Also, there is a greater choice and consequently a greater likelihood of developing the best business solution.

Because much of the cost of operating systems comes from user support, it makes sense to standardise applications software. Being 'state of the art' implies risk, because early versions of software may not be reliable. It also means that support staff need to maintain skills in several different products. The same argument for standardising applies to software, but which standards should be adopted? Choose the most appropriate package for the job, subject to the following conditions:

> The package is widely used and supported well. This means that there is a wealth of experience that can be drawn on and it should be easier to recruit people with skills in using the package.

> The supplier has a good track record and is financially sound. If the supplier goes broke, a business could lose access to user support and product development.

> The package is easy to use, and if it is part of a software suite, the user interface and functions should be as consistent as possible.

> The package is compatible with existing packages and, to a lesser extent, existing hardware.

The last consideration is the most telling from a business perspective. The concern is to get the maximum return on investment (ROI) from hardware and software. ROI is often defined as the income an investment brings in each year related to its cost. In information systems, ROI is complicated by the investment being made to reduce costs. Although all the costs are usually known in advance, the benefits in terms of income and savings may take several years to develop. A more commonsense definition would be 'value for money'. Information systems managers are judged on several criteria, one of which is cost-effectiveness. Existing systems (legacy systems) often impose constraints on what is achievable. Information systems is about the art of the possible. No system is perfect — most people have seen compromises in performance, quality, user friendliness and so on because of cost, time constraints or existing systems. The trick is to get the best compromise.

> **Reflection question 4:** Why is horizontal software cheaper than vertical software?

Stand-alone or integrated software?

In the past, most applications were independent, stand-alone packages. This approach led to 'islands' of information. For example, the effort involved in generating a report that contained spreadsheets, graphs and some simple illustrations was huge. Synthesising all the elements using separate applications programs was often complicated because one package produced output that was not compatible with another.

These problems led to the development of software packages in which all common software is available in the same software suite, for example, Microsoft Office. Several pieces of compatible software are bundled together and licensed as a single package. Many software developers have argued that Microsoft's approach to bundling software products and shipping its Internet browser with the system software amounts to unfair competition, but a major advantage of this approach is that the interface, appearance and functions are consistent. Figure 2.1 shows the presentation graphics, website creation and management, spreadsheet and word processing programs from Microsoft Office. Note the similarity in appearance and function. This improves personal productivity.

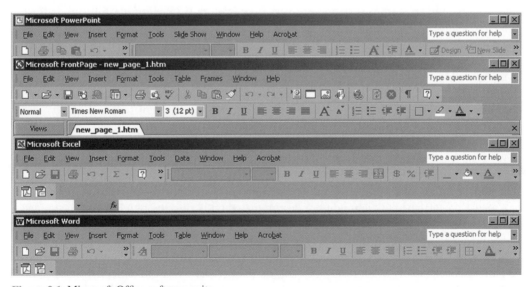

Figure 2.1 Microsoft Office software suite

Although it is true to say that there are other fully integrated office software suites, it must be acknowledged that Microsoft has more than 90 per cent of this market and that its nearest rivals have a very small slice of the action and, as a consequence, fewer profits. The Canadian software company Corel has an excellent range of offerings, but Microsoft's market domination means that large corporate users tend to select and stay with Microsoft's products simply for transparency of use, even though files can be exchanged easily between the two products. Adobe has done much to standardise file exchange between programs and platforms, but the company is at the mercy of Microsoft. In 2004, the state of Massachusetts investigated claims that Microsoft was stifling competition from unspecified Internet search engines and alleged that similar campaigns were planned against producers of other document software, such as Adobe Acrobat (Foss 2004). In the interim, other players such as Google are entering the desktop market and providing desktop software that can follow users around the world: Google Spreadsheet is the most obvious example. Microsoft will need to act to protect its US$11 billion market.

The development costs of software are the same for a mainframe, mid-range system or PC. The mainframe market is much smaller, so to ensure cost recovery and profit, the cost of mainframe software licences is much greater than that of PC licences, with $1 million to $2 million not uncommon. Correspondingly, the range of software available for PCs far exceeds that available for mainframes. A rough survey indicates that there are at least 15 000 commercial software packages for PCs, as opposed to a few hundred for mainframes. Integrating software makes people more productive because they can move data between different software applications. Think how easy it is to generate a word-processed report that includes graphs and tables generated from a spreadsheet and a database. Just as applications software can be horizontal or vertical, so integration can be horizontal, vertical or a combination of the two.

Giving it away — software for free

You are probably familiar with shareware and freeware. These are software that is available for download from the Internet or freely circulated on disk. The production values of shareware and freeware may be very low, with no guarantee of quality, user support or security. In fairness, the quality varies from very good to very poor. Naturally, most of the software is for PC or related platforms. Sometimes, a company will allow a cut-down version of its software to be downloaded to promote the professional version. Some companies may try out software that is under development (beta versions). Sometimes, a company may give its valuable program code away for nothing, as is the case with Mozilla's web browser and email software. However, you should realise that centring core business applications on shareware is potentially high risk, because a small private company in startup phase is often in danger of failing. Equally, major companies trying to break into the software market (e.g. Google) may provide reliable freeware, but the functionality, compatibility and user support may be questionable.

We obtain software 'free' in other ways. Original equipment manufacturers incorporate Microsoft's systems software into a computer that they then sell under their own brand names. Microsoft 'bundles' other products with the systems software, for example, an Internet browser or a media player. The bundle might not be completed until after the purchase has been made. For example, Macintosh buyers can download entry-level media-editing software for free. Bundling has short-term advantages for the user but might stifle competition in the longer term.

Microsoft's Internet browser came free with the system software. Netscape's browser had to be purchased separately. As a result, Netscape's market share fell dramatically. Since a large portion of Netscape's business was in building private internets (intranets) for companies, the company took the view that if it gave away the software code for its browser, software developers would develop applications that would make use of its technology.

Despite this bold move, Netscape's fortunes continued to decline until the company was acquired by AOL in 1999, and use of the Netscape browser has declined to a few per cent. AOL's motives in acquiring Netscape might have been to prevent competition, but a popular (and — more importantly — free) browser would have been of enormous benefit to AOL. Although AOL's share of the domestic US market is considerable, it is a very small percentage of the total Internet user population. If direct competition is not possible, then a widely used vendor-independent browser might be a desirable option. In 2003, AOL opted to let the Netscape name disappear and donated startup funding to the Mozilla Foundation. This is proving to be a shrewd move. Mozilla inherited all the source code from Netscape and has a commitment to open source code and documentation. Anyone can develop features for the Mozilla suite. All that is required is that developers adhere to Internet standards and that, if their code is meant for public distribution, the source code and documentation are made freely available. The current version of Mozilla incorporates an enterprise-grade email client that can synchronise with palm devices (Thunderbird); a web browser with security features built in (Firefox); Internet chat software; and a web page editor. Within the first few weeks of its release, more than a million downloads were recorded (www.mozilla.org), indicating the demand for a vendor-neutral browser suite. Care was taken to ensure that both PC and Macintosh users were fully catered for.

It is hard to give a breakdown of browser use because many sites are not able to distinguish among browsers, but reliable estimates put Internet Explorer's share of the desktop about 63 per cent, with Mozilla's Firefox browser having about 30.8 per cent of the market. (W3Schools 2006). Other estimates put Internet Explorer as having up to 80 per cent of the market. It is even harder to tell the kind of machine from which a web search or request originates, because these estimates are often based on the type of browser used. Many users will simply use the browser that their PC came with, while others will install their browser of choice. Knowing the type of browsers in use and what type of computer they are running on helps web designers to produce websites that are 'optimised' for most users and to identify market niches that need to be catered to.

The 'browser war' is not merely about domination of the computer desktop but about controlling Internet standards and information channels. Because Microsoft's Internet Explorer has such a large share of the market, many web developers often ensure that their website works best with that browser. From a purely pragmatic point of view, this is not unreasonable. Other developers have a long-term commitment to open source code and international standards. They see an Internet that is free from domination by one or two megacorporations as benefiting most Internet users. The nature of standards is discussed in the section 'Open source vs proprietary software' later in this chapter. The choices that information systems managers need to make revolve around a few important factors. Using free software can save money in the short term but could cost more later if maintenance is an issue. Freeware that is open source can reduce dependency on software suppliers but could lead to compatibility problems if the business makes extensive use of proprietary software. The question of security is vexatious: some people would argue that widely used proprietary systems are targeted by hackers, while others believe that open source freeware is inherently insecure because of poor production values and quality control. As with so many other issues in business, the best way to make a good decision is to make a thorough evaluation of needs, risks and costs.

Beware of geeks bearing gifts

When we think about hackers installing spyware and malware on PCs, we tend to imagine a disaffected individual wreaking havoc just for fun. We do not expect a major corporation to be responsible but that is just what happened in 2005. Sony BMG was using techniques normally associated with spyware and viruses to restrict unauthorised copying of its music CDs. The technology is called XCP (eXtended Copy Protection) and it makes Sony's audio tracks inaccessible to anything other than Sony's Music Player. It also prevents users from making more than three backup disks of the same CD. Customers who use PCs as media centres must accept an end-user licence agreement to install Music Player; that is, if they want to play Sony CDs that they have bought. Most users did just that but they were unaware that the installation also included spyware, which hid itself in the heart of the Windows operating system. Music Player then became the default media player and would gather information on user listening habits. Uninstalling Music Player did not remove the spyware, which continued to prevent users from making copies of CDs. Whether by intent or accident, the software seems to prevent users from making clean copies of MP3 files from noncopy-protected CDs by inserting pseudorandom noise into files. Users reported that their CD and DVD drives no longer functioned or 'vanished' from the system if they were running popular security software (abcnews.go.com). With hundreds of thousands of PCs affected, the public relations people worked overtime and soon a software patch was made available, but to download the patch, users had to supply a lot of personal information. In the interim, real hackers were beginning to exploit the security chinks that Sony had exposed. The legal battle continues and there are several class actions in progress in the United States, with several others settled. The case raises some interesting discussion points. How far can a company go to protect its copyright? How should consumers respond? Curiously, Sony managed to offend many legitimate customers and there is talk of boycotts. Despite removing the software from many of its new releases, Sony insists that its CDs will be protected. So for now the best advice for consumers is *caveat emptor* — buyer beware.

Source: Information from Veiga, A 2006, 'Sony program woes linger for AOL users', http://abcnews.go.com; Borland, J 2005, 'Antivirus firms target Sony "rootkit"', *CNET News*, http://news.com.com.

Systems software

Systems software may be divided into two main categories: the operating system, and the user interface and its associated utilities.

The operating system manages the underlying resources of the computer, such as the processor, RAM and file system, transparently and handles communication with, and control of, peripheral devices. It is responsible for booting up (starting) the computer and carrying out diagnostic checks. It handles any errors that occur during the execution of programs.

The remaining systems software provides a convenient interface between the user and the underlying hardware and between the user and applications programs. Utilities such as file management and screen savers are also provided here. Figure 2.2 shows the major functional areas of systems software.

Systems software is platform specific, so it may limit the portability of applications. Additionally, systems software may be classified according to its level of scope. There are three levels:

> *personal:* for individual desktop use
> *workgroup:* to support a small community of users
> *corporate:* to support a large organisation.

Often, organisations use all three levels of systems software. Workgroup and corporate levels normally support multiuser operation. Windows and its variants are the most widely used systems software for individual machines and workgroups. Linux is widely used for server or workgroup systems. It has about 25 per cent of the server market. The 2008 Linux servers market should be worth at least US$10 billion. Despite the availability of Linspire (a window interface for desktop Linux systems), Linux accounts for only 3.5 per cent of the desktop market (W3Schools 2006) but this may change as more user-friendly Linspire packages are developed.

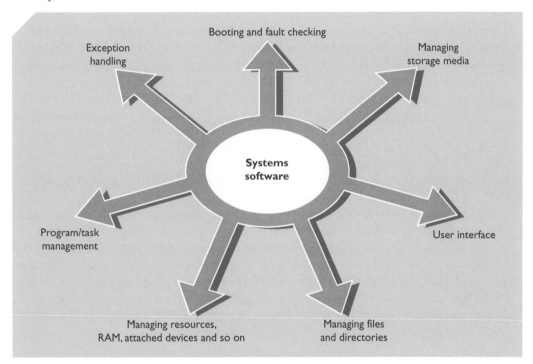

Figure 2.2 Seven functional areas of systems software

Some systems software operates at all three levels, and Unix is a good example of this. Originally developed as a teaching tool, it rapidly became commercially exploited because the source code (the actual high-level language text in which the systems software was written) was made available to anyone who had an interest in developing software for it. There are versions of Unix for mainframes, workstations and PCs. Because there are well-defined standards for Unix, and no single corporation controls its development, it is said to be 'open'. Open systems are systems that are conformant with industry standard hardware platforms and data formats, and for which anyone may develop software. This facilitates software and data portability. This contrasts with proprietary systems software, which is controlled by a single company. Standards for Unix graphical user interfaces (GUIs) were set in the 1980s, allowing it to have the ease of use of other systems software packages. However, it is apparent that Unix is losing market share to both Linux and Windows.

IS in action

Things go better with Swire

A small 1816 Liverpool trading house owned by John Swire has grown into a huge, diverse multinational corporation. A subsidiary operation, Swire Beverages, is a joint venture between Swire Pacific and Coca-Cola. It operates in Hong Kong and mainland China and has the sole right to manufacture, market and distribute Coca-Cola products in Hong Kong and Taiwan. The need to use English, Chinese and simplified Chinese as well as specialised file formats was causing technical problems for desktop software and overloaded networks. Large files were placing heavy demands on servers and were taking too long to transmit, slowing the flow of information vital to the company's operations. The diversity of language and lack of effective controls to prevent users from altering and printing documents were also causing some security concerns. These were exacerbated by the increasing number of technical reports, forms and graphs being sent over the Internet or the company's intranet.

The solution was to reduce complexity and diversity by adopting a uniform standard for documents. Swire made a commitment to adopt PDF as its preferred format and chose Adobe Acrobat as its preferred software. Over three years, it installed Acrobat onto 2000 computers, mainly to standardise document formats but also to facilitate process improvement and auto-mation. One significant benefit has been that Swire has been able to implement Coca-Cola's quality system, which requires a standardised document format.

Standardising on Acrobat has enabled offices to stop using multiple (and often different) versions of software. Now only one software package is needed to be able to view documents in English, Chinese or simplified Chinese, which simplifies the entire software platform and reduces costs. The layout and formatting of complex documents are preserved. Because Acrobat compresses files, storage loads on servers and transmission loads on networks have been reduced. The major benefit has been improved security. Only authorised users can amend, annotate or print company documents. In a nutshell, this has resulted in a simpler, faster and cheaper flow of information within the organisation.

Source: Information from www.adobe.com/products/acrobat/pdfs/swire.pdf.

❭ **Reflection question 5:** Why is it necessary to have systems software? Why are the required systems functions not included in the applications software?

Applications programs make use of systems software to perform their tasks. This division of responsibility allows development effort to be focused on applications and systems software separately. However, applications software depends on systems software to function, which has profound implications for the nature of competition in the software industry.

Communications software

This category includes all forms of computer communication. Over the past 25 years, software systems moved through the following discrete phases:

> *stand-alone applications:* totally independent software not linked to any other computer

> *networked applications:* software that can use a network if one is present, provided the user knows how to make use of the features

> *network-friendly applications:* software that can use a network to share information or processing in a user-friendly way

> *network-intrinsic applications:* applications that have been developed specifically for networks, such as client–server architectures.

The main thrust of competition in the computer industry has moved from manufacture to applications software to systems software, and now it seems likely that communications software is set to become a major battleground. Many software developers ignored this area because it is specialised, and certain companies and products managed to consolidate themselves into an expanding area. Early entry into the market allowed these companies to exert an influence on the emerging communications standards and consequently secure a competitive advantage over later entries into the marketplace. Just as systems software influences developmental trends in applications software and hardware, the increasing importance of communications means that communications software is exerting a strong influence on the development of systems software. This is considered further in chapter 4.

The nature of competition in the software industry

In the mainframe market sector, which is relatively small, systems and applications software have been very stable when compared with the PC sector. This has permitted one generation of applications and systems software to outlive several generations of supporting hardware.

In contrast, the PC sector is very large and competition is at its most intense. It is important to understand the nature of the relationship between hardware manufacturers and software developers, since this leads to the 'step–lock cycle', which currently dominates the market. A second factor in the development of the PC market sector has been the development of the graphical user interface (GUI).

The step–lock cycle

The argument for the existence of the step–lock cycle runs thus: hardware manufacturers make faster computers, so software developers make more demanding software to take advantage of the increased processing power. Hardware manufacturers then make even faster computers and the software industry responds by developing more complex and demanding software. This increases the total cost of ownership because businesses are forced to upgrade their hardware and software at regular intervals and at considerable expense.

The graphical user interface

Moving to a graphical user interface (GUI) from text-based systems in the 1980s enfranchised a larger segment of the community because interaction with the computer was less difficult, so users could carry out far more sophisticated tasks. This was part of a movement that has seen the deskilling of much of computer use. Making computers easier to use has had the effect of increasing the size of the market sector, increasing the demand for hardware, applications software and systems software as users join the step–lock cycle.

The GUI approach to computing was made possible by the invention in 1967 of the computer mouse by Doug Engelbart (CNN 1997) (see figure 2.3). Pioneered by Xerox PARC and later by Apple, GUIs allowed users to focus on higher-level issues rather than low-level systems software. Engelbart explained in an interview for *Wired* magazine (2004) that his team had experimented with the number of buttons on the device:

> We tried as many as five. We settled on three. That's all we could fit. Now the three-button mouse has become standard, except for the Mac. Steve Jobs insisted on only one button … We haven't spoken much since then.

The impact of this mouse device cannot be understated because it changed the nature of human–computer interaction totally. Up to that point, users were forced to think in a linear way, in a sequence of text. What Englebart's mouse did was to allow people to think in two dimensions as though they were working on a real desktop. Amazingly, Engelbart received no royalties for his patent: other manufacturers used different technologies to achieve the same result.

Figure 2.3 Douglas Engelbart with a prototype three-button mouse

A winning formula

Formula 1 car racing is an expensive business. Success depends as much on engineering and information systems as it does on the driver. Renault chose Symantec (a company most commonly associated with data security and storage) to provide the infrastructure for its F1 system. Up to 100 sensors monitor some 12 000 vehicle components in real time, allowing engineers to evaluate the effectiveness of their designs and make necessary modifications (in a racing season, up to 30 per cent of a car's design may change). Security of stored and transmitted data is vital to maintaining Renault's position among the elite. Symantec's high-performance solution eliminated the need for additional servers giving cost savings of $222 000.

Source: Information from Symantec 2006, 'Renault F1 team', www.veritas.com.

[**Key concept:** Divide and conquer, break a big problem down into several smaller ones.]

Apple and Microsoft

The Apple Macintosh was conceived as a total package: hardware and systems software. Technically and ergonomically, the Macintosh was a very user-friendly, well-engineered computer with a slick GUI. Whereas PC users had to understand how the computer worked to use it effectively, Macintosh users were free from this constraint and could focus on running applications. The graphical nature of the interface made the Macintosh an ideal vehicle for high-end desktop publishing software and other graphics software and although Microsoft was firmly focused on the PC market, other software companies met this demand. Apple wanted complete control of its product, so it did not allow any other company to manufacture 'Apple clones'. Consequently, while demand for home computers increased exponentially, Apple's ability to meet that demand increased in a linear fashion, resulting in increased sales but declining market share.

That the IBM PC standard was widely available ensured competition for manufacture as 'IBM clones' hit the market. This in turn increased demand for IBM PC standard software. Apple came to rely on Microsoft to supply applications software, but since the Macintosh market was much smaller than that for PCs, the software tended to be developed for the PC first. This eroded Apple's competitive edge in the market, and its market share declined further. The incompatibility of the Apple and PC platforms meant that businesses opted for the PC platform or the Macintosh platform — seldom both. Cost and compatibility issues meant that most companies opted for the IBM standard. If businesses had a need for superior desktop publishing, drafting or graphics software, they opted for the Macintosh simply because the required software had been developed specially for that platform, so was more mature and reliable (even if that meant running several types of desktop computer), and the superior graphics and ease of use outweighed cost factors. The competition between Apple and Microsoft was not purely business based. There is a long and bitter history of litigation between the two, centring on the look and feel of the Apple operating system and its rival Windows. Curiously, Microsoft's potential monopoly led to it becoming a shareholder in Apple to ensure the company's survival. Apple's market share has shrunk from its peak of nearly 16 per cent in 1992 to about one-third of that at 6 per cent (*Mac Daily News* 2007). Although the company has experienced financial stress over that time, it should be noted that the desktop arena is not Apple's only market.

Servers, printers, monitors, imaging, handheld computing, online music and media players are all part of its portfolio. Because it has now moved to use the same chipset as the PC for its desktop and laptop offerings, compatibility is no longer an issue. Whether PC users will flock to the Apple platform remains to be seen but the move is a shrewd business decision. A more interesting question is whether Apple will allow its flagship product operation system to run on the PC platform.

> **Reflection question 6:** If Apple had agreed to the manufacture of Macintosh clones, do you think that Microsoft Windows would still be the dominant systems software for the PC platform?

Linux

The development of Linux is of great interest at this point. The proliferation of the IBM PC standard fuelled the growth of Microsoft Windows. Linux is a PC version of Unix, which has the potential to weaken Microsoft's market dominance in systems software. Linux is open source code, which means that it is a recognised international standard but is not 'owned' by a large corporation. Although specialist software developers' kits can be expensive, the developer of Linux, Linus Torvalds, has made it available to software developers for no charge. Given a choice between Microsoft's system software for a large fee or Linux for little or no cost, many businesses are opting for Linux.

As the user community grows, it becomes more worthwhile developing software for the PC/Linux platform. Users are able to run Microsoft products on a PC using Linux, although there are minor problems regarding integration. Because Linux is comparatively small compared with Windows, it has the potential to run more quickly, allowing cheaper server configurations to be used. Its smaller size means that it is easier to secure and control. Linux is the dominant web server operating system for new installations, and it is likely to provide the enabling technology for high-performance, supercomputer clusters on the Internet.

> **Reflection question 7:** In your view, should hardware and software standards be determined by market forces, or should they be regulated in some way? Why?

How communications software can break the step-lock cycle

With minor upgrades to applications software every 12 months or so and major upgrades every two or three years, the average business can budget about $500 per machine per year for software. In addition, the useful lifespan of the hardware is about two years without a major upgrade, so a further $1000 per year can be added to the operating costs. Although the purchase costs of hardware and the licence costs of software are a minor component of the total operating costs, they are still significant. Most information systems managers would like to reduce costs.

A PC has a powerful processor, lots of memory, hard drive, CD-ROM and so on. If the software and some of the processing were to be carried out by a computer network, all the PC would need to do would be to communicate with the network, accept input, perform output and handle a limited amount of processing. So simplified systems software is all that is required. Instead of replacing the PC every two years or so, the replacement net computer should have a useful life of at least four years. This view has many influential advocates. The applications software would be resident on a dedicated machine (server) on the network. As mentioned, many applications now are client–server and require a network (computer–computer communication) to function. In this environment, the user desktop machines are called 'clients' and they access software, data and services from other computers on the network, which are called 'servers'. Traditional client–server systems have fat clients, in which the clients have a large amount of applications software to run. A more modern and cost-effective approach is to have thin clients, with most the software resident on the network. In this environment, the network becomes the computer.

Simplifying and standardising the client machines mean that all updates and software and hardware upgrades are performed on the network. The management and purchase costs per client machine are much reduced and the task of management is now simplified because the software exists in one place, rather than being replicated on every part of the network. It also allows better control of viruses and security. Because the requirements for the client machines are reduced, they have a longer useful lifespan.

Client–server systems make demands on network capacity, and thin clients require even more from both the network and the servers. Would-be adopters should make sure that the network is able to carry the extra traffic and that the server is suitably powerful. The breakeven point for adopting a thin-client solution is about 15 to 20 desktop machines. As chapter 4 shows, the real cost savings do not arise from the reduced cost of the hardware but from reduced system management costs.

[**Key concept:** Follow the KISS principle (keep it simple, stupid!). If it is easy to understand, then it is easy to maintain and manage.]

This approach is being pushed by some software developers but is being resisted by the major players. So long as many businesses remain locked in to their desktop hardware and software step–lock cycle, the situation is unlikely to change. To be generally applicable to members of the public, the philosophy is predicated on pervasive networking (i.e. communications and networking virtually everywhere, so that the burden of computing is offloaded from desktop machines to a network); but until the communications infrastructure improves, the general public will remain trapped in the step–lock cycle. Most people use only a very small percentage of the total functionality of their software packages, yet they are forced to upgrade to the next version of the software to maintain compatibility with the rest of the organisation and business.

Common horizontal applications software

The basic rules for information systems success in most areas of business are simple: reduce complexity, reduce diversity and automate routine functions. The most common field for horizontal software is that of office automation. Generally, office automation software performs the following functions:

> word processing

> email

> spreadsheets

> web browsing

> database

> document management

> presentation

> project management and scheduling.

Word processing, spreadsheets, database and presentation software should be reasonably familiar to you, so the coverage given here is not detailed. Word processing allows the creation and editing of documents; the use of templates and mail merges saves time and effort. Spreadsheets perform repetitive calculations and allow modelling and 'what if?' analyses of data. Databases maintain records. Presentation software was once taken to refer to products such as Microsoft PowerPoint, which allows the production of lecture slides and animations. Now the definition also embraces the production of documents for online publication and specialist publishing software. These are normally bundled as a software suite, such as Microsoft Office. Alternatively, office automation software is sometimes sold as an integrated package; that is, a single program that carries out several functions. A single program is cheaper but has far less functionality than a software suite.

Email and browser software

Email allows written communication and the exchange of documents among people. Time savings result from the reduction in handling physical mail and cost savings result from the reduction in paper. However, the predictions of the paperless office of the twenty-first century seem to have been premature. Again, the multifunctional aspect of modern software can be seen because many of these packages are integrated with web browsers, and others, such as Groupwise, incorporate groupware. Groupware is discussed in detail in chapter 3.

Web browsers tend to be an underrated productivity tool. Because many workgroup and corporate-level systems operate using client–server technology, web browsers can provide a user-friendly and convenient means of accessing applications and information over the corporate intranet. Microsoft's Internet Explorer has the major share of the PC market, but other lightweight browsers such as Mozilla are making headway. Linux/Unix systems account for less than 4 per cent of desktop machines but dedicated browsers are readily available.

Document management

In a contemporary sense, this is really about information management. Information comes into an organisation from many sources, such as fax, letters and email, in addition to the documents the organisation itself generates. Keeping track of all relevant documents, enquiries, responses and quotations is a major task. Government ministerial offices and legal offices are key users of this software.

Project management and scheduling

Project management software may be horizontal, that is, applicable to any line of business, or vertical, that is, specialised to a particular industry, such as software engineering. It often integrates with basic office software, allowing time and cost management to be handled with equal ease. Scheduling is often incorporated into groupware; for example, Groupwise allows online desk diaries to be examined and meetings scheduled at a mutually convenient time.

Evaluating horizontal software

The following guidelines may be useful when evaluating and selecting software.
> Packages should not be stand-alone if at all possible. Look for how well all the software packages can be integrated with each other and other applications that you may be running.
> Use a well-supported and widely used product. This makes technical and user support simpler. Look for something that is relatively easy to manage and upgrade at a reasonable price.

> Can the software be used by everyone? Ideally, standardise operating environments where possible.
> Is it cheaper to have a site licence or individual copies of the software?
> Is this the first release of the software? It may be better to wait until the product is stable.
> Will users require extensive training in the new software in order to become productive? Or is the software easy to learn?
> Although cost is important, functionality and ease of use are far more important criteria for evaluation.

Packaged, customised and custom built: strategic and tactical implications

In addition to packaged software, there are customised and custom-built softwares. Consultants often advise on software requirements. Some consultants are also **integrators** in that they package hardware and software to produce systems solutions for clients. The most specialised consultancy category in this context is that of the **value-added reseller**, companies that take an existing software product and customise it to meet a client's exact requirements.

IS in action

Run rabbit!

It is well known that Charles Babbage was the founder of many of the principles of digital computing and that Lady Augusta Ada Byron Countess Lovelace was probably the first real programmer. What is less well known is that they used their skills to develop a 'perfect system' for gaming. Babbage was short of cash, Ada was an inveterate gambler and their system simply helped them to lose money with increased confidence. By the 1840s, Ada had accumulated large gambling debts.

Over a century and a half later and still nobody has developed a perfect system. Gambling is about taking calculated risks and the basis of that calculation is accurate information. Greyhound-data is a free system to which users can contribute. Information is held on one and a quarter million dogs, two million races and 40 000 pictures (MySQL 2006). Complicated statistical reports based on millions of records can be generated in less than a second. Initially, the system used a proprietary database system but as the user base grew, it became obvious that it could not support the increased load. As a nonprofit organisation, keeping the total cost of ownership low was important, so MySQL (an open source product) was adopted. With the addition of a few nonstandard pattern-matching routines, a 500 per cent increase in performance was achieved, allowing a reduction in servers needed for the site, yielding significant cost savings: more than 80 per cent on hardware investment. Because MySQL is open source, it is available for any kind of hardware. When Greyhound-data moved from Intel platforms to PowerPC, the change was both quick and easy. Greyhound-data also provides information on more than 100 greyhound adoption services worldwide. Gamblers may be no more successful but they are much better informed.

Source: Information from www.greyhound-data.com; MySQL 2006, 'Greyhound-Data, dog racing site relies on the speed of MySQL', www.mysql.com.

[**Key concept:** If you don't know what you are doing, find someone else to do it.]

Packaged software

Packaged software is software that can be used 'as is'. It is usually purchased from a reseller without the need for intermediaries such as consultants. The advantages are that the cost is usually low, the product tends to be well supported and relatively error free, and the software development has already been done. The disadvantages are that the user is unduly dependent on the manufacturer and has to pay for regular upgrades and user support. If users require a feature that is not included in the package, they cannot have it. If the packaged software is vertical (specialised to a particular process or industry sector), then it is very expensive for the user to migrate to a potentially better product because of the costs of licensing fees, training and workflow re-engineering.

[**Key concept:** Don't reinvent the wheel — unless you need to.]

Customised software

Customised software is usually supplied and installed to a client's specification by a value-added reseller. Most software is customisable to a point, but customised software is specially adapted to meet the client's needs as closely as possible. Although this approach eliminates dependency on the software manufacturer to deliver the required functionality, the client is now dependent on the reseller instead. Usually, a software manufacturer will list several recommended resellers, so the risk is lessened. Customised software is likely to have more errors than packaged software because the smaller market sector will not sustain rigorous quality control. Clients are not well positioned to take advantage of the increased functionality that software upgrades provide, because to do so would mean recustomising the package. Customised software is much more expensive than packaged software.

Custom software

Companies decide to produce their own software for several reasons.
> There is no suitable package on the market to perform the required task and nothing that can be customised to suit.
> The company is looking to develop a sustainable strategic or competitive advantage and competing firms are using packaged or customised software.
> The company is hoping to recover costs and make a profit by selling the finished product.

The development time for custom software can be significant, often running into several years. Custom software is also very expensive to produce and maintain, and is more likely to have errors and bugs than packaged or customised software has. Perhaps worst of all, if a competitor has access to the package, then key features can be duplicated without the long development time that was originally required. In short, a company could spend much time and money developing a package, only to have the advantages that it confers made available to competitors for a fraction of the original cost and time involved.

Table 2.1 gives a comparison of the relative merits of packaged, customisable and custom software.

Deciding which path to adopt requires detailed analysis and consideration. Software is a commitment, not a one-off purchase. Software is an asset and from a financial perspective it should be managed as such in terms of amortisation and replacement.

TABLE 2.1 A comparison of packaged, customisable and custom software

	Packaged software	Customisable software	Custom software
Strategic advantage	Low	Medium	High
Management and maintenance costs and effort	Low	Medium	High
Specialisation	Low	Medium	High
Cost	Low	Medium	High
Cost and effort of upgrade	Low	Medium	High
Range of functionality	High	Medium	Low
Dependency on third parties	High	Medium	Low

[**Key concept:** Hardware wears out and software wears in — both will need replacing at some stage.]

IS in action

Like peas in a pod

Hosting an Olympic games is a sure-fire way to get the world's attention. Just feeding the Olympic entourage is a logistical nightmare, with more than 5000 tonnes of vegetables being consumed during the two-week event. China wants to make sure that there is no potential for contamination from pesticides and pollutants. A repeat of a 2002 food poisoning incident, which resulted in 138 deaths and more than 7000 serious illnesses, is unthinkable. The concern with food quality has been driven by China's entry into the World Trade Organization (WTO) as its food standards are brought into line with the requirements of the WTO codex. The first step in the process has been to establish a world-class residue analysis laboratory (SinoAnalytica) in Qingdao and to ensure its international accreditation.

The second step will prove more difficult. For the duration of the Olympics, every single vegetable will have its own unique reference number and file and will undergo further tests and inspections at the Olympic distribution centre. In the event of a 'safety incident' the information held will enable any contamination to be traced back to its source (Li 2006) and allow any other vegetables from the same source to be recalled.

Source: Information from Li, Z 2006, 'China vegetables are to get identity codes for Olympics', *China Digital Times*, http://chinadigitaltimes.net.

[**Key concept:** Think globally, act locally.]

The relationship among systems software, applications software and hardware

Since 1985 the nature of the relationship between hardware, systems software and applications software has changed (see figure 2.4, where it can be noted that the applications are fully integrated with the system). In the early days, there was little by way of systems software and the applications software ran everything it needed on the computer. With increasing complexity, the layer-cake view of hardware, systems software, applications software and user developed. As the systems became capable of a high degree of integration, the relationships among the components became more complex. The systems software provided a convenient interface to itself (allowing previously text-based system programs to be invoked by a simple point-and-click operation), the applications programs and the underlying computer.

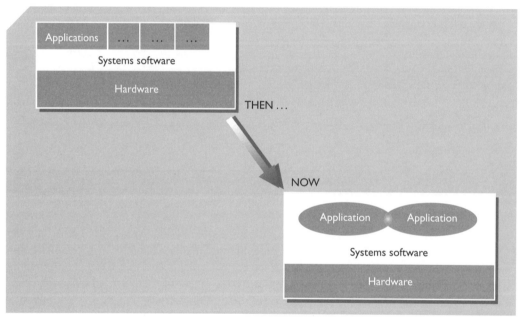

Figure 2.4 The changing nature of the relationship among hardware, systems software and applications software

Intelligent agents

In 1970, one of the biggest problems that managers faced was getting sufficient information quickly enough to run their businesses effectively. At that time, there was only about 1 per cent of the information that exists today and computer networks did not permit universal access. In the twenty-first century, finding information is not the problem — finding *essential* information in a vast sea of irrelevance is. The term 'information overload' is widely understood and there is the potential to 'inform ourselves to death'. This overload is one reason the information revolution has failed to deliver the productivity gains that were promised in the 1970s and 1980s.

This is where **intelligent agents (IAs)** come into their own. These are software entities that act on behalf of a user as an intermediary between the user and one or more systems, or between the user and another IA, autonomously. The IA is programmed according to a set of rules, and some are capable of adapting their behaviour and learning new facts and rules. Because IAs are relatively new, no single definition is accepted in the industry. However, an IA should have at least five of the characteristics detailed in table 2.2.

TABLE 2.2 Characteristics of intelligent agents

Characteristic	Explanation
Specialisation	IAs are dedicated to particular tasks of a repetitious and often complex nature.
Independence	IAs act independently and, if dealing with other IAs, cooperatively with a minimum amount of inconvenience to their initiators.
Portability	IAs should be portable across hardware, software and networks. Some agents, such as the Microsoft Access database wizard, do not meet this criterion.
Intelligence	IAs make decisions based on supplied or learned rules. Some may exhibit a high degree of 'initiative' and the ability to handle requests which are incomplete or ill defined or which contain errors.
Adaptability	Very few IAs really learn and modify their behaviour, but some are able to note user preferences and conform within certain predefined limits.
Credibility	Users should be able to have confidence in the results that IAs produce.
Friendliness	This applies to most software but it is particularly important in IAs given the productivity gains they bring.

Intelligent agents should not be thought of as true **artificial intelligences (AIs)**. In a classical sense, AIs are attempts to mimic human intelligence generally or at least within a particular domain such as geophysical interpretation. The scope of IAs is much narrower they are task focused rather than domain focused.

infobyte

Modelling terrorism — an application for intelligent agents

Intelligent agents can be used to model different scenarios in an active way as the following quotation shows:

> There are tools where they build a world in a bottle. They put down every single mosque, river, camel, and school in, say, Saudi Arabia. Then they have millions of software agents who each have desires, grievances, all these different variables. They go about their little lives and then you ask a question: What if we build a McDonald's in Mecca? Does this lead to more people joining terrorist groups or not?

Source: Gary Ackerman, director of the Center for Terrorism and Intelligence Studies in Goldstein, H 2006, 'Modelling terrorists', www.spectrum.ieee.org.

Intelligent agent applications

The following are just a few examples of how IAs can improve personal and corporate productivity. More mundane applications include having an IA control a robot vacuum cleaner.

Reducing the burden of email

Most professional people routinely wade through vast quantities of email, because this is an easy avenue for sharing information. Much of the mail received is 'spam' (junk email) and irrelevant. IAs can filter email and sort and prioritise messages, allowing users to be more efficient.

Finding and managing information

IAs help users find, categorise, annotate and retrieve information. Once user preferences and requirements are known, an IA can automatically disseminate information on a needs basis. Linking this to another IA, which manages collaboration by scheduling meetings and distributing agenda and minutes and so on, it is possible to send briefing information to participants according to the level of the pre-existing knowledge.

Finding and negotiating the best price

IAs such as Accenture's Bargain Finder, which finds the best CD price from eight online offerings, are really metalevel search engines in that they use other search engines to do their work. Bargain Finder has been around since 1996, which gives an indication of the level of maturity of IAs. More recently, complex interacting IAs have gone beyond mere cooperation to a point at which they negotiate with each other to achieve the best overall deal. The package holiday industry is an ideal application for such technology.

User interface

Desks tend to reflect the personality of their owners. Some people are tidy and others work happily with scattered paper; in-trays may be at arm's length or hidden away under piles of files — in short, desks are an expression of individuality and personal productivity. When user interfaces are considered, it is generally assumed that one size fits all, and although appearances may be changed cosmetically, few major alterations can be accommodated (Benson & Standing 2000). Microsoft introduced a family of animated agents for web pages that are either liked or despised by users according to their level of expertise. In Microsoft's Vista, users performing nonroutine tasks may be interrupted by an agent that says, 'It looks like you are trying to do X', and offers help.

Package-specific agents

A novice user of Microsoft Excel might apply borders and shading to each cell separately, or type the same entry for consecutive cells in the same column. An IA offers suggested contents to save typing. It might also suggest that there is a more efficient way to achieve the desired results or even offer to do the formatting for you. Package-specific agents such as wizards help in the creation of documents and the installation of hardware and software.

Software development

Although a high degree of creativity and intelligence is required for the production of software, many routine tasks are involved as well. Just as package-specific agents detect patterns of operation and make suggestions and offer help, so too do software development IAs. The task of embedding one application within another is a good example of something that can be supported by an IA.

Training employees

IAs can be used to train people to use complex systems and to improve their performance. Because IAs are able to adapt to the skills level of the trainee, training is customised. They can be used in simulation mode or to monitor employee performance on a live system.

> **Reflection question 8:** If IAs continue to grow in number and capability, will a point be reached at which things will run themselves?

The future of intelligent agents

It is reasonably certain that the burden of information will not diminish over the coming years, nor will the complexity of interacting information systems. Accordingly, IAs will improve in terms of functionality and capability. It is not hard to envisage a future in which IAs confer strategic and tactical advantages. These IAs could be highly individualistic, and implemented in software or embedded into firmware, and mobility will be a crucial need. Agents will duplicate themselves and search for information at source, sending only relevant results back to the user, thus reducing unnecessary network traffic. Applications for intelligent buildings and environmental control are already emerging and IAs are finding their way into motor vehicles for fault diagnosis and control (Freepatentsonline n.d.). Imbuing products with intelligence adds value to them and adds new dimensions to their use. As a simple example, think how useful mobile phones with simple organiser and alarm functions have become. IAs make previously passive technologies active, so that your DVD recorder may decide to record a program to its hard drive because you usually watch or record that program. In business systems, an agent might bring a trend or new item to your attention and will learn to adapt its behaviour to suit your needs.

Open source vs proprietary software

This chapter has touched on the topic of open source code several times. Before discussing open source code, this section needs to consider the nature and relative merits of standards. Standards come in three basic flavours:

> *De facto standards.* These are usually established by a dominant player in the market. As an example, Windows is a de facto standard.
> *De jure standards.* These standards have been ratified or defined by a legal or official standards body. As an example, TCP/IP is an internationally accepted networking protocol suite.
> *De rigueur standards.* These are mandatory for reasons that are neither de facto nor de jure, and are often based upon perception rather than reality, for example, 'this system must support Microsoft's System Message Blocking (SMB)'. SMB is a pre-World Wide Web file service that has perhaps 20 per cent of the total market (compared with Novell's 80 per cent for its Novell Core Protocol) and, although not recognised by any de jure body, is still widely regarded as a standard. An example of a de rigueur standard (now ignored): 'No one needs a computer with more than 640 KB memory.' Adobe's Acrobat document format interchange standard (PDF) is a better-known example of a de rigueur standard supported by most Internet browsers.

De jure and de facto standards are of most interest to us since these are the most dependable in a business context.

By conforming to de jure standards, one can expect certain advantages:

> De jure standards are future proof: new standards will have to be backward compatible with old ones. This reduces risk.
> Using standards should give economies of scale: because there is more competition for supply, prices should fall. This also gives a measure of vendor independence.
> Consolidating to one or two standards reduces the skills base required to run the system, so reducing training costs and dependency on key staff.
> Strategic planning is simplified.

A common misunderstanding about standards is that they are about performance. They are not. Standards are the lowest common denominator. They ensure that hardware and software will work together transparently; performance is a secondary consideration. They reduce complexity and diversity and make systems cheaper and easier to manage. Because the largest portion of the information systems budget is devoted to user support in one form or another, standards are an essential part of cost-effective management. A note of caution is required at this point. De jure standards are 'in principle' and de facto standards are 'in practice'. Software developers may follow de facto standards when there is no legal obligation to do so and ignore de jure standards because it is not in their interest to do so. Microsoft's browser included many nonstandard features (ignoring de jure standards) and its market dominance made it a virtual de facto standard. Business interest is best served when de facto and de jure standards converge.

Open source software refers to de jure standards. As an example, Linux is both open source and fully in the public domain. So anyone can develop code for Linux. If the code is intended for public distribution, it must conform to the standard. Nobody really cares what organisations do internally. Other software such as Adobe's Acrobat is freely available in the public domain and can be used to transfer documents across different hardware and software systems. However, these are not truly open because the source code is not available to developers.

Figure 2.5 shows a matrix for the classification of software according to whether it is open or closed and proprietary or public domain. The only quadrant for which there is no example is software that is both proprietary and open. Java is a universal programming language. It was developed by Sun and placed in the public domain. Although Java may be used by anyone, the source code for the Java interpreter remains private. Without access to source code, we are relegated to being mere users of someone else's software.

The advantages that arise from the use of open source software stem from the software being free. However, licensing costs are not the only factor in choosing whether to go for an open source or proprietary solution. The availability of in-house skills and user support are also significant. Microsoft's domination of the desktop systems and applications software markets simplifies decisions for information systems managers but means that there is a huge dependency on Microsoft and no ability to modify the software to match organisational needs. Other criticisms of open source code include a lack of security. However, few people would argue that most hackers and viruses have exploited features in Microsoft software. It was misreported that Microsoft was using Linux servers in 2003. The simple truth is that Microsoft was being targeted by hackers and resorted to using an Internet-wide caching system provided by Akamai. It was able to minimise the effects of distributed denial of service attacks (DOSs; see chapter 4). An irony of this is that Akamai's systems depend on Linux for their operation. However, Microsoft is a special case, and most organisations will not face the same volume of hacking or traffic and are usually able to make their Windows-based systems secure with firewalls and good internal security practices. As with most other things, the decision whether to adopt an open source or a proprietary solution is a business one. Such factors as cost and tactical and strategic benefits must be taken into account. There are no hard and fast rules. Each case must be considered in its own frame of reference.

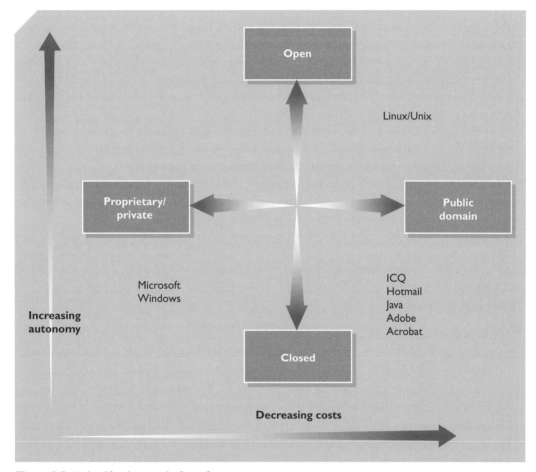

Figure 2.5 A classification matrix for software

Summary

This chapter has covered general issues relating to the history and nature of software to set a context for tactical and strategic aspects. Most companies rely on software in one form or another to maintain their competitive ability. The key points of this chapter are:

> There are five generations of software, each generation more abstract than the previous one. The fifth generation, that of natural language processing, has yet to be achieved in a realistic situation.

> The so-called software crisis of the 1970s was overcome by the reuse of programming code, the development of packaged software and the development of user-oriented query languages. Although the effects of the software crisis have been mitigated, they have not been eliminated.

> Software may be categorised as applications, systems and communications software. Applications software may be subdivided into horizontal and vertical software.

> Companies that control systems software exert great influence over the development trends of PC hardware and software.

> The pattern of business and competition in the software and processor industries is a step–lock cycle, involving the release of faster processors and more sophisticated software, which forces customers to upgrade frequently. Computer networks change this pattern by allowing systems with lower specifications to be used as client machines — so-called thin clients, which are cheaper to buy and run and easier to manage because they download most of their applications software from a server as required.

> Most companies opt to buy horizontal software, but might consider customised or custom software for vertical applications. Custom software is a more expensive option and requires investment and commitment if the competitive edge is to be sustained.

> Information overload and trivial tasks have an adverse effect on productivity. IAs allow many routine and complex tasks to be delegated to an intelligent software entity. These agents can cooperate if required and some may even be capable of negotiation.

> Standardising software (and by implication hardware) simplifies management and reduces costs.

> Although open source code seems to be free software and seems to give more control and independence to adopters, all implications — including user support and ongoing costs — must be considered.

Questions

1. The step–lock cycle forces companies to upgrade their hardware and software at regular intervals. Which of the two do you think it is more important to update and why?

2. The Linux operating system is the system of choice for most new web servers. Can you think of any reasons it is not making the same impact in the desktop market?

3. A senior staff member has announced that he has discovered a freeware financial modelling package that would be ideal for the company's day-to-day operations. He says that there is very little difference in functionality and the move would save $3500 per year in software licence fees. Would you support his proposal? Explain why.

4. If you were the information systems manager of a larger business, would you recommend being an earlier adopter of new releases of software packages? Explain why.

5. Give three reasons Microsoft's virtual monopoly of the PC applications market is a good thing and three reasons it is not.

6. Is a universal programming language achievable or desirable? Explain.

7. It has been said that good interfaces are productivity tools for users. Is the 'one size fits most' approach adopted by most large software companies good or bad? Give reasons for your answer.

8. What advantages would a company get by using an IA-based systems for staff training as opposed to training in a traditional face-to-face format?

9. Can software alone make a business more competitive?

10. Between them, Gmail, Yahoomail and Hotmail have close to 530 million users, many of them corporations and business. Why would they continue to provide a free service to profit-making organisations?

Exercises

1. Companies in Asia and Europe are now offering pay-as-you-drive insurance. This is mainly targeted at younger drivers who are seen as higher risk. Drivers pay a flat monthly fee and then a fee that depends on how much, where and when they drive. Early hours of the morning are regarded as higher risk. A GPS tracking device is able to record information and transmit it to the insurer. Additionally, stolen cars may be located more quickly. Use the World Wide Web to research other GPS/'pay as you go' applications.

   (a) Can you think of any other applications for this kind of technology?

   (b) Do you see any civil liberties or privacy issues associated with this kind of application? How serious are they?

2. Assume that you have just accepted the position of information systems manager for a sizable company. On your first day, you notice that some staff are surfing the Internet and handling personal emails. You make a rough estimate and suspect that each employee is wasting an average of 80 minutes per day in 'cyberloafing'. The company has no policy on personal use of the Internet at work.

   (a) Make a list of the main points that you would include in a presentation to senior management in relation to this problem. (Do not forget business risks and legal issues.)

   (b) What makes it so hard to control Internet use in the workplace?

   (c) What would be the essential elements in your acceptable use policy?

3. During a routine check with a senior manager, you discover that she has an illegal copy of an expensive software package on her company computer. She does not seem to think that this is a problem. What points would you make to convince her otherwise?

4. An employee admits to having a freeware version of a DVD decrypting and rewriting software package and using it on his company PC. The software is perfectly legal but using it to make bootleg copies of commercially produced DVDs is not. How would you deal with this situation?

CASE STUDY: Mervyn's garden centres

Starting as a one-person business and selling plants from the back of a truck at local markets, Mervyn has done well with his business. The business had grown over the past ten years as a result of horticultural expertise and good personal service. Mervyn was the first to admit that he was not a businessperson in the traditional sense. His wife Gail had looked after the books for him, but with the introduction of GST and the increasing complexity of reporting requirements, they needed an accountant. By purest luck, they found one who had a background

(contintued)

in information systems. They had to admit that Joe had kick-started the spurt of growth that had seen nine new outlets created and the business diversify into garden furniture, reticulation and landscaping supplies. This growth was also causing problems. The back-end office systems were struggling to keep up with the increased load and the stock control systems, which were still manual, were taking up more and more time. Apart from newspaper advertising, marketing consisted of using Microsoft Office to generate personalised mailshots to existing customers. The client–server network that supported Mervyn's business did not extend as far as the point of sale. The cash registers were just that, cash registers. Unfamiliarity with information systems and finance generally contributed to Mervyn's air of disbelief as he stared across the table at Joe:

'How much!?' he snorted.

'Just a touch under $550 000,' replied Joe calmly. 'Look at the figures. It's a small price to pay for bringing the business back under control. You are just used to paying for your computing in small instalments. You have three options: a) carry on as you are — I think we both know that's not really feasible; b) upgrade or replace the existing hardware and software, buy in a stock control system and point of sale systems and continue to pay for commercial software licences and system management.'

'And the third option?' asked Mervyn suspiciously.

'Move to an open source solution and buy a proprietary turnkey point of sales system. The main advantage of open source solutions is that they are free … ' Joe began.

'Free! I didn't have the benefit of your university education but more than half a million dollars isn't exactly free.'

There was an awkward silence. Joe knew from experience that Mervyn could be difficult to work with but once convinced, his commitment was unwavering.

'Look, there are two main things that we need to achieve, make more money and save money where we can. Sometimes we have to spend money to do this. We are always going to need hardware; the stuff we have is coming up to the end of its useful life. So that accounts for $150 000 or so,' said Joe.

'Can we sell the old stuff?' asked Mervyn hopefully.

'We could, but there are definite tax advantages in donating it to a charity,' Joe continued. 'We have two main sources of ongoing costs: commercial licences for software, networking and systems management. If we go for an open source solution, then we don't pay licence costs, but we do need to pay to get the database and accounting system converted to an open source format. I'd suggest a product called MySQL. Even though we are moving to an open solution, we don't have the expertise to handle the conversion ourselves. We need to bring people in to do it. Once it is done, we have ownership and control. The new system will be much less demanding in terms of hardware requirements, so we will need fewer servers. OpenOffice and Linux is what I am recommending for the desktop. Again, they are both free.'

Mervyn paused. The word 'free' appealed to him but all this change was somehow daunting. 'I've heard about Linux,' he said. 'It's based on something called Unix and I know that is hard for people to use. I have never heard of OpenOffice. People will need training and some of them just won't cope, Mary has used Microsoft Office ever since she came to us; how will she cope? Millions of people use Microsoft; you can get user support.'

'You are right about training,' Joe replied, 'but users won't use Linux as such … there is a Windows-like interface that is very user friendly. OpenOffice has about 16 per cent of the corporate market now, and it can interoperate with Microsoft Office to a great extent. Most of your applications are based on standard document formats, so the conversion process will be easy. Because we will be using international standards, we will never need to convert them again. We can even create PDFs directly.'

'The point of sales system is one of those open ones, is it?' asked Mervyn.

'No, it's not, but it is a well-defined "off the shelf" system, which will be able to interface with the stock control system and automate the process. I have seen the system in use and it does everything that we need it to. We should be able to reduce the stock on hand and yield some cost savings there too. It's what IS people call a "mixed" solution. We may find ourselves overstaffed.'

'Can we afford it?'

'We can't afford not to,' answered Joe.

'I was thinking,' said Mervyn, 'all those customers browsing around the garden centres, wouldn't it be good if they could get a nice cup of coffee and something to eat? …'

Questions

1. Is Mervyn's lack of expertise in information systems and finance a major problem?

2. Mervyn's business depends very heavily on Joe. How risky is this and what could or should Mervyn do to reduce the risks?

3. Joe's solution appears to be driven by a personal philosophy. Is this a good thing? Explain why.

4. How much of threat to Microsoft's market is open source technology? What is Microsoft doing to mitigate that threat?

5. Identify and explain three main advantages and three disadvantages of Joe's solution.

6. How would you go about introducing the new system to the business? (*Hint:* Think about the people factors.)

7. Joe is recommending a turnkey system with very little formal evaluation and comparison. Is this sensible? What would you do?

8. What would you suggest to improve the marketing of the business?

9. What advantages does PDF have over conventional and proprietary word processing file formats?

References

Babbage Institute 2007, 'Who was Charles Babbage?' www.cbi.umn.edu/about/babbage.html

Benson, SP & Standing, CR 2000, 'Irradiating intranet knowledge: the role of the interface', *Journal of Knowledge Management*, vol. 4, no. 3, pp. 244–51.

Britannica 2001, 'Jacques de Vaucanson', www.britannica.com.

Bromley, AG 1987, 'The evolution of Babbage's calculating engines', *Annals of the History of Computing*, vol. 9, pp. 113–36.

CNN 1997, 'Inventor of computer "mouse" finally cashes a big check', www.cnn.com.

Foss, K 2004, 'Federal court report suggests Microsoft targeting Adobe', *PlanetPDF*, www.planetpdf.com.

Li, Z 2006, 'China vegetables are to get identity codes for Olympics', *China Digital Times*, http://chinadigitaltimes.net.

Mac Daily News 2007, 'Net applications: Apple's Mac "market share" continues rise, hits 6.38% in February 2007', 1 March, http://macdailynews.com.

Meyers, J 1999, 'A short history of the computer (b.c. – 1993a.d.), www.softlord.com.

Russo, M 2001, 'Herman Hollerith: the world's first statistical engineer', www.history. rochester.edu.

SPIE — The International Society for Optical Engineering (SPIE) 2006, '$100 laptop nears launch', http://newsroom.spie.org.

Symantec 2006, 'Renault F1: the story', www.veritas.com.

Wired 2004, 'The click heard around the world', www.wired.com/wired/archive/12.01/ mouse_pr.html.

W3Schools n.d., 'Browser statistics', www.w3schools.com.

CHAPTER 3
Business information systems

LEARNING OBJECTIVES

After reading this chapter, you should be able to:

» describe the major categories and subcategories of business information systems in current use and the types of business activity they support

» understand the basic functions of databases, their management systems and the advantages that they confer

» understand the types of reports and information that business information systems produce

» understand how the various types of business information systems relate to or operate in a corporate context

» understand the difference between a database and a data warehouse and how both are used

» understand the basic functions of groupware and how it can be used to transform business operations.

Introduction

This chapter is intended to give an overview of the different types of information systems in current use. In doing so, it relates business information systems to management levels within organisations because this provides a useful conceptual framework.

The nature of work is that the higher someone is in an organisation, the less structured and more abstract that person's job is. In contrast, those people lower down the hierarchy have jobs that are highly structured. When automation is contemplated, processes that are well defined and structured are usually selected for computerisation, because the development–effort ratio makes the exercise worthwhile, because well-defined systems are easy to develop. However, functions that are high level are much more difficult to automate. A senior human resources manager who analyses skills deficits and arranges customised training is hard to replace with a computer. In short, the major impact is twofold: the automation of simple processes for which timelines and supply chains can be shortened, and providing tools that support higher-level functions. In the latter case, there are tools that support analysis and modelling to facilitate make management easier. The simple data hierarchy 'Why? How? What?' is useful as a framing context for business information systems. Table 3.1 shows this simple hierarchy and relates it to business levels and tasks.

TABLE 3.1 The relationship between management levels, data and tasks

Level in organisation	Data hierarchy position	Scope of tasks	Example
Executive level: highly unstructured activities using highly abstract information	Wisdom (why?)	Being able to apply knowledge	Planning to abandon an unprofitable line and introduce a new one
Senior management level: loosely structured tasks using condensed information	Knowledge (how?)	Understanding the meaning of information	Analysing the trends shows that a particular line is no longer profitable
Line management level: summarised data, fairly structured tasks	Information (what?)	Data processed in such a way as to reveal previously obscure trends	Summarised quarterly data expressed in chart form
Operative level: no summarised data, highly structured tasks	Data (what?)	Raw, unprocessed entries	Daily cash entries in a spreadsheet relating to sales lines

Remember the division between knowledge and information that was introduced in chapter 1. Information can be codified and stored and communicated externally, but knowledge and wisdom are imbued with meaning and therefore deeply personal. When people talk about *knowing* something such as a telephone number, they are really talking about information or what some authors refer to as *catalogue knowledge*. Understanding how to use that piece of information is knowledge. Deciding not to call someone at 3.00 a.m. is an example of wisdom. Although this may seem fanciful, the simple implication is that data and information-based activities are usually well defined and easily automated. When operating in the realms of knowledge and wisdom, most people do not automate the activity as such; it is more cost effective to provide support tools and environments in which humans can perform their tasks.

This chapter covers a wide range of topics, but the underlying themes are easily understandable. When reading the chapter, keep table 3.1 in mind — think how the business systems relate to the levels of management in the table and what they must do to enable the management tasks to be carried out. In essence, the higher the level of management, the more unstructured and ill defined the tasks become, and information becomes more summarised and less detailed. The lower the level of management, the more structured tasks become, and information becomes more detailed. It is helpful to imagine a three-level hierarchy of information systems: at the lowest level, operational matters are the main concern; at the second level, tactical issues are the main focus; and at the highest level, strategy is the principal issue.

[**Key concept:** Anything that is well structured and defined is relatively easy to automate.]

Transaction-processing systems

Transaction-processing systems are the backbone of commerce. Humans have recorded basic business transactions for tens of thousands of years, and the need to do this is believed by many to have given rise to written language. What is a **transaction**? A transaction is the most fundamental unit of commercial activity. Transactions are indivisible. For example, think about using a bankcard to withdraw money from an account using an ATM. This involves several stages: verifying the card and PIN, establishing the balance, authorising the withdrawal, debiting the account and dispensing the cash. If any subprocess in the transaction fails, then the entire transaction will fail. It is not acceptable to have your account debited but no cash dispensed. Think of transactions in binary terms: they either succeed or they fail; there are no half measures. Beyond the obvious, why do we need to record transaction data?

The law requires records to be kept for taxation and audit purposes. The provision of audit trails also allows problems and incomplete transactions to be checked and verified. For example, if an order was received, and the goods were despatched but not received, the failure probably lies with the shipping company.

Analysing transaction volumes and patterns allows managers to build and manage appropriate business systems, but more importantly this information can be used to devise effective marketing strategies and to integrate them with manufacture and distribution. This also allows inventory loss and pilfering to be quantified. For a chain of retail outlets, it is therefore possible to compare the relative efficiencies of individual branches and managers.

Customers, suppliers and business partners might need to have access to transaction details relating to themselves. This allows reconciliation among systems and improves security by lessening the chance of computer fraud. Long supply chains may be shortened if companies use **electronic data interchange (EDI)** while maintaining secure systems.

Employees might need transaction-related information to carry out their daily duties. For example, a ticketing agent needs to check the availability of theatre seats and pricing before proceeding with a transaction on behalf of a customer via through a credit card company.

Batch and real-time systems

Batch systems collect and store transaction details for processing at some later time. Immediacy and high performance are not needed, so the computing load can be spread over longer. This also means that a company can have cheaper hardware, and serial storage media such as tapes can be used instead of faster and more expensive random access storage media such as hard drives. Examples of batch systems would include running a fortnightly payroll system and how banks deal with deposited cheques. (The banks make a record of each cheque deposit but the new account balances are not calculated until later when the cheques are processed as a batch.)

Real-time systems process transactions as soon as they are received, and the need for greater speed of response means that hardware and software will be much more expensive. However, many applications have to operate in real time, such as an airline reservation system: Sabre (developed by American Airlines) handles upwards of 5000 transactions per second and has a response time of two seconds. Slower response times waste an unacceptable amount of customer time and render a system uncompetitive. Some leeway is available on retail goods: the customer may go to a competitor, but the business still has the goods to sell and overall profit may not be badly affected. However, for applications where businesses are selling time and space, for example, a hotel room, another occupant for the room may not be found and profit may suffer badly as a result.

There are many kinds of batch and real-time transaction processing systems, including point of sales systems, order-entry systems, reservation systems and general ledger systems (Turban, McLean & Wetherbe 2004).

> **Reflection question 1:** Why are real-time systems preferred over batch systems from an accounting perspective?

Point-of-sales systems

You should be familiar with point-of-sales (POS) systems from visits to the supermarket, but you may not have thought about what happens in the process. There are a few basic steps:
> The checkout operator scans in the product code.
> The system obtains the price of the goods from a database.
> These steps are repeated until all the goods have been scanned, and then a receipt is printed.
> Details of the transaction are recorded (but not committed, i.e. made permanent) in the database, including date, amount and method of payment, which includes details of coupons, discount cards, loyalty cards, frequent-flier cards and so on.
> For noncash transactions, the system verifies that the card is valid and that there is sufficient balance or credit to cover the transaction. At this point, the sales record that is held in the register is used by the system to process the request for payment from the credit card company or bank.
> Once payment has been made, the transaction details that have been recorded in the database temporarily can be made permanent. (Had payment failed, the goods would have been

returned to the shelves and the transaction would not have been processed.) The inventory system can now be updated.

A few things are worth noting here: specialised hardware is used to handle input and speed up the process — should the bar code be unreadable, the operator can still input the numeric code manually; the number of bad payers is minimised by getting approval 'up front'; at any point in time, the inventory of the store is accurately known, which allows more dynamic stock models to be developed, reducing wastage and increasing profitability; and there is a wealth of information on sales and customers, which can be used for marketing purposes.

POS systems are not restricted to supermarkets. They may be used, for example, by insurance agents selling in the customer's home and accessing the system with a laptop and a modem.

Given the high level of expertise required to develop a POS system, many companies simply purchase off-the-shelf or turnkey systems (ready-to-roll systems that are customised for a particular line of business).

Order-entry systems

Order-entry systems allow customers to order goods (such as pizzas) and services (such as magazine subscriptions) with much of the functionality of POS systems, but they also handle billing and shipping addresses. These systems usually require customers to be registered. When an order arrives by telephone, fax, email or EDI, the customer must be verified and records checked. If the customer is registered and creditworthy, the order will be processed, checked against inventory and shipping instructions issued.

Because input can come from different sources, including manual ones, verification may be handled by an operator or a computer, or both. Therefore, the potential for error is much greater than in a POS system. Operation can be real time or batch, depending on the application.

Both POS and order-entry systems can interface with specialised inventory systems that handle distribution and logistics. Consider the problems a company with advanced computerised systems has when dealing with a supplier whose systems are primitive or nonexistent. It might take as long as 30 days to place an order and receive the goods. Additionally, because payment cannot be processed quickly, it is not possible to give a discount for speedy payment. Discounts can be given for bulk purchase but this means tying up valuable capital in stock and limiting the ability to make money.

[**Key concept:** Using information systems is no longer optional — it is essential.]

Reservation systems

Reservation systems are mentioned earlier in the text in connection with airline and hotel reservation systems. In the past, these systems could be accessed only by organisations or their agents. Since the Internet became a commercial reality, members of the general public are able to make airline, theatre, car hire and hotel reservations with comparative ease. Because customers are dealing directly with the business (i.e. there is no intermediary), the profit margin is greater and discounts can be offered. Many hotels now advertise a special Internet rate.

General ledger systems

There is some controversy as to over whether accounting and general ledger systems qualify as transaction-processing systems. It is suggested here that they do, because updates (transactions) are indivisible and the systems meet all relevant criteria in terms of their need to record transaction data. In most businesses, the general ledger tends to be the confluence for all other transaction-processing systems in the business; in other words, the general ledger ties everything together. These systems tend to be sold as integrated modules consisting of general ledger, payroll, accounts payable and accounts receivable. (A database often stores records of debtors and creditors and may be linked directly to the ledger system. This can prevent needless debt reminders or legal action.) Whether they are 'true' transaction-processing systems depends on the degree of integration with other systems to which they are linked. If the updates that they perform are reflected in those systems directly, it may be assumed that the ledger system is a true transaction-processing system.

Transaction-processing systems summary

Ideally, data entry should be as simple and efficient as possible, and bar codes meet both these criteria. However, in reality the data come from a variety of sources and a lot are captured manually. For most online businesses, the customer performs data entry on a web page. As emphasised in previous chapters, the aim is to reduce complexity and diversity: standardising forms and input sources can improve manageability and save costs. For example, a large organisation using more than 20 different kinds of forms for similar activities found that by redesigning the forms, it was possible to reduce the number of them to eight.

All transaction-processing systems need to be quick, secure and reliable. Increasingly, transaction-processing systems are expected to operate 24 hours a day, seven days a week. Extra hardware and power supplies are needed to support this. Problems may arise when accessing the system over the Internet, because periods of heavy demand may reduce performance to unacceptable levels with a corresponding loss of business. Transaction-processing systems provide the mechanisms and infrastructure for the implementation of transactions. The transaction data are recorded in a database. A good transaction-processing system needs good database management and accessibility. All transaction-processing systems need to carry out validation and verification of input. The data must be of the right type (e.g. numeric) and of the right value (within a specified range, e.g. 0000–9999) and even checked for 'reasonableness' (someone entering their age as 12 is unlikely to weigh 350 kg!). Besides ensuring that the system will be able to do its job, there are good security reasons for carrying validation and verification. Hackers often input executable code and spurious links into online forms.

IS in action

Putting the clock back

Most people would remember Y2K as a significant nonevent. True, the threats were blown out of all proportion by the media, but a vast amount of work was carried out to ensure that important systems would continue to run. The true costs of fixing the Y2K bug are hard to ascertain but well-informed estimates of US$320 billion are relatively common. Many contemporary systems rely on very accurate time measurement and use a system called Coordinated Universal Time (UTC). This is based on International Atomic Time, which is harmonised with UTC by the addition of 'leap seconds', because UTC is based on the Earth's angular rotation, which is not completely regular. (Complicated, isn't it?)

UTC began on 1 January 1961. It is defined as the number of seconds elapsed since then. Different timezones, relative to the Greenwich meridian, are defined as positive or negative offsets from UTC. Curiously, UTC is referred to as 'Zulu' time because each timezone is assigned a letter of the phonetic alphabet. Modern computers use 4 byte integer to store the UTC second count, with 31 bits used for the count and one for the sign. It is likely that problems will emerge when the number of seconds exceeds 2 147 483 648, which will happen on Tuesday, 19 January 2038 at 03:14:07. At that time, owing to a quirk of binary storage formats, the UTC time will be reset for many computers to — 2 147 483 647. Ironically, this date will be Friday, 13 December 1901 at 20:45:52, so whether this will be called the 2038 bug or the Friday 13th bug remains to be seen.

What is certain is that some commercial systems will make mistakes, just finding out which systems they are would be expensive. This bug has already caused problems — AOL's server software specifies that a database request never expires by specifying a timeout of 1 billion seconds from the current time. At 21:27:28 on 12 May 2006, the billion seconds exceeded the 2038 deadline and the servers crashed. Some industry analysts say that this will far exceed the Y2K bug in terms of potential effect and cost. Disputes over how to handle the problem continue. Some argue that computers will improve and use more bytes to record time, while others suggest resetting UTC to begin on 1 January 2000. Time will tell.

Source: Information from *Advisor* 2001, 'Y2K cost: US$320Billion', http://doc.advisor.com; 'The year-2038 bug', www.2038bug.com.

[**Key concept:** You can choose to ignore the future but it will not ignore you.]

Databases

'A database is a centralised collection of data.' Thus began a 1982 database course. It is easy to criticise this definition with the benefit of hindsight but it will serve as a starting point. The word 'centralised' is not appropriate because contemporary databases may be spread over different computers and over a wide geographic area, so it is best replaced by the term 'logically related'. Next, the concepts of organisation and management need to be introduced. Any collection of data needs to be easily accessible and capable of being queried efficiently. This leads to the following working definition:

A database is a logically related collection of organised data.

Connolly & Begg (2005, p. 16) give a formal (if grammatically suspect) description of a database as 'A shared collection of logically related data, and a description of this data, designed to meet the needs of an organization' and an informal view of a database as a 'self-describing collection of integrated records'.

Just as there is a distinction between hardware and software, so there is a distinction between data and the means of accessing and managing those data. A database not only has data, it has a **database management system (DBMS)**. Essentially, the DBMS looks after the following functions:

> data storage and retrieval
> transaction and update indivisibility

> user authentication and security
> reducing redundant data (data that occur more than once in the database) to an absolute minimum
> **metadata** management. Metadata are data about data; they describe the data structures and relationships. At an enterprise level, this description is called a schema, and at lower levels the descriptions are called subschemas. The data dictionary falls into this category.

The elimination of redundant data needs further explanation because this is a major advantage of using a DBMS. Without a database, organisations would be forced to duplicate data so that staff could access them. When the data were updated, the change would need to be reflected in each duplicate copy. The consequences of making a decision on the basis of outdated data could be significant, and managing so many copies would be a major headache and very costly. By ensuring that data occur only once in the database, these problems can be overcome. (In practice, some data may need to be repeated for performance purposes but to all intents and purposes, the view of the data is consistent throughout the entire organisation.) The practice of removing repeating items from the data is called 'normalisation'. The data hierarchy is shown in figure 3.1. At the lower levels of the hierarchy, things become more detailed and less meaningful: a single byte or even a field conveys no information if it is removed from its context. Even single records removed from their context are of little value.

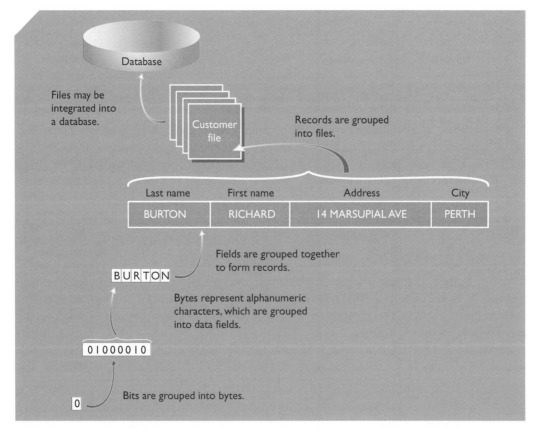

Figure 3.1 The data hierarchy

Separating data from their description (metadata) also simplifies management. If the relationships or structures need to change, then all that needs to be done is to change the description. When discussing software in chapter 2, the concept of third-generation programming languages was introduced. In these, the data were defined inside the programs, so maintenance and management were time consuming, and major alterations were difficult to complete in a reasonable amount of time.

Modern databases make use of fourth-generation languages. These are much easier to use and allow changes to be made quickly. The most widely used database organisation is based on the relational model. Here, data are organised into tables and relationships are defined within and among tables. Object-oriented databases are a newer approach, which may come to predominate over the next 15 years or so. Currently, there is so much investment in relational databases that the situation is unlikely to change in the short term. Most modern databases also make use of client–server technology (a form of information systems architecture in which desktop machines (clients) make use of a network to send requests to a server that is dedicated to a particular task (e.g. database or mail). The server then responds to the request. This is discussed further in chapters 5 and 11).

Databases do not just hold current data; they may contain huge amounts of historical data that could be analysed by management, for marketing and planning. Specialised databases that are used solely to support managerial decision making and planning for an entire enterprise are termed data warehouses. Multidimensional analysis and modelling software is available to allow management to view data in many different ways. Smaller specialised databases that focus on a single application or business unit are called datamarts (McKeown 2002). The integration of databases using web-based technology is also an important trend, which is covered in chapter 5.

Methods of data organisation

There are several ways to organise data in a database. Three approaches, each of which has its own merits, are considered here: the hierarchical database, the network database and the relational database.

The hierarchical database

In the hierarchical database, the relationship between the data elements is one-to-n, where n is an integer. Child nodes depend on parent nodes for their existence. Figure 3.2 shows this method. Note that it is not possible to access a child node directly and that deleting a parent node causes access to all its child nodes to be lost. In figure 3.2, Jones works for both accounting and finance, and the only way to cope with this is to have two separate entries for Jones, which can cause inconsistency problems. This approach is very fast for well-defined queries but potentially slow for more complex ones. This lack of flexibility in dealing with ad hoc queries makes the hierarchical approach unsuitable for anything other than simple, well-structured applications.

The network database

The network database is much more flexible than the hierarchical approach. Figure 3.3 shows this method. Note that it is no longer necessary to duplicate entries for Jones. Here, relationships among nodes can be one-to-one, many-to-one or many-to-many. Although it is much more expressive than the hierarchical approach, the complexity of link management makes it unwieldy for complex applications.

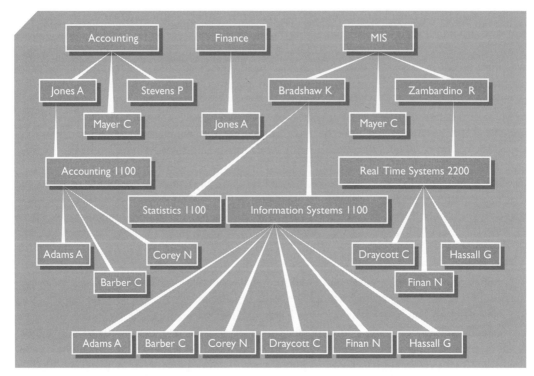

Figure 3.2 The hierarchical database

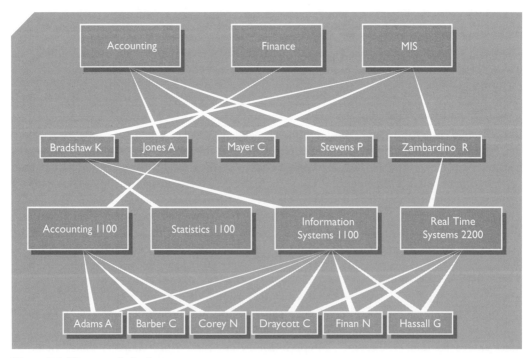

Figure 3.3 The network database

The relational database

The **relational database** is more modern and flexible than the previous methods considered. As shown in figure 3.4, data are organised as a set of relations or tables. Fields in one table can be used to find data in other tables. With the exception of key fields (fields used to find things in the database) no duplication of data is permitted. This results in databases that are easier to manage and update. The relational approach is more expressive because it can handle relationships among tables that are one-to-one, many-to-one, one-to-many and many-to-many (Carter 2000). The relational model relates very closely to database design and development. Once the data requirements have been modelled, the logical database design flows naturally. *Entities* are clearly identifiable things or concepts in a business system (such as *customer*, *invoice*, *vehicle* and so on). They have properties called *attributes* (such as *address*, *invoice number* and so on). The database analyst identifies the entities and defines the relations among them; for example, a customer may have zero or more vehicles. Placing restrictions on the relations and the attributes enables business rules to be enforced; for example, a car-hire customer must be older than 21. An introduction to data modelling is provided in chapter 6.

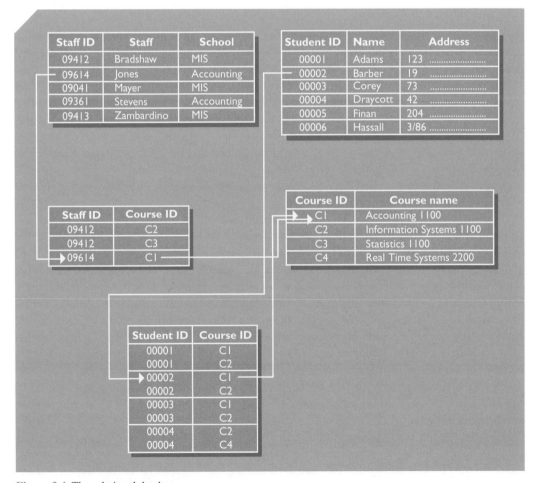

Figure 3.4 The relational database

Database organisation summary

An in-depth consideration of the relative merits of the three schemes is beyond the scope of this text. Simpler queries, such as those in restricted applications such as transaction processing, can be handled slightly better by hierarchical and network databases (Connolly & Begg 2005). However, these methods are not as flexible as the relational approach for more complex searches and queries, for which their performance is much worse than relational models. Improvements in hardware performance have meant that most new large databases have been based on the relational model. Remember that many transaction-processing systems are quite old, and a substantial number of hierarchical and network databases are still in use. Newer database technologies are based on object-oriented approaches. Although these are novel and exciting in some ways, their adoption is limited by the high level of skills needed and the demands that they place on hardware. The main limitation, however, is the potential cost of converting all the data to another storage format for a fairly limited business benefit. For these reasons, it seems likely that the relational database approach will prevail in the short-to-medium term.

Hunters and collectors

In many ways, the database and its management system are the easy part of the exercise. The hard part is achieving accurate data capture. In most cases, data entry is carried out by underpaid (and often uninterested) humans. Often, where data entry is automated, it is downloaded from other databases that practise or practised manual data entry.

Businesses want to integrate different information stores to profile or identify potential customers better. Every time someone interacts with an information system, they divulge information about themselves. Until recently, that information existed in separate data stores but lately the trend is to use the power of the Internet to create a 'big picture' of potential customers. From the business' point of view, data accuracy is of prime importance. From the customer's point of view, there are serious ethical questions.

Allowing users to input their data directly is no guarantee of success either. People mistype or fail to appreciate the importance of the task at hand and give erroneous information out of sheer frustration. A recent US study took a random sample of 15 000 voter registrations and compared them with the motor vehicle database for New York. Of the records, 20 per cent failed to match because of typing errors (Cherry 2006).

Common errors include misusing homonyms, for example, Peers, Pierce, Piers, Peirce, Jon, John; nicknames, for example, Steve instead of Stephen Benson; punctuation, for example, Mahmoud Sami al-Baroudi becomes al Baroudi or al_Baroudi; marriage, for example, Christine Barton née Fink becomes Christine Fink or Mrs Alan Barton; transposition, for example, Xue Feng becomes Feng Xue; incorrect punctuation, for example, Mary O'Brien might become Mary O Brien or Mary Obrien; double names, for example, Mary-Ann could become Mary Anne or Marianne, and hyphenated names can be split in the same way. When we add to that the complexity of titles (e.g. Doctor, Professor or Reverend) and postnominals (e.g. III, IEEE or PhD), the potential for problems is quite obvious, especially because the types of error are not mutually exclusive.

Database experts have developed automatic methods for correcting erroneous mismatches but most businesses and governments try to cut costs and do not use them. The results of mismatches could be ineligibility to vote, denial of finance for house or car purchase or erroneous legal action. The consequences of a mismatch in medical database could be lethal. Business decision making relies on well-organised, efficient databases. They in turn rely on well-organised, efficient data capture.

> **Reflection question 2:** Can you think of any downsides associated with putting corporate data into highly centralised databases?

Management information systems

Management information systems sit on the boundary between information and knowledge. They are really support tools providing management with the information needed to do the job. In essence, different kinds of information are able to be accessed and analysed, and summarised reports produced. The reports are used at the highest levels of management to produce long-term strategic plans, and in middle management to improve the quality of service and employee efficiency, or for simple operational matters such as identifying bad debtors. A management information system might access information from one or more transaction-processing systems to do its job.

Management information systems can be divided into five basic categories:

> management reporting systems
> decision support systems

> expert systems
> executive information systems
> groupware.

Each of these is considered in turn.

Management reporting system

A management reporting system supports managers who are concerned with operations management and the effective use of the organisation's internal resources. The science of deploying people and materials to achieve objectives is called logistics. At an enterprise level, when a more complete picture is required, we tend to talk in terms of enterprise resource planning (ERP).

For example, consider a company that manufactures ceramic tableware. Materials must be brought into the factory and specialist design services might be required. Kiln maintenance and management require careful production scheduling. Balancing orders and shipping against labour costs is also important. Manufacturing ceramics requires a large amount of energy, so efficient energy management is needed. Deciding which lines are profitable and which need to be replaced will have a large impact on manufacturing. An ERP system would enable all these functions to be carried out.

Besides general logistics, accounting and sales information could be presented in summarised or report form to managers. The main types of reports produced are shown in table 3.2.

TABLE 3.2 The main types of reports generated by management reporting systems, and their uses

Report type	Management level	Report content
Summary	Medium/high levels	This is usually statistical, time series information, giving an analysis of the underlying data. Generally speaking, the higher the management level, the more summarised the data. Transactional analysis is quite common.
Exception reports	All levels	Only data or information that falls outside the expected range is presented in the report, for example, an excessive number of orders placed by a customer who has not paid a bill recently, or an unacceptably high failure rate in manufacture.
Detail reports	Usually lower levels; sometimes higher management levels when summary reports are too coarse-grained to provide information needed to solve a problem	These tend to be used at the operational level. The period the report covers might be hourly, daily or weekly, depending on the nature of the business. People might want to review the efficiency of sales staff in a department store, or be able to link manufacturing problems to the replacement of tools from a certain supplier.

In addition to the main types of reports, *when* these reports are generated is important. There are three main categories:

> *Scheduled reports*. These are reports generated at fixed intervals (daily, weekly, monthly and so on) and distributed to selected members of staff. The format and content are usually determined in advance. They might feature employee production rates for operations managers, or occupancy rates for hotel rooms, or simple accounting information. They are intended to support managerial decision making while minimising information overload. In the case of a hotel, a manager might decide to reduce the cost of rooms or offer special deals to established customers to increase occupancy.

> *Event-driven reports*. These tend to be generated when an expected event or problem arises. For example, a company might have a multiphase software project to deliver. On the completion of each phase, reports are generated showing the state of progress, budget versus projected and so on. Usually, the distribution list is selective.

> *Ad hoc reports*. Sometimes, an authorised manager may wish to perform a one-off query. Most modern systems provide managers with the software they need to perform this task. A manager might want to review advertising expenditure patterns with sales trends to assess the effectiveness of a marketing campaign.

Note that whatever the type of report and its timing, these systems are intended to help managers by automating the routine parts of the job and providing accurate, timely responses. The information is provided by the system; the thinking, knowledge and wisdom (the interpretation and decision making) are provided by the manager.

Decision support system

Up to this point, all the systems considered have used data that are internal to an organisation. A **decision support system** *may* use data from external sources. The systems considered so far are retrospective, that is, concerned with the past, but a decision support system is concerned with both the past and the future. By using existing data, a manager can model possible futures and select the most appropriate strategy. This allows decisions to be made with a greater degree of confidence. A decision support system is targeted to a specific functional area.

An example decision support system might handle staff rostering and be able to cope with employee illness and leave. It might also allow a manager to see how the business would cope if an employee was to leave or be dismissed. Another might perform detailed analysis of demand, overseas suppliers and commodities, factor in overseas exchange rates and labour costs and check local manufacturing capacity and costs order to help a manager establish the viability and profitability of a particular contract or project. Figure 3.5 shows the main components of a decision support system. It is important to note that if the system is for senior management, it must be very convenient to use, so user interface design is a major issue. Decision support systems can be high or low level. the latter are usually used in situations in which staff turnover is high and the application is very well defined: baking or manufacturing schedules or leave rostering would be good examples. At high levels (which is where most are used), they deal with unstructured questions. Data from a variety of sources and are generally used to answer 'what if?' type questions.

The function of each of these components should be clear, with the possible exception of the knowledge base. This contains information about the complicated relationships between data that would be impossible to describe in a database, for example, balancing manufacturing capacity and cost against demand and profitability.

Although many decision support systems stand alone, there is an increasing tendency to rely more on humans for expertise and knowledge and use the technology to facilitate and moderate communication. **Group decision support systems** have software that improves group decision-making processes: areas of consensus and argument can be identified quickly. They are frequently used for brainstorming sessions. Usually, staff can contribute to the decision-making process with complete anonymity, which tends to reduce personality clashes and improve group focus. Special electronic meeting rooms can be used for the purpose, and the use of Internet and related technologies allows for geographic distribution of staff. The role of groupware is vital here.

Decision support and data warehouses

A data warehouse differs from a database in several respects. First, it is a management tool only; it is not part of the operational business (live) system. Second, updates to the warehouse are carried out periodically rather than incrementally, as is the case with most live systems. Third, the scope of a data warehouse is greater than that of a database, since data from several different databases may be used. Fourth, instead of information retrieval and simple report generation, **online analytical processing** tools, statistical analysis tools, **data mining** tools and geographical information systems (GIS) are all provided. Finally, the data are organised according to subject area rather than application.

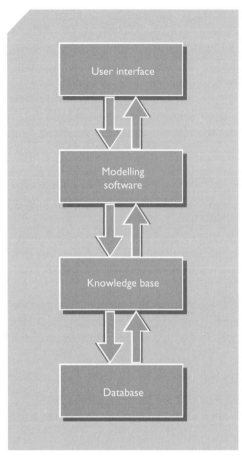

Figure 3.5 Components of a decision support system

Specialist software is used to remove any duplicate data and to fill in any missing fields before the data are organised into consistent file formats.

Data warehousing helps support decisions by allowing more sophisticated analyses than a database alone would provide. However, the degree of sophistication makes it possible to search for hidden patterns in the data, going beyond most decision support system design parameters, such as a relationship among customer, postcode and expenditure. Other applications include fraud detection, identifying profitable customers and product repositioning.

Data warehouses are expensive to set up and maintain, often costing several million dollars for large companies, but smaller datamarts may be set up for much lower costs in a short time. Datamarts are smaller and cheaper than data warehouses and usually focus on a single aspect of a business rather than having enterprisewide applicability. Datamarts may subsequently be networked into a confederated warehouse environment.

B&Q warehouses to housewares

BQI is the international arm of B&Q, a major UK company specialising in homewares and DIY. As the business expanded overseas into China, Taiwan and Turkey, each subsidiary made its own decision regarding information systems. As the growth continued into other nations, compatibility problems arose. The need to centralise control over store management and performance meant providing a single information technology platform. Based on the experience of its parent company, BQI decided to opt for SAP (a major provider of ERP software). Because much of SAP is modular, BQI only needed to pay for those modules that it actually needed for its business. In the event, it adopted the entire SAP retail package, comprising: accounts, financials, merchandising, electronic POS, shipping, purchasing (internal and external) billing, replenishment, stock management, warehouse management and business warehousing. (SAP has many other specialised modules for manufacturing, human resources management and so on.)

Although cultural differences are important, retail processes differ little worldwide. In a very insightful way, the company handling the project for BQI (CIBER Novasoft) developed a template for overseas business processes, basing it on the management of stores in Turkey. Not only did this speed development, it also reduced the amount of new programming required to customise the SAP package to less than 10 per cent. ERP systems are large in scale and notoriously slow to develop but CIBER Novasoft was able to deploy the system in only seven months, completing the business process design phase in four weeks. The world's largest B&Q store is in Shanghai, with a local population of more than 18 million, and is supported by the SAP platform.

The advantages of the system are improved employee allocation, faster processing, better inventory management, international support and much better tracking of sales and margins. All of which mean an improved bottom line.

The benefits are not short term. As new releases of SAP and upgrades become available, BQI is able to adopt them quickly. This enables ownership costs to be reduced and competitive advantage to be maintained. Again, the modular nature of SAP reduces the cost of upgrades because they are targeted. Because the approach is infrastructure based, future developments to the systems are incremental rather than quantal and this too reduces costs.

Although ERP systems are costly, B&Q is large enough to achieve true economies of scale. An important feature to note is the intelligent development process. By standardising and duplicating business process models, the development process is simplified and quickened. The resulting business operation is easy to understand and can be managed in a transparent way giving further cost reductions.

Source: Information from CIBER Case Study 'CIBER Novasoft commissioned to implement SAP's retail management solution, MySAP.com for B&Q International', www.ciber.com.

Expert systems

Expert systems mimic the expertise of humans in a specialised field. They may be used to augment human decision making or may make the decision themselves. Because they are computerised, they are faster than humans and can work reliably (and cost effectively) 24 hours a day.

Consider the nature of distribution and delivery. Many companies exist to perform this specialised function, and rates and tariffs change frequently. An expert system can be programmed with details, delivery routes, schedules and costs for many different companies. An expert system can be used to find the best company to deliver a particular shipment of goods.

In a medical scenario, an expert system can be programmed using information from many human experts. Details of individual case histories might also be available for statistical analysis. A doctor diagnosing a patient's condition would be prompted to input the symptoms and might be asked further questions for clarification. The system might recommend further tests for the patient or be able to identify the condition and provide a list of one or more possible causes with their associated statistical probabilities.

Unlike most computerised systems, which require certainty, expert systems can usually handle uncertainty. Expert systems software consists of the three main components shown in table 3.3.

TABLE 3.3 Components of expert systems software and their descriptions

Component	Description
Interface	This is intended to make the system as easy to use as possible, because it may not be used by experts or domain specialists. A good interface will improve users' productivity.
Inference engine	This uses the knowledge base to answer a particular query. It might be simple information retrieval or require the application of deductive logic. Most inference engines incorporate a module that allows a user to see how the facts and rules have been applied.
Knowledge base	This is not knowledge in the true sense but rather where facts and rules concerning the domain of expertise are stored. This 'knowledge' is captured from one or more human experts.

Although some expert systems are developed from scratch, more often companies purchase off-the-shelf packages called 'expert systems shells'. These provide the interface and inference engine, and all the company has to do is build its knowledge base. (This is often referred to as knowledge engineering.)

It would be useful at this point to explain the distinction between backward- and forward-chaining approaches to expert systems. Expert systems have facts (e.g. Jane is a postgraduate information systems student) and rules (if X is a postgraduate student, then X needs work). Take a simple system with three rules:

(a) If X is a postgraduate information systems student, then X needs a job.

(b) If X is a postgraduate information systems student, then X lives on campus.

(c) If X needs a job, then X will get a job as an information systems tutor.

Now add a fact:

Jane is a postgraduate information systems student.

A backward-chaining system will do nothing until prompted by a query. If we ask 'Is there anyone who will become an information systems tutor?', the system will first explore the facts to try to find an answer. But in this case, the only fact is inconclusive, so the rules need to be explored. The rule that would answer that query is rule (c) but this does not allow the query to be answered because we need to know who needs a job. Rule (a) is relevant but can be resolved until the facts have been checked. In this case, the only fact allows the rule to be resolved and the original query answered. 'Jane will become an information systems tutor.'

A forward-chaining system, as it name implies, will be active and try to generate new facts and rules as information is entered into the system. Adding the fact 'Jane is a postgraduate information systems student' will make the system check all rules whose conditions were not true before this fact was entered but are now. This will create two new facts: 'Jane lives on campus' and 'Jane needs a job'. Adding the fact 'Jane lives on campus' will not create any new facts because rule (b) need not be reciprocal — living on campus may be a necessary but not of itself sufficient condition for being a postgraduate information systems student. (As a more mundane example, all of John Lennon is dead, but not all dead people are John Lennon.)

Many people regard expert systems as specialised types of decision support systems, but they are actually systems in their own right. Although some authors to regard expert systems as part of a **knowledge management** strategy (which is for a community of users in an organisation and is facilitated by groupware), expert systems are usually for individual use as a support.

infobyte

Checking out the competition

UK supermarkets have diversified into many different areas, including petrol sales, car servicing, financial services, travel and wine, but Tesco is the first to offer its own brand of software. Basic antivirus software will cost £10 and Internet security and office software will be priced at £20, with user support being web-based only. The move could be described as bold because the companies producing the software are relatively obscure and they are competing with well-established brands and open source or free products. Tesco has a huge presence in the UK market and its brand image is associated with quality and value for money. A key factor in the success of the venture will be the provision of file compatibility with major products such as Microsoft Office. Given Tesco's aggressive pricing strategy, the move has the potential to increase competition in the software industry, which has to be good for consumers.

Source: Information from www.tesco.com.

Executive information system

The information needs of high-ranking executives are different from those of lower and middle management. An **executive information system** tends to have an enterprisewide focus and makes extensive use of external data. Superficially, it resembles a design support system but it emphasises data synthesis, display, and trend and cause analysis rather than modelling.

An executive information system may make use of hard information (information that is known to be reliable and has a factual basis, e.g. monthly sales figures) and soft information ('speculative' data, such as industry forecasts and the views of business gurus). The interface of an executive information system needs to make the system very easy to use, because senior executives may not have good typing skills. Because the work at this level is highly unstructured, the underlying software has to be very flexible. Most executive information systems allow an executive to browse the underlying information without making a query, recognising that humans often discern trends intuitively.

A main objective of all executive information systems is to facilitate communication between staff, often as part of a coordinated knowledge management strategy. Increasingly, this is groupware oriented (see the next section) and supports remote access by executives who are interstate or overseas. Executive information systems incorporate 'environmental' sensing and actively select news items that executives need to see. A subscription to Reuters or other services may yield more than 10 000 items per day, so the system allows filters to be set so that only news items that relate to set criteria (commodity prices, competing companies and so on) are selected. Because much of the news is still in hardcopy form only, some organisations choose to pay staff to select, classify and scan news items into the system.

Many executive information systems are relatively slow in operation. This is because they tend to rely on relational database technology, which does not handle complex queries well. With improvements in hardware and moves towards object-oriented databases, this will change, because it is important to deliver performance where it is most needed.

IS in action

Pride and seek

Have you ever wondered how a search engine actually works? One of the best known is Google and one of its main features is the speed with which it is able to retrieve information. This speed is achieved by using a distributed network of thousands of low-cost computers. Processing is said to be massively parallel and performance is high. There are three main components to Google: Googlebot (the web crawler that finds and fetches web pages), an indexer (this sorts every word on every page and stores them in a massive database) and a query processor (this compares your query with the stored index and recommends the pages that should be most relevant). Googlebot is a web 'spider' (possibly because of association with the term World Wide 'Web') and some people visualise the spider traversing the Web. In practice, the 'spider' stays put and does what any web browser does, it finds and retrieves pages but it does so much faster than an ordinary browser. It finds pages in two main ways: by finding links while web 'crawling' or by people registering a web page with Google. When Googlebot finds a page, it retrieves all the links from that page and puts them into a list for future crawling. Retrieving links in this manner is called deep crawling. This is a lengthy process, which can involve almost any web page in existence.

Although simple in principle, Googlebot must be able to handle some difficult problems. Because there are thousands of simultaneous requests for pages, the 'visit soon' list must be compared with the index and duplicates eliminated. The next problem is to decide how often to revisit a page. There is little point into reindexing an unchanged page but on the other hand users expect up-to-date content. The compromise is to have Googlebot perform a fresh crawl, and pages that are known to change frequently, such as news and weather services, are downloaded more frequently.

Googlebot gives the indexer all the text from the pages it finds. These are sorted alphabetically by search term and stored in the index, where they are cross-referenced against documents containing those terms. In theory, this should give rapid access. To ensure that searches are not impeded, Google does not index common words such as 'the', 'for' or 'how' (called stop words) and ignores punctuation marks.

The query processor has a user interface (the search box), a search engine (which matches evaluated queries to documents and a results formatter. To do its job more effectively, Google uses special techniques to rank a page, the more relevant a page is deemed to be, the higher its ranking. The algorithm used to do this is a closely guarded secret because hackers and spammers could exploit that knowledge. Additionally, Google learns about relationships among stored data and is able to cope with alternative spelling and common typing errors. The advanced search options allow users to search for terms in defined areas of the document, such as in the heading, in the body and in links to the page.

So what seems to be a simple desktop-driven query actually involves thousands of computers, complex corporate databases and a high degree of software intelligence, which could span the globe.

Groupware

Most groupware operates at enterprise, group and personal levels. Figure 3.6 shows the four main functional components of groupware. The boundaries between the components are deliberately fuzzy because there is a high degree of overlap. The four areas do not fill the groupware area entirely, which implies that there is more to groupware than these four components. Staff, intelligent agents (IAs), access to decision support systems, extranets, order-entry systems and so on might also be considered to be part of a particular groupware system.

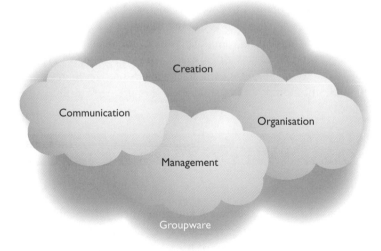

Figure 3.6 The main functional areas of groupware

The four functional areas shown in figure 3.6 are found at every level of groupware use, whether at personal (stand-alone), group or enterprise level. In essence, companies use groupware to create, share, organise and manage information. Many of these functions have been developed separately and are integrated in packages such as Lotus Notes. The communications aspects are handled at a physical level by local area networks and at a logical level by intranets and specialised software. There are many references to groupware with more specialised features (i.e. focused on specific tasks rather than on general tasks, as is ordinary groupware). This groupware forms the basis for computer-supported cooperative workgroups and group support systems. Notwithstanding, most authors would regard groupware as horizontal software.

Communication

Communication may be divided into two main categories: synchronous and asynchronous. In addition, communication may be local or remote.

Synchronous means 'at the same time', so the communicating parties are engaged in immediate communication. Local synchronous communication includes electronic meeting room systems. Remote synchronous communication includes video conferencing and interactive multiauthor screens.

Asynchronous means 'at a different time' and email and bulletin boards are good examples. The messages can be read later and replied to when convenient. Obviously, groupware needs to support all communication modes.

infobyte

Water, water everywhere

It's a sad fact of life that computers become hot and need to be kept cool. It is true of automotive engines too and early automobiles used water-based thermosiphon systems to prevent overheating. The same cooling methods are now being used in home PCs. Although commonly used in upscale computers, liquid cooling has been comparatively rare in desktop PCs, until recently. So why bother? In countries such as Japan, where people tend to live in small apartments, the PC often doubles as an entertainment unit. Cooling fans cutting in and out detract from the viewing and listening experience and mean that PCs are not as quiet as stand-alone DVD players. NEC now offers a PC with Blu-ray drive digital TV tuner, dual 250 GB hard drives, a 20-inch LCD screen, flat speakers and a remote control, giving virtually silent, high-definition output. In businesses where the need to think and concentrate is paramount, silent PCs will also be a boon.

Source: Information from ITworld.com 2006, 'NEC to sell water-cooled PC with Blu-ray drive', www.itworld.com.

Organisation

Because companies wish to have fast, efficient and convenient information retrieval, the documents stored must be classified and cross-referenced meaningfully.

At an enterprise level, many businesses opt for a mixture of databases and web-type technology, in which the cross-references become active links to information. Users may need to be alerted to new information, and information may need to be 'aged' or deleted as it ceases to be relevant. Because the documents that need to be cross-referenced might be in a variety of formats — graphics, text file, email, hypertext markup language, scanned text and image files — this is a complex area, usually requiring dedicated staff for its care.

At a personal level, there are fewer cross-references, so the task is usually much simpler, for example, filing and categorising emails by content and author for later retrieval, or linking files together to form a book or web page.

Creation

Staff need to create a variety of files in their everyday activities: spreadsheets, jpegs, databases and so on. Many of these are single-author and use files that do not need to be shared. However, some files will need to be shared and some, such as shared files in group decision support systems, will have multiple authors. Editing is included in this area because when a document is altered, a new version of that document is created. Groupware provides templates for memoranda, web pages, emails and so on, and usually supports widely used software packages such as Microsoft's Expression web. Providing templates ensures rapid development, consistency of style for corporate image, and ease of management.

Management

Single-author, nonshared files do not need to be managed at a high level. However, as soon as information has to be shared, it needs to be managed. At its simplest, this might involve restricting access to certain information for some staff. It might entail automating and authenticating vote-counting for group decision support system purposes. Active environments will notify relevant staff when information has been updated. A business might want to restrict email access to some employees, and so on. Essentially, the business is concerned with coordinating the activities in the environment. The word 'environment' is deliberate, and is a good way to think of groupware: a pervasive infrastructure that makes personal and business activities more convenient and efficient (Andriessen 2002). Return on investment is quite high in this area — it is necessary to consider where the main cost savings are to be found and why.

Besides the static rule-driven aspects of management, there are tools that possess a high degree of intelligence, which can carry out tasks autonomously, such as IAs, which are very useful in a groupware setting. Suppose that it is necessary to arrange a meeting or video conference with five members of staff. An IA can scan their electronic diaries, find a mutually convenient time for everyone, update the diaries accordingly, book the meeting room and video-conference facilities and supply briefing materials to the participants. It can also, if necessary, inform the catering staff and arrange for refreshments during the meeting. (IAs are also used in decision support systems and executive information systems to scan the environment for news and so on if it is necessary to brief staff.) IAs supporting specialised tasks such as project management and problem and progress chasing are increasingly common. Basic scheduling software that accesses employees' electronic desk diaries is provided by Microsoft's Outlook and Schedule Plus, as well as products like Powercore's Netscheduler 3. Unfortunately, employee conformance may be a problem. The software works only if all concerned keep their 'diaries' up to date and check the system frequently. These are major implementation and management issues.

Mobile agents

Mobile agents are a variation on the theme of IAs. As the name implies, they are able to 'move' from one computer to another carrying out their work at source. Although mobile agents have been slow to catch on, they do offer certain advantages. Their main advantage is the reduction of network loads. For example, think of downloading a large data set across a network and then performing the analysis. A mobile agent could perform the analysis and send the results via the network.

Problems with groupware

There are several problems with groupware (in addition to the purely technical ones):

> *Information overload.* Because it is so easy to share information, people can be overloaded and unable to sort out important from trivial information in a reasonable time.

> *Inappropriate sharing of information.* This might include unauthorised access to personnel files or (more commonly) people using the system to socialise and exchange nonwork-related information, such as jokes and cartoons. Again, productivity may suffer.

> *Time wasting.* Because it is easy to arrange meetings and conferences, there will be more of them. Many meetings are not productive or essential.

> *Human factors.* Managers often encounter resistance from staff who are opposed to change in the workplace. Careful planning and consultation can do much to ensure a smooth transition.

Despite these problems, informed opinion is that groupware is a cost-effective investment.

Groupware and knowledge management

Definitions of data, information and knowledge are given in chapter 1 and reviewed in this chapter. The subjective nature of knowledge is problematic from a management point of view. Whereas the transfer of data and information can be built into computer systems, the transfer of knowledge often relies on social systems for its implementation. Many authors divide knowledge into two basic categories: explicit and tacit. Explicit knowledge is procedural information that can be codified, for example, how to use a software package, who to contact in the event of x happening. Explicit knowledge is a formal (and usually incomplete) expression of corporate culture.

Tacit knowledge is personal knowledge: experience, and ethical and judicial ability. Tacit knowledge makes use of formal and informal networks and structures, which are hard to codify. When working in teams, people rely on one another's expertise, and learn by observing the techniques and thinking of others and adapting them to their needs. This is a combination of social constructivism (where optimal learning takes place through dynamic interactions among people) and learning by doing. The problem that managers face is that key members of a team may leave at short notice, taking their expertise with them.

The challenge is to make as much knowledge as possible explicit and to create working environments that encourage tacit knowledge transfer. For example, think about a company that has an annual performance review of staff before deciding whether to award a payrise. If financial resources are limited and a person has a high level of expertise in a particular area, then sharing that knowledge with others effectively undermines that person's bargaining position. New paradigms require new reward structures. As indicated, information systems is a people business. Many of the problems are motivational not technical. Adoption of best practices and industry benchmarking is essential if a competitive edge is to be maintained, and this applies to knowledge management too. Knowledge must be applied to knowledge.

Tacit knowledge relies heavily on social interaction. Some groupware, such as video conferencing, can support such interaction. Under certain conditions (single-site, small and medium-sized entities), tacit knowledge transfer gets better as the computer systems get worse. This seems counterintuitive until you realise what is happening. Because the systems do not support knowledge sharing, users are forced to move around the building and talk to other users. In so doing, they are exposed to a wider variety of people and views than they would encounter via through the computer system. Face to face is a very rich form of communication because nonverbal aspects are included in the exchange. This should not be taken as an apology for bad systems. Rather, it is an argument for much better systems that support rich communication.

> **Reflection question 3:** As a manager, how would you go about creating an environment that encourages learning and knowledge sharing?

IS in action

Groupware

As an example of the use of groupware, consider a nationwide department store chain. Ideally, each store needs to operate as independently as possible, but it is sometimes possible to negotiate better deals with suppliers for larger quantities. The time and cost of each purchase should be minimal. Advertising and marketing need to be coordinated at a national level. Expenditure also needs to be matched to budgets, and traditional accounting systems tend to report at fixed intervals. This can cause managers to overspend budgets in certain areas.

Examine figure 3.7 (overleaf). The processes are almost self-explanatory but a few things are worth comment. All documentation is electronic, avoiding paper-trail delays. The groupware server and the main business system exchange financial data each night, allowing purchase requisitions to be checked against budgets (actual and committed). Requisitions meeting set criteria are approved automatically by the groupware server, but those that do not meet the criteria are referred to one or two levels of management at head office for approval. Approved requisitions are then linked to the main business system and orders are issued. The progress of any purchase requisition can be checked with a web browser, and email notifies all relevant personnel of outcomes. Internal ordering systems are simpler and faster. Because payment can be effected on the same day as delivery, suppliers will give discount for prompt payment. Purchasing decisions are based on the most current information available. All in all, this system is more responsive than a traditional system.

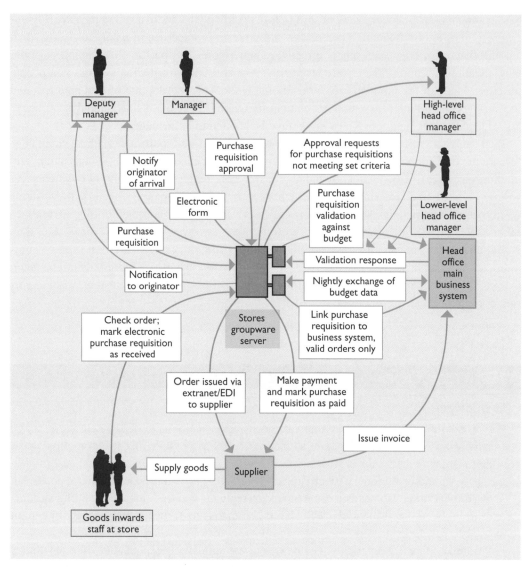

Figure 3.7 An overview of a groupware-supported purchasing system

[**Key concept:** If a process or subprocess does not transform data or add value in some way, eliminate it.]

Putting things into context

This chapter presents a hierarchy of data and information before discussing various types of information system. It would be useful to bring direct the discussion to providing a context and a hierarchy for the systems covered. Figure 3.8 shows systems in terms of their complexity of processing, informational needs, input/output and level of routine. Remember that the higher the position in the hierarchy, the less structured, the more complex and the harder to automate the application becomes.

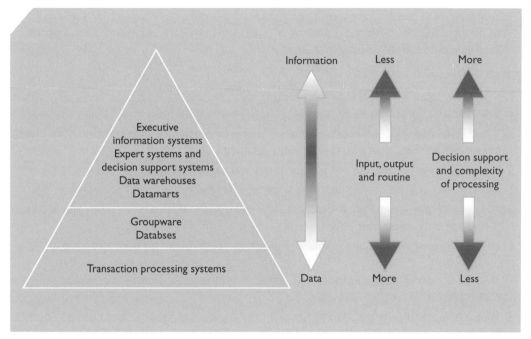

Figure 3.8 The information systems hierarchy

Summary

The coverage given in this chapter has been both broad and selective. Details such as precise database architecture have been omitted so as not to lose view of higher-level concerns. The key points of this chapter are:

> Business information systems cooperate in a connected hierarchy. The lower the position in the hierarchy, the more detailed the information is.

> Lower-level systems are usually concerned with the automation of basic operational processes, for example, transaction processing. Higher-level systems are concerned with less structured activities, provide a wider variety of easy-to-use tools and use more summarised (condensed) information.

> Most organisations have logically related collections of data called databases, which are where day-to-day transaction data are recorded. These live systems can be used to generate middle-level management reports. Data warehouses hold archived data from a wide variety of sources and are updated infrequently. Data warehouses are used for multidimensional analysis to support marketing and decision making. Datamarts are 'mini data warehouses', focusing on a specific business area. A group of datamarts may be integrated into a quasi data warehouse.

> Decision support systems are intended to aid the decision-making process. Expert systems mimic human decision making in specialised areas.

> High-level systems are more likely to make use of information from outside the organisation.

> Groupware is an integrated environment that supports document creation and management and communication. Groupware improves productivity by shortening timelines, improving communication and integrating systems.

Questions

1. SQL is an international standard for storing data and metadata in databases. Why would software companies choose to support it and why would business prefer that it be used?

2. Which kind of expert system do you think would be preferable: one that backward chains or one that forward chains? Explain your reasoning.

3. How does an expert system differ from a decision support system?

4. Is it possible to put a dollar value on corporate data? How would you go about the task?

5. Give at least two examples of hard and soft information. What sort of information system would be likely to use soft information?

6. Logically speaking, it does not matter whether a database is physically centralised or distributed over different machines. It is often much cheaper to adopt a distributed solution. Despite this, many organisations still opt for a physically centralised system, suggest reasons for this.

7. What characteristics would a transaction processing system need to have before you could say that it was truly reliable?

8. Explain how knowledge differs from information. Can they be managed in the same way?

9. Suppose that you are managing a project that introduces groupware to more than 400 staff. Identify and briefly explain four things that you would do to make sure that the implementation went smoothly and that the system was used by staff.

10. What are the significant differences between a database and a data warehouse?

11. This chapter presented a simple information hierarchy (data, information, knowledge and wisdom). Knowledge management is an important topic in business. What sort of classification scheme would you use to categorise knowledge?

Exercises

1. You are the manager of a large hotel in a major city. The hotel trade is very competitive and your occupancy rate has dropped to less than 70 per cent. There is a comprehensive guest history database. How would you use that database to develop a better room type and pricing mix? And how would you use the database to develop a marketing plan?

2. Suppose that you were in charge of a project that would develop an information system that would be used in restaurants to record orders and handle billing. The system would provide handheld computers for use by wait staff. What would be the five most important features of the system and how would you market it to the restaurant trade?

3. A large motor vehicle manufacturer is in the process of establishing a national dealer network. Their vehicles will be covered by a five-year warranty. Quality of product and service is a major concern. Briefly explain how the company could use a database and a datamart to address the quality issues. Remember to consider data capture in your answer.

It was not much to look at, 1200 square metres of floor space with three-metre-high ceilings, but for Ruth and Ken it represented their dream and a 600 000-dollar loan secured over their home. Within a month the remodelling was complete. The yellow and green colour scheme that would later come to signify their brand was freshly painted and 60 pieces of cardiovascular training equipment, 64 cable weight machines and six racks of free weight equipment had been installed. A glass wall separated an aerobics room from the rest of the gymnasium, while downstairs a small lap pool, spa, sauna and shower blocks completed the fit-out. That was more than ten years ago.

The first couple of years had been difficult, but Ruth and Ken had actively marketed their gym to individuals and corporations and after 18 months, they had sufficient members on the books to be self-sufficient. They had both worked in the fitness industry as group and personal trainers and as the business grew, they found it necessary to offer more types of classes and to take on other groups and personal trainers, so their management responsibilities increased.

In 1997, the opportunity to acquire another gym presented itself and by 2002, Boomer's Fitness had nine gyms at strategic locations around the metro area. Of their members, 85 per cent were aged between 23 and 35. To Ruth and Ken, Boomer's was still a family business, and a major part of their business philosophy was based on personal service. Ruth and Ken used their computers to generate mailshots for marketing purposes and would send customers reminders of when their memberships were due for renewal. Though quite a large business, Boomer's had kept its staffing base relatively low, employing only administration, maintenance and sales staff. Trainers were independent contractors who paid Boomer's for access to its members and training facilities. Additionally, they were obliged to pay for corporate dress.

Things started to unravel in 2004. Against the advice of their accountant, Ruth and Ken had acquired their (unlucky) thirteenth gym, refinancing their new home to do so. Rises in interest rates had some effect but the main problem was increased competition in their market. One overseas health club chain was targeted exclusively at women. An interstate chain was also muscling in on their territory. Both these companies were advertising aggressively and Boomer's was losing customers and some of its best trainers and staff to them. In 2006, the situation was grim. For the first time since its inception, Boomer's was losing money. At that point, the losses were small but the figures painted a very gloomy picture.

A meeting of all Boomer's staff was called. When everyone was present, Ken walked over to the whiteboard and listed the options as he saw them.

Option 1: Do nothing — and we go out of business in nine months.

Option 2: Sell the business to one of our competitors while it is still worth something — we would get less than it is worth but most of you would keep your jobs.

Option 3: Downsize — about half of you will lose your jobs and we stay in business … I don't know how long for …

There was an awkward silence. Xue Feng, an overseas student working part time for Boomer's as a personal trainer, raised his hand.

(continued)

'I have another option ...' he began. Ken handed him the whiteboard marker and sat down.

He wrote the word 'Franchising' in large letters. 'Basically, you get other people to buy into your business; they manage individual branches; you retain control over advertising, branding and so on and take a percentage — more money up front, less money longer term but the chance to grow because you will not be involved in so much management.

'There are a few things that need to be done. First, there is the need for cash flow. Inviting people to become franchisees will provide an injection of capital, which you can use to advertise. The next task is to look at what you do and change it. I hear lots of things that customers say they want. Being able to go to any Boomer's club is one thing that they want ... having to pay for a full membership when they only use certain facilities at certain times is an annoyance to others. The aerobics room here is only used for 28 hours a week but you pay for it all week — I can't think it will be different at the other clubs. Is there something different that you can do here? You need to use technology to compete more effectively. You need a member database and you need to be able to track members and training programs. You have to be much more selective and targeted in your marketing. And you need to retain your good staff.'

He walked over to Ken and returned the whiteboard marker. Ken sat for a moment or two and then strode over to the whiteboard and wrote, 'Just do it'.

Questions

1. If Boomer's goes ahead with the franchise option, how will its information management need to change?
2. How would you recommend that Boomer's go about selecting potential franchisees? (*Hint:* How or where can it find the information that it needs?)
3. Outline the essential elements of a marketing plan for Boomer's. How can it widen their customer base? How should they promote their Brand image? In particular focus on the information needs of the business and how they could be met.
4. A business like Boomer's depends on the expertise of good trainers. What can be done to improve the retention rate of trainers and what part would information systems play in this?
5. Consider the problems of operating off-peak memberships (between the hours of 10.00 a.m. and 3.00 p.m.). What would be needed to make this work in terms of information systems?
6. Why do you think that Xue Feng is so keen on the idea of customer tracking? How would you see that being implemented?
7. How could Boomer's make use of a website?
8. How could the member database be used for marketing purposes?
9. Suggest possible applications for expert system and decision support system use in Boomer's business operations. Explain how these applications could pay their way.
10. Do you think that a poor information system played any part in Boomer's current problems? Assuming that the franchising strategy could save the business, make suggestions for changes that would help to prevent similar problems in the future.

References

Andriessen, JHE 2002, *Working with groupware*, Springer-Verlag, London, p. 4.

Carter, J 2000, *Database design and programming*, McGraw-Hill, Maidenhead, pp. 25–30.

Cherry, S 2006, 'The next voting debacle', *IEEE Spectrum*, October, pp. 8–9.

Connolly, T & Begg, CE 2005, *Database systems: a practical approach to design, implementation and management*, 4th edn, Addison-Wesley, Boston, Massachusetts, pp. 48–53.

McKeown, PG 2002, *Information technology and the networked economy*, 2nd edn, Harcourt Brace, Orlando, pp. 127–40.

Turban, E, McLean, E & Wetherbe, J 2004, *Information technology for management*, 4th edn, John Wiley & Sons, New York, pp. 330–6.

CHAPTER 4
Communication and networks

LEARNING OBJECTIVES

After reading this chapter, you should be able to:

» comprehend the differences among digital and analog information, signalling and communication
» understand the differences between asynchronous and synchronous communication
» explain the terms 'simplex', 'half duplex' and 'full duplex'
» appreciate the difference between circuit and packet switching
» define the term 'protocol' and give suitable examples of local area network (LAN) and wide area network (WAN) protocols
» understand some of the different types of communication media in use today, their limitations and their applications
» explain the basic principles and implications of wireless and cellular networking
» understand the purpose and use of firewalls
» discuss the differences between LANs and WANs and understand why each evolved
» give working definitions of 'local area network', 'wide area network', 'backbone network', 'metropolitan network', and 'personal area network' and understand their basic technologies
» define the terms 'Internet', 'intranet' and 'extranet', and appreciate how they change the nature of business
» understand the principles behind client–server networking
» explain the basics of TCP/IP and domain name service (DNS).

Introduction

This chapter describes the communications and network technologies on which many information systems rely. Developmental trends and possible futures of communications technology are also covered.

Mainframe computers transformed the way businesses operated in the 1960s and 1970s, but the advent of the PC in the 1980s demanded communication to fulfil its potential. This combination of information technology (IT) and communications technology had a remarkable impact, and with the addition of Internet-based technologies in the 1990s, this impact became truly profound. This was the dawn of a new age, heralding the imminent demise of corporate management information systems in the accepted sense.

Although many organisations have realised this and have undertaken business process re-engineering (BPR) to gain maximum advantage of the new technologies, there are some that are losing the ability to compete as they cling to the past. When the president of Western Union, William Orton, was offered the exclusive rights to Alexander Graham Bell's telephone for $100 000, he refused, saying, 'What use could this company make of an electrical toy?' (Casson 1910, p. 58). Now, as then, it is vital to think about the future and take advantage of all that technology can offer.

The most obvious manifestations of current technological developments are fusion (fewer devices but with greater capability, e.g. using a mobile telephone to surf the Internet) and fragmentation of society and the market into increasingly specialised (and smaller) areas. This fragmentation arises as a result of increasing media diversity and poses particular problems for advertisers and marketers. From a management point of view, it is possible to construct small and effective teams of people to work on specialised tasks. These teams can be housed in a single location or distributed nationally or internationally. In all cases, communications technology links members of the team to their client base and to one another.

To appreciate the business advantages of networking, it is necessary to review some fundamental aspects of communication. For communications, the following are needed: information, a sender, a receiver and a medium that links them.

Digital and analog information

Analog and digital information should be familiar to you from everyday life. Digital information is discrete (discontinuous and almost particulate in nature) and has an allowable range of values. Days of the week are a simple example: as the clock ticks over 2400 hours on a Monday evening, the transition is from Monday to Tuesday; at no point is it Monday *and* Tuesday. It is the same with integer numbers or notes on a piano. There are no intermediate values. The keys of a piano are digital, and there is no value between E and F. The best-known example is binary code: 0 and 1 for computer use.

Analog information is continuous and there is an infinite set of values between any two points. A violin allows you to have as many notes as you wish between E and F. The human voice is analog information, consisting as it does of a range of frequencies. Most music is recorded in analog form but is often converted to digital for ease of storage and processing, as is the case with CDs. For example, to show the word 'hello' as analog information would mean using the exact shape of the entire sound wave. To store it in digital form, only representative values of the information need to be held and those representative values can be used to recreate a close approximation of the waveform. The more samples there are, of course, the better the approximation becomes.

Digital and analog signalling

A simple fact may help you to remember the difference between digital and analog signalling: the only time it is possible to have true digital signalling through a cable is when a voltage can be directly applied. In the simplest case, there is a level for 0 and another for 1, so that there is no distinction between the signal and the information. (In practice, there might be several discrete voltage levels: as an example eight would allow all the binary digits from 000 to 111 to be transmitted. This is called pulse code modulation.) Whatever the signalling scheme used, it is important to note that there is the rate at which signals can be generated (the baud rate, which is limited by the carrying capacity of the medium) and the bit rate (the number of binary digits transmitted per second), which is a measure of the rate of information transfer.

In nondigital forms of signalling, the signal is a model, representation or analog of the information. Analog signalling involves combining the data with a carrier signal (an electromagnetic sine wave) and is referred to as **modulation**. Put simply, a wave is modified to represent information. Its amplitude (AM) or frequency (FM) could be modified or the phase of the wave (PM) shifted even.

There is no relationship between the data or information type and the signal type: digital information can be sent in analog form and vice versa.

Digital signalling tends to be used for relatively short distances, principally in LANs for interdevice communication. Direct digital signalling is also called **baseband** modulation and allows only one channel to be in use on a medium at any point in time. Baseband uses **time division multiplexing** to share the use of the medium on a 'turn-taking' basis.

Analog signalling is used for:
> TV and radio
> much of the telephone network
> microwave communications.

Digital signalling is more modern, and is cheaper, faster, simpler and more reliable than analog. Most of these advantages derive from analog systems tending to use a spread of frequencies for transmission and, consequently, the equipment needing to be more complicated. Digital signalling simply requires that a signal can be interpreted as a '1' or a '0'; the absolute level of the signal is not important. In contrast, analog signalling requires the entire envelope or shape of the signal to be fully recovered and processed. Accordingly, absolute signal values are usually very important in analog signalling; small changes to the shape of the wave caused by interference can have a dramatic effect on the signal.

For radio, TV and telephone communications, an analog carrier wave is modified to convey information. This modification process is called 'modulation', which is a key function of a modem. Because a microcomputer uses digital information and signalling, and the user parts of the telephone network are analog, it is necessary to change the computer's digital information to analog for transmission purposes, a process that will need to be reversed at the receiving end. This is why a modem (modulator–demodulator) is needed.

Analog signalling is also called broadband transmission. Broadband allows several channels on different frequencies to be in use at the same time (e.g. watching one TV channel and video-taping another channel simultaneously), which is called frequency division multiplexing. Digital communication is superior to analog communication in most cases. This is discussed in the next section.

Digital and analog communication

You now understand the difference between analog and digital information and analog and digital signalling. Digital communication may use any possible combination of these, with the exception of analog data and analog signalling. In other words, analog information sent using digital signals, digital information sent using analog signals, and digital information sent using digital signals are all examples of digital communication. As mentioned, the only time digital signalling is possible is when a voltage can be applied to a cable directly. Accordingly, a digital mobile telephone does not use digital signalling. What makes digital communication superior to analog communication?

People who have used an analog mobile telephone network will be aware of the pops, hisses and crackles that became part of the signal during conversations. Because analog signal reception involves recovering the complete envelope or shape of the wave, the overall communication quality is poor because the waveform is degraded during transmission.

Many analog transmissions use a range of frequencies in the signalling process. The high-frequency parts of a signal are the first to be weakened during transmission. For example, think about hearing someone's sound system from a few streets away — at a long distance all you hear are the low, bass components of the sound; at a medium distance you can hear the mid-range frequencies, too; only when you are close to the source of the sound can you hear the entire frequency range.

High transmission speeds require high-frequency waves but these do not travel for long distances. Lower frequencies give greater transmission distances but do not give high transmission rates. Cable transmission distances may be extended by using repeaters and amplifiers, but this adds to the cost and complexity of the systems. Because the signal is being distorted by the weakening of high-frequency components, these devices must be quite sophisticated because they must amplify high frequencies more than low frequencies. This means that most analog communications systems are a compromise, with cost and complexity balanced against performance.

[**Key concept:** Perfection is not achievable. The 'best' systems make the right compromises.]

Digital communication (using analog signalling) is usually restricted to a single frequency, so the amplifiers can be simpler and, consequently, cheaper. Because signals can travel further before being amplified, fewer amplifiers are needed, reducing the cost more. Also, because less processing is involved, the process is faster. All in all, digital communications are cheaper, faster and more reliable than analog communications.

Returning to the digital mobile telephone, the voice data are digitised and sent by a restricted analog signal using a single frequency. The data are compressed, too, so that they take less time to transmit. When the signal is received, the handset recreates the voice data using the digitised data. Thus the effects of interference and distortion (compared with analog systems) are almost eliminated.

However, there is another advantage: digital communication can make more efficient use of the bandwidth or carrying capacity of communications media. Table 4.1 gives a comparative summary of analog and digital communications.

Bandwidth is the range of frequencies that a communications medium can carry. The greater the bandwidth, the greater the data-carrying capacity of the medium. Conventional analog transmission, which uses a spread of frequencies, is very wasteful in terms of bandwidth. Regulatory bodies allocate bandwidth to broadcasters, and it is not a good idea to have two radio or TV channels too close together or they will interfere with each other. Accordingly, there are guard bands between stations, which enforce channel separation. Digital communications eliminate the need for guard bands, allowing many more communications channels in the same bandwidth. Figure 4.1 gives an idealised pictorial comparison of analog and digital communication bandwidth usage. Moving to a digital broadcast standard with conventional-definition television allows for many more TV channels.

TABLE 4.1 Comparison of analog and digital communications

Analog communications	Digital communications
Signal may consist of more than one frequency	Signal usually consists of one frequency
Prone to error	Relatively error free
Relatively costly and complicated	Cheaper and simpler
Slower	Faster
Not very efficient use of bandwidth	Good use of bandwidth because no guardbands are needed

infobyte

Cable TV revisited

Whereas most people see ultra-wideband (UWB) communications as replacing older cable systems, Pulse-Link Inc. sees UWB as a means of increasing the capacity of older cable TV networks. The underlying concept is simple: inject low-power UWB signals into digital and analog cable TV systems. These signals will coexist with existing TV signals and (because the amplifiers have to cope with a broad range of the spectrum) are able to travel over the entire network. The attraction is that retrofitting high-speed Internet and high-definition TV technology to older cable networks will be a relatively cheap option. Tests have shown that downstream speeds of 1.2 Gbps with upstream speeds of 120 Mbps are feasible, opening up a new range of applications.

Source: Information from www.pulse-link.com.

Although the superiority of digital over analog has been emphasised in this chapter, analog transmission is far from obsolete. Telstra, the main Australian telecommunications company, is providing asymmetric digital subscriber line (ADSL) connections to many Australians. ADSL runs at up to 20 times the speed of a normal dial-up Internet connection. The 'asymmetric' part of the name refers to different speeds being used for the downlink (from the provider) and the uplink (from the user). Because most users are net consumers rather than producers of information, this is acceptable. Technically, ADSL provides digital services, but the transmission remains analog. ADSL and broadband services are discussed further later in this chapter.

However, while Telstra has the largest share of the Australian market, it is not the only player in this market. Cable TV companies, independent wireless network providers and even power companies are competing in this sector.

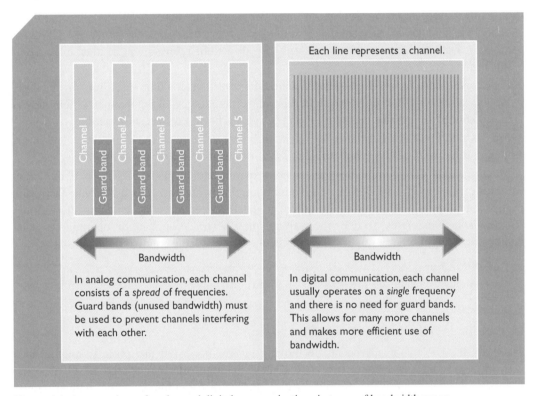

Each line represents a channel.

Bandwidth

Bandwidth

In analog communication, each channel consists of a *spread* of frequencies. Guard bands (unused bandwidth) must be used to prevent channels interfering with each other.

In digital communication, each channel usually operates on a *single* frequency and there is no need for guard bands. This allows for many more channels and makes more efficient use of bandwidth.

Figure 4.1 A comparison of analog and digital communications in terms of bandwidth usage

Asynchronous and synchronous communication

Asynchronous communication means that there is no real-time relationship between the sending of component parts of a message and their eventual receipt and possible reply. To clarify this, think about sending ten letters to someone over a period of three days. The letters need not arrive in the order in which they were sent and it may be many days before you get a reply (if at all). Letters are asynchronous communication.

Synchronous communication incorporates a real-time element (here and now) and is connection oriented, for example, a telephone conversation or a TV broadcast. 'Connection oriented' should not be taken to imply that there has to be a medium that relates (connects) the communicating parties in real time. It should be noted that many applications such as Internet telephony and video streaming seem to be 'real time' but are not, because errors may occur during transmission and sections may need to be resent. However the receiver buffers information it receives, giving a sort of 'time shift' playback. At the speeds at which humans operate, the quality is acceptable because the application is error tolerant. Although it may seem to be error free and synchronous, the real-time aspect is not quite there in the strictest sense.

Switch technologies, which were previously used in telephone and WANs, are now being used in LANs, an example of technology fusion. It also means that voice, video and data communications can all be handled by the same network, reducing costs and simplifying management.

Communication modes

Communication systems can operate in one of three distinct modes. These define the operational characteristics of the system.

〉 *Simplex*. Data or information flows in only one direction. Television is an ideal example of this mode.

〉 *Half duplex*. Data or information can flow in both directions but only one direction at a time. Walkie-talkies or CB radios operate in this well-ordered, turn-taking manner. Often there is an acknowledgement that each part of a message has been received successfully.

〉 *Full duplex*. Data or information can flow in both directions at the same time. The information flows need not be symmetrical in terms of quantity of data transmitted or speed.

Most practical data communications operate in full-duplex mode because half duplex is wasteful of bandwidth. To explain this, think about throwing and catching a ball. When the players are close together, the time is equally divided between throwing, catching and waiting. As the distance increases, so does the waiting time. A typical application operating in half-duplex mode might waste as much as 80 per cent of the available bandwidth in waiting.

〉 **Reflection question 1:** There are cases when the communication link is full duplex but the communicating parties use it as though it were half duplex. What reasons might there be for this?

Circuit and packet switching

These are the two major approaches to moving information from one place to another in a network, that is, how the medium is used. Circuit switching works in much the same way as the telephone. A connection is established for the duration of the communication, data are transmitted and finally the connection is closed. This approach permits synchronous applications such as video and telephony. Most WANs use this approach, but circuit switching can suffer from the same problems as the telephone system; that is, once a circuit is in use, it is usually not available to other users. This means that long messages may cause delays for other users. Circuit switching allows synchronous applications for the communicating parties for the duration of the interaction. Access time (the time spent waiting to use the medium) is not constant and, as a consequence, pure circuit switching may cause problems in nonbroadcast situations.

Packet switching involves breaking a message into small components (packets), which are then forwarded through the network to their destination. Each packet may follow a different path to its destination, so each must carry addressing information, sequencing instructions and error-control information. Packet switching is used by most LANs and does not support synchronous applications. Packet switching reduces the delay time by interleaving packets from different sources, although the individual delay time for long messages is likely to increase. The Internet protocol TCP/IP (a protocol in this context is just the set of rules that govern the exchange of information; it says what must be done in the event of an error, resetting a connection and so on) is the predominant WAN protocol and is able to operate on a circuit or packet basis. TCP/IP stands for transmission control protocol/Internet protocol.

Fast circuit switching is a modern hybrid technology (although the concepts were published in the early 1980s), which combines the simplicity and fairness of packet switching with the synchronous transmission abilities of circuit switching. A connection is established for each packet sent, and the access time is so low as to make true synchronous applications possible. It is likely that most networks will migrate to a variant of this scheme. This provides yet another example of technology convergence.

Communications media

Detailed coverage of cabling and media in current use is beyond the scope of this book. However, media can be subdivided into hardwire and softwire.

Hardwire media are media that can be touched. Twisted pair, coaxial cable and optical fibre are all hardwire. The initial installation costs are lower than for softwire systems but they are more expensive to maintain and manage. Because the final connection to a networked device is by means of a cable or fibre to a designated network connection point, hardwire systems do not allow a high degree of user or device mobility. Hardwire systems have been around for a long time and standards are well developed, so performance is better than it is for softwire systems.

Table 4.2 gives a simple comparison of hardwire and softwire media.

TABLE 4.2   Comparison of hardwire and softwire media

Hardwire	Softwire
Setup costs low	Setup costs high
Ongoing management costs high	Ongoing management costs low
Not flexible, no mobility	Very flexible, allows great mobility
Good standards and high speeds	Standards now well developed and speeds approaching hardwire capability
May not be an option for an architecturally significant building, because the alterations required to install cabling and powerpoints may not be permitted under local regulations	Can be used anywhere

Softwire ('wireless') media are broadcast systems. They use radio waves, microwaves or free-space optics to handle the communication. They cost more to install than hardwire systems, but are easier (and cheaper) to manage. They allow a high degree of user or device mobility but do not give as good performance as hardwire systems. However, for a temporary installation, one that requires a high degree of flexibility or one for which architectural constraints preclude the use of hardwire systems, they are excellent. Satellite systems are very good for broadcasting but not so useful for ordinary communication owing to the long propagation delays that they introduce. Satellites are also affected by sunspot activity and magnetic storms, so most Internet service providers do not choose to use satellite links as their only source of Internet bandwidth.

Another way to classify media is to divide them into electrical, radio and optical categories.

> *Electrical media*. These include telephone, twisted pair and coaxial cable. Of these, twisted pair is the most commonly used medium in local area networking. Category 5 cable (CAT5) is baseband twisted pair and operates at 100 Mbps over 50 m. Coaxial cable gives similar performance but over longer distances and tends to be used in network backbones. Both are giving way to CAT6 cabling, which runs at 1000 Mbps. All electrical media are prone to interference or induced currents caused by lightning strikes.

> *Radio*. Apart from radio and TV broadcasts, this category also includes microwave communications such as satellites and mobile telephones. As are electrical media, this category is prone to interference, and for some applications may represent a security hazard because the signals are broadcast.

> *Optical*. This may be a softwire system using infra-red light (not unlike a TV remote control) but more commonly uses **optical fibres**. Optical fibres do not suffer from interference. The limitations here come from absorption of the signal and signal loss at fibre joins. Optical fibres are resistant to interference and lightning strikes, making them ideal for the safe interconnection of buildings in a LAN environment. Because they are not electrical, they cannot be tapped externally, and because they are so thin, they are virtually impossible to tap internally. This high degree of precision makes optical fibres expensive because of the engineering needed to make connections, but this cost continues to come down as the technology becomes widespread. A single strand of multimode fibre can replace 1800 pairs of telephone lines, which gives some idea of its huge carrying capacity. Fibres are much lighter than copper cables: 1 km of coaxial cable could weigh much more than 1000 kg; the same length of a single optical fibre can be carried easily in one hand. Of course, because much of the installation cost of any cabling is labour, more fibre than immediately needed should be installed to allow for growth.

[**Key concept:** Labour is a significant cost, so it is better to overengineer the system in the short term than to pay for expensive upgrades in the medium term.]

More on optical fibres

Fibres come in two main types: multimode and monomode. Multimode fibres propagate the signal by total internal reflection and are able to use **light-emitting diodes (LEDs)** as light sources. They are much cheaper than monomode fibres and tend to be used for distances of less than 5 km. They are usually capable of delivering at least 150 Mbps. They tend to be used for metropolitan area networks and shorter–haul, high-speed links, although they are starting to be deployed in ordinary LANs.

Monomode fibres have a much smaller aperture (diameter) than multimode fibres; they are so narrow that they approach the physical wavelength of light. At this point, the ray model of light fails and the light can be propagated only as a wave — hence the name *mono*mode. Monomode fibres are very expensive and have to use lasers as light sources. They are used for long-haul communications links (often more than 20 km) and have a much higher carrying capacity than multimode fibres do. In theory, their bandwidth is in excess of 5 Gbps. Speeds in excess of 10 Gbps are possible, but rely on a technique called dense wave division multiplexing, which is similar to frequency division multiplexing. Table 4.3 gives a comparison of common communications media.

TABLE 4.3 A comparison of common communications media

	Network	Typical speed	Typical distance	Error rate	Security	Cost
Hardwire medium						
Twisted pair CAT5/6	LAN LAN backbone High-speed server links	100 Mbps (CAT5) 1000 Mbps (CAT6)	100 m	Low	Average	Low
Coaxial cable	LAN backbone	150 Mbps	500 m	Low	Average	Moderate
Optical fibre	Any	100 Mbps To 160 Gbps	Up to 40 km	Extremely low	Excellent	Very high
Softwire medium						
Radio	LAN	~ 10 Mbps	< 500 m	Moderate	Poor	Low
Infra-red	LAN backbone	16 Mbps	< 100 m	Moderate	Poor	Low
Microwave	WAN	4–32 Mbps	< 30 km	Low to moderate	Poor	Moderate
Satellite	WAN	Up to 8 Mbps	Very long	Low to moderate	Poor	Moderate

Communications networks

'A communications network is a set of independent devices that may exchange information.' This definition is rather more inclusive than many but it has certain merits. First, the word 'independent' implies that no individual device is in control of the communication process: the master–slave relationship of the old mainframe days is all but over. It reflects the empowerment of users through PCs. Second, the word 'devices' is used in preference to 'computers' to convey the idea that networks have types of devices other than computers, for example, smart printers, servers, interconnection devices. Last, the word 'information' may be construed to mean simple data, processed data, instructions, requests, graphics files or just about anything. This is indicative of the huge changes that have occurred in business computing in the past decade or so.

Networks are the enabling technology that allows modern systems to function. Some people have described them as the 'glue' that holds corporate systems together. The importance of networks is evidenced by communications costs far outweighing data-processing costs for the vast majority of businesses. There are many reasons for networking, and most of these will emerge from a consideration of basic network types and their function.

WANs and LANs

Wide area networks (WANs) evolved first and had their origins in telephone network technology. These allowed staff at different mainframe sites to communicate. There were two driving forces behind this: the first was simple commerce (the need to make money) and the second was defence (largely driven by the Cold War between major Western powers and the then USSR). However, in terms of applications, the original emphasis in wide area networking was communication and this has not really changed in the past four decades. WANs tend to be connection oriented and the separation between communicating parties is usually in the order of tens of kilometres but may span several hundreds of kilometres. Many companies do not build their own WANs but find it cheaper to buy in communications from a third-party provider or to use the Internet. Increasingly, companies are using a **virtual private network (VPN)** on third-party-provided WAN services and, more recently, on internal local area networks (LANs), too. A VPN is a sort of network within a network, invisible to all but its authorised users.

[**Key concept:** It is usually more cost effective to use someone else's network than it is to build and manage your own. This is especially true for WANs.]

LANs developed a little later than WANs. Initially, the emphasis was on sharing resources, such as printers and disk drives, and the networks tended to be oriented towards specific functions such as localised data processing or controlling automated industrial processes. The advent of the PC in the 1980s and reduced technology costs allowed the original emphasis of resource sharing to be extended to include communication functions. LANs now provided the information and communications infrastructure for many businesses. They provide basic communications functions such as email and support network-intrinsic software such as groupware. Increasingly, they also provide high-quality video-conferencing, media streaming and the like. Most LANs are contained within a single site (and many within a single building) and the separation between communicating parties is usually in the order of a few thousand metres.

Backbone networks

A **backbone network** is a special kind of LAN that interconnects everything on a single site, including other smaller LANs (LAN segments), into a single, cohesive whole. The backbone may operate at a much higher speed than other parts of the network and may use different networking technology from the rest of the site.

Personal area networks

Personal area networks (PANs) have evolved in recent years to support the increasing number of peripheral devices that PCs need to communicate with. Operating at a variety of speeds and over short distances (see later in this chapter), the emphasis is on the convenience of local mobility. Typical products for home use would include Bluetooth and WiFi networking.

Storage area networks

Enterprise networks now frequently include a storage area network (SAN). This is a special high-speed network (or subnetwork) that interconnects many different kinds of data storage devices and servers. These networks carry out archival and retrieval of data, backup and restoration of data and disk mirroring (copying an entire hard drive in case of failure). SANs also provide for business continuity in the event of technical problems and sometimes disaster recovery in the event of major problems.

Cellular and wireless communications

Few people would have expected the take-up rate for the various forms of wireless communication now available. Essentially, there are three main uses: telephony, data transfer and communication between PCs and peripheral devices (personal area networking). The cellular and wireless approaches are examined here.

Cellular communication systems

The principle of cellular communication is simple. The service area is divided into 'cells', each of which has a low-powered transmitting station at its centre. As a user moves from one cell to another, the stations negotiate a graceful handover so that the communication does not drop out. The use of low-powered stations means that transmission frequencies can be reused in non-adjacent cells to increase the service coverage. To achieve a handover, the cells must overlap as shown in figure 4.2 overleaf (where the overlap is shown for *some* cells by means of circles, but conventionally cells are represented as hexagons). To prevent interference, adjacent cells must use different frequencies.

Cells come in several varieties. *Macrocells* are for low population density areas, and the transmitters are more powerful than ordinary cells. *Microcells* are created by splitting a normal cell as the demand increases, and the transmitters have much lower power than an ordinary cell. Microcells can be further subdivided to create picocells. *Umbrella cells* are sometimes used to improve the effectiveness of a microcell cluster. Someone driving a car through such a cluster would require many handovers. So when the speed of a user unit is sufficiently high, it is handled by the umbrella cell rather than the microcells. *Selective cells* are used whenever a 360-degree transmitter is impractical, or not needed, such as at tunnel mouths or adjacent to high-power electricity installations.

Cellular systems underpin mobile telephone technology. Contemporary mobile phones do much more than handle voice communication; they are also able to handle data communication. Older systems used **cellular digital packet data (CDPD)** to allow users to surf the Web, but the speeds were very low. CDPD is regarded as obsolescent technology. Code division multiple access (CDMA) has replaced CDPD with current versions operating at speeds of 2–4 Mbps, but this technology too is rapidly approaching the end of its useful life and will soon disappear. The Australian replacement is Telstra's 3G850 network. This will operate on the same frequency as CDMA (850 MHz), using the same antennae, with very similar overall coverage to CDMA. This will be supplemented with high-speed downlink packet access to give consumers mobile broadband services such as video calls and music. Initial speeds were between 500 Kbps and 1.1 Mbps but increased to 14 Mbps in 2007. Because many other companies worldwide are using the same technology and standards, this should give true global roaming in 140 countries.

However, combinations of high speed and low download limits could make this an expensive option for ordinary consumers.

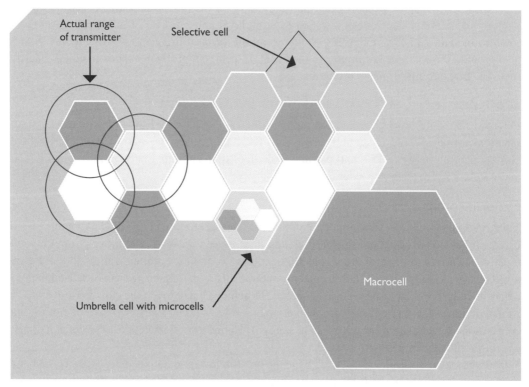

Figure 4.2 A simple cellular network showing different cell types

Mobile commerce is expected to make extensive use of mobile phone technology, but the lack of global standards is posing obstacles in the medium to short term. Mobile phone tariffs tend to make mobile data communication an expensive option, and the small displays and keypads on phones do not make for good-quality web surfing. 3G networks may improve this.

Bluetooth

Bluetooth was developed to support communication between PCs and peripheral devices, but the technology soon found its way into mobile phones and handheld computers. Bluetooth (named after Harald Blåtand, the tenth-century Danish king, known as Bluetooth, who united Denmark and Norway) can operate in either packet or circuit modes at speeds less than 3 Mbps for voice and data (typical circuit operation would be no more than 1 Mbps). It uses a cellular approach, and a Bluetooth picocell allows up to eight devices to be networked within a 10 m radius. A picocell has one master and several slave devices. Up to ten piconets can be overlapped to form a scatternet. Frequency limitations prevent more than 80 devices being used in a scatternet. Although the range of a picocell is normally restricted to 10 m, it is possible to increase it to 100 m by boosting the power of the transmitter.

The founding companies (Ericsson, Nokia, Toshiba, Intel and IBM) have been at pains to ensure that the technology remains relatively inexpensive, but it seems likely that higher-speed wireless networking such as IEEE802.11a,b or g will eventually supersede Bluetooth on the grounds of superior performance, despite promises of vastly improved performance. In the interim Hewlett Packard is shipping personal digital assistants (PDAs) that support both standards in the interim, but most businesses will prefer supporting one standard instead of two. The Institute of Electrical and Electronics Engineers (IEEE) has been active in defining networking standards for many years. Its '802 family' of standards addresses local area networking. Standard IEEE 802.11 refers to a networking technology loosely called 'Ethernet', which is the most widely used local area networking technology. It is discussed in more depth later.

Wireless networking

Given that Ethernet is the dominant standard for local area networking, it is logical to expect a mobile version. There are three main varieties. IEEE 802.11 is the 'umbrella' standard for these networks. A newer kind of wireless networking called ultrawideband supports very high speed transmission over short distances, and this will support high-definition multimedia in the home. Working groups are in progress to use the technology to improve Bluetooth.

Pervasive networking

The take-up rate for mobile and wireless networking is sufficiently high to support pervasive networking. All the term 'pervasive networking' means is that networking technology is finding its way into many different kinds of technology. Televisions, DVD players, video cameras, cars, refrigerators and so on are having networking capability installed. Even devices that already have networking capability are having to support several communication protocols. PDAs are being shipped with Bluetooth, IEEE 802.11b as well as the usual infra-red communication ports. Table 4.4 gives a comparison of the different technologies in terms of range and speed. There is some debate about which will come to dominate, but it seems likely that most devices will support several networking standards, if only because of the substantial market penetration already achieved. Ultimately, slower standards are likely to be superseded and the newer IEEE 802.11n seems set to do just that.

TABLE 4.4 Comparison of range and speed of technologies

	Speed (typical)	Speed (maximum)	Range (indoor)	Range (outdoor)
Bluetooth (faster versions under development)	1 Mbps	3 Mbps (maximum, usually 1 Mbps)	10 m	100 m
IEEE802.11a	25 Mbps	54 Mbps	25 m	75 m
IEEE802.11b	5.5 Mbps	11 Mbps	35 m	100 m
IEEE802.11g	25 Mbps	54 Mbps	25 m	75 m
IEEE802.11n	200 Mbps	540 Mbps	50 m	125 m
Ultrawideband	500 Mbps	880 Mbps	5 m	15 m

Note: The information given in this table is indicative. Actual speeds and ranges vary with local conditions and the class of device used.

What are the practical implications and applications of pervasive networking? Freedom from cables in the home is one major advantage; apart from power cables, monitors, TVs, printers, scanners, speakers and so on will need no direct connection to each other or a PC. A whole new range of geography-specific applications will become available, and homes will become more user-friendly. A PDA will function as a universal remote control, not only for entertainment devices but also for communicating remotely with home lighting, security and climate control systems.

Increasingly networks make use of wireless technologies, and some devices are able to support synchronous communication and operate as 'wireless switches'. The potential down-side of pervasive networking is the increased vulnerability to hacking and eavesdropping. Although techniques such as frequency hopping (changing frequencies so that eavesdroppers only receive part of a message) and encryption (encoding a message so that it cannot be read without a key) are available, portable devices do not usually have a lot of processing power to spare. So security is problematic.

[**Key concept:** The smaller you are, the more you will pay for bandwidth.]

infobyte

BigDog's bark worse than his byte, a case of tall puppy syndrome

Transporting things around under battlefield conditions is a risky occupation for a human, which is why Boston Dynamics has developed a robotic Great Dane that can transport 55 kg of equipment up a 45-degree incline at a little more than 5 km/h, tackling terrain that wheeled and tracked vehicles cannot. What makes BigDog special is that it is aware of its surroundings and its triple-jointed aluminium legs can be repositioned more than 500 times per second. The current version is remote controlled and requires secure battlefield communications, but future versions will be intelligent and unleashed.

Source: Information from Lerner, P 2006, 'Robotic dog of war', *CNN online*, www.cnn.com.

Differences between LANs and WANs

The obvious difference between LANs and WANs is that of operating distance, but the implications of this are a little more subtle. Because WANs operate over long distances, they tend to use third-party lines and cables, which seldom support high-speed communication. The error rate in WANs is higher than it is in LANs, which means that the protocols must be more complicated and consequently less efficient. Most WANs are connection oriented but are much slower and more error prone than LANs.

Because LANs operate over much shorter distances than WANs and tend to be totally owned by one party, they have much better-quality cabling than WANs. In turn, this means much higher transmission rates (often in excess of 100 Mbps) and lower error rates. LAN protocols can be much simpler and more efficient than WAN protocols.

Metropolitan area networks

Metropolitan area networks (MANs) are a relatively recent phenomenon. The advent of reliable, high-speed communications media such as optical fibres has allowed simple, efficient

LAN protocols to be used over much greater distances. The emphasis in MANs is one of interconnection: they allow dissimilar networks on different sites to interconnect and cooperate. MANs often provide gateway (access) services to remote networks and applications. Even here wireless networking is becoming more important as WiMax technologies (a generic term for broadband MAN technologies based around the IEEE 802.16 standard) are used. In theory these could deliver 70 Mbps over long distances (greater than 50km) and could be used to provide high-speed Internet access to consumers. In practice, this is only true of 'line of sight' operation. Most consumers could expect 10 Mbps over 2 km, which is still a respectable speed. WiMax is an obvious competitor with 3G networks.

Table 4.5 provides a comparison of the different network types.

TABLE 4.5   A comparison of different network types

	PAN	LAN	BN	MAN	WAN
Emphasis	Peripheral interconnection	Resource sharing	Interconnection	Interconnection	Communication
Speed	Low to high	High	Very high	Very high	Relatively slow
Protocol	Simple and efficient	Simple and efficient	Simple and efficient	Simple and efficient	Complex and slow
Distances	Very short	Short	Campus scale	Metropolitan scale	Long

Other reasons for networking

Resource sharing and communication have been the prime movers in the development of networks. Another reason for networking is the need for systems that have 'failsoft' potential. (Failsoft is the ability of a system to detect component failures and temporarily modify its processing to prevent irretrievable loss of data.) If part of a networked system goes down, because processing and data are distributed, it is possible for the business to continue its operations by using other parts of the network, e.g. if a local server goes down a business might be able to use a remote server. Performance will be reduced for the period of the outage but the business can continue to trade. Some organisations operate on a 24/7 basis (i.e. 24 hours a day, seven days a week) and make extensive use of redundant networked hardware. In the event of faults, the system will continue to function at a normal level and identify the faults for later repair. Larger organisations may have several servers devoted to the same task to improve both performance and reliability. In such cases, allocating loads to servers can be a complex task. The ability not to lose business far outweighs the extra hardware and management costs. To put this into context, the management costs for a LAN for one year will far exceed the purchase costs of all the hardware and software.

Basic local area networking technology

LANs consist of devices that allow PCs to access the network, communications media, devices that interconnect cables, and software that facilitates network management. These are considered in turn.

PC network interface card

Each computer and networked device such as a server or printer needs to have a network interface card (NIC). In a PC, the NIC is installed in one of the spare expansion slots on the computer's motherboard (refer to chapter 11). The NIC allows the computer to 'talk' to the network.

Cabling

At a physical level, the network makes use of a communications medium. Although softwire (wireless) media are available, most installations will use cables of some kind. LAN cables come in three basic varieties:

> *Twisted pair.* This is the most widely used medium in local area networking. CAT5 cable runs at 100 Mbps, which is more than sufficient for most desktop devices.

> *Coaxial cable.* This is similar in appearance to the cable that is used for TV and was often used for network backbones (the core cabling of a LAN). Advances in twisted-pair cabling (e.g. CAT6) and optical fibres rendered coaxial obsolescent for most LAN applications.

> *Optical fibre.* This is the most expensive and the most reliable medium. Because it uses light instead of electricity, it is immune from interference. It gives very high-speed transmission (frequently in the order of gigabits per second) and is very secure because it is almost impossible to tap. It is also used for long cable runs between buildings to avoid the effects of lightning. Expense prevents its use for desktop connections but it is widely used in high-speed network backbones.

infobyte

Plug and play

Most people would be familiar with the concept of power over Ethernet: using network cables to power remote devices such as security cameras. Using power cables to handle Ethernet connections is a little different. For home networking, most users deploy a variant of WiFi and wireless technologies to share a broadband connection. However, the speed and range are restrictive and the systems can usually only handle three channels simultaneously; the wireless signal can be affected by interference, thick walls and metal. Large multi-storey homes with simultaneous users are especially problematic for wireless access. Netcomm have developed a turbo HomePlug system that can use the electrical wiring of a building to transmit Ethernet signals at speeds of up to 85 Mbps over 200 m. This gives great flexibility and excellent performance. Games consoles, computers and media devices can be networked easily and wireless access can still be provided. The system is very useful for conventions where temporary systems need to be set up quickly and easily.

Source: Information from www.netcomm.com.au.

Interconnection devices

Interconnection devices tend to operate in two ways: broadcast, in which a message is transmitted throughout the entire network (a hub operates in this way), and directed, in which messages are 'targeted' to their destination. Directed devices may operate at a hardware level, as do switches, or at a higher level in software, as is the case with routers. Of course, for messages to be sent, received or forwarded, every device in a network has to have an individual address.

Routers process network traffic and forward messages along preprogrammed paths (hence 'router' because they route messages) and in larger networks find an alternative path in the event of circuit failure. Routers have a high degree of software intelligence, and because they operate at a higher level than switches and hubs, they are able to provide privacy and security. They can be used to restrict access and create closed user groups and 'virtual networks' (a virtual network is a network within a network, visible only to authorised users). Routers are also able to handle several different LAN protocols, allowing them to be interconnected. However, because a full consideration of routers and hybrid devices is beyond the scope of this text, the discussion is restricted to the most commonly used devices in LANs, that is, hubs and switches, with an emphasis on switches as the dominant networking device.

LANs use interconnection devices to provide connection points among computers and other network devices. These simplify the process of network design because the developer can focus on the central infrastructure of the network. The main tasks are to design efficient cable runs and to ensure that the network has scope for growth. Most developers install more and better cable than is required initially, and make sure that interconnection devices have spare ports to accommodate growth. If this seems extravagant, remember that the yearly operating costs of a LAN far exceed the installation costs. Remember, too, that most of the cable installation costs are for labour, and return visits for upgrades are relatively expensive. The basic infrastructure for a LAN should have an effective lifespan of five to seven years. Hubs may be hardwire or softwire, such as WiFi hubs.

Ethernet-type networks (the most commonly used local area networking strategy) are mainly switch-based hubs that are really broadcast devices, that is, everything that is input on one port is automatically output on every other available port. This is wasteful because every computer will receive a message whether it needs to or not. However, for a small, lightly loaded network, this may be permissible. Hubs cannot support modern synchronous applications and will likely become of historical interest only.

Switches are selective (i.e. directed), and make connections only between computers or devices that need them. A 32-port hub can handle only one communication at a time but a 32-port switch can handle up to 16 communications between pairs of computers or devices at the same time. Switches allow synchronous applications and give much better performance than hubs. Accordingly, many newer LANs are based around switch technology. Switches are usually able to operate at more than one speed, which allows for a very fast link to a server and relatively slower links to the desktop.

Network operating system

A network operating system (NOS) is also required. Although most computers are now shipped with operating systems that are network friendly and incorporate networking function, a network operating system is different because it is dedicated to the network and not limited to the desktop machines and servers. The NOS helps in basic network operations management and allows user accounts and so on to be set up easily. Novell Netware, Linux and Windows-derived products are well-known examples. Although these provide 'nuts and bolts' features of network operations, they should not be confused with higher-level software whose function is network management. The distinction is analogous to that between word processing and desktop publishing software.

[**Key concept:** In LANs, performance is vital, so if the budget will stand it, opt for high-speed synchronous communication.]

Ethernet

Ethernet is the dominant local area networking technology. The original standard was published in 1976 by Robert Metcalfe and David Boggs. Since then, it has undergone many revisions and the standards have been extended to include switch-based operation, very high-speed versions and wireless technologies. Its dominance of local area networking technology seems unlikely to change. This dominance ensures that competition for the manufacture and supply of components is sufficient to keep prices relatively low and to reduce dependencies on one or two key suppliers. Its dominance also ensures a degree of future proofing, because future developments will be backward compatible with the existing standards.

Satellites

In 1945, the science fiction writer Arthur C Clarke, in an article in *Wireless World*, proposed the idea of using geostationary orbits for communications satellites (he did not, as popular opinion has it, actually invent the communications satellite). In Clarke's view, three satellites would have been sufficient to provide world coverage, with each satellite acting as a line-of-sight relay for communications. The link has to be line of sight because satellites use microwaves. Astonishingly, Clarke never patented his idea because he thought it would never be achievable in his lifetime, as he commented in an interview: 'It is with somewhat mixed feelings that I can claim to have originated one of the most commercially viable ideas of the twentieth century, and to have sold it for just $40'.

The 'Clarke' orbit is at a distance of 35 680 km above the equator, and here a satellite tends to maintain the same position relative to the Earth. (Some variations in orbit occur because the Earth is not perfectly spherical; accordingly, satellites burn fuel to maintain their position. Eventually, the fuel runs out and the satellite's orbit decays; hence the interest in using the space shuttle to carry out repairs and servicing to satellites in orbit.) Approximately 150 satellites can be accommodated in the Clarke orbit (called **geosynchronous earth orbit**; **GEO**). The uplinks and downlinks of a satellite operate on different frequencies to avoid interference, and the area covered by a satellite's transmissions is called the 'footprint'. The larger the footprint, the weaker the signal and the larger the receiving dishes have to be.

Advantages of satellites

Satellites have several advantages:
> They can carry huge amounts of data.
> Communication costs remain the same irrespective of the number of receivers or the distance between the sending and receiving stations.

> National boundaries and control are hard to apply to satellite communication.

> Transmission errors occur randomly, and error-handling techniques yield good results.

> Users can be highly mobile while using the communication links.

Disadvantages of satellites

Satellites also have several disadvantages:

> A one-way circuit may have a delay of 0.25 seconds, and a two-way link may have a delay of 0.5 seconds. Obviously, this is not suitable for telephony.

> Transmissions are not secure because they can be received by anyone in the footprint area. Encoding can overcome this, but it adds to the cost at the receiving end.

> Restrictions on launch vehicle payload mean that satellites do not carry or generate much electrical power. This can result in weakened signals.

> Some frequencies used tend to be affected by interference and atmospheric conditions.

> Satellite links can be costly.

For some applications such as intermittent operations in remote locations, satellites are the only real option. Not all satellites are in geostationary orbits. Medium earth orbit (MEO) is used for communications and earth resource mapping. MEOs are inclined to the equator at a height of about 9600 km. Because these satellites move in respect to the Earth, more are needed than for GEO systems. However, GEO satellite locations are overcrowded, and MEO systems are cheaper because they do not cost so much to put into orbit. MEO systems do not need to be as powerful as GEO systems, which yields further cost savings. Finally, MEO systems have a much smaller signal delay time than GEO systems.

There are also low earth orbit (LEO) systems, positioned at a height of 640–1600 km. Launch costs are much lower than for other satellite types, and because the distances involved are much less, both satellites and users can handle less powerful signals. Many more satellites are needed to provide coverage, because they frequently change their position relative to Earth. LEO satellites were the underlying technology of the Iridium project (a system that originally proposed 77 satellites and for that reason was named 'Iridium' after the element with the atomic number 77). The underlying idea was simple: take the cellular concept of a mobile phone and put the base stations into orbit. This would give a worldwide mobile network for voice and data communication. (The quoted coverage of current mobile phone networks tends to be based on percentage of population with access, rather than geographic area in which the service is available.)

The Iridium concept was bold and total project costs were to be in excess of US$5 billion for hardware alone, but it was decided that the potential profits justified proceeding. However, the project was not a commercial success and Iridium went bankrupt in 2000. Other LEO systems (e.g. Globalstar) are still in use.

The Internet

The Internet is a network of networks, each network having its own acceptable use policies. Nobody owns the Internet, and it exists in many different countries. The term 'Internet' is not to be confused with the World Wide Web (the Web, or WWW); the Internet (or Net) is the hardware and the Web is the hypertext environment that sits on top of the Net and makes it easy to use. The concept of hypertext had been around for some time: HG Wells and Vannevar Bush were notable proponents. Ted Nelson and Doug Englebart are generally credited with inventing hypertext in the modern sense of the word, intending it to be used to share academic papers. Tim Berners-Lee pushed the use of hypertext to a new level when he applied it to the (then) emerging Internet to develop a more interactive database. He then proposed a global hypertext project, which would ultimately become the World Wide Web.

The Internet has its origins with the US military. The need for reliable communications and networks that could still operate if they sustained heavy damage led to the development of the routing methods and addressing schemes that became TCP/IP (the world's most widely used network protocol). This resilience has been a double-edged sword as far as governments are concerned, because it is almost impossible to control the Internet and still maintain adequate performance. The Internet spans national boundaries and so the question arises as to which jurisdiction should apply. As hackers are wont to say: 'The Internet finds a way'.

> **Reflection question 2:** Is it possible to censor the Internet?

The combination of Internet and web technologies has allowed users to access Internet resources in a relatively friendly way. Graphical browsers such as Netscape mean a simple point-and-click style of operation. The downside of the Internet is that performance is variable since it depends on network loads. There is a huge investment being put into re-engineering the Internet to deliver the performance people require. In the early days of public Internet access, little was needed other than simple text transfer. Currently, users expect interactive chat, graphic file transfers, Internet telephony and video-conferencing technologies. Much of the revenue needed to fund the technology comes from Internet advertising.

Security is another major issue. There is no intrinsic security on the Internet, so all that can be done is to take precautions at the sending and receiving ends. This might entail physical measures such as proxy servers (devices that hide internal network details from outsiders) and logical security measures such as passwords, authentication and encryption.

Earlier, a reference was made to the phenomenon of technology convergence. All networks simply move information from one place to another, so why does the technology have to be different? You may have used Internet telephony, a piece of software that allows your $3000 computer to emulate a $20 telephone handset. Currently, the quality is not ideal, because the Internet's routing protocol introduces delays into the communication, but if the infrastructure is in place, performance can be very good. Products such as Skype and Vonnage are now widely used. The cost savings more than compensate for performance issues; a local call to your Internet service provider costs a few cents and you can talk for as long as you wish. It is much cheaper to send faxes over the Internet using secure technology, and many companies in the United States do this as a matter of routine. At the 1997 International Switching Symposium, World Telecommunications Congress, more than 2500 professionals were surveyed about whether they thought that the telephone systems and the Internet would be separate technologies by 2010. The overwhelming response was 'no'. Also, when the infrastructure of the Internet is sufficiently good, video and music is likely to be reticulated into the home. Here, again, the data communications and media technologies may be seen to be converging.

Internet access

Within most sizable businesses, the networking is high speed and high quality, but when it comes to home and small-business users, high performance is often difficult and expensive to maintain. In Australia, the main telecommunications provider (Telstra) has enjoyed a virtual monopoly because it owns most of the infrastructure and has some measure of protection enshrined in legislation. It would be not be in Telstra's interests to provide new products and services requiring massive investment. In the interim, customers have access speeds that are slow and expensive by international standards. Because the infrastructure is limited, many Australian users still have simple dial-up access and, owing to line quality and modem pooling (i.e. how Internet service providers (ISPs) share out the bandwidth) few if any are realising the 56 Kbps speeds that their PC modems can reach.

Broadband services require a special kind of modem and provide a higher-speed access (although usually much less than 0.5 Mbps). These are based around digital subscriber line (DSL) services, which have the advantage of not tying up phone lines for network access. In most DSL variants, including ADSL, data transmission uses different frequencies from those allocated to voice transmission. ISDN is an older technology that is still available, but both ISDN and ADSL are relatively expensive options when download limits and speeds are considered. In areas where cable TV systems are well developed, it might be possible to get high-speed downloads through the TV cable; however, the uplink to the ISP must be made by telephone. One- and two-way satellite options are available, but these are also quite expensive. For many Australian businesses, dial-up access and ISDN are the most cost-effective options because they are restricted to the telephone system for historical reasons. Currently, Australian dial-up customers are just in the majority but that seems set to change with increasing competition. The Australian G9 consortium (comprising Optus, AAPT, Internode, iiNet, Primus, Macquarie Telecom, Powertel, Soul and TransACT) is committed to developing its own very high-speed network with the intention of providing high-speed Internet access. Telstra (a potential partner) decided not to take part in the project, There are many issues to be overcome, including design and finance for the $4.1 billion project, but SpeedReach (the umbrella company that will build and run the network) could be a serious contender offering speeds of 12 Mbps as a minimum to at 4 million customers. Equally, the download speeds that Telstra offers to broadband customers are limited to 1.5 Mbps as an administrative convenience. The controlling software can be reconfigured to increase the speeds by a factor of four or five (Tay 2006). It may be a few years before SpeedReach achieves its goals but competition can only be good for consumers.

Although the actual infrastructure of the Internet is relatively good, 'last mile' connections are where most delays occur, most notably where the telephone infrastructure is obsolescent. Here, wireless DSL might provide an effective solution. As a final comment, note that good communications speeds are not synonymous with good Internet performance from a user point of view. Internet performance requires efficient DNS (running at the local Internet service provider) and good subscriber-to-connection ratios.

> **Reflection question 3:** Given advances in Internet technology, do traditional telephone companies have a long-term future?

[**Key concept:** The smaller you are, the more you will pay for Internet use.]

Intranets

The problems with the Internet from a corporate perspective are lack of performance; too much information to search through; potential lack of security and an inability to restrict access and an inability to impose control on content and presentation aspects.

If a company had its own privately owned and controlled internet, then these problems are not an issue. This is the guiding principle behind the development of intranets, which have user-friendly graphical browsers and make corporate information resources available to staff in a convenient way. Think of them as a privately owned and controlled internet for use within a single organisation. Content management service provider Numotion e-business suggests the return on investment (ROI) for intranets is 1000 per cent (Numotion e-business website), and there are suggestions ROI may even reach as high as 2000 per cent for a well-developed and managed system. Think about maintaining a web-based telephone directory for an organisation with 3000 staff and a high staff turnover: the listing would be up to date and available at all times, and would save on time and paper over a hardcopy. The range of services that may be accessed might include groupware, organisational charts, staff directories and corporate databases. Restricting access to specific groups is a simple matter of network management.

IS in action

More than content but less than happy

As intranets have come of age, much of the hype surrounding their adoption is now subject to critical analysis. For well-focused systems, the ROI figures can be very high. As an example, human resources management systems that allow employees to manage their own leave, superannuation details and so on can save about $400 per employee a year. As some intranets have grown, they have lost that sharp focus because managers have tried to make them all things to all people. To improve productivity, the content presented on screen needs to be relevant to the task in hand. It also needs to be very easy to find. Being able to move easily from one part of the intranet to another relies on good design and sophisticated link management. Interviews with corporate clients suggest that the initial ROI productivity gains have not been sustained as intranets have increased in scale and scope. The performance of technology is not at issue. The problem would seem to be that staff can not find the resources that they are looking for efficiently, and consequently waste time and money. If the intranet is really bad, then staff will actively avoid it and ask colleagues for help. Most intranets have a search facility that enables staff to locate the resource or information that they are looking for, yet many of these are less than optimal in performance. In contrast, a search on Google will yield results in a tenth of a second. What this tells us is that many organisations are still locked into twentieth-century thinking and managers view the corporate intranet as a repository for information. Simply buying into a superior search technology like Google will not solve the problems. Staff generate content that may be second rate. Because the intranet is seen as a document management system, little or no thought is given to link management or contextual help and support. The lesson? Intranets are so much more than document management systems; to achieve the high ROI, information needs to be considered holistically in conjunction with business processes.

Extranets

Whereas intranets are for internal use and the Internet is for general use, extranets are somewhere between those two. Extranets are networks that form umbilical links between a company and its suppliers or customers. Extranets frequently (but not exclusively) make use of Internet technologies such as browsers. The connections between sites can be private or public. In the latter case, security and data encryption are very important.

While intranets shorten timelines and improve the delivery of information inside an organisation (and consequently improve knowledge management), extranets do the same for suppliers and customers. Shortening timelines improves cash flow and increases the competitive edge. (Just-in-time delivery systems are discussed earlier in this text and are revisited when e-business is discussed in chapter 9.) There is an important psychological aspect to extranets: they make customers, clients and suppliers part of the enterprise. As mentioned in chapter 1, Harley-Davidson Motorcycles uses 'materials as needed' (MAN, not to be confused with metropolitan area network) in its factories, and its extranet allows parts and product information to be disseminated to its North American distributors and dealers. The dealerships are then able to give better service to their customers and reduce their investment in parts on hand. The benefits move up and down the supply chain.

Client–server issues

In client–server environments, client machines (usually desktop or laptop machines) make requests for a service (e.g. printing, Internet access) and a dedicated device on the network responds to the requests. Most modern databases operate in this way.

[**Key concept:** In any system, try to allocate computer processing so as to minimise the load on critical central resources.]

Client–server architectures have been a major force in the development of both application software and LANs over the past two decades. The distribution of processing between client and server is a major factor in design. Sometimes, the client merely provides an interface to the server-based system, whereas in other approaches the client may carry out a substantial amount of processing. There are two things to note:

> Client–server architectures give a very clear division of responsibility between client and server. Placing critical data and applications onto dedicated servers means that they are easier to control and manage (duplicating corporate data and applications on every desktop would be a managerial and security nightmare). There is a third component in the client–server system: the network. Each component in the system may be developed and managed separately, allowing a clearer management focus.

> Client–server systems are network intrinsic. Their very nature places huge demands on the networks that support them. Client–server systems generate a lot of network traffic, that is, they have been responsible for a rise in LAN numbers and are a driver in improving network performance.

Usually, servers are accessed through a LAN, but there is no reason they should not be remote. Client–server architectures may be simple two-tier systems or they may use other devices as intermediaries between the client and server (so-called N-tier client–server systems). An interesting variation made possible by networking is that of 'thin clients', discussed in chapter 2. They are discussed in a little more depth in chapter 11, in covering IT infrastructure issues.

Often, when general-purpose (horizontal) software is being used at an installation, it is downloaded onto the client from the server each time it is required. This places a huge demand on the network, so why is it done in this way? Software licences may only allow a certain number of people to use the package at any one time, and because not every employee needs to use the package at the same time, a cost saving is possible. It also ensures that every user has the 'correct' version of the software.

TCP/IP and DNS explained

To understand the threats to networks using Internet technologies, you need a grasp of how Internet works. The various services available are discussed in chapter 9, but provided here is a 'nuts and bolts' explanation. The concept of a protocol (the set of rules which govern the exchange of information between networked devices) has been touched on; the following text provides an overview of the protocol suite that makes the Internet possible, TCP/IP. It is suggested that you treat this as light reading and not worry if you do not understand all of it, so long as you have a grasp of the fundamentals.

Looking at the acronym, you might think that it looks like two protocols and you would not be far wrong. There are a whole suite of protocols but TCP/IP are the two most important. TCP stands for transport control protocol and IP for Internet protocol. The need to get networks of any kind talking to each other was the driving force behind the development effort in the early 1970s. Until then, network developers had taken the view that the networks had to be perfectly reliable. Consequently, networks were expensive, complex and somewhat slow because of the complicated protocols they needed to support. Robert Kahn (a pioneering networker) and Vinton Cerf made two major conceptual breakthroughs: the first was to make the networked hosts and devices responsible for reliability, the second was to use a common internetworking protocol to hide all the differences between networks. Because the role of the network was reduced to that of a simple communications medium, it became possible to get almost any network to talk to any other network. The devices handle the TCP part of things and deal with errors and network resets. The networks handle the IP part and are concerned with delivery of information.

The IP assigns a unique address to each device on a network. The addresses are valid for a particular network. The address consists of four octets separated by dots. Each octet can vary in value from 0 to 255, so 131.15.171.242 is an example of a valid address. Sometime these addresses are assigned permanently (static IP addresses) but most often the network's DHCP (dynamic host configuration protocol) server assigns one of its pool of available addresses to a PC on request.

IP addresses allow for unique identification of devices but using IP addresses to locate devices on the Internet would be cumbersome. This is where DNS (domain name service) comes into its own. Put simply this allows a symbolic name such as www.pretendsite.com to be used to represent an IP address. (Not only are domain names easier to remember than numeric addresses, but they can be valuable commodities in their own right as part of 'branding' a corporate image.) When you make a request to access a website, your system accesses a DNS server, which will resolve the IP address from the domain name.

We are now up to version 6 of IP. This standard was backward compatible with the still widely used version 4. The main difference was to extend the addressing scheme to allow for growth in demand, but improvements were made to allow the payload size of data packets to increase. The number of available addresses increased from nearly 4 billion to 340 282 366 920 938 463 463 374 607 431 768 211 456, with the intention of providing for the allocation of addresses to household devices, mobiles and vehicles. Despite the 'improvements', businesses have been slow to adopt the new standard, in part because of the costs involved but also because the use of proxy servers (see later in the text) allows users to share a single IP address.

Threats to networks

Networking is a two-edged sword. The very openness we need to make business systems really useful leaves us vulnerable to hackers. The effects of computer viruses can vary from the irritating to the catastrophic. Even the threat of a virus can cause huge disruptions to business as information systems managers take preventative measures. Less well known are denial of service (DOS) attacks. The intent behind a DOS is to prevent users from consuming its available resources (such as RAM or disk space) or forcing it to reset, or to block communications by overloading the system with spurious traffic. High-profile websites are appealing targets for hackers, and attacks are much easier if the IP address of a potential victim is known. So steps must be taken to keep IP addresses secret.

Besides hacking, problems could be caused by employees. Consider the liabilities that a business might face if a staff member used the Internet from a company computer to access illegal material, make libellous statements or harass members of the public. Obviously, codes of behaviour and policies have some mitigating effect, but better controls are needed.

Firewalls

A firewall is a system intended to prevent unauthorised access to (or from) a network and can be implemented in hardware, software or a combination of both. All network managers have to make a compromise: you can have a very secure network or a very fast network — seldom (if ever) can you have a network that is both fast and secure. A firewall examines incoming and outgoing messages and only allows them to pass if they meet the security criteria set by the network manager. Firewalls can work as packet filters (packet level), accepting or rejecting packets on the basis of IP addresses, or as application gateways (application level), denying or allowing access to certain applications.

A packet-level firewall inspects source and destination IP addresses of incoming and outgoing data packets. Only packets with acceptable addresses are allowed through. Obviously, this does not prevent hackers obtaining the IP addresses of trusted business partners and using those to sneak their packets through the firewall. Because every packet entering or leaving the business must pass through the firewall, there is no time to inspect the contents because this would cause processing delays. Consequently, another kind of firewall is needed to protect individual applications. An application-level firewall carries out 'stateful inspection'; that is, it examines the contents of the data packets to make sure that their content is appropriate for the application being guarded (checks might be made concerning the user, location and time before granting access). In either case, only 'good' packets are allowed through. It is best to think of a packet-level firewall as the first line of defence, eliminating most of the suspect packets by simple filtering. The application-level firewalls (usually one for each mission-critical application) need to do much more processing to decide whether to permit or reject access but work on fewer packets, so overall performance should be at an acceptable level. Firewalls impose delays because of all the processing that they need to do. They also require managing. The complexity of management causes cost and logistical problems for many businesses. Few organisations can operate on excessively strict rules and controls. If someone needs to work in a different section of the company and needs different access privileges, locations and times, then the systems needs to be capable of handling that. However, every exception is an administrative overhead.

Firewalls give limited protection against viruses and DOS attacks. Because many computer hacks depend on network addresses being known, other methods are needed to conceal internal network details and control access. This is where proxy servers come into their own.

Proxy servers

A proxy server forces clients to make indirect connections to network services. This may seem an unnecessary inconvenience but there are distinct advantages to be had in using a proxy server: in the areas of security, control, cost and performance.

Web proxies

The concept behind all proxies is simple: devices are addressed indirectly through the proxy. The easiest kind to understand is a simple web proxy. Instead of accessing the Internet, PCs access the proxy and the proxy in turn accesses the Internet. The web proxy also stores web pages and files that are available on remote web servers, so that they can be accessed more quickly. Recently accessed material is available from the proxy server's cache (an area of server storage). When a request for a web page is made, it goes to the proxy and the first place that is searched is the cache. If the required web page is found, then it is returned to the client machine, otherwise the proxy accesses the Internet to find the requested resource.

Because all Internet access for an organisation is channelled through the web proxy, it can be used to enforce acceptable use policies. Censorware applications run by the proxy can prevent access to offensive websites and may filter out viruses and malware (a broad term used for all hostile software that infiltrates computers without permission). Other proxies may reformat web pages for specific technologies such as handheld computers and mobile phones. Although local web proxy servers can block offensive websites, it is still possible to access offensive material. Once a user visits an external website that is a CGI proxy (a website that is on the 'approved' list but allows anonymous access to nonapproved websites), he or she is then able to visit other websites that are blocked by the organisation's web proxy. The user's IP address is not disclosed to the websites visited, so there is an element of anonymity. However, every Internet access leaves traces on the corporate LAN and on the local client machine and specialist audit software can be used to track and trace this. Another way around the proxy server is for the user to reconfigure his or her web browser to avoid it. Because low-level configuration management is burdensome for network managers, this strategy is often successful. Many firewalls make use of network address translation (NAT) to conceal IP addresses from the outside world and to enable a single IP address to be shared by several computers. 'Real' IP addresses are replaced by fictitious ones assigned by the NAT server. Obviously, clever users can configure their browsers to connect directly to the NAT server and so bypass the acceptable use policy.

Intercepting proxies

Intercepting proxies combine the features of a proxy with a NAT server. Any request from a client web browser to the NAT server is automatically redirected to the proxy. The user need not be aware of this and the network manager does not have to bother with the browser settings of each and every user. Sometimes ISPs will use an intercepting proxy to provide a shared cache for all their customers. This reduces their upstream bandwidth needs and improves performance.

Another way to improve performance is to use a split proxy. In essence, this is a pair of proxies on two different computers. Communication between the two halves of the split proxy is much faster than communication with websites, so they can be used to improve the performance of slower links. When the remote half of the proxy accesses a website, it does not need to send all the information needed to display the page because the other half if the proxy already has it. Combined with data compression, split proxies form the basis of many web accelerators, such as that provided by Google.

Reverse proxies

These are the most complicated kind of proxy. To understand them needs an expansion on two reasons for networking: reliability and performance. The key to success here is duplication of resources, so instead of having one web server (or any other kind of server for that matter), there are several. This will give us much better performance. If one server goes down, then there will be backup servers ready to take its place. This leaves the problem that every server has a unique IP address. If there are several different servers, there will be major problems with DNS because address resolution would not be unique. A reverse proxy can take incoming requests and rewrite the addresses so that they can be handled by the first available machine. For outgoing traffic, a single IP address is listed as the source address. As far as the users are concerned, they are dealing with a single server and address. In reality, that single address is used to distribute the processing load to several servers, allowing us to balance loads more evenly. Reverse proxies can also improve performance by handling encryption (encoding transactions to make them indecipherable to anyone but the intended recipient) and performing data compression. As do all proxy servers, they also improve security.

Firewalls, intelligent switches and virtual networks

As mentioned, routers can be used to filter network traffic. It should be apparent that filtering is intrinsic to firewalls. In large networks, there are just too many routers. Not only are they slow, but they require costly individual management. They need to know exactly what traffic to permit, what to disallow, when restrictions need to be in place and the path that messages should take. Switches are much faster but have no software intelligence, so sophisticated management is not possible. Combining the software intelligence of a router with the hardware of a switch gives an intelligent switch. These devices can handle far more physical connections than a router, so fewer are needed. This in turn simplifies the management process and saves costs. Intelligent switches can be programmed to ensure that critical applications and important users always receive the network performance and can have firewall functionality built in. They are very important in virtual networking. As defined, a virtual network is a network within a network visible only to authorised users. It can be implemented by restricting access on the basis of user ID or network address, but as an additional measure of security they often use encryption to maintain the privacy of data. They are commonly described as VPNs. A problem faced when managing a large network is its sheer size. Deploying several VPNs on the same physical network allows a systems manager to 'divide and conquer', managing each VPN as though it were an entirely separate network.

IS in action

Burgers and broadband

Timing can be crucial in information systems. Krystal Co. decided to offer free broadband to any one who wanted to eat a burger and surf the Internet. It had already made the decision to upgrade its network to improve performance when handling credit card payments, so the timing was right. Krystal Co.'s core business is food. Providing free wireless broadband access is just another way of promoting the business. Other food chains also provide Internet access but generally charge for the privilege. The idea came about because University of Tennessee campuses became fully wireless and Krystal Co. staff thought that they might be able to tempt local students and staff to eat in return for free broadband. Because technicians were already visiting every Krystal location, it was a simple matter to add wireless broadband installation and maintenance to their portfolio. Although marketing was the prime mover in making the service free, information systems and IT logistics was the deciding factor. Most of the costs involved in providing free wireless broadband are associated with processing the payment, making sure that only people who have paid get to use it, enforcing time management and looking after passwords and so on. Implementations being simple, 'plug and play' and repeatable was a key factor in success. If technologies are mature when they can be thought of as a simple commodity, then wireless broadband has come of age.

Source: Information from Schuman, E 2005, 'Restaurant CIO: would you like wi-fi with that?', *CIO Insight*, www.cioinsight.com.

[**Key concept:** Networked systems tend be a compromise between high security and high performance.]

Future developments

Currently, more than half the world's population has never even seen a telephone, let alone used a computer to access the Internet. These people are being asked to leapfrog several generations of technology and culture, and it must be acknowledged that this is a huge shock to the psyche. However, most people's view of the information systems world is very PC oriented, which influences the way they think. The basis of competition in the industry is basically a step–locked loop. Manufacturers make faster PCs and software companies write more demanding software. So every so often, people are obliged to upgrade their hardware and software. Two technical drivers might change the PC emphasis. The first of these is wearable computing, with its emphasis on portability, and the second is wireless communication. Using a keyboard can be a very slow and inefficient method of interacting with a computer, especially for handhelds and devices with small keyboards. PDAs, which use a stylus for input, are even slower. Voice recognition and speech processing systems offer a way to speed things up.

Steve Mann of Toronto University has a different vision. He has been involved in personal cybernetics and wearable computing since the 1970s. His inventions include WearComp (wearable computing with networking capability) and Eyetap, a technology that provides visual information fed to the human eye. Eyetap can be concealed in spectacles or in contact lenses. The eye operates as both camera and display, enabling people to link into information resources and to communicate with each other. A third invention of Mann's, which comprises a brainwave monitor as another input/output to the WearComp, gives rise to a 'telepathic' experience. Kevin Warwick of Reading University has implanted microprocessors into his own body to communicate with computers (Warwick 2003), and more recently with similar devices implanted in his wife. In all of this, mobile communications is the prime driver.

These sorts of scenarios lead us to ask whether the PC will still be with us in a recognisable form ten years from now or whether wearable and portable devices will predominate. Everything you want to access by way of music, information and video will be available. Given that writing evolved as a way of making information more permanent and widely available, what impact will all this have on literacy? Will people still send memos when they can send a videogram? What will be the effect on business? The wireless technologies that enable mobile commerce will see the PDA or mobile phone become the nexus point at which conventional retail and e-commerce meet.

IS in action

The man from Del Monte says yes to VOIP

Merging two large organisations will create opportunities for consolidation and such was the case with Del Monte and HJ Heinz's food operations. Nearly 100 systems were removed and the new entity standardised on ERP, data warehousing and supply chain management. The aim was to reduce diversity and complexity and hence save costs. Calls to the help desk (usually a very expensive area) have reduced to 10 per cent of their previous levels, and just 104 staff support more than 8000 users. Combining information from the supply chain management system and vendors' POS systems allows accurate tracking of inventory levels which can be used to generate business intelligence to distinguish between slowing

(continued)

sales of a product and sales that have reduced because of a lack of stock on hand. A startling initiative was to transform corporate telephony by migrating to voice over IP (VOIP). This was intended to reduce operating costs but it was soon realised that new strategic advantages emerged. Any staff member could click on a database entry for an employee and be connected with that person wherever they were in the organisation. Initial quality issues are in the process of being resolved. Major telecommunication companies have reduced the cost of long distance calls to reserve their market share so the cost savings come about because offices can be created or relocated very quickly without worrying about PBX infrastructures and the new offices can be managed centrally. Longer term, VOIP can be used to integrate multimedia communications and the systems will make it easy for employees to deliver multimedia content via the network. This is an excellent example of information systems and IT enabling organisational transformation and delivering competitive agility and cost savings.

Source: Information from Schuman, E 2005, 'Del Monte cuts help desk calls by 90%', www.eweek.com.

Discussion

Hardwire and softwire systems are discussed early in this chapter. There is much talk in the business community about which will come to predominate. Mobile phones are commonplace now and Internet technologies are finding their way into many handheld devices. The technology for portable DVD players using special headsets that give the perspective of large-screen TV is already available. Information-carrying capacity (bandwidth) is not a problem, but cost is the current deterrent. Most information systems professionals hold the view that hardwire technology will persist for long-haul communications and most LAN applications for the next ten to 15 years, whereas softwire (mobile) communications will predominate at the personal level.

The direct impact of Internet technologies on business is substantial; few businesses' style of operation will not be changed to a great extent. The implications of this are rather more subtle. In the past, businesses used proprietary technologies to manage internal affairs. Very few businesses actually used those technologies to communicate with the world at large. Now the situation is different: businesses are still maintaining those older legacy systems but, increasingly, access to them and other corporate resources is tending to be web-based, that is, the systems or access to them is more distributed than before. The merging of communication technologies with Internet technologies is worthy of mention. As the basic Internet infrastructure has improved to the point at which it can provide good-quality service, applications have arisen to take advantage of it. Internet telephony is commonplace and IPTV (TV over the Internet) is becoming popular.

The fundamental nature of corporate information systems has undergone an irrevocable paradigm shift. The technology used inside the organisation is virtually the same as that used between the organisation and its clients and customers and the market at large. The difficulty management information systems managers face is where to place the boundaries between internal and external systems. It is quite clear that people will not be able to think about corporate information systems in quite the same way again.

Summary

Networking has transformed the way many companies do business. It has enabled small business to operate globally and made it possible for companies to form strategic alliances and partnerships in their supply chain and customer relationship management. Communications have changed the cost balance of technology and so offer ways to save money (thin clients would be an obvious example). Mobile communications are in the ascendancy, and it seems likely that many people will access network services in this way, even though this has security implications. Larger networks such as those that form the Internet are most likely to remain with hardwire communications, simply because they can carry much more data at much higher speeds. Networking allows the crossing of state and national boundaries with relative ease and connection of businesses to customers and suppliers. This openness comes at a price because allowing outsiders to access systems through a network can pose significant security risks from hackers and computer viruses. Firewalls can improve network and system security but they add to the cost and complexity of network management.

The key points of this chapter are:

> Networks are the 'glue' that holds systems together, and economics favours networked rather than centralised systems. Although mainframe computing will be the only option for some organisations, that market is contracting and consolidating. Physically distributing the components of a system also helps to improve its resilience to failure.

> The number of networked applications continues to increase but networks themselves are converging. Historically, there were data, telephone and media networks. Increasingly, networks are able to handle any kind of traffic.

> Business and domestic users are demanding high-speed synchronous applications, such as video conferencing. Many existing networks will have to be replaced or upgraded to meet this demand.

> As with other hardware and software, adherence to internationally recognised standards is important, strategically, tactically and financially. The fewer the standards that can be used in an organisation, the easier management will be. The more people who adopt a standard, the bigger and more competitive the market becomes.

> Hardwire systems will continue to be important in larger networks, but PAN access is increasingly wireless.

> Information systems security is always important but it is even more so in a networked environment. Firewalls and proxy servers can go some way towards protecting important applications and data resources, but there is a trade-off. Secure systems tend to be slow, fast systems tend to be insecure. It is important to establish a level of security that is commensurate with risk.

Questions

1. Microsoft is embedding many security features into its flagship operating system. Briefly discuss the pros and cons of this.

2. Briefly explain two advantages and two disadvantages of softwire systems when compared with hardwire.

3. Delivering digital TV via the Internet offers many more channels than analog systems. Is this a good or bad thing for (a) the consumer and (b) business? Give reasons for your position.

4. Currently the Internet is a level playing field, in that all network traffic is treated equally. It has been suggested that there should be differential tariffs and services so that businesses that pay more have their content delivered more quickly to users. Is this a practical idea and what are the implications?

5. Why is satellite communication less suited to telephony and video conferencing than media and entertainment applications?

6. Will optic fibre render satellite communications obsolete? Explain your answer.

7. Compare optic fibres with satellite communications and coaxial cable in terms of cost, speed and security. Are there any other reasons for using optic fibres other than speed and security?

8. RFID tags use wireless technologies to allow goods to be tracked within retail outlets with great accuracy. How could you use RFID tags and networking to improve merchandising and sales at a large store that sells clothing?

9. It has been said that mobile commerce is merely another channel for Internet-based commerce. Do you agree with this statement? Can you provide examples of applications that can only be carried out in a mobile commerce environment (i.e. could not be effected using conventional Internet access)?

10. Why are domain names more useful to businesses than fixed IP addresses?

11. The advances in digital TV are allowing for a greater degree of interactivity with consumers, and pay TV systems offer a much wider choice of channels. Interactive TV allows goods and videos to be purchased with the TV remote. Why would companies prefer this mode of operation rather than Internet-based e-commerce? Would this mean the end of e-commerce? How could e-commerce companies react to prevent this and is it likely that media networks will replace the Internet in a domestic situation?

12. Is it possible to make a networked system too secure? Explain your answer.

Exercises

1. Using the World Wide Web or your personal experience, produce a list of seven significant threats to e-businesses and identify appropriate controls or countermeasures.

2. Use the World Wide Web to find out how Google Web Accelerator works and prepare a briefing document explaining it to others.

3. Use the World Wide Web to research spyware. What symptoms would you expect if your computer was infected with spyware?

We tend to take cinema for granted and while we may be aware of the major advances that have taken place in the field (sound, colour, surround sound, widescreen formats and so on), most people think of cinema as a developed rather than a developing technology. Yet we are poised on the edge of a technological revolution that will transform cinema and extend its reach to remote communities and the home. Disney's *Glory road* became the first motion picture to be released in a standardised digital form, indicating that celluloid movies are about to head the same way as traditional camera films.

Many of the problems faced by movie theatre managers are in relation to duplication and distribution. Making the many thousands of copies of films needed for wide release leads to a degradation in the quality of the copies, with each generation of copy being worse than the previous generation. Subtleties of hue and sound may be compromised. As each copy is shown, mechanical damage takes place and the copy is further degraded. The existence of so many copies also poses a security hazard. Special formats such as 3D are hard to achieve in traditional film format but would be relatively easy in digital forms (Wintner 2006).

Until recently, the digital movie revolution was held up by two major problems; the lack of internationally recognised standards and the lack of technology that was good enough to compete with the century old 35-mm film resolution. The first of these was solved in 2000 with the new JPEG standard and recently digital projection systems that have 2048-line horizontal resolution and 2 000 000 projection mirrors provide cinema-grade quality. Figure 4.3 (on page 132) shows the distribution process in outline. Theatre owners were reluctant to invest in digital technology for the simple reason that there were no guarantees that the systems they purchased would be compatible with the every studio's movies.

The breakthrough came in 2002 when seven major studios — Disney, Fox, MGM, Paramount, Sony Pictures Entertainment, Universal and Warner Brothers Studios — agreed to set up Digital Cinema Initiatives to define standards for digital cinema. The brief was that the standards had to be as good as film, with the potential to be better. Movies will most likely continue to be made on film and distributed in digital form. This is mainly because the size of the files that would be needed to handle an uncompressed and unedited movie would be in excess of 6000 terabytes. For logistical reasons, the files have to be compressed and customer expectations would not permit unreliable products.

Digital movie distribution systems vary in their specifics, but all must take movie files, convert them into the standard digital format, protect them from pirates, get them to the multiplexes, distribute them to the correct movie theatres and project them onto the big screens. Today, most distributors truck digital movie files to the theatres, but in the future, satellite distribution will play a bigger role.

Estimates are that more than 60 per cent of North American cinemas will be digital by 2009. The cost of converting 36 000 screens in the United States and Canada to digital will be in excess of US$3.5 billion. So where are the cost savings to justify the investment? The savings for studios are quite apparent: the cost of each print copy of a movie are estimated to be about US$2000 plus distribution, yielding potential savings of about US$1 billion for the North American market. For the movie theatres, setting up a digital screen will cost about

(continued)

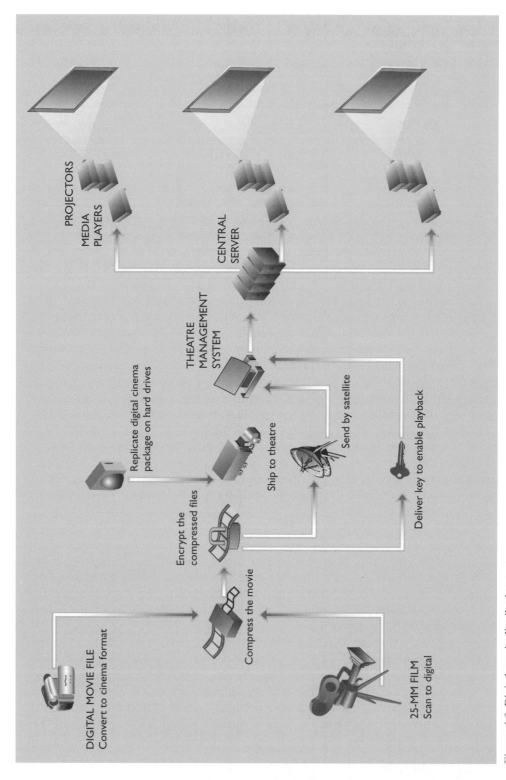

PROJECTORS

MEDIA PLAYERS

CENTRAL SERVER

THEATRE MANAGEMENT SYSTEM

Replicate digital cinema package on hard drives

Encrypt the compressed files

Ship to theatre

Send by satellite

Deliver key to enable playback

Compress the movie

DIGITAL MOVIE FILE Convert to cinema format

25-MM FILM Scan to digital

Figure 4.3 Digital movie distribution systems
Source: www.spectrum.ieee.org.

US$100 000, about three times the cost of a traditional screen. It is likely that the studios will help theatres move to the new format. Currently, two distribution modes are envisaged: satellite downloads and physical distribution of hard drives onto which the film has been copied. A typical feature film, even after compression, is likely to be in excess of 300 GB. Satellite distribution, although more expensive and requiring more users to make it economically viable, is the preferred option because it allows processes to be automated. Having to distribute hard drives is easier than distributing and handling film packs but in a digital age, in which information is transported instantly, this is rather like going back to traditional 'snail mail' methods of distribution.

The other major problem that has beset studios is piracy. The decreasing size and increasing quality of handheld cameras allows 'pirates' to smuggle in a recording device and make illicit copies of the film. The standard provides for the date and location of the movie's showing to be displayed on the screen in a format that is invisible to humans but will be visible to recording devices. If piracy cannot be prevented entirely, it can at least be detectable — and provable in a court of law.

Proponents of digital cinema describe it as the biggest shift in the industry since black and white films gave way to colour. They could be right.

Questions

1. Advances in home theatre technology allow cinema-quality displays in the home. Does this trend imply that public cinemas will disappear and that consumers will watch new-release movies in the home?

2. Identify and explain three ways that a movie theatre could save money in its day-to-day operations by moving to a fully digital solution.

3. What is the overwhelming characteristic that the technology should possess from the consumer's point of view?

4. Optic fibres are much faster, more secure and more easily controlled than satellite links. Why do you think that the movie studios are not pushing fibre-optic technology for movie distribution?

5. What are the main advantages to consumers in digital cinema?

6. Identify and explain three ways that a movie theatre could generate additional income as a result of digital cinema technology.

7. How does digital cinema make content protection easier? Is there still a risk of piracy? If so, what can be done to prevent it?

8. Consider Porter's competitive forces model. Does digital cinema make the threat of new entrants more or less likely? Explain your answer.

9. Does digital cinema make it easier to market films? Briefly discuss the possible linkages to e-commerce systems.

10. This case has focused on North America. How applicable is it to a country such as Australia? What factors would be likely to prevent the adoption of digital cinema?

References

Casson, HN 1910, *The history of the telephone*, McClurg & Co., Chicago.

Jones, WD 2006, 'Blood test', *IEEE Spectrum*, November, pp. 11–12.

Numotion e-business solutions website, www.numotion.net.

Tay L 2006, 'G9 plans FTTN for Australia without Telstra'. *Computerworld*, www. computerworld.com.au.

Warwick, K 2003, 'The potential for implant technology', *Proc. European Journal on Engineering in Information Systems Applications*, vol. 5, no. 1, pp. 1–7.

Wintner, R 2006, 'Bits on the big screen', *IEEE Spectrum*, December, pp. 37–42.

CHAPTER 5
Systems integration: information systems at work

LEARNING OBJECTIVES

After reading this chapter, you should be able to:

» discuss the relative merits of centralised and distributed information systems organisation

» explain how the information systems function is funded and the advantages and disadvantage of different approaches

» explain the various job types that are available in the information industry, what they entail and what abilities they require

» understand what outsourcing is, what may be outsourced and the considerations that must be taken into account before outsourcing

» appreciate the need for systems integration and the various strategies for achieving this

» understand enterprisewide client–server architecture

» understand what is meant by enterprise resource planning (ERP) systems, the advantages that they confer and their applications

» know what is meant by the term 'application service provider (ASP)' and how small-to-medium entities may take advantage of ASP services for systems integration and ERP.

Introduction

This chapter focuses on two broad aspects: the organisational aspects of information systems, including the staffing function, and systems integration. Hardware, software, communications and different kinds of business information systems have been considered in previous chapters. This chapter looks at how all these interact in a commercial context. Organisations are seldom, if ever, in the position of having a 'clean slate' when devising systems solutions. In the case of a small business, it is sometimes more cost effective to start from scratch. But in most medium and large enterprises, systems have been developed without reference to each other that are crucial to the operation of the business. A classic example is a company that has several different PC networks and runs a mainframe for much of its transaction processing. The development effort for the mainframe systems is measured in hundreds of people-years, and because those systems still meet the requirements, they will not be replaced in the near future. These are termed 'legacy systems'. The challenge is making the different systems in a business become a well-integrated, cohesive system that is convenient to use. Success often depends on appropriate organisational structures.

Information systems management — centralised or distributed?

In general, management consists of five basic functions: planning, organising, directing, controlling and staffing. For the purposes of this chapter, only organising and staffing are covered.

There are three terms that are frequently confused: information systems infrastructure, information systems architecture and information systems organisation. *Information systems infrastructure* is all the hardware, software, systems and people of the information systems division. Infrastructure is about providing an information systems environment within which corporate systems can operate. Infrastructure-based approaches are usually geared to maintaining the status quo and often lack detailed focus. *Information systems architecture* is a framework or plan that shapes the hardware aspects (including future trends) of corporate systems. *Information systems organisation* defines reporting responsibilities, organisational structure, mode of financial operation and managerial responsibilities.

Centralised information systems organisation

Many of the arguments that suggest that databases are better than a collection of independent file systems can be used to justify the centralised model. Centralising resources eliminates duplication and achieves economies of scale. Less expenditure on hardware, software and personnel is needed. These advantages are not limited to information systems; human resources management, purchasing, legal and other areas can all be centralised. Certainly, in a centralised environment, it is easier to maintain control over processes, people and systems. However, the downside of this approach is twofold. First, unless business processes are highly streamlined, the information systems division can take too long to respond to the needs of its clients. Most organisations respond to this problem by making sure that the public face of information systems (the help desk) has a very visible presence and a fast response time. Second, there is the risk of costs rising because information systems personnel are too far removed from the business processes. Much depends, of course, on the size of the organisation. In smaller businesses, the information systems division *has* to be centralised because it is so small. Usually in the centralised approach, a single person, the **chief information officer (CIO)**, has responsibility for the entire information systems function. This arrangement is shown in figure 5.1.

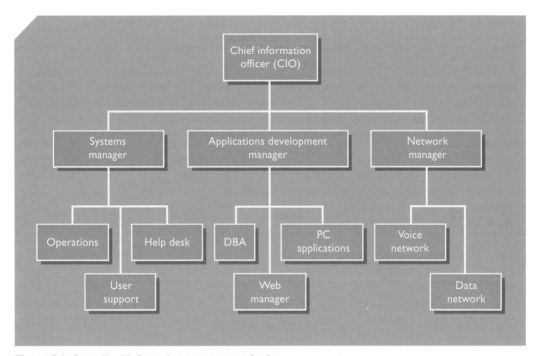

Figure 5.1 Centralised information systems organisation

Distributed information systems organisation

This view is perhaps best regarded as a set of centralised information systems divisions within an umbrella management structure as shown in figure 5.2. Here, the mini-information systems divisions are contained within separate business units. Now there are **divisional information officers (DIOs)** who report to their divisional managers, but they may also report to the corporate CIO (if the CIO role remains, then that person is usually equal in status to a divisional manager).

Devolving responsibility to divisional level allows divisions to select the most appropriate solution to their systems problems based on local knowledge and experience. Because the locus of control is much closer to the client, responses should be quicker. Divisions have their own hardware, software and staff.

Most DIOs are concerned with vertical systems (not companywide systems but systems specialised to the needs of the division). Accordingly, the corporate CIO retains responsibility for the development and management of systems that span business units. The disadvantage is that there may be substantial duplication of resources. Equally, there may be a greater capacity to meet the systems needs of the divisions, which in turn may confer a business advantage that outweighs the cost of duplicated resources. Additionally, the reporting structure tends to produce a matrix-like model.

Organisations that have distributed their information systems division tend to duplicate hardware, software and personnel. For example, one organisation had 15 separate web servers, when only five (plus a backup) were needed. The excessive hardware and management costs were reduced after rationalisation. Additionally, the organisation employed several web developers, four of whom were underworked. Another problem with the distributed approach is the potential loss of tacit knowledge transfer between information systems staff as staff in the core information systems division are reduced.

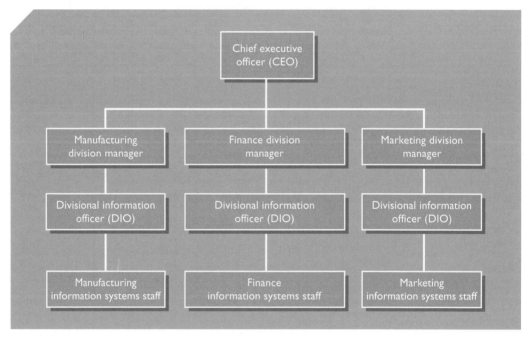

Figure 5.2 The distributed information systems function

Hybrid information systems organisation

Many businesses opt for a mixed structure, in which systems development is devolved to the divisions, but all live systems are managed centrally. This reduces unnecessary duplication of resources but still permits a high degree of autonomy for divisions. As with the distributed approach, managers have to ensure that information systems staff maintain skills and that each division is aware of systems under development by the other divisions.

Funding the information systems function

There are three basic approaches to funding the information systems function. The division may operate as an unallocated cost centre, an allocated cost centre or a profit centre. Each of these approaches is examined in the following sections.

Unallocated cost centre

In the **unallocated cost centre** model, the information systems manager receives a one-line budget to cover expenditure for the whole year. This sum is usually taken off the top of everyone else's budget before allocation. In short, information systems is considered to be an organisational cost. If the information systems division is providing services to several large divisions, there is bound to be conflict among those various departments regarding which information systems services and innovations are required. So budget allocation can be politically difficult if there are many competing requests. The information systems manager has to be tactful and professional to make this work well. Requests from users or clients need to be supported by cost–benefit analysis. This means talking to internal clients at length about needs and plans. From the perspective of other division managers, there is a loss of control and status that follows the flow of funds from their budget to the information systems budget. If accounting controls are not rigorous, information systems costs can escalate.

Allocated cost centre

Operating as an **allocated cost centre** within the company means that costs are allocated for services to internal clients. Although no money will leave the company, there is still the added complexity of internal accounting and budget transfers. However, this has some advantages. First, it may eliminate any cross-subsidy from one division to another. Second, it makes for a more responsive relationship between the information systems division and the internal clients. Third, the accounting information is very useful for planning purposes because it reveals patterns of use and growth that enable the information systems division to meet the future needs of the organisation. This prevents the demand for information systems services exceeding the capacity to meet it. Usually, load thresholds are set: besides the disaster threshold (the point at which the business fails), there is the pain threshold (the point at which the business begins to suffer). Most responsible information systems managers raise an alert when the load comes within 20 per cent (or some other arbitrary value) of the pain threshold. This gives the information systems division some time to respond to the problem and develop avoidance strategies.

[**Key concept:** Anticipate clients' needs. Ideally, the only time a client should know that there is a problem is after it has been fixed.]

Profit centre

In the **profit centre** model of operation, internal and external clients are not distinguished, and the information systems division competes for both kinds. This allows users to choose who will carry out the information systems function on their behalf, with a chance that the work will go outside the company. The information systems division is in direct competition with external companies, so it is motivated to be as efficient as possible, but there is still a risk of the operation being outsourced. Perhaps most significant of all, costs to other divisions are likely to rise. Divisions that operate as profit centres tend not to carry out developmental and experimental work because this has to be done on a cost recovery plus profit basis.

Some information systems job descriptions

All information systems staff need to have good problem-solving and communication skills, and need to be flexible and adaptable and able to work on several things at the same time. Creativity and attention to detail are important. Depending on their level within an organisation or project, information systems staff may also require organisational and managerial skills.

Curiously, some employers seem to put hard technical skills a little lower on their shopping list. A graduate looking to find a first position in the information systems industry should have the following skills:

> a working knowledge of basic business disciplines and processes
> basic computer literacy
> the ability to identify information requirements
> the ability to outline design requirements or specify system requirements or both
> the ability to program in a third- or fourth-generation software product
> experience in using a software development tool.

Business knowledge is at the top of the list because information systems exist to support business. If you understand what the business does, it is much easier to build a system to help the business to do it. If not, you are at a disadvantage. However, if you are lacking in some of the other skills in the list, do not despair — in the authors' experience, more than a third of information systems professionals did not have an information systems background before they entered the profession. There are examples of biology, philosophy, liberal arts, history and literature graduates who have made the transition into information systems and done very well. The demand for information systems professionals exceeds the supply that universities are able to produce. Most employers accept that they will have to train graduates before they become profitable.

> **Reflection question 1:** Is it valid to assume that a background in mathematics and logic is a prerequisite for a career in information systems?

As with much else in the information systems industry, job titles, descriptions and terminology vary greatly from organisation to organisation. In the following sections the most common terms are used.

Chief information officer (CIO)

The position of CIO is synonymous with director of information systems, director of management information systems, manager of information systems services and so on. Essentially, this person is responsible for all information activities and resources, and reports to the most senior levels of management. It is important that the position has sufficient status within the organisation because much effort is devoted to organisational politics. Besides leadership, planning and organisational skills, the CIO requires good people skills, because the job requires negotiation with staff and motivating them to achieve goals. CIOs also spend a lot of time educating management about information systems and management information systems from a strategic perspective. Basic financial skills are also needed, because part of the brief is to secure all the resources required for the information systems division.

In companies that are too small to support a full-time CIO, the role is often given to the head of accounting or finance, because cash flows and information flows often coincide.

In some larger organisations, the CIO role may be augmented by separate DIOs for each business function, as shown in the distributed information systems organisation in figure 5.2.

In the past, cynical information systems people would say that CIO stood for 'career is over'. The thinking behind this was the CIO was as far up the hierarchy as an information systems professional could rise without a business or management qualification. This has been seen in other disciplines and it explains the popularity of MBA courses. More recently, information has come to be regarded as a strategic resource and CIOs are now being promoted to the highest levels in the organisation. Other authors also tend to this view (Kerrigan 2002).

Systems manager/operations manager

The systems manager/operations manager is responsible for the entire day-to-day running of the information systems division from an operational perspective, overseeing technical staff who maintain and upgrade hardware and software. All operational policies and procedures fall within this area. Service-level agreements, maintenance and backup schedules are all carried out here. Monitoring the systems and gathering information for planning and security purposes is also a major responsibility. Budgeting and acquisition may form part of the portfolio. Depending on the organisational structure, the help desk and user-support functions are frequently the systems manager's responsibility.

> **Reflection question 2:** Help desk functions should be centralised for planning and control purposes. But they also should be distributed so that users receive prompt assistance from a familiar and friendly person. What are the relative merits of each approach?

Database administrator

Very few companies have separate data and database administrators, preferring the single viewpoint that a combination of these positions gives. Therefore, the database administrator (DBA) operates from an enterprisewide perspective, establishing data requirements for projects and applications. Additionally, the DBA refers to company policies, establishes all necessary data access and security policies and translates business rules into data integrity constraints (e.g. 'a client may not have more than $30 000 credit' is a business rule that is enforced by the database). Database design, data organisation and maintaining the data dictionary are all within the DBA role. More specifically, the DBA performs database backups and disaster recoveries and ensures that the database delivers the required level of performance to users.

Network administrator/manager

The network administrator/manager is responsible for all corporate network local area networks (LANs) and wide area networks; increasingly, this includes voice networks. The role usually entails planning and staffing for network function. Network administrators are also responsible for the day-to-day running of the networks and operational management. As noted in chapter 4, corporate communications are vital and, accordingly, network administrators are better paid than most other technical managers. This role requires a strong technical emphasis and most network administrators have technical qualifications only.

> **Reflection question 3:** If there is a single corporate LAN that handles voice and data communications, which does it most resemble, a data network or a telephone network? Why?

Solutions architect

When organisations use systems that have enterprisewide significance, reconciling the needs of different stakeholder groups and applications is an essential role. A solutions architect usually has a technical background, with good business knowledge and excellent communication skills. Much of this job is about eliciting information and knowledge requirements throughout the organisation, consolidating and rationalising those needs and then providing infrastructure-based solutions. Solutions architects are especially useful in ERP settings. The job title is relatively new and is something of a superset of software engineering and business analysis.

Project architect/applications development manager

In larger organisations, there is the potential for several departments to develop similar software packages leading to duplication and waste of resources. The project architect/applications development manager monitors and helps coordinate all software development activity. As earlier chapters discuss, it is important to reduce diversity and complexity, and this usually entails strict adherence to hardware and software standards. The project architect is involved in the definition and enforcement of these standards. In centralised information systems organisations, this role is frequently subsumed under the CIO role. However, in distributed information systems organisations, the project architect position is particularly important. Leadership, organisational ability, communication skills and people skills are very important in this role. Typically, project architects have experience as analysts and programmers but this is not always the case.

Many systems have the potential to cost vast sums if they malfunction. It is cost effective in these situations to use rigorous design and specification methods and strict quality control and testing. It is important to design systems with testing in mind. Testing may be carried out by the project team (benevolent testing) or by people from outside the team (adversarial testing). In larger organisations, the project architect is responsible for developing and implementing quality procedures. In smaller organisations, testing is often the duty of systems analysts and programmers.

Project manager

A project manager is usually assigned to a particular project for its duration. The goal is to deliver systems that meet user requirements and corporate standards on schedule and within budget. Because much of the work involves supervising technical work, the project manager often has a technical background. Much of the rest of the work involves human resources management, so managerial skills are also valued. Sometimes, the project manager may provide business expertise in a particular area (domain specialist), in which case the reporting structure expands and the project manager may report to, or liaise with, a technical manager. Although most project managers are appointed for the duration of the project only, some are regarded as permanent management positions.

Web manager/administrator

Web-based technologies are used to facilitate systems integration, provide uniform interfaces for corporate information and so on. A company's intranet resources are often overseen by a web manager/administrator. This person has responsibility for the development, delivery and integration of all web resources, and works with the DBA and network administrator to ensure that systems are safe and secure. The web manager usually has a background in web development.

Systems analyst/business analyst

Although the systems analyst/business analyst role is sometimes the graduate-entry position into the information systems industry, most information systems graduates tend to enter the profession as programmer–analysts (developer–analysts) and progress to the business analyst role. The systems analyst is involved with every aspect of the system development lifecycle with the exception of programming. The definition of requirements and design and specification of the system are where most of the effort is expended. The whole system lifecycle revolves around the analyst, who acts as a liaison point between technical staff and business clients, translating business requirements into system requirements. Business skills are usually crucial to this role.

The analyst requires excellent communication and presentation skills, organisational ability and an understanding of the programming process.

Although the analyst is distanced from the technology, increasingly companies look for analysts who have experience in using computer-aided software engineering (CASE) software. There is a tendency to call any analyst with CASE experience a software engineer, but software engineers are much closer to the actual process and often perform detailed design work and develop and test codes. Software engineers generally do not have business expertise. In the authors' experience, analysts are involved in the system requirements definition, whereas software engineers are not. Most companies will train their analysts in the use of CASE tools, but do not necessarily train software engineers in business.

Programmer

As the job title implies, a **programmer** produces software. However, the definition of software is now far broader than it used to be and most businesses include web development (with the exception of specialist graphic design), customisation of packaged software, fourth-generation products and high-level code as part of the programmer's portfolio. The role is often combined as programmer/analyst.

Programmers do not need to have a business education, although it may restrict their progress at a later date if they lack one.

Most employers expect an applicant for a programming position to have two-to-four years of tertiary education and the ability to program in at least one language or product. Industry-based qualifications and certificated courses are very well regarded by employers.

Within the programmer role there is the position of specialist or **virtuoso programmer**. This person specialises in certain problematic areas of coding. For example, a virtuoso programmer might rewrite parts of systems software to improve performance of an application, or write code which integrates one application with another. Virtuoso programmers produce very efficient code and their background is steeped in technology.

Chief technology officer

Many organisations do not have a **chief technology officer (CTO)**, so the role is taken on by the CIO. Larger organisations often find it useful to have a person in this position. The CTO is responsible for keeping abreast of technology and the market, briefing other staff on his or her findings and outlining plans under which the business could take cost-effective advantage of the new technology within its existing information systems framework.

Some businesses prefer to distribute the role among industry specialists, such as network administrator and database administrator. These people meet at intervals to brief one another on their own area and combine their views. The existing information systems plan can then be reviewed in the light of their findings. In many ways, this has advantages over having a single CTO because individual excesses tend to be moderated by the group. It also makes people more aware of what their colleagues actually do, and consequently helps divisional activities to be more concerted.

Training officer

The training needs of information systems professionals are sufficiently different from those in other business areas to warrant special treatment. In fairness, only large organisations actually have a special person in this role. Most training needs are determined by line managers and staff themselves.

Organising training in the use of a new system for end-users usually becomes the responsibility of the project manager. The importance of the training should not be underestimated. Users can make or break a system. If they are trained to use it effectively, they will accept the system and be more productive. If they are not trained or are badly trained, then they will make mistakes and criticise the system. You should view training as relationship marketing and encourage others to do the same.

[**Key concept:** Appearances are not everything, but if you do not look professional, you will not get the job.]

> **Reflection question 4:** From a personnel management perspective, are older staff unsuited to modern systems development? Justify your answer.

infobyte

Backup should not be a solo effort

If you have ever experienced the trauma caused by a hard drive crashing or a virus wiping out data, you will know the importance of backing up. The chances are you will also know how tedious the process of keeping backups can be. Carbonite.com (the name seems to owe something to Star Wars) has simplified the entire matter. For a small monthly fee, customers can install and use a simple piece of software that automatically backs up unlimited amounts of data without degrading Internet performance. Confidentiality is guaranteed because the data are encrypted before they leave the customer's PC. If a computer is damaged, lost or broken, all a customer needs to do is visit Carbonite's website to retrieve all the data.

Outsourcing

Most companies choose to maintain their own information systems infrastructure, enabling them to exercise control over the whole information systems domain. But there are other options. Outsourcing means paying a third party outside the organisation to perform specific functions such as data processing, application development, communications, or electronic data processing audit. In so doing, organisations try to reduce the size of the information systems infrastructure and the number of staff, and so cut costs. The trick is to achieve these things without compromising the organisation's short-, medium- and long-term ability to compete.

However, outsourcing can be high risk. Having divested itself of its information systems equipment and staff, the organisation no longer has the infrastructure to perform the outsourced functions itself if a problem arises with the service provider.

Advantages of outsourcing

Considerable advantages can be gained from outsourcing, so long as the conditions are right to do so.

> It has the potential to reduce costs. The word 'potential' is used advisedly, because even when an application is outsourced it is important to maintain strategic management in-house. Another factor that is often overlooked is the cost of overseeing the outsourced contract — making sure that the provider delivers the levels of service in the contract and that all submitted accounts are correct. If employees are to be made redundant, the costs of payouts need to be considered.

> It allows consolidation of the information systems division. In many organisations, the information systems or information technology (IT) division is in a support role, yet represents a major cost centre. Outsourcing allows the information systems division to be reduced to a core of strategically important staff, thus saving salary costs.

> It reduces fluctuations in staffing levels. As new projects are undertaken, it is necessary to take on new staff to complete them. Besides the expense of salary and on-costs, employment legislation can make it difficult to shed staff. Additionally, increase in demand may be seasonal or related to peak workloads, forcing companies to employ more staff than they really need to. Outsourcing may be a solution.

> It reduces dependency on key personnel. In areas in which it is hard to attract and retain staff, for example, SAP development, the outsource provider will have several staff who are capable of performing key roles. Without outsourcing, a business might depend on a single person's expertise, which makes it very vulnerable to market forces.

> It allows management to focus on business rather than on technical issues. The infrastructure is someone else's problem.

> It gives improved reliability and system availability (the service provider can justify a higher level of investment in hardware because it enjoys the benefits of economies of scale).

> [**Key concept:** If it is not your problem, do not take ownership of it (unless you really have to).]

Disadvantages of outsourcing

Although undoubted benefits can be gained from outsourcing, the activity is not without risk. Outsourcing has the following downsides.

> It removes knowledge of business processes from the organisation, with an associated loss of control. This is why it is not advisable to outsource anything that is of strategic importance, the business may lose the ability to perform the outsourced functions for itself.

> It leads to a loss of corporate culture and experience if existing staff are made redundant. When problems arise, it may not be possible to use similar situations that occurred in the past to help formulate useful strategies.

> Using information strategically can be made difficult. If the information systems division is outsourced in its entirety, a business may not have sufficient control to take action. The selection of technology platform lies with the outsource provider and many outsourcing

agreements are geared towards maintaining the status quo. It may have the information it needs but not the control to use it effectively.

> It ties the company to the service provider, often denying any competition. This is especially true of specialist or niche outsource providers. If there is little competition, prices are likely to be higher than they need be.
> It may increase costs. If a business fails to carry out thorough cost–benefit analysis, it may overestimate the cash savings. The need to oversee a contract and retain strategic management are both factors that are commonly overlooked.
> It prevents the consideration of enterprisewide information systems and may restrict strategic planning because control has been surrendered to a third party.

What to consider when outsourcing

ABC — assume nothing, believe nothing, check everything — is particularly useful advice in the outsourcing context. There are many things to consider, and the following is a selection of the most important.

> What is the track record of the provider? Is it well established and dependable? Most providers are large companies with a substantial asset base. Businesses need to feel confident that their choice of provider is not a risky one.
> Is the application that is being outsourced of high strategic value? If the answer is yes, then outsourcing may not be a good idea because you will lose control over your competitive edge.
> What is the nature of the relationship of the organisation to the provider: customer? client? partner? Power differentials are important here. This also relates to the type of provider. Those operating in the 'me too' category, providing general services, are easily replaced, but specialist providers operating in niche markets have high profit margins and are juicy targets for takeovers. Few if any can be said to be partners. After all, they are providing services for your competitors as well as for you.
> How flexible is the contract? What happens if things go wrong? Is there a get-out clause and provision for damages?
> How is the service to be monitored?
> What is the pricing structure? Is it possible to renegotiate charges at intervals? Hardware becomes faster, smaller and cheaper, so your provider's costs will fall and its profits will rise. This should not be at your expense.
> What is your investment position? If you have just invested heavily in hardware and software, the outsource provider is unlikely to save you enough to recover your costs. After all, the bulk of the depreciation occurs in the first month and the provider will not buy your second-hand equipment at brand-new retail prices. On the other hand, if you are approaching the end of an investment cycle, then the equipment and software are verging on the obsolete. It may be a good time to outsource.
> Does the application vary substantially in load and throughput? It may be a good thing to outsource because it is costly to employ sufficient staff to meet peak demands.
> Is this an area in which it is difficult to attract and retain staff? Again, this is a suitable candidate for outsourcing.
> What are the privacy, security and intellectual copyright positions? Can the provider guarantee that your data will remain confidential? If you have developed software for a particular

application, does the provider have the right to use and develop it? If that software gives you an advantage in the market, can you prevent the provider using it for other clients?

> Are you diversifying into a new area and wish to reduce your capital commitment? Outsourcing may provide a cost-effective option to try out an idea for a new line of business before fully committing to it.

IS in action

A healthy option

Singapore Health Services Pte Ltd (SingHealth) treats more than three million patients a year and has revenues of about $1.23 billion. The potential for both problems and costs savings are considerable. Because it is so large, it can offer a much wider range of services than small private hospitals and the economies of scale mean that it has much greater purchasing power. Most of the hospitals and clinics in the group were using SAP (a leading ERP software package) to manage human resources, financials, supply chains and patients.

The main problem was that each hospital and clinic in the group operated as an independent entity, with its own SAP systems. This lack of integration meant that SingHealth could not achieve the potential for synergy in its large and diverse business operations. Cooperation among different parts of the business was at the best of times consuming and complicated. Without a centralised patient database, patients would need to be registered at each hospital where they received treatment. The lack of pertinent information and the potential for wrongly identifying patients were also causes for concern. Delays in billing processes were affecting cash flow.

From an information systems/IT management perspective, things were also difficult. Because each installation was independent, there was a high degree of duplication of data centres and hardware but the killer was the lack of organisational standards. This meant that when the management teams made strategic decisions regarding IT implementations, each installation had be handled individually. As a consequence, IT across the organisation was very expensive to run and very difficult to scale.

SingHealth turned to IBM to deliver a single, integrated solution for its business. IBM centralised the patient database and brought the systems together using high-performance, fault-tolerant hardware with inline backups. This solution is easily scalable and provides excellent disaster-recovery potential. Realising that installation management was not part of its core business, SingHealth outsourced management to IBM, which has had the effect of reducing costs.

SingHealth now spends far less on IT administration and is able to make changes more quickly. Its systems are 'future proof' in that they are scalable and robust. Centralising inventory management allows the entire group to act as a single purchasing authority through demand aggregation, with the economies of scale pushing down costs. Billing is much quicker, which has improved cash flow. Patient care has been improved, referrals are simple and all relevant information is available when needed. SingHealth is now more flexible and better able to compete.

Source: Information from IBM website, www.ibm.com.

[**Key concept:** If you do not know what you are doing, it is not a good idea to do a lot of it.]

> **Reflection question 5:** You are negotiating an outsourcing contract. Your costs per transaction are $1.20. The outsource provider has offered a price of $0.80 per transaction and has guaranteed to hold the price for the next seven years. Assuming that everything else in the contract is acceptable, would you accept the offer? Explain your answer.

Outsourcing: the current picture

Outsourcing was a major trend in the 1980s and 1990s and is still popular. It needs to be considered in a climate of corporate downsizing and the corporatisation of government. Although many case studies have been published that present outsourcing in a positive light, there are some disaster stories. However, very few companies wish to publicise failure. Of those companies that consider outsourcing, approximately 60 per cent choose not to proceed. Also, many companies that have outsourced in the past are now rebuilding their infrastructure. A loss of control can affect a company's ability to compete. Outsource providers tend to be large, well-established companies such as IBM, with a long history and a secure asset base.

Not all outsourcing is necessarily high risk, nor need it involve a bona fide provider. In areas that are well defined, a business might look to establish a strategic complementary alliance with a third party. For example, consider an organisation that has retained its mainframe systems but has provided a PC-based network to improve the performance of its applications. The distributed system has removed much of the load from the mainframe, which is now under-used and is no longer a cost-effective option. An agreement with another company that is in a similar position could lead to both companies sharing a mainframe installation. Cost savings are substantial, with virtually zero impact on control, staffing and planning. Disaster recovery and contingency arrangements can also be handled in this way. Two companies might agree to provide mainframe data processing for each other in the event of a systems failure. Companies frequently outsource long-haul communications and Internet service provision.

A strategy that yields cost savings similar to those of outsourcing is competitive tendering. If the information systems division runs as a profit centre, then it tenders for work in the same way as external companies, but this can lead to overcharging for some services to subsidise a tender to secure the contract for new work. The amount of developmental work carried out also tends to be less (see the preceding discussion on profit-centre information systems).

Islands of information and proprietary systems

Many large organisations still have complicated heterogeneous hardware platforms and applications. A typical portfolio might include:

> old, high-volume, mainframe-based transaction-processing systems using **proprietary systems** software and nonrelational proprietary databases. The centralised application usually has a large network of nonintelligent terminals (IBM's IMS is a good example)

> moderately old divisional or departmental management information systems-operational applications running on proprietary midrange computers using relational but proprietary databases

> online applications that make use of divisional or departmental client–server LANs

> relatively new divisional or departmental operational applications running on open (non-proprietary) client–server platforms; often these are Unix servers hosting open relational database products such as Oracle.

This scenario leads to the development of 'islands' of information, that is, corporate information that is not universally accessible throughout the organisation. Although individual processes may be automated, the business as a whole is not, so islands of automation also develop. Applications cannot share data easily and users cannot access all relevant corporate data from their desktops. This limits the ability of the organisation to compete effectively. Because the architecture is fragmented, information systems staff cannot change the information systems infrastructure to reflect changes in business requirements in a reasonable time. Moving to a position where changes can be made in a reasonable time and systems can be integrated normally involves the use of open systems.

Open systems

Chapter 4 discusses the importance of standards in networking to simplify communication among computers. Discussions in earlier chapters also highlight the importance of standardising hardware platforms. Systems are said to be **open systems** if:

> they can be connected to other standard components easily

> they can exchange data easily

> they are hardware platform independent

> they use internationally recognised standards rather than proprietary ones.

Open systems reduce cost and risk because future systems are guaranteed to be compatible with present ones. Accordingly, changes to systems will be evolutionary rather than revolutionary. Oracle, a relational database company, specialised in converting corporate data into standard formats and ensured that its database software was available for every industry-standard platform. This allowed business to break free from proprietary traps and achieve openness at the data and application levels.

However, although a company may be committed to an open systems path, there may be problems handling **legacy systems**. These often impair a company's ability to make changes to application functionality without changing the existing information systems infrastructure. Changing the infrastructure is usually not possible without changing the way in which business applications operate. Legacy systems are usually (but not always) mainframe based, with huge development efforts invested in them. There are three basic ways of handling legacy systems in the corporate information systems plan: forward engineering, reverse engineering and wrapper engineering.

> **Forward engineering** is how systems are usually developed, but the presence of legacy systems can hinder the introduction of new ones. However, if it has been decided that a new system is justified, then processes can be re-engineered and the legacy system replaced by the new one. In many cases, simply discarding the legacy system is not a cost-effective option.

> When a company depends on the legacy system and there is insufficient system documentation or a lack of knowledge about the underlying business processes, then **reverse engineering** may be the only option. Here, the behaviour of the system is used to derive a new set of system requirements, which, in turn, are used to design an optimised system. Again, the legacy system is discarded, which may prove costly.

> Usually, financial constraints and the risk of introducing a massive amount of change in one go prevent companies adopting forward- or reverse-engineering solutions for legacy

systems. A more conservative approach is to leave the old systems as they are but 'wrap' them in newer, more friendly systems, thus providing a more convenient interface to users and other systems. This is termed **wrapper engineering**. This makes it easier to integrate the legacy system into the corporate system. Usually, there will be a migration plan for the legacy system's final replacement. Many ERP systems operate in this manner, making older systems more flexible and useful.

infobyte

My tunes make fortunes

What sort of music do you like? You cannot necessarily identify a particular band that appeals; some of their recorded tracks may not float your boat. Even categorising your likes by genre may be too general to be useful. This problem was tackled by a group of musicians and technologists a few years ago, and their solution was to launch the musical genome project: the most comprehensive analysis of music ever undertaken. As Tim Westergren comments, 'We set out to capture the essence of music at the most fundamental level. We ended up assembling literally hundreds of musical attributes or "genes" into a very large Music Genome. Taken together these genes capture the unique and magical musical identity of a song — everything from melody, harmony and rhythm, to instrumentation, orchestration, arrangement, lyrics, and of course the rich world of singing and vocal harmony' (Westergren 2000). This genome project now forms the basis for pandora.com: an Internet music service that allows you to create your own 'radio stations' based on your musical preferences. Input your favourite song and the system will make suggestions from more than 300 000 available tracks. Your feedback is used to refine the playlist. The free version includes advertising but advertisement-free services are available on a subscription basis for US$36 per year.

Source: Information from Pandora website, www.pandora.com.

Systems integration

It is not only legacy systems that cause problems for systems managers. Often, modern systems have been selected for their particular ability to handle a specialised application. Differences in data formats and networking standards may prevent these systems from being integrated into the corporate information systems resource. This has an effect on productivity and effectiveness. There are three aspects of systems integration:

> *External integration* entails interconnectivity and interworking between business partners' systems. This was touched on in earlier chapters when discussing using information systems to form umbilical cords between companies. Web browsers, computer networks and electronic data interchange (EDI) play a large part in this process.

> *Internal integration* refers to the integration of the company's web-based systems with the company's core application systems. It also implies that the core applications themselves are closely integrated. There is an underlying assumption that the applications are built with standard **application program interfaces**. This allows new functions to be added quickly and with minimum risk on a modular basis. Some authors refer to this as **componentisation**.

> *Infrastructure integration* refers to the integration of information systems infrastructure and applications. It also includes the integration of infrastructure components. It is important that the applications are independent of, and insulated from, the underlying infrastructure because this allows either to be changed without the need for expensive and disruptive changes to the other. This differs from internal integration in that every internal system, including networking and communications (not merely the applications and web-based applications), is integrated along well-defined lines. Some authors refer to this as service-oriented architecture.

Two schools of thought predominate when it comes to managing systems integration. The first is to have an overall migration plan in which the current systems are moving towards a more uniform solution, which uses fewer standards. The second ignores the technical problems of hardware and software integration and seeks to achieve integration at the application level by using high-level software that enables all information resources to be accessed in the same way regardless of hardware platform or data format. This is termed **enterprise application integration**. Organisations with a slowly evolving information systems portfolio tend to opt for the former, whereas organisations with a diverse and rapidly changing portfolio tend to opt for the latter.

Enterprisewide client–server architecture

It is not simply a matter of connecting existing applications. The different networking standards and data formats actively prevent this. A more reasonable approach is to allow users to access a wide variety of applications directly from their desktop machines, using a Windows-based graphical user interface. This includes the mainframe legacy systems. This relies on open client–server architectures on an enterprise-wide scale. In short, the legacy systems may be left as they are, but extra functionality in one of the nonserver tiers in the client–server architecture needs to be added. Accordingly, a new application might take data from several legacy systems, remove redundancy, pool the data, and present it again for information or analysis in a new, more meaningful format. This approach improves the performance of older applications by removing unnecessary work from legacy mainframes and presents opportunities for downsizing.

Faced with a choice between rewriting or redeveloping existing applications (forward and reverse engineering) or replacing or augmenting the systems using a companywide ERP package such as SAP, many organisations have opted for the latter.

Implementing a modern ERP system, which includes applications and technical infrastructure, is an expensive option, but the advantages that it confers may justify the investment. Specifically, ERP provides:
> applications software that yields functionality in line with industry best practice
> complete horizontal and vertical integration throughout the enterprise
> applications that are tailored for their environments, which includes languages, currencies and legal frameworks
> simplified applications development because of componentisation.

Besides overcoming the islands of information and automation identified, ERP systems are intended to support **business engineering**. This is more than just the automation and improvement of existing processes: here, the emphasis is on organisational flexibility. This means that a business is better positioned to respond to a changing environment quickly. With business engineering, processes are considered in a rich information environment and their relationships with other processes are important. Businesses are still trying to reduce product-cycle times, speed cash flow and improve customer service, but ERP (when properly deployed) should grow individual and team creativity. In terms of chapter 1, this is the transition from the industrial age into the information and knowledge age.

Extended ERP systems

SAP is the best-known vendor of ERP solutions. Typically, the modules provided on the mySAP.com e-business platform include:
> mySAP Workplace
> mySAP Supply Chain Management
> mySAP Customer Relationship Management
> mySAP E-Procurement
> mySAP Product Lifecycle Management
> mySAP Business Intelligence
> mySAP Financials
> mySAP Human Resources
> mySAP Marketplace
> mySAP Industry Solutions.

All these are predominantly internally focused except for E-Procurement, Supply Chain Management, Customer Relationship Management and some aspects of Business Intelligence. Supply Chain Management requires the interconnection of all partners: business-to-business (B2B) links from suppliers are referred to as 'upstream links', and business-to-customer (B2C) links are referred to as 'downstream links'. Extended Supply Chain Management involves both upstream and downstream links. An ERP system is said to be an **extended ERP (EERP)** system if it incorporates e-commerce functionality.

Upstream links are used for **supply chain management** (the practice of linking one's suppliers into core business processes). Large organisations have been practising supply chain management for some years because they can justify the huge investment required for internal ERP systems. About 65 per cent of SAP's customers are large companies with revenues in excess of $250 million. ERP deployment typically costs several million dollars and extends over several years. The question arises what can be done to ensure that small-to-medium entities (SMEs) can realise the potential benefits of ERP.

As networking and e-commerce technologies (such as EDI) have improved in their capabilities, so the supply chain management systems that they support have increased in their levels of sophistication. From handling the needs of a single factory, so the systems are now complicated systems of interconnected online hubs, as shown in figure 5.3.

[**Key concept:** There is a trade-off between integration and flexibility: the better integrated a system is, the more difficult it is to make changes to it.]

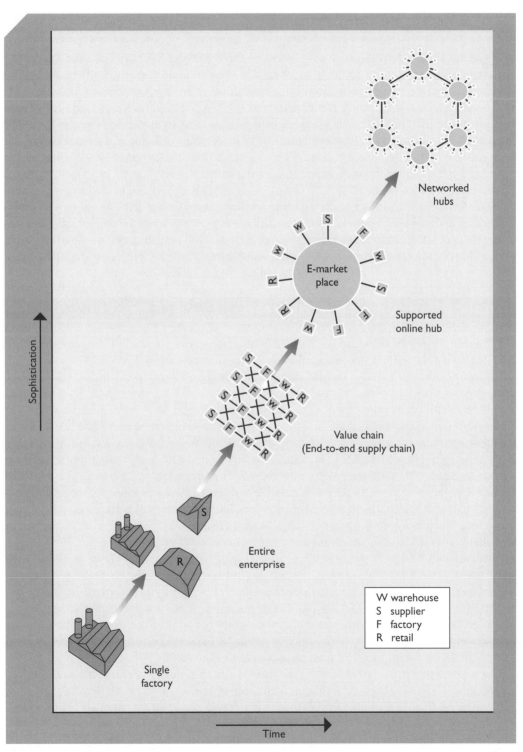

Figure 5.3 The evolution of supply chain management systems

ERP and small-to-medium entities (SMEs)

SMEs cannot afford the huge investment required to build ERP systems, and the cost of using EDI networks is prohibitive for smaller organisations. Usually, SME customers are not connected to the supply chain electronically, and if they are, they may have proprietary networks and systems that actively prevent interconnection. The inclusion of web-based e-commerce components in ERP packages (shopping carts, catalogues and so on) reduces barrier costs and improves accessibility for B2B and B2C links. However, when ordering a computer online, for example, the web-ordering system needs to interface with the distribution systems, manufacturing systems and component supplier systems, so that delivery can be guaranteed within a certain period. Given the need for just-in-time delivery, this integration is vital to the business process. Most ERP systems usually lack the intelligence to search through masses of transaction data and make suggestions. Nor, as a rule, are they able to sense the environment and use external data in decision-making processes. For supply chain planning, business partners need to be aware of each other's patterns of demand and the implications for their own manufacturing and supply systems. Good ERP systems should provide these features.

Application service providers

The use of web-based technology in ERP systems provides a level of convenience when accessing the system that fits well with SMEs. The cost of ERP systems is a deterrent, so a form of outsourcing has emerged that enables SMEs to have access to ERP technology and permits a cheap 'implementation'. An **application service provider (ASP)** is a person or a company that installs (and possibly customises) prepackaged software applications (such as ERP) on its own computer systems and then allows its customers to access those applications. Payment schemes are usually similar to rental agreements, because pay-for-use approaches might reduce cash flow to the ASP. The initial costs associated with implementation and ongoing costs associated with management are now the ASP's responsibility. Of course, the ASP will rent the application to as many clients as possible to increase income. Figure 5.4 shows a typical ASP scenario, in which all that the SME needs is Internet or virtual private network access using Java-compliant web browsers running on thin clients. (Recall from earlier chapters that thin clients simplify management and reduce costs under most conditions.)

As mentioned, a major business trend is to deal directly where possible. The independent software vendor could fill the role of the ASP itself. It is difficult to generalise about the ASP market, but it would seem that ASPs come in three main types. Each poses risks for businesses.

The first is the specialist ASP. Its profit margins are high because the expertise required is of a high order. Specialist ASPs are unlikely to suffer bankruptcy but they are often subject to takeover bids. In this event, the distinctive nature of the service ensures that it has a strong identity in the new structure. The strategic advantage of the service is high.

The second group has a broader focus, usually on an industry sector. This means more competition, so profit margins are smaller than those of specialist ASPs. These ASPs are more likely to be involved in friendly mergers than in direct takeovers, but because they are providing services that are already provided in a competitive market, they can lose their identity in the new business. This in turn can pose problems for their clients because the services provided might deteriorate or be reorganised.

The last type of ASP is the generic provider. These ASPs provide nothing special, and competition is intense and profit margins low. Takeovers and mergers are common, and bankruptcy in the face of fierce competition is nothing unusual. The effect on a business is disruptive but not catastrophic. Here, the strategic advantage of the service is low.

The simple rules in choosing an ASP are pretty much the same as they are for any other outsource provider. You are looking for an organisation that is big enough to maintain its identity in the face of competition and can deliver the required services at an affordable price. Usually, the larger the organisation, the greater the pool of skills it has to draw on. What is not immediately apparent from figure 5.4 is the effect that supply chain management has had on geography. Locality is much less of an issue because supply chain management can be Internet enabled. This in turn allows smaller companies to take part in the processes, increasing competition and reducing prices.

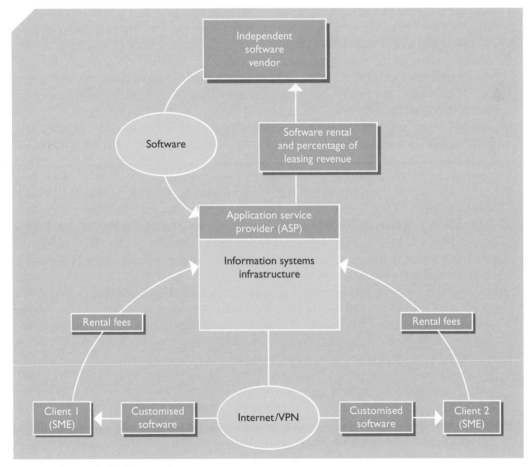

Figure 5.4 A typical ASP scenario

Just how much money can an SME save by using ERP through an ASP? Forty per cent is a typical figure. Products such as PeopleSoft carry an annual licence fee of about $180 000, which does not include the cost of support, service and hardware and software infrastructure. It is true that the rental costs will accrue rapidly, but if the SME is not in a position to deploy its own ERP system owing to cost constraints, this is the only way in which it can obtain the competitive advantages that ERP gives. Careful cost–benefit analysis is vital in reaching a decision.

> **Reflection question 6:** Why would it make good business sense for an ERP software company to let companies have its software for free?

IS in action

Seven questions to ask before adopting CRM software

1. Do you have customers or clients? A call centre-type operation has people sitting at their desks all day dealing with highly structured processes and highly structured data, so information gathering is easy. By contrast, a business analyst is away from his or her desk for extended periods dealing with unstructured processes and unstructured data, so gathering the information that you need to make customer relationship management (CRM) useful is messy and unproductive.

2. Are you managing or creating customers? CRM is very useful for managing customers you already have (which is fine for large companies) but of limited use in creating new ones. This means that you should question the viability of CRM for small business and recent startup companies.

3. Are your data transactional or transformational? Most CRM systems are databases with specialised forms added. Basic transaction-type data are well structured and easily managed. However, a lot of information that is really useful is highly unstructured, for example, background client and industry information needed to negotiate a new contract for the supply of services to a client. The simpler the needs, the more likely it is that CRM will be useful.

4. How do you motivate staff? CRM means making users update the system frequently. Put simply it adds to their workload. If rewards and motivations are insufficient then updates will not happen. Some companies actively withhold salary until the updates have been completed. Human factors are very important.

5. Are you certain about your information needs? When you buy anything of significance, the chances are that you will use the Internet to find out about it. Being ignorant leaves you open to exploitation by sales staff. This applies to the supplier as well as the consumer. Can the system provide you with the business intelligence you need to be effective?

6. Is it really 'easy' to use? Most CRM systems have a steep learning curve you have to climb if you want to do useful things. Easy is a relative term. People who work in information systems and IT every day may have no problem with the CRM system but mere mortals may struggle, with consequent loss of morale and efficiency.

7. Do you have a real need for CRM? Salespeople can be persuasive and CRM is surrounded by media hype. The only case that supports the use of CRM is a business case. If cost–benefit analysis says do not do it, then do not do it.

The global CRM market exceeds $13 billion and there will be a lot of pressure from sales departments to buy into technical solutions. The simple rule of thumb is that the cost of implementation should be less than the perceived benefits. The difficulty is that the costs are easy to ascertain, whereas the benefits are uncertain.

Problems with introducing ERP or other changes

Introducing any new system has associated risks. People generally are resistant to change, and too much change in one go can destroy a business. Chapter 1 states that information systems is a people business and that it is important to make sure that integrated solutions are achievable from a personnel point of view. The following guidelines are useful in this context:

> Involve staff in the planning process and project management. They are stakeholders in the enterprise, so they should be stakeholders in the new system.

> Provide incentives for change, productivity-based payments or a more manageable workload.

> Introduce change gradually. When introducing groupware, it may be best to start with a small group of technically able people who will benefit most quickly from the new system. From that point, good training programs will allow the system to 'snowball'. However, this is not an option for all systems.

> Job descriptions change. Moving to a distributed database environment with web-based interfaces has the potential to render employee skills surplus to needs. For example, consider COBOL programmers who were not needed after the transition to relational databases. Fear is natural, but if opportunities for training and career change are offered, most people can make the transition fairly comfortably.

> Gather information on the performance of the new systems from the users, and involve them in the shakedown trials.

> Take the opportunity to introduce total quality management, quality circles or other forms of participative management.

When attempting to integrate business systems with ERP or by other means, it is important to realise that there may be some mutually antagonistic departments or divisions. It is vital to find the best all-round compromise. As with any system, there is a need to focus on four views:

> the business view (why is the system needed?)

> the functional view (what will the system do?)

> the technology view (how will the system be constructed?)

> the implementation view (how will the system be deployed, managed and updated?).

Most systems have a degree of complexity but enterprisewide systems need to cope with conflicting needs, complexity, diversity and uncertainty within the confines of a single architecture. To make progress, operate on a divide-and-conquer principle (this is common to many design and management exercises). Reducing the overall problem to a set of manageable chunks allows progress to be made in several areas concurrently. In practice, these 'chunks' are referred to as 'views' or 'domains' — they are really stakeholder perceptions of the underlying system. In this context, a stakeholder could have a business or technology perspective or a combination of the two. A solutions architect normally carries out these functions, matching the required functionality to available ERP components and subsystems.

[**Key concept:** There is a limit to how much change an organisation can take at any one time — maximise the effectiveness but minimise the impact.]

Six principles for successful CRM implementation

1. *Define a vision for CRM:* this should conform with the company's strategic plan. The system itself is largely defined by business rules, but ultimately it will be customers who make it a success so involve them at an early stage.

2. *Find champions and advocates:* all important projects need to be driven at the highest levels of management, and technology is a major driver of CRM. However, it is middle management who must carry the message to staff, and that message must be clear.

3. *Seek employee endorsement for the vision:* personalise the benefits and avoid presenting information in an abstract way. Instead of talking about a 'typical customer', talk about George, the production manager of company X.

4. *Set realistic milestones:* the key to most successful projects is people management. If goals are too large, complex and far off, staff tend to lose motivation. A good project plan will ensure that staff experience success regularly.

5. *Manage staff with a degree of sensitivity:* change causes problems. If staff are properly informed — for example, being told: 'Things will be difficult for the next two months while the new systems are bedded in' — their expectations and coping strategies will be realistic. Compare this with being told: 'Everything will be wonderful from day 1.'

6. *Ensure that improvement continues:* once the system is in place, every aspect of it — technology, training and so on — must be re-examined from customer, company and employee perspectives with a view to maximising effectiveness and system satisfaction.

Summary

People are as much a part of the system as hardware, software and communications, and in many ways people are the most important part. Understanding the various jobs and roles in the information systems industry is essential if you are to appreciate how the entire enterprise operates. Integrating the various islands of information and automation into a cohesive enterprisewide system pays dividends because it extends the range of control over all business processes including B2B and B2C links. The key points in this chapter are:

> Jobs in the information systems industry are many and varied and subject to continual evolution. Most require good communication skills and business knowledge. Even 'hard' IT firms place business analyst skills high on their shopping list.

> Systems integration is important in reducing costs and maximising the return on investment in older systems. It also improves the ability of an organisation to compete.

> Outsourcing is often a key part of the information systems plan.

> Integration may be vertical (specialised to a business function) or horizontal (general enterprise functions).

> Systems integration should be accompanied by business engineering to ensure the effectiveness of the processes. The integration may be achieved by redeveloping systems (forward and reverse engineering) or incorporating them into a modular ERP system.

> Most ERP systems are expensive but give good tactical and strategic advantages, such as freedom from proprietary systems, application and data independence, easier infrastructure planning and change. Usually, ERP systems are viable only for large organisations.

> The development of ASPs has allowed SMEs to have access to ERP and other software.

> When introducing systems integration, ERP or any system, it is vital that the process of change is handled well. This involves stakeholder analysis and an inclusive management style. People make or break systems.

Questions

1. Why do most organisations decide against a decentralised information systems and IT management structure?

2. Why is it important for a large company to have strict hardware and software standards (IT governance) in place?

3. What problems would an organisation face if it had to change its ERP software vendor? Is there anything that could be done as a preventative measure to mitigate the impact of change?

4. To shorten timelines for important large-scale projects, businesses often outsource the software development. What problems could stem from this stratagem? What are the potential rewards? Why might a company choose not to develop its own staff?

5. Which do you think is more important for a systems analyst: a business background or competency in software development? Give supporting reasons for your answer.

6. What factors make wrapper engineering a useful technique?

7. Although operating as an allocated cost centre is the preferred option for many information systems divisions, difficulty arises in allocating costs to departments. Identify some costs that are difficult to allocate, and suggest a workable solution.

8. With any large-scale project such as ERP implementation, staff turnover is a major problem. Suggest strategies to (a) avoid the problem and (b) minimise the effects of staff turnover on your large-scale project.

9. Smaller companies needing ERP software often use an ASP to save time and money. What are the relative merits of this approach? Is it a valid option for larger companies?

10. Is business engineering the same as business process re-engineering? Explain.

11. Are CRM systems necessarily good for customers? Explain your answer.

12. Many businesses see ERP systems as being necessary but no longer of strategic advantage. The view they take is that there is a disadvantage in not having ERP. Do you think this is a return to more traditional modes of business competition, or is the technology still a prime influence on business strategy? (*Hint:* Porter's five forces model may be useful to you.)

Exercises

1. You have been placed in charge of the implementation of a large ERP project. The information systems and IT group is competent but morale is very low and one or two people have an attitude problem. How would you set about making sure that the project is delivered on time without major problems?

2. One of the major factors in successful ERP implementations is making sure that staff-members receive the training that they need to be effective. How would you go about devising a training program for a large organisation? Bear in mind that people whose skills are in demand tend to have a higher turnover rate than less valuable staff do. Is there anything that you could do to mitigate the 'brain drain' problem?

3. CRM systems allow you look at your existing customer base in more interesting ways than usual. How would you see a CRM system being used by a university management team to provide services to students in a cost-effective and efficient way? What sort of information would be needed by the system?

4. Modern management methods attempt to empower rather than control staff. Implicit in this approach is that staff members know exactly what is required of them and what they are allowed to do. Some companies actually produce a bill of rights for employees. Identify seven rights and their associated responsibilities for employees. Remember that the goal is to make the business more effective. If you are working in a small group, discuss the proposed rights and identify the seven most useful proposals.

CASE STUDY: Toy Time

Toy Time has been a rag doll-to-riches story of corporate Australia. From its first soft toy line (Smiley Sally) in 1976, it has now grown to have an annual turnover in excess of $37 million, employ nearly 400 staff and have 35 main product lines. It emerged from the high interest rates of the 1990s leaner and more efficient than its competitors and able to compete with businesses in countries where labour is cheap and plentiful. Toy Time has invested heavily in flexible manufacturing systems and ERP software. Toy Time has enjoyed four years of competitive agility and growth.

The changes have not been painless. Besides the considerable financial costs of buying into the technology, Toy Time has shed staff and has had to re-engineer many of its business processes to conform to the requirements of the software package. After three years of effort, the systems are stable and are really beginning to deliver the returns that were promised. The maintenance contract with the software vendor (WYTE) has another 12 months to run, and the vendor issues four service packs a year to tackle errors in code and add minor upgrades to functionality. Toy Time was lucky enough to get in on the ground floor of a product that was obviously going places but now finds itself with something of a dilemma.

'Please tell me you are not serious?' said Phil Deakin, Toy Time's managing director and founder. 'I gave you your first job; I promoted you; I put you in charge of our IT operations — and now you tell me this?'

'I am serious ... and so are they,' replied Rachel Sherwood. 'They know that they are in a position of power and they are not too worried about using it to their advantage ... It's not all bad though. Potentially difficult but not necessarily bad per se. WYTE-ERP is poised to become a major player in the ERP sector but to get the really big corporate client base, they need to add a lot of functionality to the product and they need to recover the developments costs of the new package ... '

'I don't mind it costing them plenty, I object when it costs us on such a large scale. We paid $500 000 for the software and we pay $100 000 each year for maintenance. If it's so damned good, why does it need to be maintained so much? It all affects our bottom line. In the 1970s, we just made things, sold them and made more things to sell: life was simpler. So now they want $400 000 for an upgrade. What do we get for that?'

'Life might have been simpler, but you worked 60-hour weeks and drove a second-hand car — just a little different from today's Jaguar and overseas holidays…' Rachel responded. 'The question you need to ask is "what will it cost us not to upgrade?". The simple answer is most of the company. We have re-engineered our work process to suit WYTE. Our suppliers and customers are linked into our systems and our cash flow depends on it. Legally, WYTE has to support us for the next 12 months. After that, we are on our own.'

'But we still own the software — what's the problem? Why can't we just carry on using it? Surely we can just buy the quarterly service packs?' Phil asked.

Rachel sighed. 'It's like this. You remember the huge gains we made when we moved to WYTE?' (Phil nodded.) 'Well, the upgrade will give us about a 50 per cent improvement in functionality and that in turn will make us more competitive. We could shed 20 clerical positions if we adopt version 2. Don't forget, our direct competitors can jump directly to the new version. WYTE are giving us a better deal because we have been in on this from day one. We get four service packs a year, but each pack has to be installed, have any modifications and improvements loaded over it and then tested thoroughly to make sure that all the features work as intended. So if a single improvement we make to the software provided by WYTE costs us $50 000, we spend another $40 000 implementing and installing it. We make four significant improvements a year. The most recent was so that we could handle Taiwanese suppliers. Eventually, the gap between the version we have and the current version of the WYTE will become so great that we won't be able to install the service packs and then we'll be really stuck. One option we have is to come off maintenance. We have a sizable and well-trained information systems and IT division. We could hang fire and move directly to version 3 in two years. Version 2 has been out for two years and WYTE will be moving to a three-year product cycle. They support the current version and the previous one. They will still sell us version 3 for $400 000: we save $200 000 in maintenance and maybe AUD$120 000 on service packs. The downside is that we would be early adopters of version 3 and we would have to install it over version 2, which we would then get for free.'

'And the costs to convert to version 3?' asked Phil.

'The original project cost us nearly $1 million,' said Rachel. 'A major upgrade like this is going to cost about 80 per cent of that. Moving to version 2 now would be about $500 000 and we could move to version 3 in three years for about $400 000. Version 3 will need fewer improvements — say one a year — and version 2 would need two a year, I guess. ERP projects are never really finished… just be grateful that we are not a small company or we'd really be feeling it. It's your call, Phil. What do you want us to do?'

Questions

1. As best you are able with the figures given, work out the costs for skipping an implementation and moving to version 3 in three years and for moving to version 2 and then version 3. Which option would you recommend and why?
2. Why is Rachel concerned about being an early adopter of version 3? Are her concerns justified?

(continued)

3. Do you think that Phil's views on software pricing are appropriate?

4. Would the situation be better if Toy Time was a late adopter of version 3?

5. How confident should Phil feel in Rachel's advice? What would you do in his position if you had any doubts?

6. What questions should Phil be asking of Rachel?

7. Are there any other options available to Toy Time? If so, discuss their relative merits.

8. Why did Rachel tell Phil 'just be grateful that we are not a small company or we'd really be feeling it'?

9. Given that Toy Time has a large and well-trained information systems and IT division, why has it not developed its own ERP software?

10. Rachel said that ERP projects are never really finished. Is she justified in saying this? Explain why.

References

Kerrigan, P 2002, 'The changing role of the CIO', http://au.fujitsu.com.

Westergren, T 2000, 'The music genome project', www.pandora.com.

CHAPTER 6
Introduction to systems development

LEARNING OBJECTIVES

After reading this chapter, you should be able to:

» understand the components that make up the systems development environment

» explain the purpose of the systems development lifecycle (SDLC)

» describe the skills needed by systems analysts

» describe each stage of the systems development process

» explain the purpose of computer-aided software engineering (CASE) tools

» compare the variety of data- and information-gathering techniques

» provide an overview of data and process modelling

» explain the role of methodologies in systems development

» provide an overview of alternative systems development approaches.

Introduction

This chapter provides an introduction to the topic of building information systems otherwise known as **systems development**. The **systems development lifecycle (SDLC)** serves as a framework for developing information systems. The classical phases of analysis, design, implementation and maintenance provide a logical and structured approach for building systems. Data are valuable resources in organisations and require effective management. Data and process modelling provide the **systems analyst** with methods to manage and document the data and the processes that modify the data. Software such as CASE tools is commonly used for improving the development process, and techniques such as rapid application development (RAD) and joint application design (JAD) can be used for speeding up project timelines. Different problems require alternative systems development methodologies. Some situations may need softer, people-centred approaches rather than structured engineering methods, especially where there are differences of opinion about what is best for the organisation.

This chapter is concerned with explaining general development approaches and techniques that are applicable to most types of systems development situations. The World Wide Web affects many systems development projects today, and specific details of web applications development are covered in chapter 10.

The systems development environment

Chapter 1 explains that an information system in a business environment is made up of several components. These usually include people, hardware, software, policies and procedures, data and information. The components of the information system do not operate in isolation but are closely interwoven with the fabric of the organisation. Information systems are often complex systems that operate in complex environments. Systems development methods are techniques, often diagrammatic, that aim to simplify this complexity both for developers and users. A systems analyst needs to understand these methods and develop a toolkit of methods and techniques to manage existing systems and to help in the creation of new ones. Two key techniques for information systems professionals are the modelling of 'data' and the modelling of 'processes' in organisations.

[**Key concept:** 'A picture is worth a thousand words.' Systems development uses diagrams and tables, wherever possible, to model the system.]

The development processes used in building an information system involve following a series of steps. Although information systems could be developed in an informal way, there is usually a more formal process, or methodology, that is used in organisations.

The systems development lifecycle (SDLC)

Every systems analyst has heard of the SDLC. It is important to become familiar with the basic concept. The SDLC is a structured framework for developing information systems. It breaks down the development process into various phases and provides a project management context to work within. The main phases are analysis, design, implementation and maintenance (see figure 6.1), and these are briefly outlined in the following sections.

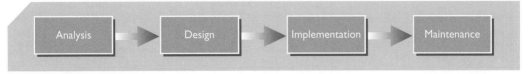

Figure 6.1 The systems development process

[**Key concept:** Divide and conquer: break up the problem or task into smaller components and solve each subproblem.]

› *Analysis.* The analysis phase concentrates on gathering information about the current and proposed systems. It is important that the feasibility of making changes is continually assessed. The requirements of the new systems are gathered and form the basis of the logical design, which details what data and information will be processed but not the technologies that will be used. This phase uses modelling techniques to describe the processes and the data within the organisation.

› **Reflection question 1:** What are some of the potential consequences of a poor analysis phase?

› *Design.* Once the requirements of the new system have been obtained, the new system has to be designed in detail. This involves specifying all components of the system including the design of the database, network infrastructure, the policies and procedures and the software.

› *Implementation.* After the design details have been worked out, the system must be constructed and put into place. The software has to be written, or set up if it is an off-the-shelf package. A large amount of testing and training takes place before the system is finally handed over to the users.

[**Key concept:** Analyse, design and then implement is the basic problem-solving approach underlying much of systems development.]

› *Maintenance.* You will notice businesses changing how they regularly interact with their customers. Most information systems undergo changes as time passes. These may be the result of changing requirements or errors being detected in the system. As a consequence of the need for change, resources must be set aside each year for maintaining a system.

The four commonly used phases can be broken down into further stages (figure 6.2 overleaf). Systems development textbooks have different names for some of the stages or some stages may be combined or even further broken down, but the seven stages in figure 6.2 form a logical breakdown of the SDLC. The lifecycle can be amended for alternative systems development approaches such as prototyping (discussed later).

The broad phases of analysis, design, implementation and maintenance are used in many situations. Building a house, for example, requires a systematic approach. The requirements of the owners need to be considered in relation to major specifications such as the size of the house and the number of rooms. All the requirements need to be specified in a design drawn by the architect. The implementation phase involves the actual building of the house and, of course, as every home owner knows, continual maintenance is needed. Perhaps later down the track the home owner will require some major structural modification such as an extra bedroom or a kitchen extension.

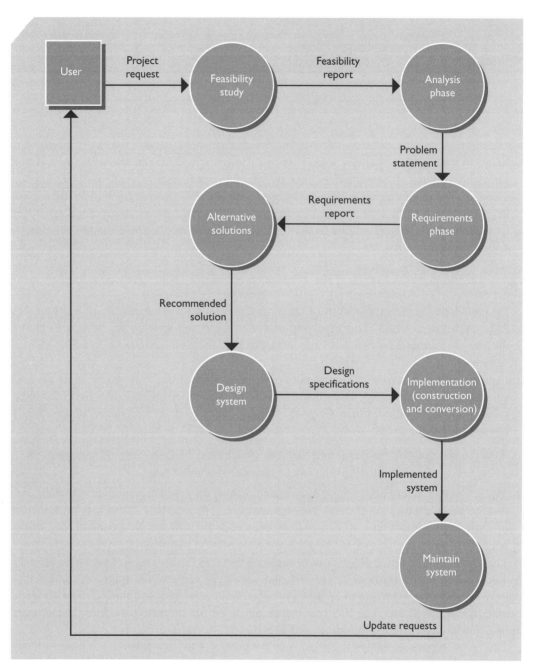

Figure 6.2 The systems development lifecycle

The structured lifecycle approach evolved as a reaction to the problems of developing information systems in an ad hoc or unsystematic way. Several dangers are inherent in developing an information system without some type of framework. Table 6.1 lists some problems that could arise from not following some basic guidelines in the systems development process.

infobyte

Waterfall methodology

The SDLC approach is sometimes termed a 'waterfall methodology'. This is because each phase of development is completed, reviews are conducted at the end of each stage and decisions are made whether to continue to the next stage. This cascading approach has many benefits for ensuring reliability and quality because the project does not move to the next stage until everything has been completed. Others view this approach as old-fashioned and consider it a slow and inflexible approach, not mirroring the way people work. However, the word 'waterfall' provides a memorable metaphor for a key project management technique of making sure each phase is well done and documented before moving on to the next phase.

TABLE 6.1 Some problems associated with an informal approach to systems development

Problems	Possible causes
The completed system is not what the users want.	Users' requirements were not properly gathered.
The customers do not use the system.	Users were not involved in the development process.
There is much conflict in the development of the system.	Benefits of the system were not stressed.
Resources are wasted.	Team management is poor.
Developers suffer from poor motivation and low morale. People may have to work harder than needed.	Team members are not working together and do not share work.
The system does not produce the right information.	Requirements were not gathered or were not checked.
The system is not finished on time.	Developers are inefficient and do not use time-saving methods.
The developers get a bad reputation. The system is difficult to maintain.	There is poor communication with user management and a lack of documentation on the system.

> **Reflection question 2:** Can an approach to developing information systems be too structured?

The skills required by systems analysts

The systems analyst requires a wide range of skills to develop information systems effectively. Many of these are general skills, which are important in most aspects of business and will need developing throughout the analyst's career. As you read through the next section, ask yourself where your strengths lie and which skills you should work on. Making a frank appraisal of your skills set is sometimes a painful exercise but a necessary one if you want to improve your chances of landing that challenging job or gaining that important promotion.

Communication and interpersonal skills

Have you ever heard anyone stand up and give a marvellous yet seemingly effortless presentation, which informed and entertained the audience at the same time? Chances are that the person making the presentation had worked hard on his or her presentation skills for years and had also put a lot of preparation into the presentation itself. The same applies to that wonderfully constructed memo, letter or report.

Systems analysts require effective writing skills because they have to write many reports, memos, emails and letters throughout the systems development process. Well-structured and well-presented reports are important tools for communicating with users and senior managers. Oral presentations are also important in helping to guide the team in the development of the system, to report to managers on progress, and in requests for resources. At times, analysts will need to be enthusiastic in 'selling' the system to users and managers. The ability to relate to people, form working relationships and effectively negotiate are useful skills, which the analyst should develop.

infobyte

So what are the business skills that IT staff need?

What exactly are business skills? Generally, employers and professional computer societies say that knowledge and skills related to the business domain are important. For example, if an information technology (IT) developer works for a bank, it is helpful to know how a bank works from a process perspective, how customers interact with the bank and what tasks the staff complete as part of their everyday work. It also means that IT staff should have some idea how business value is delivered within that business context. If IT staff know how their business works, they are more likely to be able to deliver systems that provide value to the organisation rather than just technical solutions. Other business skills can include basic financial skills related to developing a budget or assessing costs for a project or putting a financial value to the benefits of a system. Of course, many see good communication skills as an essential business skill.

Analytical and problem-solving skills

Many problems arise when dealing with computerised information systems. The analyst must be skilled in analysing and solving problems. Rather than looking upon them as a continual series of problems, many analysts see them as challenges and opportunities for improving the system.

The solution of problems may require creative thinking. This is an especially useful skill in the systems design phase, where multimedia interfaces can provide a competitive edge.

Technical skills

Systems development requires an understanding of the technical issues related to technology to make sound recommendations concerning the systems design details. Programming, for example, is usually a very involved and intricate task, which demands a 'technical' aptitude and eye for detail. Project management skills include managing resources and people as well as time, and require technical methods, techniques and software. Project management is a fundamental skill, which the analyst must be conscious of and make every effort to develop.

[**Key concept:** Systems development requires a blend of business, communication and technical skills.]

infobyte

Trends in IT

e-skills.com (www.e-skills.com) is a UK-government-sponsored initiative to provide information on the IT industry. In partnership with Gartner, it has produced a list of key trends that will affect the IT workforce over the next ten years:
> globalisation of business and international outsourcing
> technology standardisation
> the implementation of new channel strategies
> remote and collaborative working
> an increasing focus on privacy and security
> transformation of IT into a utility-style service.

Source: Information from www.e-skills.com.

The tasks involved in each stage of systems development

This chapter earlier introduced the four key stages of systems development: analysis, design, implementation and maintenance. The following describes in more detail the tasks that need to be carried out as part of the SDLC. Not all information systems projects require that every stage and task be completed fully. Remember, the SDLC serves as a framework for development and does not need to be used in exactly the same way on all projects.

Information systems planning

Information systems planning is an important issue for many information systems managers, and is covered in more detail in chapter 7. However, it is worthwhile looking at information systems planning in relation to the SDLC. Because of the rapid changes in IT, organisations are seeking to harness technology to help drive the business.

Information systems plans are seen as a way of strategically positioning the organisation in terms of its use and development of information technology. An information systems plan includes broad directions for the technology platform, the network infrastructure, the software architecture, and the key data and processes of the business, as well as identifying the information systems and IT expertise and skills required by the organisation. Future project requests can be assessed from the perspective of whether they fall in line with the information systems plan. This can reduce the danger of becoming sidetracked by projects that are not aligned with the organisational strategy and goals.

Feasibility phase

A project is initiated as a result of a user request, a management initiative or the analyst's suggestion. The feasibility phase has a simple aim: to determine whether the suggestion or proposal is worthwhile. It may involve gathering information on, and understanding, the current system if there is one. Problems are identified and the benefits of solving them are assessed. If no current system exists, then research may be carried out on similar systems in other organisations. The feasibility phase is a preliminary investigation, which tries to identify the scope of the project and determine the project's validity. On occasions, potential broad solutions are suggested and estimates of costs and benefits are made. Of course, at this stage, all the costs and benefits are difficult to identify and quantify. A more detailed cost–benefit analysis is often left to subsequent stages, when more detailed information is known. The outcome of this stage is a feasibility report on the project, which is typically presented to management. A decision must then be made on whether to move on to the next stage of the lifecycle, to cancel the project or to shelve it for the time being until conditions become more favourable.

Feasibility can be assessed from three perspectives. All three are important. The first is operational feasibility, the second technical feasibility and the third economic feasibility.

Operational feasibility

The acceptability of a solution is a measure of the system's operational feasibility. The system must work in practice. For example, if a system is developed for the Internet but the web interface is just too difficult to use, then it is not operationally feasible. Another aspect is the controls built into an application. If the security control measures within the system are inadequate, then the system fails operationally.

Technical feasibility

Technical feasibility is about assessing whether the application can be developed within reasonable limits of complexity. New technology is being developed and marketed continually. However, leading-edge technology may not be tried and tested. As a result, it might be too high risk to employ within a business organisation in which high reliability is required. Some solutions may require a great deal of expertise to complete, which may not be available within the organisation or even within the region. Without the skills, the solution becomes technically infeasible to develop.

Economic feasibility

The economic benefits of a system should outweigh the costs of development and running the system. Some benefits may be difficult to quantify. For example, better public relations is a difficult aspect to put a monetary value on. However, attempts should be made to try and quantify the improvement. Even increasing sales orders on the Web is difficult to assess. It could be argued that some customers would seek the more traditional sales outlets if they did not have access to the Web option.

[**Key concept:** Anything you do in systems development requires justification.]

IS in action

Feasibility studies are the same the world over — an example from the Punjab

Information Technology Policy Manual
Feasibility Study Guidelines
For Information technology Projects
Government of Punjab
Prepared by:
Department of Information Systems & Reforms

Outline for an IT Feasibility Study

The concerned Government Department must make a crucial decision during the early stages of an information technology (IT) project: whether to seek funds to support full-scale development and implementation or to suspend project activities due to a lack of clear benefits (tangible, intangible, or both), and/or overwhelming risks. The feasibility study is a structured, modular process to accumulate the information needed to support stakeholders in making this crucial decision.

A Department will prepare the feasibility study when sufficient functional and technical design has been completed to articulate the major objectives of a project and define the work necessary to achieve those objectives with a high degree of confidence. This means a Department has completed a Project Definition, a Requirements Analysis, and a General Manual Design. As a result of this work, the Department has far more information in hand about the expected costs, benefits, and risks of a proposed project than it did when preparing the Project Definition. It is critical this new information be applied to a 'go/no go' decision before committing significant funds to development.

Source: Department of Information Technology of the Government of Punjab, 'Feasibility study guidelines for information technology projects Government of Punjab', www.doitpunjab.gov.in/IT/feasiguide.pdf.

Analysis phase

A systems development project usually involves an examination of the current operations and systems. For example, in assessing the development of a new order-processing system, the existing system should be analysed to gain an understanding of its strengths and weaknesses. The problems associated with any information system fall into broad categories (see table 6.2). The costs associated with the problems can then be estimated. This information can be used to justify the expense of the new development. If the proposed system is completely new, then this phase can be used to research systems in other organisations.

When analysing the current system, analysts conduct a detailed investigation that uses various information-gathering techniques, such as interviews, observation and questionnaires (see the later section on information gathering). The study phase typically requires considerable end-user involvement. Data-flow diagrams are commonly drawn to document the existing system, and form part of the documentation for the stage together with a study phase report, which identifies the key problems and associated costs.

TABLE 6.2 Common problems found in information systems

Symptom of problem	General problem
Managers find it difficult to make decisions.	Information is lacking.
Customers complain about invoices.	Data are inaccurate.
Reports are not used.	Level of information is inappropriate.
Complaints about delivery times are received from customers.	Systems are too slow in producing information.
Users do not know how to query the database effectively.	Information is available but underused, so it becomes an expensive resource.

[**Key concept:** Information systems problems usually fall into the categories of speed, accuracy, relevance, availability and expense.]

Requirements phase

After studying the current system, analysts must try to define the requirements for the proposed system. Again, this phase requires much end-user involvement and uses a range of information-gathering techniques. This phase of the SDLC is logical. The emphasis is on defining what is required in terms of the information requirements, rather than how the system should be physically implemented.

The requirements of the proposed system can be documented using process models (data-flow diagrams; DFDs) and data models (entity relationship diagrams; ERDs). A CASE tool can be used to develop and store the documentation of the system. A presentation can be made to user management at the end of the stage to communicate the essential requirements of the proposed system.

infobyte

Have you really considered all the users?

A significant percentage of users, particularly of websites, have some form of disability. Indeed, many vision-impaired people rely heavily on the Internet for information. Because these people use screen readers, careful attention should be given to each web page to ensure that table content is summarised, graphics and videos have text summaries, and that the page is effectively formatted when read by screen readers.

The role of CASE

Computer-aided software engineering (CASE) is used in the development process to manage the vast amount of data and information that is gathered. It provides diagrammatic modelling tools and, in many cases, validation of the logical and physical designs (see figure 6.3). The data (or project) dictionary is the repository of data input through templates in the CASE tool (see figure 6.4). Eventually, every aspect of the system is modelled and recorded in the software and the record should be kept up to date once the system is implemented. Upper CASE tools focus on the analysis and design phases of the SDLC and lower CASE tools concentrate on the implementation and maintenance phases.

The advantages of using CASE tools are:
> They improve the quality of system documentation (i.e. better presentation, fewer errors and omissions).
> They improve the quality of the completed system.
> They improve communication between analysts.
> They improve maintainability of system.
> They can potentially speed up the development process.

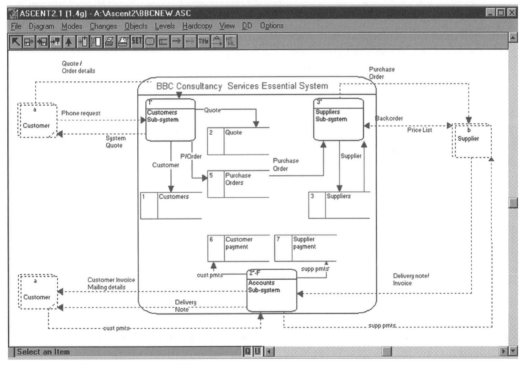

Figure 6.3 Data-flow diagram drawn in a CASE tool
Source: This diagram appeared at the Knowledge Base website.

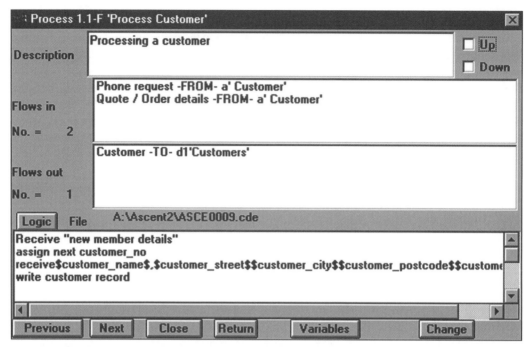

Figure 6.4 Data dictionary entry in a CASE tool
Source: This diagram appeared at the Knowledge Base website.

Alternative solutions phase

The **alternative solutions phase** involves identifying possible implementation solutions for the requirements. Ideally, the analyst proposes several options, rather than one, and presents them to management to decide on one. They might include a fully automated system, a partly automated system or alternative technology. The option of keeping the system as it is should be included as a yardstick for comparing the proposals. The technical details of each alternative system are specified and the costs estimated. The level of detail for each specification depends heavily on the resources and the type of system being developed. Time constraints do not usually allow the developers to specify all candidate solutions in absolute detail.

[**Key concept:** Always assess the implications of making no changes to the current system.]

Design phase

Systems design is a physical stage of the SDLC because it concentrates on how the proposed system will be designed. All aspects of proposed systems have to be designed (see table 6.3). Database design is a common and critical part of the systems design phase. The characteristics of a well-designed database are many, but this section focuses on the key characteristics:

> *The system minimises redundancy of data.* This requires that data are specified only once in the database. Although it is not always practical to do this, the objective is to minimise the amount of redundancy or duplication of data that is likely to create update problems in future.

> *The database should be flexible to the needs of users.* In other words, a user should be able to create reports and obtain relevant information on the basis of their own requirements. If the database is designed with flexibility in mind, this should be achievable.

> *The data within the database should be reliable and accurate.* If the database is properly designed, it is more likely that the correct data will be input and errors will be trapped. Also if data are not duplicated, an update requires the updating of just one dataset rather than two or more.

> *The database should be designed to respond quickly to requests.* Careful design and fine-tuning of the database will provide fast retrieval of data.

Of course, a database that is well designed should be easy to use and understand.

TABLE 6.3 Activities of the systems design phase

Activities of systems design	Description of tasks
Software and hardware acquisition	Sourcing and buying hardware and software Evaluating vendor recommendations
Database and file design	Setting up the database Fine-tuning the performance of the database
Network design	Designing the data communications infrastructure
Input design	Designing forms and input screens
Output design	Designing reports and output screens
Interface design	Designing the user interface (usually graphical user interface)
Software or program design	Designing the software for modularity and reusability
Design of methods, procedures and controls	Timing of events and specifying the conditions they operate under

IS in action

Off-the-shelf or customised software?

The advantages of buying off-the-shelf software or accessing software over the Web as opposed to developing software in house is widely recognised. Even so, customised application development is still a significant part of the IT world. For some companies in rapidly changing sectors such as telecommunications, financial services, technology and pharmaceuticals, the costs of developing software are very high. Banks, for example, still spend large amounts on developing software. Even when companies choose to buy software packages, they may add modules to provide specific capability.

Some companies that develop customised software have begun to take a modular approach to their applications development, so that modules can be written and reused in other

(continued)

applications or even packaged and sold to other companies. If modules are written with flexibility in mind, then new applications can be developed more quickly. Functions such as 'customer calls' or generic software tools can all be reused if designed and developed to be reused. It could be argued that this approach is only suitable for very large companies that develop many software systems.

Source: Information from Marwaha, S, Patil, S & Tinaikar, R 2006, 'The next generation of in-house software development', *Information Age*, April/May, pp. 3–8.

Hardware and software acquisition

Hardware and software may have to be acquired for the proposed system. If there is to be a substantial investment in technology, then this task needs considerable effort. If company officials are sure about the hardware and software required, then they can approach various vendors and ask for quotes for the products. Warranty agreements, price of products, quality of equipment and reputation are all factors to be considered in choosing a supplier. Other factors, such as whether the supplier is a local company that will collect equipment under warranty for repair, can be important because delays are usually involved when distances are greater.

If the decision makers have not chosen particular hardware and software, they will require vendors to make recommendations with justifications in this area. The requirements of the organisation should be outlined for the vendors, which should respond with their suggestions. The vendors' proposals can be ranked using a scoring system that allocates points on a scale of one to ten, for example, for each feature of the recommendations.

IS in action

Systems integration at CRT

The CRT Group is a transport, warehousing and high-value food ingredients business, which has more than 250 staff in Australia. CRT decided to replace its in-house developed IT systems (five in total) with a new enterprise resource management solution. This system would integrate financial, warehouse and transport logistics management with the ability to link to customer systems.

From the start the project had senior support. A steering committee was developed, headed by senior management, with representative users from each functional area. A short timeline was stipulated, so the scope of the project was made more narrow than the original plan. The project was divided into two stages. Phase 1 was financial management and warehouse management. Phase 2 included transport management, container tracking and replacing the entire rates and billing system. The new systems streamlined business processes, improved data integrity and provided more timely and accurate data.

From a systems development perspective, this project was complex and dealt with critical systems. It was a worthwhile project because the five systems developed in house were not fully integrated. Examples of good practice demonstrated during the project included obtaining top-management support, having representative users involved and breaking the project into two major phases to manage complexity.

Source: Information from http://download.microsoft.com.

Implementation

Implementation is the phase in the SDLC when the system is built and tested (construction phase) and then handed over (conversion phase). Of all the phases, this usually takes the most amount of time. A lot has to happen during implementation.

Major tasks to be completed during implementation include:

> altering rooms and buildings
> coding programs
> testing programs
> installing hardware
> setting up systems software
> installing applications software
> installing the network
> setting up the database
> keying data into the database
> further testing
> putting security measures in place
> testing security measures
> training staff
> updating documentation
> handing over the system
> reviewing the system.

> **Reflection question 3:** Which of the tasks mentioned are not necessary when a software package is bought rather than developed?

The most important aspect of systems implementation is project management, which is the scheduling of events and the organising of people to achieve set goals. Many projects run over time or over budget because of poor project management. Projects may run over time for several reasons:

> Estimations of task duration may have been overoptimistic. This often happens as a result of trying to win contracts or being too eager to please project sponsors.
> Poor project management skills on the part of the project leaders can lead to a failure to see all the tasks involved and the capabilities of the team.
> The project team may be poorly motivated. It may be lacking incentives to complete the project on time.
> Clients may be poorly motivated. Staff can drag their heels and put up obstacles if they are resisting change.
> The skills of the project team may be inadequate for the tasks. Its members may not be the right people for the job or they may not have had sufficient training.
> People may be unwilling to be accountable and take responsibility for corrective action.

Testing

Computer-aided mistakes can have severe consequences. Mistakes that result from software or hardware problems can lead to loss of life or loss or damage to property, or financial loss. Computers are used in many critical situations such as:

> controlling air traffic
> flying aeroplanes
> for hospital treatment
> in manufacturing processes.

The effects of undetected errors in such systems are potentially disastrous. Recent cases have involved giving cancer patients too great a dose of radiation over a prolonged period (software error) and an aircraft falling from 9000 to 6000 metres in a few seconds (software error).

The seriousness of cases such as these is apparent. Mistakes in the business world can also be very costly; for example, a bank recently processed the debits and credits twice for one day (software error), and mistakes have been reported to occur in mortgage calculations.

Determining who is responsible and consequently liable for computer-aided mistakes can be a legal minefield. Factors such as the following have to be taken into account:

> whether the error resulted from a mistake in the program (developers)
> incorrect data stored in a file or database (the users or possibly the developers)
> whether the person using the computer was incompetent or was badly trained (users)
> inadequate requirements provided (users or developers)
> inadequate requirements gathered (developers).

In other words, the problems in relation to a computer system not working properly can result from a wide range of factors. Testing aims to minimise the number of errors appearing in a system and to ensure that the system performs adequately. These might seem straightforward objectives but testing is far from straightforward.

Testing is a continual task. After every phase of the SDLC, developers test the accuracy of the system by:

> going over the work
> going through the documentation with users
> referring back to earlier stages of the SDLC and overall project goals and aims to see if everything is consistent.

The main focus of testing is during construction and delivery of the system. The testing is carried out by the systems developers and the users of the system.

The systems developers test the software as it is being written and then the system as it is being put together. There is some time during implementation when the developers work with the users to test the system. There is usually some time after the system is handed over when the users test the system alone and report back to the developers (see figure 6.5).

Systems conversion

Systems conversion is a stage in the project when processing changes over from one system to another. Conversion can be carried out in several ways.

> *Direct conversion.* On a set date, dispense with the old system and start with the new.
> *Parallel conversion.* Run both systems for a time.

> *Pilot conversion.* The system is tested in one location before others are converted.
> *Phased conversion.* Subsystems are implemented one at a time.
> *Evolutionary conversion.* This takes the perspective that a system evolves in small increments rather than by radical changes from old to new.

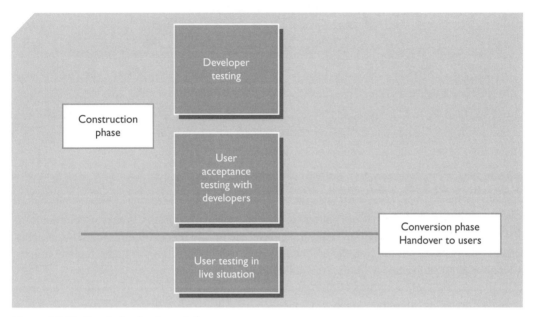

Figure 6.5 Testing during implementation

Maintenance

Maintenance projects can be divided into two categories. The first category concerns correcting errors in the system. The errors may have been detected during the systems development process but left to a later date for correction. The second category concerns detecting errors when the system has been running for some time. The problems are logged and attended to in batches if they are deemed not to be critical. If they are critical to the system, they must be attended to as soon as possible.

Changes will need to be made to the system at various times because requirements change. These changes may come about because of new regulations, changed preferences or new techniques that can improve the performance of the system. A change to a system can be a significant project in its own right and may require following the SDLC, albeit a shortened version.

[**Key concept:** The cost of maintaining a system often amounts to more than the initial cost of developing the system.]

The lifecycle for small systems

Clearly, in a small business or where a small system is concerned, not all tasks will be performed to the same level of detail. However, the SDLC is still a good framework to work within. The emphasis with small systems will be on the needs assessment and associated cost assessment leading to the technology design (see figure 6.6 overleaf).

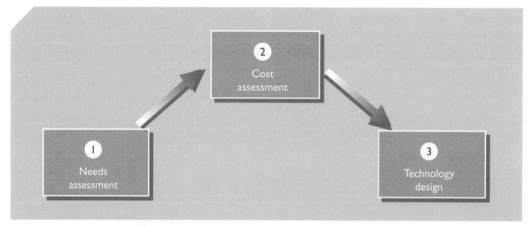

Figure 6.6 Key stages in the development of small systems

Information gathering

Fact finding or information gathering is undertaken at various stages throughout the SDLC. It is particularly important in defining the problem or problems and requirements. Researching design options and the technology also require information-gathering techniques. There are nine common fact-finding techniques:

> analysing company documentation
> analysing forms, files and database records
> visiting other organisations
> researching topics in magazines and journals
> observation of the systems in action
> questionnaires
> interviews
> informal conversations with users
> joint application design.

> **Reflection question 4:** Is there any particular order in which information gathering should be carried out?

The systems analyst must be skilled in gathering information. Table 6.4 gives some of the strengths and weaknesses of each method. Much can be determined by accessing the various types of data and information within the organisation. Analysing company reports and brochures can provide valuable background information about the current system. Observing organisational processes in action is a useful technique to find out the glitches in a system, but the analyst should be aware that people often modify their behaviour when they are being watched. Questionnaires are used in many areas of business but considerable thought must be used in the design of the questions; otherwise, the information can be worthless or too difficult to collate and interpret. The same hazard applies to conducting interviews. The right people must be interviewed, and they should be asked the right type of question or they may feel that their time is being wasted.

Joint application design (JAD) takes the form of intensive workshops with key personnel and a skilled facilitator. The aim is to define the essential requirements of the new system. JAD can reduce the time required for defining the requirements and can be very effective if the workshops are properly organised and structured.

[**Key concept:** The systems analyst must be skilled in gathering information.]

TABLE 6.4 The strengths and weaknesses of information-gathering techniques

Method	Phase or phases used	Strength of the method	Weakness of the method
Analysing company documentation	Feasibility Analysis	Gives good background information	May be out of date May not reflect reality
Analysing forms, files and database records	Feasibility Analysis	Good for detailed information	May be out of date
Visiting other organisations	Requirements	Learn from others' mistakes	May not be possible to gain access to other organisations
Researching	Design	Valuable sources of information from experts	May not be easy to find relevant information
Observation	Analysis Requirements	Can find out first-hand how things work	May give a distorted view of events and work
Questionnaires	Feasibility Analysis Requirements	Can involve many people in a cost-effective manner	Not easy to construct, or few may reply, or difficult to get detail
Interviews	Feasibility Analysis Requirements	Can get detailed answers	Time consuming and sometimes difficult to arrange
Informal conversations	Analysis	Good for finding out problems	Can give a distorted view
Joint application design	Requirements	Shortens the time to define requirements	May not be possible to get key people for enough time

Systems modelling

At this point, it is worth introducing an overview of systems-modelling methods. As noted, data modelling and process modelling are part of the systems analyst's toolkit. The two most commonly used types are entity relationship diagrams (ERDs) (data) and data-flow diagrams (DFDs) (process). The two methods are complementary but were never originally designed as cohesive modelling techniques. However, some systems development methodologies use both modelling approaches. An ERD represents a static view of the data in a system and the DFD is used to model the dynamic aspects of the system or how the data are changed (processes). Most CASE tools facilitate the development of both techniques, and the details and cross-references can take place in the data dictionary.

Data modelling

Data modelling is a method of organising and documenting a system's data. The models produced are considered to be logical models because they are implementation independent. They form the early stages of the database design. Although the data are always changing in a business, the types of data collected are fairly stable. Data are usually more stable than processes, so some methods put the emphasis on data modelling. One methodology that does this is James Martin's information engineering (Martin 1989).

[**Key concept:** Data change less than processes.]

Entity relationship diagrams (ERDs)

The entity relationship diagram (ERD) is a data-modelling technique that shows the relationships among the data within a business. It is not a technique to show how data are implemented, created, modified or deleted. Figure 6.7 shows an ERD for a company's order-processing system. This ERD forms the basis of the database design and, as can be seen from the diagram, implies that data will be stored on customers, products, orders and so on.

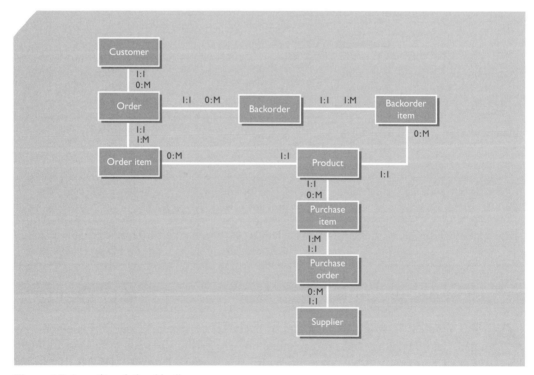

Figure 6.7 An entity relationship diagram

A data entity is anything, real or abstract, about which we want to store data. A rectangle is used to denote a data entity. Each entity has a list of attributes to describe it with one or several of them acting as the key or unique identifier. The following is a list of example entities:

> Machine
> Book
> Contract
> Applicant
> Borrower
> Contractor
> Order
> Client
> State
> Campus
> Patient
> Customer
> Project
> Purchase_Order
> Quote.

A data relationship is shown by a line between the entities. The relationships among entities can be made more explicit by defining their degree. The degree of relationship among entities is denoted by:

0:M — zero or many

1:M — one or many

1:1 — only one.

The ERD in figure 6.8 shows products being ordered from suppliers and can be read in the following ways:

> A purchase order is filled by one and only one supplier. This is a 1:1 relationship.
> A supplier fills zero (no orders being completed) or more orders. This is a 0:M relationship.
> A product is contained on zero or more purchase orders. This is a 0:M relationship.
> A purchase order contains at least one product. This is a 1:M relationship.

Figure 6.8 Part of an ERD to show the ordering of products from suppliers

Of course, all entities are described in the data dictionary within the CASE tool (see figure 6.9 overleaf).

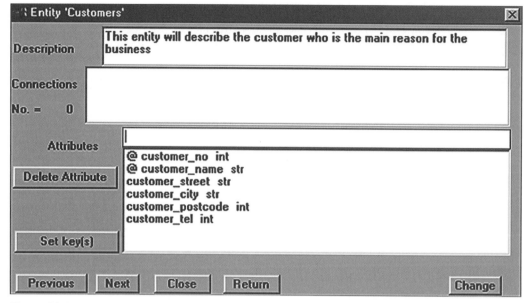

Figure 6.9 Data dictionary entry for an entity

Steps in developing an ERD

1. *Identify entities and relationships among them.*
   These can be identified by discussions or formal interviews with staff or by analysing forms, reports, files, current systems or existing database (if they exist).

2. *Define unique identifiers (keys) for each entity.*
   A key is a unique identifier for an entity. For example, a student entity could have an ID field to provide a unique identifier. Some entities require two or more fields to form a unique key.

3. *Draw a rough draft of the ERD.*

4. *Identify the items that describe the entities.*
   These are called data attributes (see figure 6.10).

5. *Match the entity attributes to entities.*

6. *Conduct data analysis.*
   See the following section for details on data analysis.

7. *Redraw ERD with the new group of entities.*

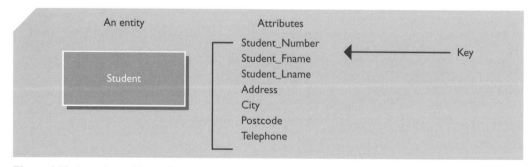

Figure 6.10 An entity and its attributes

Data analysis

After the initial data modelling has been completed, each entity has to be analysed to assess whether all of the attributes describe one entity. The process is called data analysis or normalisation. Normalisation rules are designed to prevent update anomalies and data inconsistencies in the future database. This section deals with three levels in normalisation. These are termed first, second and third normal form. There are a further two levels (fourth and fifth) but this chapter is not concerned with those because they deal with special cases of data that you are less likely to come across.

First normal form

First normal form excludes variable repeating fields and groups. If you look at the data in table 6.5, you can see a repeating component. This format would create much redundancy in a database because all of the order details would have to be repeated for every part or if the cells were left blank, they would create ambiguity. The solution to this problem is to split the entity into two separate entities.

TABLE 6.5 Data in unnormalised form

ORDER				
ORD-NO	DATE	COMPANY	PART-NO	QTY
0001	3/6/2008	J Smith	P1	10
			P2	30
			P7	10
0002	4/6/2008	XYZ	P2	10
			P7	20

TABLE 6.6 Order data in first normal form

ORDER		
ORD-NO	DATE	COMPANY
0001	3/6/2008	J Smith
0002	4/6/2008	XYZ
0003	4/6/2008	A Capp

(continued)

ORDER_LINE		
ORDER-NO	PART-NO	QTY
0001	P1	10
0001	P2	30
0001	P7	10
0002	P2	10
0002	P7	20

The data in table 6.6 is in first normal form. The objective of doing this first step was to reduce the many-to-many relationships to one-to-many relationships, alleviating update and redundancy problems. The creation of the new entity Order_Line reduces the many-to-many relationship to a one-to-many relationship. The key combines the keys of the original table and the repeating group.

Second normal form

Second normal form is violated when a nonkey field is a fact about a subset of a key. It is only relevant when the key is composite, that is, consists of several fields.

TABLE 6.7 Part and warehouse data

PART_WAREHOUSE			
PART	WAREHOUSE	QUANTITY	WAREHOUSE_ADDRESS
P1	Alpha1	4000	20 Singleton Road, Bunbury
P1	Beta2	250	10 Desert Road, Geraldton
P2	Alpha1	2235	20 Singleton Road, Bunbury
P3	Alpha1	965	20 Singleton Road, Bunbury

The problem with the data in table 6.7 is that Warehouse_Address is a fact about the Warehouse alone and not the Part. Warehouse_Address is repeated in every record that has a part in that warehouse. If the address of the warehouse changes, every record for that warehouse must be updated. Data may become inconsistent because of the redundancy. At some time, there may be no parts stored in the warehouse, so no record in which to keep the warehouse address. The record should be decomposed into two. This data in table 6.8 is in second normal form.

TABLE 6.8 Part and warehouse data in second normal form

PART_WAREHOUSE

PART	WAREHOUSE	QUANTITY
P1	Alpha1	4000
P1	Beta2	250
P2	Alpha1	2235
P3	Alpha1	965

WAREHOUSE

WAREHOUSE	WAREHOUSE_ADDRESS
Alpha1	20 Singleton Road, Bunbury
Beta2	10 Desert Road, Geraldton

Third normal form

Third normal form is violated when a nonkey field is a fact about another nonkey field. In table 6.9, Department_Location is a fact about Department and not about the Employee_No. The main problem with this data is the repetition of Department_Location. The redundancy of this data has the potential to lead to data inconsistency.

TABLE 6.9 Employee data

EMPLOYEE

EMPLOYEE_NO	DEPARTMENT	DEPARTMENT_LOCATION	DATE OF BIRTH
1011	Accounting	Joondalup	23/01/59
1012	Information Systems	Churchlands	17/11/60
1017	Accounting	Joondalup	10/01/75

The problem is resolved by breaking up the data into two entities (see table 6.10 overleaf). Department is included in the Employee table and acts as a foreign key because it forms a link between the two tables. A foreign key is the name given to a key from one entity that is repeated in another entity to form a link.

TABLE 6.10 Employee data in third normal form

EMPLOYEE		
EMPLOYEE_NO	DEPARTMENT	DATE OF BIRTH
1011	Accounting	23/01/59
1012	Information Systems	17/11/60
1017	Accounting	10/01/75

DEPARTMENT	
DEPARTMENT	DEPARTMENT_LOCATION
Accounting	Joondalup
Information Systems	Churchlands
Accounting	Joondalup

Once the data is in third normal form, it is considered normalised data. The process results in more smaller tables or entities. Even so, it is more efficient because there is less duplication of data overall and fewer errors in the data are likely to appear as a result of this. Normalisation may seem a strange process and it usually takes quite a bit of practice to be able to do it with accuracy.

Process modelling

All the actions that take place in a company, such as an order being received and dealt with, are processes. Process models using DFDs model system processes and are commonly used by systems analysts. They can be used to model both the existing and the proposed system.

Reports as a form of communication have partly been replaced by diagrams in systems development for several reasons: diagrams are less ambiguous; diagrams show relationships better and diagrams summarise material.

Data-flow diagrams (DFDs) can either show the physical details of implementation or be logical diagrams without the physical details. As figure 6.11 shows, they can be used:

> in the problem definition phase during analysis (physical DFDs)
> to view the current system logically (logical DFDs)
> in the requirements definition phase (logical DFDs)
> to describe alternative solutions (semiphysical DFDs)
> in the design stage (physical DFDs).

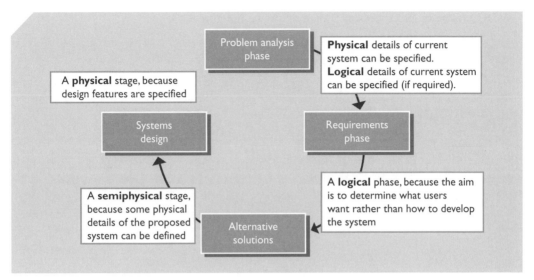

Figure 6.11 Physical and logical stages of systems development

Logical DFDs are implementation-independent models. They remove biases that are the result of how the existing system is implemented, or how one person thinks the system should be implemented. Implementation-independent models reduce the risk of missing functional requirements because of a preoccupation with technical details. They allow the analyst to communicate with the user in a nontechnical way when gathering requirements.

[**Key concept:** Avoid specifying physical features of the system before you know the information requirements.]

There are four symbols used in DFDs (see figure 6.12(a) to (d)):
> The *data-flow* symbol shows the flow of data (a).
> The *process* symbol shows the processing of data (b).
> The *entity* symbol shows data coming into and going out of the system (c).
> The *data store* is a symbol to show the storage of data (d).

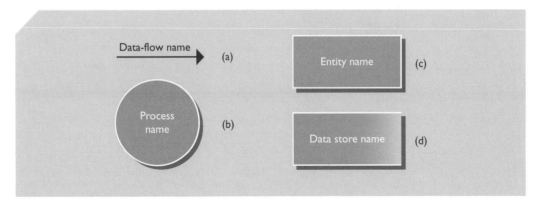

Figure 6.12 Symbols used in DFDs

A DFD for an order-processing system is shown in figure 6.13.

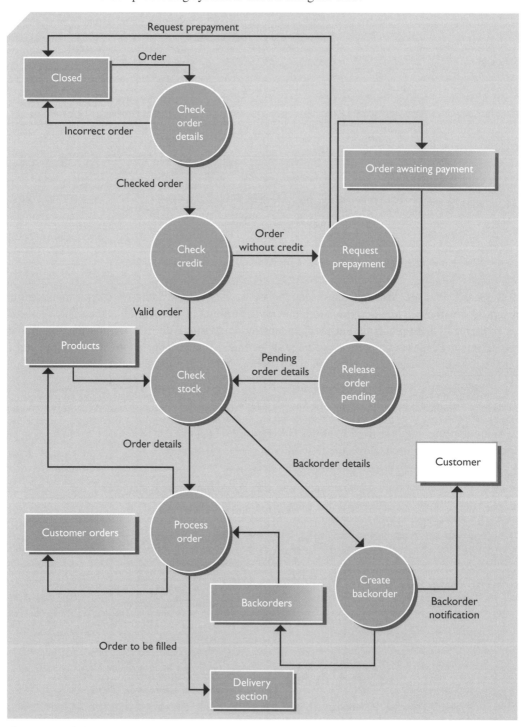

Figure 6.13 Order-processing DFD

DFDs are developed in increasing levels of detail for a system to form a hierarchy of diagrams.

Context diagram

The context diagram (see figure 6.14) has one process and delineates the system boundaries. The process describes the system that is being examined. It could be the company, subsystem or department within the company; it all depends on the scope of the system being examined.

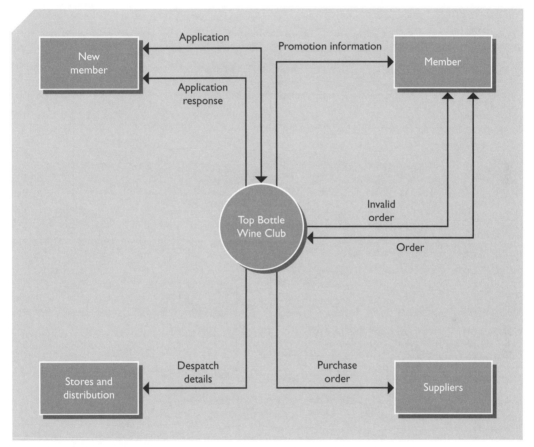

Figure 6.14 Context diagram

Subsystem diagram

The context diagram does not show much detail. If the process from the context diagram is broken down further, subsystems can be shown. The subsystem diagram (see figure 6.15 over-leaf) is sometimes referred to as the systems diagram or the overview diagram. This diagram shows the data flows between subsystems; it may even include shared data stores.

Detailed DFDs

The subsystem diagram can be decomposed further into middle-level diagrams and then primitive-level diagrams. The middle-level diagrams are not always necessary; it depends on the size and detail of the systems under study. Primitive-level diagrams (as shown in figure 6.13) show detailed processes for a self-contained task for the system.

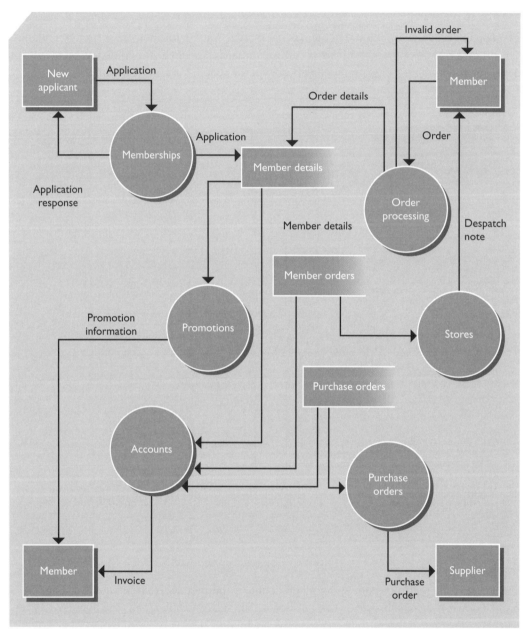

Figure 6.15 Subsystem diagram

Data dictionary entries

Processes need to be documented because many involve several steps. These will not be obvious from the DFD. Many of these processes will form the software component of the new system, so they need to be specified in detail so that the programmers can accurately implement them. The processes that are not implemented in the software are manual procedures that still need to be recorded.

Although the processes could be explained by a process description in text format, they may be ambiguous to another reader. Decision tables and structured English are two ways of unambiguously presenting the steps involved in any process.

Decision tables

A **decision table** is a method of describing process logic (see figures 6.16 and 6.17). Decision tables are used when the process is sufficiently complex to warrant a clear explanation in a table. The stages in developing a decision table are as follows:
> Identify the conditions.
> Identify the rules and their values.
> Specify the actions.
> Complete the bottom right-hand corner of the decision table by identifying the actions that result from the combination of conditions.

Conditions	Condition values
Actions	Action values

Figure 6.16 The structure of a decision table

CONDITIONS	RULES											
Credit rating	A	B	C	A	B	C	A	B	C	A	B	C
Over 26?	Y	Y	Y	N	N	N	Y	Y	Y	N	N	N
Employed more than three years	N	N	N	N	N	N	Y	Y	Y	Y	Y	Y
ACTIONS												
No credit						X						
Credit level A			X	X	X	X			X	X		X	X
Credit level B	X							X			X	

Figure 6.17 An example decision table

Structured English

Process logic can also be defined using **structured English**. The decision tables are used for defining business policies and structured English can be used for defining business procedures.

The two are complementary techniques (see figure 6.18). Structured English uses a restricted set of terms, file and attribute names to describe the high-level logic. There is no set vocabulary for structured English but its style must be brief and to the point. It relies on the use of repetition, condition and sequence statements.

For each credit application

    Case 1 (credit rating A) then

      If age 26 and employed three years then

        assign credit level A

    else

      assign credit level B

    end If

    Case 2 (credit rating B) then

      assign credit level A

    Case 3 (credit rating C) then

      If age 26 and employed three years then

        assign no credit

    else

      assign credit level A

    end If

    End Case

Figure 6.18 An example of structured English

Systems development methodologies

So far in this chapter, you have gained an understanding of the SDLC and common systems-modelling techniques. The principles of the SDLC form a framework for developing information systems. Because the SDLC is a general approach, it needs an extra slice of formality to be really useful in organisations. This formality commonly takes the form of a standardised set of rules and procedures for developers of information systems to follow. When the extra formality is added, the approach is called a methodology. The aim in this section of the chapter is to present an understanding of information systems methodologies and to provide insights into a number of well-known information systems development approaches.

An information systems methodology can vary from a series of steps used in solving a problem to a general approach to problem solving, or it can even be a philosophical approach. Depending on the nature of the problem and the contextual environment, any one or a combination may be appropriate to use in the systems development process.

An information systems methodology is defined here as a collection of philosophies, phases, procedures, rules, techniques, tools, documentation, management and training for developers of information systems.

Generally, its components describe:

> how a project is to be broken down into stages
> the tasks to be carried out at each stage
> the outputs to be produced
> the actions or events to be carried out
> the constraints to be applied
> the support tools to be used.

A methodology is often used as a project management tool to create a better end-product, a better development process and a standardised process. There are two main types of information systems methodologies: structured and behavioural methodologies. The lifecycle discussed in this chapter is characteristic of traditional structured methodologies. Examples of these include information engineering and structured systems analysis and design methods. Structured methodologies, although not really scientific, tend to draw on the credibility of the scientific method.

[**Key concept:** Choose a methodology appropriate to the situation.]

Behavioural methodologies

Behavioural methodologies take an organisational perspective. The real complexity in an organisational setting comes about as a result of the interaction of the components of the system. The system encompasses such things as the people, technology, protocols, procedures, organisational culture and politics and the wider business environment. The soft systems methodology (SSM) is perhaps the best-known behavioural methodology used in information systems (Checkland & Scholes 1990).

Examples of information systems methodologies

Information engineering

Information engineering (Martin 1989, 1990) is a methodology that takes a data-driven approach. This means that data models and data modelling are at the heart not just of any one system but of the organisation as a whole. The enterprisewide approach to systems development is also the reason it puts such an emphasis on systems planning. Process modelling is given some attention but is not given the same priority as data modelling. The methodology is supported by a CASE tool called information engineering workbench.

Object-oriented methodology

Although object-oriented development has much in common with the structured approaches described in this chapter, it differs in that it focuses on the notion of objects that encapsulate both data and methods (processes). This means that objects can be developed and then reused in other parts of the system without worrying greatly about their internal structure. For example, suppose that there is an object that is a picture. It could be developed to include the method to display it on the screen, so that if the object is reused in another part of the system, it carries with it the code to display it. The object acts as a self-contained feature of the system.

Traditional structured techniques were developed when data was mainly text based. Increasingly, systems have to store multimedia information, so object-oriented methods are seen as a more appropriate way of handling these diverse forms of data. Object-oriented development has also made an impact on web applications through the use of Java applets. Java is an object-oriented programming language, which can be used for developing web applications or stand-alone applications.

A class serves as a template from which to create objects. The class defines the properties (data values) that can be stored for an object and the methods or functions that can be performed on the data. For example, a STUDENT class could be created that provided a template that included a student's personal details, such as First_Name, Last_Name, Date_of_Birth, Sex and so on. The methods could be Add_Student(), Delete_Student() (see figure 6.19(a)). This class could then be used to create objects that store students' actual personal details (see figure 6.19(b)).

Student	Student: 095614
PROPERTIES	PROPERTIES
Student_ID:	Student_ID: 095614
First_name:	First_name: James
Last_name:	Last_name: Jones
Date_of_birth:	Date_of_birth:
Sex:	23021980
METHODS	Sex: Male
Add_student()	METHODS
Delete_student()	Add_student()
	Delete_student()

(a) Class for student   (b) Object for student

Figure 6.19 A class and object

Inheritance is another key concept of object-oriented development. A superclass or parent class can have subclasses or children. These subclasses inherit all of the data (properties) and methods (behaviour) from the parent class. In addition, a subclass can have properties and methods of its own. This means that properties and methods are being reused at the subclass level. For example, a university is made up of staff and students. Both require an ID, name and address and other personal details and methods to create a new university member and to delete a member. However, the student class will record data about courses enrolled in, grades and so on, whereas the staff member will need a method to process payment details (see figure 6.20). When classes are arranged in a hierarchy, it allows the reuse of properties and methods, which in turn improves efficiency.

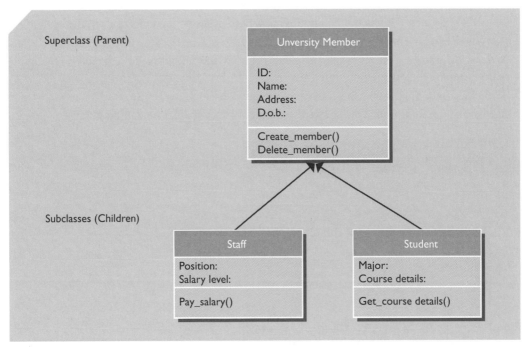

Figure 6.20 Inheritance in object-oriented development

Object-oriented approaches have several advantages from a systems development perspective:

> *Reuse of objects is encouraged.* This cuts down on the development time required for new systems because objects are reused when new subsystems are developed.

> *Systems are more reliable.* Because an object is a self-contained entity with its own data and processes, it should be reliable, robust and less likely to have undesirable effects on other parts of the system. Also, the reuse of objects that have been tried and tested improves the reliability of systems.

> *The development paradigm is consistent.* Object-oriented approaches cover analysis, design and implementation by object-oriented programming languages.

> *Flexibility is improved and complexity is reduced.* The basic objects can be used like building blocks, which can be drawn into the development of new subsystems.

> *Objects are based on features of the business that are unlikely to change rapidly as opposed to the specific information needs of users at any given time.*

From a systems development perspective, objects need to be defined along with their relationships to other objects for the system being developed. This is termed **object modelling**. The properties (data) and methods (procedures) for each object would then need to be detailed.

Although a range of object-oriented methods have been developed, the Unified Modelling Language (UML) has become widely accepted. UML includes a range of modelling techniques for identifying and presenting the objects in a system and the relationships between them. Some of the most commonly used UML diagrams are (Kendall & Kendall 2005):

> *Use-case diagram.* This describes how the system is used. Figure 6.21 is a simple use-case diagram illustrating how a customer interacts with a company in relation to orders.
> *Use-case scenario.* This is not a diagram but text to describe the behaviour in the system.
> *Activity diagram.* This shows the flow of activities.
> *Sequence diagram.* This shows the sequence of activities taking place reflected by the inter-actions among the objects through time.
> *Class diagram.* This shows the classes and relationships.
> *State transition diagram.* This shows the different states that an object might have.

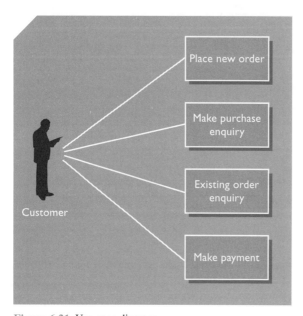

Figure 6.21 Use-case diagram

Prototyping

Prototypes have been used by engineers for many years. They generally develop a small-scale working (or simulated) model of a product. In systems development, a prototype is used to supplement the SDLC to define requirements or try out designs. Structured methodologies were seen to be concentrated on documentation and were perceived as inflexible. If the users were uncertain about their requirements, the methodology became a barrier to the progress of the project. Developers became frustrated by this scenario and many questioned the need for full documentation on all projects. Prototyping was seen as a part solution to some of these problems. It relies on tools that enable the interface to be specified quickly. Examples of proto-typing tools are Microsoft Access and Visual Basic. It can be used as part of rapid application development (RAD), the main aim of which is to quickly put together a system shell by using structured methods, joint application design (JAD) techniques and prototyping methods.

Four types of prototyping have been identified: feasibility, requirements, design and implementation prototyping (Whitten, Bentley & Dittman 2000).

Feasibility prototyping

This is used to test the feasibility of a specific technology approach that might be used for an information system. For example, a college wants to improve its enrolment procedures, because too much time is spent on keying in the data, and it is believed that students could input the data directly into the computer system. So a prototype is designed to test a range of student reactions to inputting the details of enrolment. In other words, it allows some input and simulates some basic searches. On the basis of the students' reactions, the college can decide whether to go ahead.

Requirements prototyping

This type of prototyping is used to define the users' requirements. It is used as a tool to encourage interaction between users and developers. The prototype is composed of screens which have menus, icons and forms to illustrate the types of data to be captured or output. Users can then use the screens as a prompt to give further information. The actual design of the screens is not really important.

Design prototyping

The user interface of the system can be developed and shown to users. The users assess the ease of use, the layout, the order of input fields, help messages and so on, and provide feedback to the developers, who can then modify the prototype. After several iterations, the interface should be in line with what the users find acceptable to work with. However, the prototype may not become the finished system; another tool may be seen as more appropriate for implementing the software.

Implementation prototyping

When the design prototype is extended to become the actual system, it is called an implementation prototype. In this case, it would not include certain editing and security features, which would be added later.

Prototyping is not a return to development without a methodology and documentation. The development process needs to be managed and, ideally, used alongside another methodology. It should be used with set objectives in mind, such as for a small project or as part of the design of the interface of a large system. It is not a panacea for all systems development problems.

Rapid application development (RAD)

Rapid application development (RAD) is a systems development approach that is aimed at speeding up the development process. It combines prototyping, CASE and JAD in an iterative cycle until the users and developers are satisfied with the system designs. JAD involves collecting requirements in a group-based situation. The developers and users work closely together, with an emphasis on getting the system developed. It was put forward by Martin as a reaction to the problems with methodologies that followed a more traditional SDLC, in which the development process was thorough but often seen as time consuming.

> **Reflection question 5:** Why do you think developing systems quickly is of concern to systems developers?

Agile software development

Agile software development can be defined as a method of software development that aims for customer satisfaction through the early and continuous delivery of useful software components. The approach tries to reduce the failure rate associated with many software projects.

It is really a bundle of ideas based on the following principles:

> Start with only the essential requirements.
> Develop, complete and accept code in small increments.
> Use small development teams.
> Have members of the team work together on writing and checking code.
> Involve non-IT executives in project teams.

Extreme programming is a development method derived from the agile development approach with the same aims of improving software development times and reducing the risk of project failure.

Soft systems methodology (SSM)

Soft systems methodology (SSM) grew out of dissatisfaction with structured techniques for their underestimation of the issues associated with defining the problem or problems with the current systems and in defining a way forwards. Peter Checkland developed the methodology not just as an information systems methodology but as a general problem-solving approach (Checkland & Scholes 1990). SSM has seven stages but has, at its core, the development of 'rich pictures' and the ethos of empowering users to decide on the acceptability and desirability of any changes to be made. The rich picture is a freeform sketch drawn by the user. It incorporates such things as concerns, challenges, issues, politics and competition. The SSM sessions are facilitated so that they promote open discussion, based on the idea that real progress cannot be made until the issues and concerns are acknowledged.

Figure 6.22 is a rich picture that illustrates the problems that a merged company called 'New Accounts' is experiencing. Briefly, a successful accounting company called Taskers merged with another, Account-Right, to form New Accounts. However, each company has different IT systems and there is a need to integrate the two information systems to be effective. The separate systems are costing the company a fortune and the director of New Accounts can see money being wasted. Account-Right's systems are old and out of date but it has a support and maintenance contract that runs for another year. To break it would cost money but the chief information officer (CIO) is considering doing so because it may still save the company money to have an integrated system. To add to this, the support company is quite a distance away in Faraway Town and is not always responsive to their needs. The CIO is wondering whether she should take the axe to this system and abandon it altogether and go with the system that seems to be working well at the Taskers' premises. The staff at Taskers are well trained (almost to the level of computer Olympiads!). The cultures of the two firms now need to be brought together because the staff at what was once Account-Right think Taskers staff have a much better environment to work in. To add to the problems, there are two positions vacant in the IT department, one for a web developer and one for a systems developer. The CIO has spoken to some IT consultants but so far, they all seem to be expensive.

It is not expected that the rich picture will have a lot of meaning to someone who is not involved in the system but to those who are, the symbols and icons can usually easily be recognised.

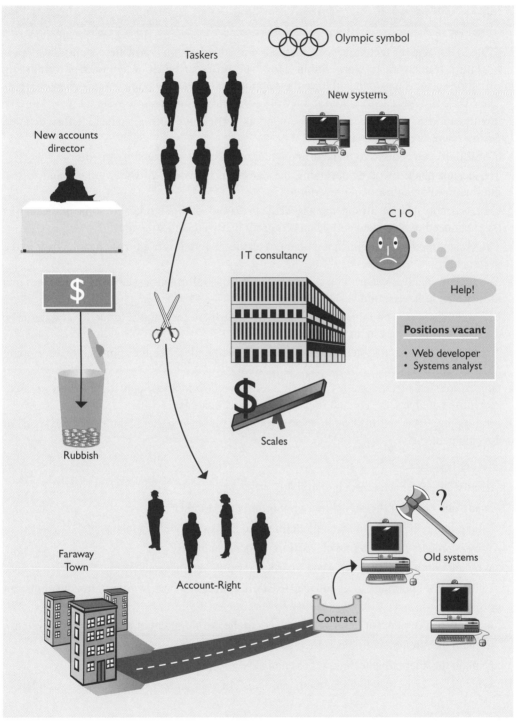

Figure 6.22 An example of a rich picture

Summary

The SDLC and the techniques and methods embedded within it provide systems developers with a framework to work within. However, different types of approaches to building information systems exist, and all have their applications. The key points in this chapter are:

> The SDLC provides a structured framework for building information systems.
> Identification of problems and requirements is carried out during analysis before detailed design issues are considered.
> CASE tools can be used to manage and document the development of systems.
> The design phase involves designing the database, network, software, reports and forms, interface and organisational procedures.
> Cost, warranty, leasing arrangements and the proximity of the supplier are some of the factors that may need to be considered when acquiring hardware and software.
> The system requires a significant amount of testing before it is eventually handed over to the users.
> The systems analyst needs to be skilled in the various information-gathering techniques and ideally should have sound business skills.
> ERDs, DFDs, decision tables and structured English are techniques to model and describe the data and processes in an organisation.
> The term 'information systems methodology' is used to describe the approach to developing an information system.
> Object-oriented methodologies form an alternative development approach, which involves specialised analysis, design and implementation techniques.
> Prototyping, RAD and JAD are methodologies that emphasise user involvement and speed of development.

Questions

1. Briefly describe each phase in the SDLC.
2. Is any one phase of the SDLC more important than another?
3. Where in the SDLC would data modelling and process modelling take place?
4. Why is process modelling a vital skill for systems analysts?
5. Why are communication skills so important for the systems analyst?
6. Is it always important to conduct a feasibility study as part of a systems development project?
7. Is there an argument for not involving users in the development of an information system?
8. Explain the strengths of object-oriented methodologies.
9. Explain the alternative techniques to changeover from one system to another.
10. What are systems development methodologies? In your answer provide some examples.

Exercises

1. Use the Internet to gather information on prototyping. Compare and contrast the different styles of prototyping used in information systems development.

2. A real estate agency manager is considering buying personal digital assistants (PDAs), including mobile phone, for his workforce of estate agents. The PDAs will have a calendar, email access, camera, personal organiser tools and can be synchronised with desktop applications. Assess the broad benefits and costs associated the idea.

3. Review the skills required by a systems analyst. Assess your capabilities and limitations in relation to these skills. Try to give yourself a score (out of a maximum of ten) for each skill. Justify your decision, and provide an example that demonstrates your use of the skill in the past. Present the skills analysis in a table.

CASE STUDY: Content management systems at Kromann Reumert

Kromann Reumert is a top law firm in Denmark, which employs about 500 people. The company has offices in Copenhagen, Aarhus, London and Brussels. The company provides full legal support to the corporate sector. Two companies merged to form Kromann Reumert, which created a need to design a new content management system. Searching for information can take up considerable time in a law firm that has thousands of documents. The aim was to create a new system that would enable employees to quickly and easily find information. It had to fit with the way people worked, rather than staff adapting to the way the software worked.

One of the two firms had a content management system but it was not working well. The functionality was basic and the vendor did not bring out regular upgrades to the system. Overall, the system was slow and the database was unstable. Much time was spent on rebuilding the system database, which meant that staff could not get on with their work.

It was decided to look at a new centralised content management system, rather than stay with the existing system. The key requirements for the new system were that it had to be an intuitive system and provide comprehensive functionality around the sharing of documents and collaborative working. It was also important to find a vendor that would upgrade the software so that it would develop as the company developed.

Several software systems were investigated. A steering committee was formed, which consisted of people from across the company. The vendors gave presentations and demonstrated the systems. The committee scored the systems on a range of criteria that covered their requirements. The software finally selected met all of their requirements.

The implementation of the software was done as part of a major IT infrastructure project, in which most of the systems in the company were replaced. The new system was seen as a building block that would fit with the other systems. Each building block of the IT infrastructure was implemented in turn. After a short pilot project, the content management system was rolled out live across the company. The users were sent on a two-day course to learn about the new system.

The company have used surveys of the users to identify any problems with the new system. They then discussed these with the vendor and made sure they were dealt with. Today, all employees are using the system. Documents that once were printed and stored in filing cabinets, which took up considerable office space, are now stored in the enterprise repository.

(continued)

This has also helped the sharing of knowledge across the organisation. Collaborative work spaces improved team productivity. Overall, the system integrated seamlessly with other corporate systems.

An evaluation of the system was conducted three months after implementation to determine whether all of the expected benefits were being realised. The company found that it had significantly reduced the time spent on retrieving documents, which was providing substantial savings. The system meant that client needs could be met more quickly, so customer satisfaction improved. Staff were highly satisfied with the system and the level of support provided by the vendor was excellent.

Kromann Reumert is now looking to extend the system with further modules, such as one that provides reports and statistics on what documents people are spending the most time on or do not use at all. This will enable the company to streamline processes even further.

Source: Information from www.hummingbird.com/us/kro.

Questions

1. Why could Kromann Reumert not use the content management system that was in place in one of the premerger firms?

2. What were Kromann Reumert's requirements for the new content management system?

3. How did Kromann Reumert go about selecting a vendor and system?

4. What did the company opt to conduct a pilot implementation before full implementation?

5. What were the key benefits of the new system?

6. Was a post-implementation evaluation really necessary?

References

Checkland, P & Scholes, J 1990, *Soft systems methodology in action*, John Wiley & Sons, Chichester.

Kendall, K & Kendall, J 2005, *Systems analysis and design*, 6th edn, Prentice Hall, Upper Saddle River, NJ.

Martin, J 1989, *Information engineering*, vol. 1, Prentice Hall, Englewood Cliffs, NJ.

—— 1990, *Information engineering*, vols 2 and 3, Prentice Hall, Englewood Cliffs, NJ.

Whitten, JL, Bentley, LD & Dittman, K 2000, *Systems analysis and design methods*, McGraw-Hill, New York.

CHAPTER 7
Strategic information systems management

LEARNING OBJECTIVES

After reading this chapter, you should be able to:

» explain the significance of strategic information systems planning in organisations

» explain how information systems and information technology (IT) can be used as a strategic driver

» describe the components of an information architecture and its importance in information systems strategic planning

» describe various forms of strategic analysis that can be used in information systems planning

» explain the advantages and disadvantages of outsourcing the information systems function

» explain the resource-based view of strategy development and how information systems and IT can be used to support it.

Introduction

Anyone who owns a PC will know how quickly technology changes. Those who use technology at work or at home may sometimes think how they can make their work or life easier, be more efficient or just have more fun with hardware upgrades or new software. Large business organisations are no different — with the exception of fun, perhaps. In the rapidly changing business environment, managers must constantly assess the contribution that technology and new or improved information systems can make to their organisation.

Who is responsible for keeping an organisation at the forefront of information systems and IT developments so that it is competitive in its business sector? Although good ideas can come from anyone in an organisation, the bulk of the responsibility for developing leading-edge information systems rests with the senior information systems management team. It must give considerable thought to these issues. Leading-edge information systems strategies rarely happen by accident. Information systems managers have the responsibility for developing information systems strategy and managing the day-to-day information systems operations of the organisation. This chapter focuses on the process of developing information systems strategy and chapter 8 examines the operational aspects of information systems management.

Information systems strategic plans can be developed in several ways. It is not the aim of this chapter to cover them all, but rather to explore some examples of information systems strategic thinking to provide insights into how information systems can be maximised for organisational advantage. The concept of competitive advantage is examined, together with how information systems can be used to gain it. Other strategic approaches include developing an information systems and IT architecture, using information systems and IT to support the business goals of the organisation and to improve efficiency and effectiveness through value-chain analysis.

The importance of strategy

A strategy is a plan for achieving medium- and long-term goals. When this is specified for an organisation in a document that covers such things as the vision and mission of the business, the organisation's goals and how it will achieve them, then it is called a strategic plan (Bartol et al. 1998).

Strategic planning has been much maligned in recent years. Some critics pointed to all the strategic plans that were resting on the shelves of senior executives that were never referred to after they were completed. However, this is not a fault of strategic planning itself but rather a failing of management to follow through and implement the plans. Critics may argue that in a rapidly changing business environment, developing large-scale detailed plans that quickly become out of date has little point. Those in favour of strategic planning argue that a loose-fitting, general framework or plan is better, one that can accommodate changes in technology and in the business environment. As you work through the chapter, consider this argument and make up your own mind about the usefulness of the approaches.

> **Reflection question 1:** Can you think of other reasons strategic plans might never become reality?

A strategic plan is important for two main reasons. First, it provides the organisation with a focus and clear mission, which can be communicated to employees, suppliers and customers.

The problem with CRM systems

An Association of National Advertisers/Booz Allen Hamilton (ANA/BAH) survey on CRM has found that most CRM projects fail to deliver expected returns because the information systems and marketing strategies are not aligned with the organisational strategy.

The Customer Communications Group (Inc), a North American company specialising in CRM implementations, has found recurring problems with CRM initiatives:

> no corporationwide CRM strategy; failure to develop a shared management perspective of CRM opportunity
> lack of clearly defined and measurable business objectives
> attempts to develop skills and infrastructure too quickly, looking for the 'big bang'
> little or no attention paid to employee skills and abilities; too great a focus on tools and hardware, not humanware
> change in the organisation is not managed well, leading to functional barriers as well as philosophical roadblocks. Everyone must see and understand where they will benefit
> inappropriate sequencing plan for CRM investments (e.g. building technology before strategy or expectations)
> failure to understand which business processes must be optimised to support the strategies
> program not in line with the brand position and customers' expectations
> quality of data not properly considered
> failure to create rigorous controls and testing.

CRM is multidimensional. It has a functional component, which includes the services and technology, and a strategic component, which includes the vision, mission and culture of the organisation. According to the Customer Communications Group (Inc), 'One cannot succeed without the other, and they must be developed and executed harmoniously'.

Source: Information from www.customer.com.

People work better and more productively when they understand what the aim of the business is. They can make decisions more easily and effectively if they have a clear understanding of the organisation's goals. A clear strategy can be useful externally, because suppliers and customers know what the organisation stands for.

[**Key concept:** Strategic planning enables a company to focus on what is important.]

Second, in the process of developing a strategic plan, the organisation should be able to identify where its strengths lie and how it can create or maintain a competitive advantage over other organisations.

Information systems strategic planning is concerned with helping the organisation achieve its strategy. For example, if a business had a strategy to tap into global markets, then information systems management would look at how the information systems could support this. One option would be to look at how the Internet could be used to reach new markets. This would need to be specified in the information systems strategic plan. You might be thinking that the information systems strategic plan is constantly changing, and to some extent you are right, because the information systems strategic plan is a dynamic entity and needs to be continually updated in line with the organisation's strategy. However, because a strategy contains high-level goals, it stays relevant for longer than many would think.

Customer relationship management (CRM) is a business strategy to manage customer relationships long term to add value. CRM becomes a strategic focus for the organisation when it embraces management, strategy and organisational culture. Therefore, it cannot be effective if viewed solely as a technology solution.

Information systems and IT as a strategic driver of the business

In the early years of computerised information systems, the focus was on automating the day-to-day transactions of the business and consequently producing significant cost savings. These transaction-based systems contained great volumes of data in files that could be interrogated and summarised to produce management information. Decision support systems were more interactive systems that managers could use to improve their decision making. However, the view of the role of information systems was one of supporting the rest of the organisation. In more recent times, information systems have in some cases taken on the role of **strategic driver** in organisations. In other words, the information systems are not just supporting other functions in the business but are the main reason for a company improving its position in relation to its competitors. In this sense, the information systems become a strategic driver for the business.

For information systems to be considered strategic, they should be helping the organisation achieve its goals and objectives and not just playing a role in the operational aspects of the business.

[**Key concept:** New technologies create opportunities for improvement and competitive advantage.]

Information systems management in organisations

Information systems management in larger organisations operates on several levels. A key person is the **chief information officer (CIO)**, who has overall responsibility for the information systems and for developing the information systems strategy for the business. The CIO does not typically get involved with operational (day-to-day) activities of the information systems function, but works with functional managers to ensure the information systems are delivering the desired services.

The executive board of a business is responsible for developing the strategy of the organisation and will be led by the **chief executive officer (CEO)**. The CIO advises the board on information systems issues and strategy and implements the board's directives.

The CIO may be called the information systems manager in smaller organisations but has similar responsibilities. However, the position may call for more involvement in operational activities and any crisis that might arise.

Other management members with responsibilities within the information systems function include the project manager, who takes charge of particular projects, and senior systems analysts, who are responsible for managing other analysts and programmers.

The role of strategic planning

You may have heard the saying 'If you fail to plan you plan to fail'. This is true of running a business. It is important for any business organisation that wants to operate effectively over the medium and long term to have a vision and strategic plan. A strategic plan should provide a focus for an organisation. Without a strategic plan, a company will concentrate on the day-to-day activities and lose sight of the big picture. The 'big picture' in this case is developing the goals and strategies to stay ahead of competitors. Strategic plans can be developed at several levels of the business and should ideally be integrated. The plan should be communicated to all stakeholders. Stakeholders can include employees, shareholders, the board of directors, customers and suppliers. An effective strategic plan that is properly communicated has the potential to radically improve the fortunes of a business. Any new CEO or CIO will work hard on developing a strategic plan for the company. It is the best chance of getting things working in the required way.

> **Reflection question 2:** Can you think of personal examples from any area of your life when you used a form of strategic planning?

A strategy is a large-scale plan used to achieve long-term goals. However, a corporate strategy is made up of a number of components (see figure 7.1 overleaf), which are discussed in later sections of this chapter. An organisation should have a vision statement, which defines in a few sentences the company's main purpose.

IS in action

Woodside's vision and mission

The Australian company Woodside Petroleum has the following vision and mission statements:

> Woodside's vision is to be a preferred partner of governments, joint venture participants, customers and communities due to delivery speed, commercial acumen, cost focus, technical capability and values.

> Woodside's mission is to create outstanding growth and shareholder wealth while conforming to its core values.

By achieving the company's mission and striving towards its vision, Woodside will satisfy shareholders while increasing the quality of life by meeting society's energy needs in ways that make people working for the company proud.

The people who work at Woodside have values based on strong performance, care and respect, integrity and trust, initiative and accountability, creativity and enterprise and working together.

Interestingly, Woodside's vision statement is concerned with providing service and being part of a network of organisations. IT can clearly play a big role in supporting Woodside's vision and mission by facilitating interorganisational relationships and communication.

Source: Information from Woodside Petroleum, 'Woodside mission, vision and values', www.woodside.com.au.

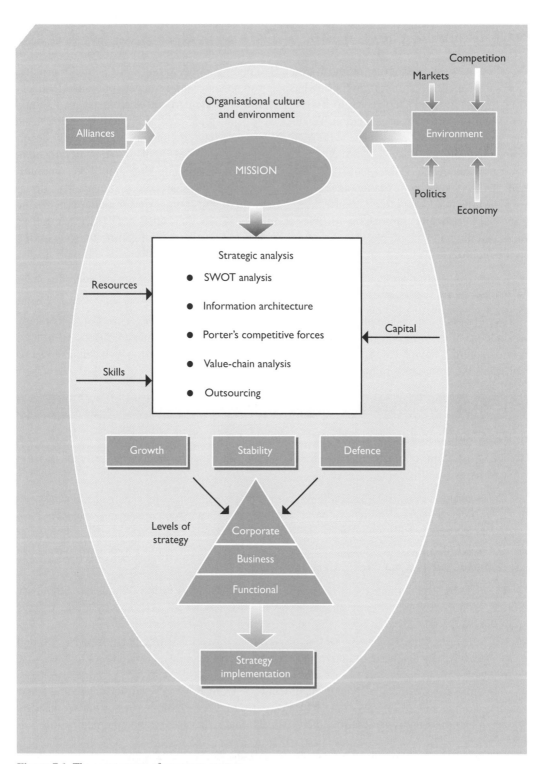

Figure 7.1 The components of corporate strategy

A vision statement can be expanded further to communicate broad organisational aims in a mission statement. These aims should provide a steering mechanism for the functional units where more detailed objectives and goals can be specified along with strategies to achieve them.

[**Key concept:** A holistic or systems perspective recognises that everything is connected to everything else and is important in achieving organisational success.]

A vision statement and mission statement are only two components of a strategic plan. Organisations typically develop strategies at three different levels: corporate, business and functional (see figure 7.2). The corporate-level strategy is developed by the senior people in the business. It can cover new business directions, the closing of some operations and the allocation of resources between branches of the company's operations.

Business-level strategy applies to organisations that have (semi)autonomous businesses operating independently. These businesses need to develop their own strategies as they are usually in the best position to do so. However, the business strategy should support the broad aims of the corporate strategy. In smaller organisations, the business unit level is not applicable.

Functional-level strategy is concerned with plans at the functional business level such as marketing, information systems and finance. Effective strategies at the functional level can provide a competitive edge to the organisation as a whole. For example, the development of e-commerce through a well-designed website has the potential to improve market share for an organisation.

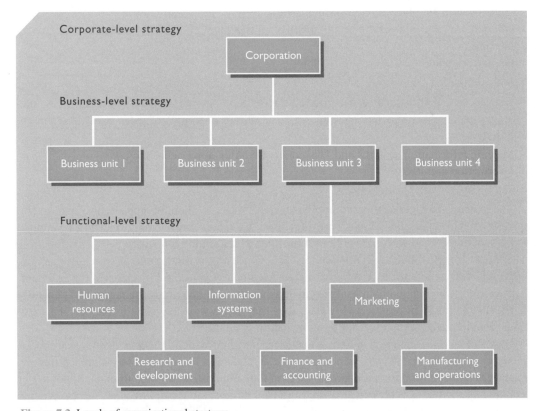

Figure 7.2 Levels of organisational strategy

Coordination of the different levels is essential for strategic planning to be effective. Corporate strategy must be backed up by aligned plans at the business and functional level.

[**Key concept:** Information systems strategy formulation follows a top-down approach.]

The aims of information systems strategic planning are to improve the performance of the business, to gain a competitive advantage, to add value to business processes and to improve productivity or reduce costs. It should not be driven by the desire to adopt technology as an end in itself. In other words, there should be sound business reasons for adopting the technology. However, this does not prevent the technology, in some circumstances at least, becoming a business driver. In business organisations, strategic planning should aim to add economic value. From an information systems perspective, strategic planning should result in improved economic value, although in government and nonprofit organisations, the emphasis may be on delivering a better service even if it costs the organisation more money.

Strategic analysis approaches

Information systems can contribute to the strategic direction of an organisation in many ways. The following sections examine several strategic planning approaches, each with their own strengths and weaknesses. They can be broadly divided into general managerially based strategic planning approaches and specific information systems strategic planning approaches.

General strategic planning approaches include:

> competitive analysis: Porter's competitive forces model, SWOT analysis, value-chain analysis
> business process re-engineering (BPR)
> outsourcing
> resource-based strategies focused on the internal competencies of the organisation. Knowledge management and the learning organisation are examples of more specific resource-based approaches.

Specific information systems and IT strategic planning approaches include:

> information architecture
> IT alignment with business goals.

The general managerially based approaches are strategic planning approaches that are frequently used in strategic planning at the organisational level. However, they can also be applied at the functional level within an organisation, such as within the information systems function. There are strengths and limitations associated with using a more general strategic planning approach within the information systems area. Methods such as SWOT analysis, Porter's competitive forces and value-chain analysis are reasonably well known by managers and generally fairly easy to apply in practice. However, they may not always translate to the specific functional requirements of an area such as information systems.

How does an information systems function determine which strategic planning approach is most suitable for them? This depends on the organisation in question, the approach that the managers feel comfortable with and the method they think is most suited to their situation. For example, if a company is feeling pressure from competitors, more emphasis may be put on using competitive analysis approaches, even at the functional level. If a company feels that they have many systems that do not integrate well, then it may want to stress an organisational information architecture. Of course, nothing stops an organisation using a combination of approaches, such as a competitive analysis, BPR and an information architecture plan. It should be remembered that strategic planning approaches did not evolve as a coherent group of methods. They have all developed independently. This section of the chapter provides an introduction to each method and how it can be used in the information systems field.

Competitive analysis

Competitive strategic analysis takes into account the competition in the business environment and the potential of using information systems and technology to gain a competitive advantage over other companies. There are several versions of strategic analysis. This section examines Porter's competitive forces model and SWOT analysis.

Porter's competitive forces model

A commonly referred to framework for analysing the competition within an industry is Porter's competitive forces model (Porter 1985), as discussed in chapter 1. Although the model was not initially intended for use in IT strategy formulation, it can prove useful for IT strategic planning.

The five forces can form a framework for analysing potential threats. Information systems managers can examine how information systems can be used to alleviate the competitive forces. For example, a company might look at how the Internet could be used to promote cost effectiveness in acquiring products from suppliers, or it could set up an electronic marketplace (e-market) or join one to have more flexibility in choosing suppliers. (An e-market is a market-like environment conducted over the Internet, in which buyers and sellers are matched with one another. An example would be eBay.) A way of controlling the threat from competitors is to form some alliance or merger with them. In this respect, the external industrial forces become internalised. Information systems can be used to support such changes.

Some might argue that Porter's model is a reactionary approach to strategic planning because changes may not be proposed until the threat becomes severe. It is also mainly concerned with competition — if there is little direct competition, there may be no impetus for change and improvement.

SWOT analysis

SWOT analysis is another form of competitive analysis (Thompson & Strickland 1995). The competitive situation for a company is assessed by examining its strengths (S), weaknesses (W), environmental opportunities (O) and threats (T). The competitive analysis will yield different results for each business examined. However, some broad categories of strengths and weaknesses may be a useful aid in the analysis (see table 7.1 overleaf).

The 'S' in SWOT analysis relates to the internal strengths of the business, such as stream-lined administrative systems or technologically adept staff. The internal weaknesses of the organisation can be detailed in much the same way. The wider environment can be scanned for economic, technological and social trends that can be exploited. New government legislation may create an opportunity for some organisations; for example, government departments may require suppliers to conform to new software standards. This creates opportunities for software consultants and IT-training organisations, which could help companies become accredited. The external threats need to be considered because future prosperity depends on how the organisation deals with these.

Consider the travel industry, for example, and in particular the role of the travel agency. A strength of many travel agencies is the personal customer service they provide. This, in turn, often results in a high level of customer loyalty. Many travel agents have expert knowledge on certain holiday destinations and have a wealth of experience in the industry. One of the weaknesses of travel agencies is that they typically offer only what is available through their customer reservation systems, which is a quite restricted set of options. Many travel agencies also operate on small profit margins. Of course, there are opportunities in relation to using the Internet. Threats come from all sides: airlines offering direct ticket sales to consumers and online travel agencies and travel brokers marketing directly to the consumer.

TABLE 7.1 SWOT analysis examples

| Internal to organisation | | External to organisation | |
Strengths	Weaknesses	Opportunities	Threats
Sound management	Poor administrative procedures	Growth market	Skills shortage
Greatest market share	Low profit margin	New government legislation	Recession in economy
Latest technology infrastructure	High staff turnover	Advantages of new technology capitalised on	New product developments create obsolescence of current materials
Highly skilled staff	Poor market image	Expand into new markets	Increasing competition
Low-cost product development	High-cost product development	Niche product	New legislation

infobyte

Spreadsheets are not enough!

As business in general becomes more complex, small companies are being faced with problems that are more common for much larger companies. Greater competition brought about by the forces of globalisation, new technologies and tougher tax compliance legislation are all making life more difficult for small business. Many small businesses use spreadsheets to record data and provide basic charting analysis but some have started to look at more sophisticated modelling tools to provide business intelligence. Business intelligence software can summarise and present data graphically to provide a high-level overview as well as allowing a detailed perspective of operations. This class of system can enable small companies to make decisions quickly, which in turn can create a competitive advantage.

Gathering information about the business environment from various sources is known as environmental scanning. Environmental scanning is not a form of competitive analysis in its own right but rather a technique for helping in competitive analysis. It can be used, for example, to identify opportunities and threats in the business environment as part of a SWOT analysis. The Web can be a useful environmental scanning tool.

IS in action

The following is an executive summary from an IT plan. You will notice many of the key features of planning from this chapter highlighted in the overview.

United States Patent and Trademark Office
Office of the Chief Information Officer Strategic Information
Technology Plan FY 2005 – FY 2010

EXECUTIVE SUMMARY

The mission of the Office of the Chief Information Officer (OCIO), in support of the U.S. Patent and Trademark Office (USPTO), is *to provide quality information products and services for our customers*. In support of that mission, the Strategic Information Technology Plan links the OCIO's goals and objectives to the USPTO's 21st Century Strategic Plan to assure that the OCIO meets customer business needs using agile, productive, and innovative approaches. Additionally, the Strategic Information Technology Plan supports the USPTO's efforts to comply with the government-wide initiatives in the President's Management Agenda.

The **Introduction** to the Strategic Information Technology Plan provides a general view of the OCIO's mission, vision, and principles and how they position the USPTO to face key challenges, including the move to the new Alexandria Headquarters, the growth in patent and trademark applications, increased business dependency on information technology, an increasingly remote workforce, and the need for international coordination. This section also provides an overview of the accomplishments to date and how the OCIO will build on these achievements in the future.

The **Strategic Goals and Objectives** sections describe the four strategic goals along with the specific objectives and tasks that support each of them. Goal 1, *Enable the USPTO to implement electronic government in its patent and trademark business areas to reduce paper handling and enhance business processes*, provides a focus for the development of innovative and agile services. Goals 2, 3 and 4 summarize the OCIO's commitment to operational excellence and to a clear linkage between business processes and technology. Goal 2 is to *Provide and support a world-class information technology operation that meets or exceeds end-user needs*. Goal 3 is to *Leverage enterprise architecture to improve information technology efficiency, effectiveness, and quality*, simplifying and unifying through initiatives such as high availability architecture. Goal 4 is to *continuously improve the delivery of OCIO information products and services to meet USPTO business objectives*.

(continued)

The OCIO strategic goals represent a five-year blueprint for implementing USPTO's information technology that supports its mission. The **Conclusion** summarizes a longer-term vision of the USPTO as those plans come to fruition. By 2010, the OCIO's internal and external customers will interface with a quality-focused, highly productive, responsive organisation meeting and exceeding customer requirements through continuous improvement of products and services. Initiatives in support of electronic government (e-Government) will have reduced reliance upon, and in some cases eliminated, inefficient paper processes. Electronic communication of applications and documents with applicants will occur seamlessly, facilitated by an integrated customer-facing government-to-business and government-to-citizen electronic government approach that brings the USPTO closer to its customers and stakeholders.

Source: This article appeared on www.uspto.gov.

>**Reflection question 3:** What types of information may be difficult to find on the Web?

[**Key concept:** Use the tools around you to maximum advantage, in this case, the Web for environmental scanning. Most people use only a small percentage of any tool's potential.]

Information architecture

The management information systems function of the organisation should develop its own strategic plan that supports the corporate plan. This will cover its own mission and strategic directions, and identify opportunities and threats. The management information systems strategic plan's main thrust is to develop and explain the information architecture that will provide the best return for the organisation. The information architecture defines the data, processes, information, organisational network and the stakeholders; it explains IT trends and opportunities and it outlines the technology to support the business aims of the organisation.

Clearly, the information architecture should be aligned with organisational business goals. The terms 'information architecture' and 'IT architecture' are sometimes used interchangeably. However, the IT architecture is actually a subset of the overall information architecture for an organisation.

The IT architecture defines the computer hardware and network infrastructure, and includes the network, systems and applications software. Your own university or college will no doubt have put considerable thought into its IT architecture, so that it can provide the best service possible to students. IT staff would have taken into account the need for general and specialist software, such as PCs running Windows software and desktop applications and more specialist scientific applications. The university's IT management would have thought through the effectiveness of the network and the compatibility issues of machines with different systems software. It will also be aware of the issues related to students connecting to the university systems from home. The aim in this type of environment is to provide a high level of service to each student but at the same time make the systems work together in a cost-effective manner. If the organisation has a general IT architecture that is regularly updated, serious issues related to performance, support and compatibility will be avoided.

The data systems within an organisation should be considered as part of the information architecture. A company that takes an enterprisewide view of its data and information is more likely to manage it effectively, so that data redundancy, duplication and errors are minimised. Compatible database systems, data warehouses and web databases all need to be considered.

The adoption and use of applications software within a company require planning. The unregulated adoption of software packages has implications for incompatibility of files, training and support for the software and the expense associated with separate licensing agreements.

The organisation of the information systems function needs to be considered. For example, the information systems function must decide whether to be concentrated as a group or release some staff to work closely with users in other departments and build up specialist knowledge.

[**Key concept:** Developing a coherent information architecture is always near the top of an information systems or IT manager's wish list.]

infobyte

Some people in the IT profession argue that we are no nearer achieving IT alignment in the business world than we were 20 years ago. This is despite the issue of IT alignment still being top of the list for IT executives. IT alignment refers to the process of aligning the IT systems with organisational strategy. However, it is unclear just which part of the business strategy the IT should align with! Should it match the mission, vision, competitive strategies or the business goals. Many times in organisations, the strategies are broad and the goals unclear, so the art of alignment in IT is to convert the strategies into specific goals. Even if the goals are clarified, there are always many ways to achieve them. Information systems and IT professionals therefore need to understand the business and be able to be creative in their solutions to really deliver benefits for the business.

Alignment of information systems with business goals

The development of information systems is usually considered a business decision, not just an IT decision. There are IT decisions to be made, of course, but any IT development should be driven by the business needs of the organisation. Generally, information systems should follow a top-down approach, so that the resulting systems are aligned with the strategic objectives of the organisation.

Woodside's mission statement, discussed earlier in the chapter, suggests the need to align the information systems function strategically with the organisational goals. Information systems can be used to help manage mineral-resource projects. The global focus of the company means that its systems are tightly integrated to facilitate global communication. Systems to provide information for decision-making purposes to save costs would be aligned with the goal of maximising shareholder value. This may include business intelligence software to provide an extra level of analysis and data mining. Information systems can also be used to support the safety of employees. Safety data can be gathered, analysed and presented through simple modelling tools such as a spreadsheet package.

It is worth considering potential outcomes from developments that are driven by IT without due consideration of the strategic directions of the business. These types of projects can result in systems that:

> take too much time and money to develop because they do not have the full backing of senior people

> do not provide a significant return to the organisation because they are peripheral to the core business needs

> displace other, perhaps more worthwhile, projects from being developed because they consume organisational resources

> are not maintained effectively and eventually become a problem for the business. The information systems may be poorly perceived by the customers, employees or both.

There is a place in organisations for experimentation. Systems may be tried out and the returns monitored. However, they must be recognised as experiments with appropriate budget allocations which the organisation can afford to write off if the experiment does not produce worthwhile results. Projects that use leading-edge technology or use technology in an innovative way and are aligned with corporate strategy have the potential to provide a competitive advantage for the business.

It should be recognised that while strategic alignment of the information systems with the business strategy is important, it is a continually moving target. An organisation's strategy is continually evolving and therefore the process of aligning the information systems is one that is continually changing also.

Hirschheim and Sabherwal (2001) have identified three strategic information systems alignment profiles for three business strategies:

> *Utility profile: alignment through low-cost delivery.* The business takes a defensive position and is concerned with lowering costs and making efficiencies. The information systems function has itself to be economical and is based on a centralised and outsourced model of operation.

> *Alliance profile: alignment through partnering.* The information systems supports the existing business operations but also helps identify opportunities for new products and services. The information systems function plays a role in building partnerships among organisations and needs to be flexible. This model typically sources information systems selectively.

> *Infusion profile: alignment through business leadership.* The information systems is used to change the market, so it is a catalyst for business innovation. Information systems in-sourcing is used to develop the necessary expertise and competencies. The information systems function is typically decentralised to be closely aligned with business units.

Business process re-engineering (BPR)

The concept of business process re-engineering (BPR) emerged in 1990 (Hammer 1990) and was further developed in a work produced by Hammer and Champy (1993). They define BPR as the fundamental rethinking and redesign of business processes to achieve dramatic improvements in critical, contemporary measures of performance. Their approach implies a radical approach to business change. Manganelli and Raspa (1995) suggest that a clean-slate approach to re-engineering is not always necessary because the business may have great strengths that require developing and improving. Therefore, incrementally improving or replacing key processes may be the preferred strategy. BPR is helped by IT and takes an added-value customer focus to the redesign and integration of organisational processes.

For example, an organisational process in a university is the student enrolment process. Many universities re-engineered this and related processes so that they could be conducted over the Web. Before re-engineering, students completed paper forms and queued up at enrolment time to submit their enrolments for that semester. The forms were checked by the administrative clerk and passed over for input into the computer system. If a student changed his or her mind, a change of enrolment form had to be completed. This involved a great deal of time from the perspective of both student and administration. Re-engineered enrolment systems on the Web have the advantage of flexibility since students can enrol from home or work at any time of day or night. The university does not need as many staff to receive and check forms and input the data, because data are now input directly by students. The re-engineering of this function has saved universities considerable money and provided a more flexible and convenient system for users.

Using value-chain analysis for strategic analysis

Value-chain analysis is, perhaps, a lower-level form of strategic analysis than, for example, SWOT analysis. It considers the organisation as a large input–output system. The inputs are resources brought into the organisation, processed in some way to add value, and then marketed and sold as outputs. The chain is usually supplemented by aftersales service. Value can be added at various points throughout the chain, such as acquiring products or resources more efficiently. The costs associated with each step and task in the value chain are determined. The costs are then compared with competitors' costs, and changes can be made to gain or sustain a competitive advantage.

Figure 7.3 is a value chain, showing where web applications can contribute at each stage. The value chain consists of primary and support activities. The primary activities are the key tasks and processes that return the most value. The secondary activities support the primary activities and do not provide the same level of returns. These include administration, research and development, human resources management and information systems development. Web applications can contribute to both primary and secondary activities. The approach results in incremental improvements to the organisation.

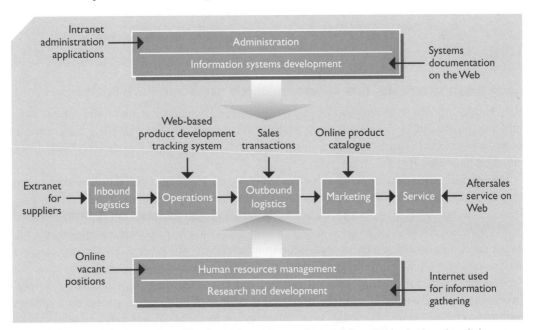

Figure 7.3 Uses of the Internet to add value to the primary and secondary activities in the value chain

Making improvements to the value chain through enterprise resource planning (ERP)

US wine and spirit business Brown-Forman Corporation employs 6500 people and sells into 130 countries. Its brands include Jack Daniel's and Southern Comfort. Although about three-quarters of the company's sales are from wine and spirits, Brown-Forman also manufactures and markets high-quality consumer goods such as china and luggage.

To ensure profit growth in an increasingly competitive international environment, the company needed to reduce costs and improve service. The solution was to ensure that production, inventory and distribution capabilities met the demands of the market by developing new supply chain processes. The proposal put forward was strategic in nature, with the following goals:

> to improve performance relative to that of competitors
> to reduce lost sales caused by lack of stock
> to lower inventory levels to reduce production and carrying costs
> to strengthen partnerships with distributors and suppliers.

These goals were achieved in part using ERP software (mySAP Supply Chain software). From a value-chain perspective, the major areas of focus were inbound and outbound logistics and inventory. The results of the project were that over 12 months, global inventory levels were reduced by 23 per cent; product availability was maintained at more than 99.9 per cent; transportation costs were decreased by reducing the number of carriers from 140 to 35 and airfreighting urgent shipments was generally stopped. A major benefit of the software was that it avoided the need to increase staff numbers by 80 per cent in the area of planning support.

Source: Information from: SAP AG 2003, 'MySAP supply chain management at Brown-Forman', SAP case study, www.sap.com.

Outsourcing as an information systems strategy

For strategic reasons, some organisations have decided to outsource some or all of their information systems and IT function. Outsourcing in this context means offloading the responsibility to an external organisation. One of the main reasons cited for doing this is to save costs, although there are others.

Various forms of IT outsourcing exist. For example, the external organisation might be used to manage the project but the people actually developing the system are internal to the organisation. This arrangement would be made when complex project management skills are required or when there is a history of projects not being completed on time or budget. On the other hand, a company might write the requirements definition and manage the process but have the external service provider actually develop the systems.

What are the benefits of information systems and IT outsourcing for a company? Several benefits are shown in table 7.2. But the strategic importance of information systems and IT in an industry sector and to an individual company is the key issue. Much depends on the resources and skills available in house and how the existing systems are integrated with critical business processes. The benefits assume that a suitable and effective external agent is available and that the company is satisfied with the service provided.

TABLE 7.2 The benefits of outsourcing

Benefit	Reason
Savings in information systems and IT	Reduces staffing levels
	Reduces information systems and IT training
	Reduces cost of information systems and IT recruitment
	Saves on hardware and software (some data may be processed at external service provider's site)
Better planning	Easier to determine budget and, therefore, to plan
Better decision making	Management free to focus on other areas of business
Access better skills	Recognises that external agency is the expert
Access better hardware and software	Recognises that information systems and IT are the core business of the external agency
Knowledge transfer	Possibility of internal staff learning from external agency

The literature on outsourcing suggests that the benefits outlined in table 7.2 do not always eventuate. For example, over time, the external service provider may increase prices significantly, posing the question whether it is cost effective to outsource. A company might feel that the level of service declines but it is locked in to the service provider contractually.

It may be difficult to gain a strategic advantage from information systems when the main responsibility for information systems is handed over to an external agency. Although service providers may work hard to keep the contract, it is unlikely they would be as strategically focused as the company employing them.

infobyte

Offshore partnering

Outsourcing across continents is increasing rapidly. This is termed 'offshore partnering', and it is driven in many cases by the desire to reduce costs. High-quality labour in such countries as India is the answer for many companies in the United States, UK and Australia. More and more senior executives with offshore experience are willing to look at this type of option. However, outsourcing internationally is not without its problems, especially in relation to working across timezones and in different cultures.

> **Reflection question 4:** What are some other problems associated with information systems and IT outsourcing?

[**Key concept:** There are always at least two sides to any information systems and IT issue.]

Resource-based strategies

Most strategic analysis approaches are based on outlining a strategic direction with complementary goals and objectives. Many organisations use one or a combination of strategic analysis methods, such as SWOT analysis, Porter's competitive forces model or value-chain analysis. However, another approach to developing an organisation's strategic competency is to focus less on the external environment and the threats from competitors and more on the internal competencies of the organisation. This approach can be classed as a resource-based view. The resource-based approach to strategy development focuses less on the external competitive environment and more on the internal resources of a company. These include physical resources such as machinery and technology but also intellectual capabilities, employee skills and even organisational culture. An IT function or department can take the same perspective in that it can develop the information systems and IT infrastructure and capability, as well as the information systems and IT expertise within the organisation. These features then become part of the resource base of the organisation and dictate its performance in the marketplace. According to one view of resource-based theory, 'what a firm possesses would determine what it accomplishes' (Das & Teng 2000).

In the fast-changing business world of today, it is advisable to create a dynamic and creative environment, which organically spawns ideas and develops effective courses of action. A more traditional approach to planning is one in which senior management set the strategic agenda and take into account the external competitive environment, whereas in a resource-based approach, the focus is on developing the expertise within the organisation, especially within knowledge-based industries. The aim of a resource-based view is to develop the internal resources of the organisation so much that this becomes the source of advantage by creating an organisational culture in which ideas and innovation are valued. Although the two approaches may seem opposed, they are not mutually exclusive. Making the development of the organisational resources and environment a key focus does not preclude strategic analysis in other forms being carried out. Goals, objectives and action plans are still needed but there is likely to be a much wider ownership and responsibility for setting strategy.

So what is behind the push for dynamic environments and new organisational forms? In a rapidly changing business world, companies need to be able to innovate to maintain a competitive advantage. Organisations must also be agile and able to change quickly to take advantage of opportunities and innovations. These attributes require new company structures. For example, rigid hierarchical management structures are notorious for slowing the decision-making process and, indeed, for killing innovation. Newer management approaches and organisational structures are moving towards the characteristics shown in table 7.3.

When an organisation embarks on creating its organisational culture afresh, it needs to develop appropriate information systems. The technological infrastructure in 'learning organisations' (i.e. companies with an ability to learn quickly), in which knowledge workers predominate, is typically quite sophisticated. It consists of widespread use of email, groupware for document management and control, a multifunctional intranet for knowledge management, heavy use of the Internet and the Web, powerful database query interfaces and perhaps business intelligence software.

Other aspects of creating a dynamic organisational environment are examined in later chapters. This section examines one particular approach that is related to creating a learning environment and managing knowledge effectively as an organisational strategy. The two concepts have a great deal of overlap, so they are discussed together. The aim with both is to develop the intellectual capital within the organisation and in so doing achieve greater success against competition.

TABLE 7.3 Features that characterise innovative business environments

Organisational feature	Traditional company	Dynamic company
Structure	Hierarchy and bureaucracy	Dispersed personnel and outsourcing
Defining features	Optimising existing processes Slow and methodical Conflict covered up	Innovation — create new processes Speed as a competitive edge Openness
Boundary role	Clear boundaries between functions Knowledge 'silos' Computers play support role	Few boundaries, knowledge sharing Networks and alliances Computer systems and networks essential
Business approach	Company defined by product and structure	Company defined by service and innovation
Decision making	Precision and certainty Avoid risk Centralised decision making and ideas	Live with uncertainty Take risks Decentralised decision making — ideas come from anywhere

Knowledge management and the learning organisation

Knowledge management and organisational learning have been proposed for years as methods by which organisations can improve productivity and sustain a competitive advantage in increasingly knowledge-based economies. They can be classified as resource-based approaches because they are concerned with developing the knowledge capital within a company. Despite the interest in knowledge management, the term still has some ambiguity, particularly in commercial circles, where it is sometimes used interchangeably with information management. However, knowledge management can be viewed as the process of creating, storing, managing, accessing and sharing tacit knowledge (in a person's head) and explicit knowledge (documented in books, intranets and so on). It relates to the corporate memory of an organisation and its intellectual capital.

Knowledge can be classified simply as follows:
> know-why: explanatory knowledge, scientific knowledge of principles (laws of nature)
> know-how: skills, the ability to organise resources to achieve desired outcomes
> know-who: social knowledge, referring to specific social relations, for example, who controls the resources needed in a particular situation

> know-when/know-where: economically useful knowledge about markets
> know-what: catalogue knowledge.

Many diverse companies are effectively developing knowledge management programs. These are applied to reducing costs, improving processes, improving productivity, improving time to market and increasing innovation. The types of applications include frequently asked questions, best practices, problem-solving software, decision support systems, resource management systems and asset management systems.

The term 'learning organisation' was used by Peter Senge (1990) to describe companies whose ability to learn quickly will provide them with a competitive edge. Although a learning organisation might generate new knowledge, it might not necessarily manage it effectively. This is where the learning organisation and knowledge management go hand in hand. Companies need to learn quickly in a rapidly changing environment, and efficiently manage and share the knowledge gained.

IS in action

Developing a knowledge management culture

William Baker worked for Texas Instruments (TI) in the United States for many years. In 1997, TI was bought out by Raytheon. Baker found the organisational culture at Raytheon very different from that at TI.

'Texas Instruments was a sharing, cooperative, collaborative environment,' Baker recalled. 'We went to Raytheon, and it was a whole other world, so bureaucratic that you had to ask the chairman and CEO to do anything. The good news was that I survived and became corporate knowledge management and benchmarking champion.' His role was to facilitate knowledge sharing within and outside of the company. It did not take long before Raytheon exhibited similar characteristics to TI.

The key characteristics of a knowledge-sharing culture are: encouragement of cooperation, and recognition of those who share knowledge, use knowledge shared by others and improve upon knowledge that is in the collective consciousness.

According to Baker and his colleague Michael English, simple knowledge transfer is not enough for an organisation to be effective. They argue that it requires rapid knowledge transfer, which combines knowledge management and systematic improvement methodologies in one place to create a knowledge-enabled culture. The methodology they propose has four phases:

1. searching for and importing best practices
2. learning, understanding and sharing knowledge
3. creating intellectual capital
4. converting that capital into value and profits.

Source: Information from Bolch, M 2006, 'Share and share alike', *The Manufacturer US*, www.themanufacturer.com.

[**Key concept:** The success of information systems is inextricably tied up with how the organisation functions as a unit. Information systems are not islands.]

Enterprise architecture versus service-oriented architecture

The concept of enterprise architectures arose in an era that emphasised the hardware architecture. Now people are talking about service-oriented architectures. According to some, service-oriented architecture is the bit that matters to everyone outside IT — and that is services! Service-oriented architectures define the processes that deliver value within the business for the users and customers. However, enterprise architectures should co-exist with service-oriented architectures because it is difficult to achieve a high level of service without a cross-enterprise view of IT and a set of standards. Even better enterprise architectures should include the expertise of the staff and not be just viewed as standards and hardware.

Summary

Strategic planning seems to be more of an art than a science. There are many ways to go about using information systems within organisations and no one strategic planning approach can guarantee business success. However, the methods presented do provide a starting point and framework for examining the potential of IT and information systems in organisations. The key points in this chapter are:

> A strategy is a medium-to-long-term plan outlining the goals of the organisation.
> The information systems plan in an organisation should be aligned with the organisation's strategic plan.
> Information systems managers can use one strategic planning method or several, including various forms of competitive analysis such as Porter's competitive forces model and SWOT analysis.
> On occasion, IT can act as a strategic driver in its own right.
> The information architecture is a plan for the organisation's information and technology infrastructure.
> Creating an effective knowledge-based organisational environment is a strategic direction facilitated by information systems.

Questions

1. Why should an information systems and IT plan be aligned to an organisation's strategic plan?
2. How can information systems be used to competitive advantage in organisations?
3. 'If you fail to plan, you plan to fail.' Discuss in relation to IT planning.
4. What is meant by an 'information architecture'?
5. What role can value-chain analysis play in strategic planning?
6. What are the likely consequences for organisations that do not perform any information systems strategic planning?
7. Describe and explain the strengths of three information systems strategic planning methods.

8. What are the perceived benefits of outsourcing the IT facilities of an organisation?

9. What is a resource-based view of strategic planning and how can information systems strategy support this?

10. How does knowledge management differ from information management?

Exercises

1. Choose an organisation with which you are familiar — it could be your own university. Outline what you consider to be the information architecture of the organisation.

2. In small groups, discuss how you acquire, record and share knowledge as part of your university or college course. Try to make the distinction between information and knowledge. Share your experiences as a group with the rest of the class. What role (if any) does technology play in your knowledge management experiences? Do you think students in universities have a knowledge-sharing culture?

3. What do you think are some of the problems with outsourcing information systems and IT operations overseas? Does it make sense in the long run?

4. Apply Porter's competitive forces framework to an organisation you are familiar with. For example, think of a travel agency and apply Porter's framework and how IT can be used to overcome some of the issues or threats.

5. Perform a SWOT analysis on an organisation with which you are familiar. How can information systems and IT be used to build on the strengths or take advantage of opportunities? How can information systems and IT be used to alleviate any of the weaknesses?

CASE STUDY: AP Consulting Group

AP Consulting Group is a leading management, information and technology consultancy, operating worldwide from 35 offices. It was started in North America more than 30 years ago. The company took over a consulting group in the UK 18 months ago and a consulting group with offices in Singapore, Hong Kong and Japan six months ago.

AP draws on the knowledge and expertise of 2000 employees, whose skills span a wider range of capability than any other major consulting firm. Its consultancy services — strategy, performance improvement, IT, technology, human resources, recruitment, program and project management — are helping its clients to transform their businesses to achieve significant increases in value, profitability and effectiveness.

Recently, AP re-examined its business processes and found that its offices and service groups did not communicate as well as they could. Expertise was not being used to the fullest to create a competitive advantage.

The success of the consultancy is based on being able to provide total business solutions on a global basis. Historically, parts of the AP Group had been insular because they were geographically distant. Now with the acquisition of the UK group and the group in Asia matters have become worse. The offices in each region have a different culture on a regional and organisational (group) level. The group based in Japan, Singapore and Hong Kong has a particular type of organisational culture, and the UK offices are often quite bureaucratic, which has tended to work against the creation of ideas and innovation. There is a perception that the UK offices do not want to be dictated to from North America and prefer to work autonomously.

The aim now is to come together globally and share not just best practice but also common and standard practice throughout the firm. For example, AP has built up methodologies over many years, but they need to be shared. There is a real need to communicate and share knowledge among service practices, industries and regions. Basically, it wants to manage knowledge more effectively.

The IT infrastructure is fragmented. Each region has its own systems and ways of providing IT support. There is a need to integrate these systems and set some standards for the organisation as a whole.

Overall, the IT and information and knowledge management problems reflect the problems associated with integrating the newly merged companies into one entity. The company's board realises that strategic thinking is required in relation to IT.

Questions

1. Explain how various strategic IT planning approaches could help AP Consulting Group in its current situation.

2. What are likely to be some of the benefits of integrating IT, data and knowledge better throughout the organisation?

3. Should AP Consulting Group concentrate on getting the basic IT infrastructure integrated first before it looks at managing knowledge more effectively?

References

Bartol, K, Martin, D, Tein, M & Matthews, G 1998, *Management: a Pacific Rim focus*, 2nd edn, McGraw-Hill, Sydney.

Das, TK & Teng, B 2000, 'A resource based theory of strategic alliances', *Journal of Management*, vol. 26, no. 1, pp. 31–61.

Hammer, M 1990, 'Re-engineering work: don't automate, obliterate', *Harvard Business Review*, July–August, pp. 104–12.

Hammer, M & Champy, J 1993, *Re-engineering the corporation: a manifesto for business revolution*, Nicholas Brearley Publishing, London.

Hirschheim, R & Sabherwal, R 2001, 'Detours in the path toward strategic information systems alignment', *California Management Review*, vol. 44, no. 1, pp. 87–108.

Manganelli, RL & Raspa, SP 1995, 'Why re-engineering has failed', *Management Review*, pp. 39–44.

Porter, ME 1985, *Competitive advantage: creating and sustaining superior performance*, Free Press, New York.

Senge, P 1990, *The fifth discipline: the art and practice of the learning organisation*, Doubleday/Currency, New York.

Thompson, AA & Strickland, AJ 1995, *Strategic management: concepts and cases*, 8th edn, Richard D Irwin, Inc., Homewood, Illinois.

CHAPTER 8
Managing the information systems function

LEARNING OBJECTIVES

After reading this chapter, you should be able to:

» explain how information systems managers manage
  people and relationships

» understand the role of power, politics and culture in
  information systems

» describe the key areas that information systems and
  information technology (IT) managers need to monitor
  to maintain the performance and effectiveness of the
  information systems

» understand the main issues related to information
  security and data privacy in organisations

» explain methods and approaches for effective
  management monitoring of information systems
  projects and development teams

» explain how charts are used in project management

» understand the capability maturity model for software.

Introduction

Information systems managers have the responsibility of managing the tactical and operational activities related to the running of the information systems service. Tactical issues relate to short-term plans, procedures and policies, whereas the operational activities relate to the day-to-day tasks that must be carried out to maintain the information systems service effectively for the organisation. How they carry out these tactical and operational activities is shaped to some extent by the organisation's existing short-, medium- and long-term strategies. A well-managed information systems function in an organisation should have a strong alignment between the information systems strategy and information systems tactical and operational activities. These activities involve managing people and relationships, delivering an effective information systems service to a range of users and managing information systems projects. This chapter examines each of these three interrelated activities in turn, starting with the management of people and relationships.

Managing people and relationships in the information systems function

An important part of an information systems managerial role is the effective management of people and relationships. These include information systems professionals, users of the systems, senior management, customers, suppliers and external alliances. Managing the relationships between these different groups requires some guiding principles, which are discussed in the following.

> *Responsibility of management*. The information systems manager must take the responsibility for making things happen; in other words, being active. This is especially true in flatter organisational structures because the manager cannot rely on being given orders from above. On the tactical and operational levels, decisions have to be made to resolve problems, avoid problems and take advantage of opportunities. The strategic plans discussed in chapter 7 will guide much of this decision making but the manager must be prepared to take responsibility and make decisions.

> *Development of boundary roles*. Information systems managers cannot afford to have an inward focus. Although day-to-day operations need managing within the information systems function, managers should become involved in boundary relationships. These are, for example, the interfaces between the information systems function and other departments of the organisation and the interface between the information systems function and suppliers or customers. Boundary relationships were once the responsibility of either executive managers or more junior people in the organisation responsible for selling and purchasing. These should be considered strategic focal points and consequently require managing on an operational level.

> *Development and use of communication systems*. Information systems management must effectively develop and use communication systems to encourage relationships between information systems staff, users, customers and suppliers. This needs to take into account what will be communicated, how often it will be communicated and how it will be communicated. For example, an information systems manager might hold short weekly briefings or

meetings to keep information systems staff aware of project developments and organisational issues. Email might be directed at relevant individuals or groups or communicate urgent information. If a dialogue exists between the information systems function and its clients, misunderstandings in relation to expectations are less likely, which should lead to a better working relationship.

〉 *Create and maintain an effective working environment.* An open and transparent management style is characteristic of the network style of management and is more likely to engender trust between groups (Limerick, Cunnington & Crowther 1998). Trust is seen as a key value in the network organisation. Managers cannot monitor their employees — or, for that matter, their business partners — all the time; nor should they try to. They have to communicate core directions and values, support employees along the way and trust that they are responsible enough to do their jobs well. If employees are empowered rather than monitored, they will be more innovative and probably work harder and longer. In this model, the manager becomes a facilitator in the network rather than a custodian of resources.

Information systems may be used to support the status quo or power brokers in an organisation. Although this is sometimes desirable, information systems become part of the problem when they become rigid and prevent organisational progress. For the information systems manager, knowledge of changing organisational structures and the reasons behind them is important so that even day-to-day decisions are informed by where the organisation is heading and the potential role that information systems and IT can play. Indeed, even on a personal level, the managerial style of the information systems function will need to be sensitive to the changing world of work and the aspirations of the staff and users.

〉 **Reflection question 1:** Do you think there could be resistance from some managers to changing their management styles?

[**Key concept:** Information systems can be used to transform organisations.]

infobyte

Looking for a mentor?

Ever wondered what it takes to get on in the information systems profession? Certainly, information systems skills are important, as well as the more generic communication and problem-solving skills. However, many consider that a mentor is important too. A mentor can provide medium- to long-term career advice and advice on how to solve difficult business problems. The mentor might typically be someone who displays qualities that you admire in how they work and make decisions. It might take time to find a suitable mentor because that person might not be in the same organisation as you. Some suggest that the mentor should not be your manager because it should be someone higher up in the organisation with more senior experience. You have to be comfortable with your mentor and be able to speak openly with them. Professional societies are excellent for developing a network of contacts and for finding potential mentors.

〉 **Reflection question 2:** If information systems managers are struggling to keep up with the rate of change in each area of information systems, how can they manage effectively?

Managing information systems professionals

An important aspect of information systems operations is acquiring and training effective staff. High-quality staff will have considerable input into information systems developments. They will influence the medium- and long-term returns from the operations. Companies that take a longer-term perspective of their endeavours will create a staffing plan that identifies responsibilities for current staff and a plan for acquiring additional staff.

All information systems professionals should have regular performance reviews with the information systems management and plan their training requirements. Motivated information systems professionals require challenges in their day-to-day responsibilities and are very concerned about developing skills that are in demand. The manager needs to allow staff the opportunity to work on exciting projects rather than being involved entirely with maintaining older systems.

Managing internal and external relationships

The information systems management team must manage the relationships with other departments and functions in their organisation. This would involve working with senior management throughout the organisation to obtain high-level requirements and feedback on the service provided by the information systems function. A service mentality is very important because if the image of the information systems function is poor, it is unlikely to obtain high levels of funding, and it might even find that more information systems services are outsourced. Users of the information systems must be trained adequately and effectively supported through responsive help desks. Surveys should be conducted regularly to obtain feedback on the level of service being provided.

The information systems function in a large organisation is likely to interface with a wide range of external organisations and individuals. These can include customers, suppliers, banks and partner organisations. The information systems managers must develop good relationships with these groups to meet their requirements and to be perceived as being responsive and active.

The role of power, politics and culture in information systems

No discussion of information systems management would be complete without explaining the role of politics and power (Jasperson et al. 2002). Since the late 1980s, researchers in the information systems field have been increasingly interested in the importance of the social and political factors in information systems development (Hirschheim & Newman 1991). In this context, 'political' refers to the clash of conflicting agendas that can surface in the struggles for recognition, resources, career progression, power and influence. Political struggles can be seen in the situations that involve user resistance. According to Grover, Lederer and Sabherwal (1988, p. 145), 'user resistance to management information systems is common'. Systems succeed or fail for various reasons, but recognising the role of politics is crucial to understanding user resistance. In some circumstances, user resistance might be caused in part by a perceived threat regarding a reduction in someone's autonomy, an increase in workload or an invasion of territory.

Politics has been given some attention, especially in its relation to power, by organisational behaviourists (Thompson & McHugh 1995). Managers often tend to rationalise their activities in terms of technical skills and to choose to ignore the influence of politics. Pfeffer defines the internal politics of organisations as '[t]hose activities within organisations to acquire, develop and use power and other resources to obtain one's preferred outcomes in a situation where there is dissension or uncertainty about choices' (Pfeffer 1981, p. 10). Therefore, people seeking influence often have to work within sectional interests or networks (coalitions).

> **Reflection question 3:** Why do you think people often assume that organisational politics is a bad thing?

[**Key concept:** Information systems are social systems, not just technical systems!]

The information systems manager must be able to manage and promote projects and relationships within and outside the organisation. The political component is the development and management of the relationships. Internal and external promotion of activities requires support in terms of people and resources. The information systems manager requires a good understanding of the organisation and its internal politics, and must be skilled in developing coalitions. Political skills can help a person sell his or her ideas, acquire resources and get things done.

Successful individuals in organisations spend a great deal of time developing relationships. This process is termed networking. It enables the individual to relate to subcultures in the organisation and to become aware of the internal political processes.

Culture has been recognised as being an important consideration in information systems development and management. Organisational culture and national culture are two main levels at which cultural issues can be seen. Organisational culture can be defined as the shared values and norms that exist in an organisation, which involve common beliefs and feelings, regularities of behaviour and a historical process for transmitting values and norms (Vecchio, Hearn & Southey 1997).

Organisational culture can have a positive influence on organisational effectiveness when it supports organisational goals, is widely shared and is internalised by organisational members (Bartol et al. 1998). It can be influenced through time by such things as policies, procedures and management strategies, in addition to the recruitment of people from different backgrounds and age groups. Organisational culture is generally seen as a unitary entity, although it could be argued that it is possible for radically different cultures to exist in the same organisation (McKenna 1999).

Information systems managers are increasingly working with clients and suppliers from different countries that do not share the same business culture. Multinational companies might assume that cultural differences are not great enough to present problems in their own organisation, but this is unlikely to be true. Hofstede (1991) classified culture in relation to several attributes. 'Power distance' is how much the members of a society accept that power in institutions and organisations is distributed unequally. 'Uncertainty avoidance' is how much the people in a group or society feel uncomfortable with uncertainty and ambiguity. This can lead to beliefs that support the promise of certainty. If high, it is characterised by conformity. The 'masculinity/femininity' metaphor is used to convey the tendency in a society to value achievement, heroism, assertiveness and material success (masculine), as opposed to a preference for relationships, modesty, caring for the weak and the quality of life (feminine). The last characteristic of culture is 'individualism/collectivism'. Western culture is often described as individualistic or independent, whereas Eastern culture is seen as being collectivist or interdependent. Individualistic (independent) cultures focus on the self and what makes the individual different from others. In collectivist cultures, a person's feelings and thinking are more influenced by social relationships with others and the individual's role in the group. In independent cultures, individual goals dominate and ties between individuals are weak. In interdependent cultures, strong groups with lasting ties dominate (Hofstede 1991).

The trend of organisations outsourcing software development to a company in another country is increasing. Many information systems departments now have experience of dealing with cultural differences. Their awareness of these differences and their ability to manage culturally diverse teams are likely to influence the success of the project (Walsham 2002). It is argued that culture has been looked at too simplistically because a country often has culturally diverse groups that need to be considered (Myers & Tan 2002).

[**Key concept:** When working in teams, always take cultural differences into account.]

❯ **Reflection question 4:** Can you think of an example of the possible influence of cultural differences on the development of information systems?

Innovation and creativity

There is no simple answer to the question of how to be creative or how to be innovative. Some people are better than others at being creative and some organisations seem more innovative than others are. However, approaches, techniques and skills can be used to develop a more creative and innovative environment.

For organisations to be successful in today's business world, they must accept that what they did yesterday may not be appropriate for tomorrow. In other words, organisations must not only accept change but also be prepared to encourage it.

To become more innovative, organisations need to value people with ideas and encourage brainstorming sessions. When expertise is not available internally, it should be brought in by new people or consultants. Organisations should become learning environments and should learn from the successes and failures of other organisations. Innovation and entrepreneurship should be rewarded. Risk taking should be encouraged and some failures tolerated. Of course, organisations should invest in training, and help staff experience new situations and new working environments. All the points mentioned apply to the information systems arena also. Staff who can creatively use information systems and IT to solve organisational problems are in big demand.

Managing information systems operations

The overall performance and effectiveness of information systems need to be managed. This involves making sure that the operational activities (daily activities) are aligned to the information systems strategic plan. The information systems strategic architecture serves as a framework for guiding the daily decisions that have to be made.

Harnessing brainwaves

Globalisation, increasing competition and changing customer demands mean that doing the old stuff more efficiently is no longer enough. Commercial success in the early 21st century requires something else – innovation.

Traditionally, when asked about their innovation strategies, many organisations would point proudly to their research and development labs. There, nestled among racks of expensive equipment, highly trained people would toil diligently at the task of developing the 'Next Big Thing'. But times have changed. Generating new ideas is no longer the exclusive domain of a select few within organisations. Successful companies realise the ideas that will help them in the future can come from anywhere. What's needed is a method of capturing them and putting them to work. As this new wave of innovation washes through the corporate landscape, the ways in which technology can help are also being reviewed. There is widespread agreement that, to successfully support an innovative organisation, underlying technology must be able to quickly respond to changes in business requirements. There's little point in spotting a fantastic new opportunity and claiming first-mover advantage if progress is stymied by a lack of support systems. Such flexibility and agility, however, does not necessarily require large investments in the latest applications or hardware. Many organisations find they already have the elements they need. It's just a matter of using them more intelligently. Sara Sauce, managing director of IT advisory firm Technology Choices, says many companies have invested in systems that are not being used to capacity or delivering all the benefits they should.

Traditionally, companies could opt for one of two models when it came to technology, insourcing or outsourcing. While each has advantages, Lamble says, it is a combination of the two that provides the best platform for innovation in a company.

'Technology is an important enabler of processes, but the way we have traditionally sourced it has been an inhibitor to the ability to innovate,' he says.

There is a growing trend towards so-called multi-sourcing, he says, whereby some processes are dealt with internally while others are handed over to external parties.

'If IT-enabled innovation is the way you want to go, then multi-sourcing can work very well,' he says. 'It provides a flexible framework that allows a business to change course quickly if market conditions require.'

Following a multi-sourcing strategy challenges the traditional relationships between businesses and their technology suppliers. For it to work properly, a business must be prepared to share its commercial priorities and future plans.

Such an approach can bring other benefits as the company finds itself exposed to new ideas and processes from outside its traditional operations. Lamble says this two-way flow opens up avenues and opportunities that may not previously have been considered.

Source: This article appeared in *The Australian IT.*

> **Reflection question 5:** Have you any other ideas for encouraging creativity in employees?

Operational management includes monitoring and evaluating the performance of the computer systems and quality of information systems service provided. This usually involves monitoring all aspects of performance, including:

> *Data quality*. Data produced by the systems must be accurate and have a high degree of reliability.

> *Response times*. Time to retrieve data from database systems must be acceptable to the users.

> *Network and server reliability*. Network access should be maintained at high levels of reliability. If access to the network servers falls below a certain level (e.g. for accessing email), then users will start to complain.

> *Hardware reliability*. Computer systems, printers, scanners and so on must be reliable.

> *Licensing agreements*. These need to be adhered to.

> *Web access performance*. Previously, the focus was on accessing internal systems but now most organisations are accessing data and information from outside the organisation.

> *Security issues*. System security needs to be continually monitored and any breaches rectified.

Policies and procedures related to these points should be developed and communicated throughout the company.

A related issue is the enforcement of standards across the organisation for the acquisition of hardware and software. Some of the benefits of these standards are:

> Support costs are reduced.

> System complexity is kept to manageable levels.

> Training costs are reduced.

> Discounts are available for bulk purchasing.

> Expertise is built up more easily.

infobyte

Motivating employees

For IT staff to perform at a high level requires them to be effectively managed. Motivating staff is not just a case of providing additional monetary rewards. IT professionals need to feel valued. During performance appraisals, staff members need feedback on their strengths and weaknesses and how they can develop as professionals. To increase or maintain motivation levels, it is a good idea to provide staff with a variety of opportunities where useful skills can be acquired. Rewards can be part of a motivating package but they should not be the only tactic. Poor performance also needs to be adequately dealt with; otherwise, it can become a demotivator for the high-performing staff to see some people getting away with less effort or substandard performance. Managing poor performance should involve a serious attempt to resolve issues by setting targets, providing adequate feedback and encouragement.

> **Reflection question 6:** Which issues or areas are likely to cause most problems for IT managers?

[**Key concept:** Performance and effectiveness of information systems can always be improved.]

Typically, new technology is adopted at different times by organisations (see figure 8.1). The timing of adoption can be classified into five stages. The innovators are a small minority who adopt the technology very early on. They are followed by a more significant minority who are still early in the adoption cycle. A larger percentage of companies are not leaders but still adopt before many other organisations. The other 50 per cent of adopters can be divided into late adopters and laggards. There is plenty to be gained by being an early adopter of technology but many companies do not want to be innovators because they want the technology to be tested in the marketplace before they use it, reducing the risk of problems associated with it.

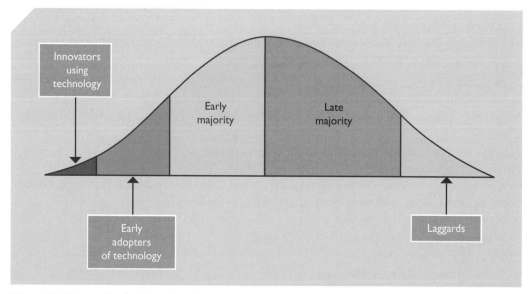

Figure 8.1 Stages of technology adoption

Information systems continuity planning and security management

Information systems continuity planning is concerned with protecting the organisation against disruption to the running of the information systems, the failure of systems or subsystems, and disasters such as fire and floods affecting the information systems. Information systems continuity planning is one part of business continuity planning, and the two should not be confused. 'Business continuity planning', as the term suggests, examines the entire business and would typically include areas that are less dependent on information systems.

Information systems continuity planning encompasses security measures. Developing a continuity plan should be high on the agenda of any information systems department. It should outline the general policies in relation to continuity planning and security, the levels of security that should be adopted, the key risks related to the systems, disaster recovery procedures and the people responsible for maintaining continuity and security.

Security includes the physical environment as well as the software environment. Once in operation, the security measures and procedures need to be monitored and evaluated for effectiveness.

Security risk analysis

Developing adequate security measures is all about the assessment of risk. Even with the costliest of safeguards put in place, there can be no guarantees that the system will be 100 per cent secure. Therefore, the levels of security required are determined by factors such as the value of the data being protected and the types of threats to the system.

Putting security measures in place has costs. Some of these are purely financial costs and others may be considered as an inconvenience. Information systems professionals should assess the value of the data and information they are about to protect, what the likely cost of system disruption would be and the possible loss of business that would arise from a disruption. For instance, putting high-cost security measures in place to protect low-value data and information has little point. However, only the organisation can put a value on the loss of business or the data being protected. There is always a trade-off between the ideal level of security and the costs associated with it.

The systems designers must assess where the main threats to the system are. Do they come from within or outside the organisation? Are the main threats likely to be deliberate acts of malicious damage or accidental events? Most of the problems in any security environment arise from not attending to basic security measures adequately.

infobyte

Employees and ethical issues

Ethical perspectives on how employees use their computer systems are constantly being challenged. For example, how many employees keep personal documents and photographs on their work computer systems? The percentage is likely to be much higher if employees are using laptops that they take home. It could be argued that personal files should not be kept on a work computer but how realistic is this? This has led some companies to relax their stance on what can be stored on work computers. Because employees are often accessing work-related emails from home, there is a recognition that there needs to be some 'give and take' on these issues. Examples such as these highlight the blurring of work and leisure time and the need for a rethink on what work computers can and cannot be used for.

Physical security

Physical security aspects of information systems include protecting the hardware, monitoring access to buildings and taking backups. Servers and other hardware should be in a secure location with a locked door, with access only for authorised personnel. However, this issue is probably not so significant within a networked environment, because the software and data on the web server or accessed through it can be modified or deleted by a variety of methods.

Access to buildings should be monitored because unauthorised people are a potential threat to computer system security: they may access confidential data both on the system and from printouts. Many companies have a sign-in procedure in which the 'visitor' provides a reason for being there and is given a badge to wear while on the premises. Anyone not recognised and not wearing a badge is challenged. In high-security situations, guards are employed to challenge people at the entrances to buildings. This level of security and associated expense are warranted if valuable data are stored or a high level of confidentiality is required.

The web server, application server and database server, if these are being used, should be protected against power surges. After a system crash, there should be adequate procedures for the rebooting of the system and restoring the service to the users.

Backups of any transactions should be taken and a copy stored off-site in case of fire or other accidents. How often should you take backups of your data files? It depends on how much the files have changed since the previous backup. For a small business, it is generally worthwhile taking backups daily. Do not overwrite the previous day's backup but work on a three-day cycle so that by the fourth day, the backup is overwriting the data from three days previously. This should always leave some data to fall back on. Taking backups daily might seem a lot of bother — but not when you think about the time and trouble involved in recreating a day's lost work.

Software security

Software security for information systems could be the subject of a book in its own right. The following covers the main issues from a security management perspective.

Network security

A firewall (see chapter 4) can protect a network or system by separating the organisation's intranet from other systems within the organisation or outside the organisation. Note that not all threats come from outside the organisation.

Developing an effective firewall system is not easy. There can be a tendency to become too severe in what is allowed in and out of the organisation and also in monitoring too much of the communication. If a security policy has been developed for the organisation, this will help in defining the level of firewall security needed.

The management of virus attacks

When corporate networks have a connection to the Internet or allow files to be transferred from disks, they run the risk of virus infection. The Internet is a threat to security through the use of email attachments and downloaded files. Each user needs to have an up-to-date virus scanner, which can detect and delete the most recent strains of a virus.

The number of people accessing data over the Internet has become a major security issue for companies. As far as downloading files is concerned, users should be aware of several things. They should avoid or minimise the downloading of files, whether software or documents, from sites that have no reputation to lose. Major software vendors bring some assurance that the files will not contain code that has malicious intent; files are more likely to have been checked and their quality assured before they are released to the public because the company has its reputation on the line. A personal site does not have the same type of reputation at stake when providing free downloads. Free software should also be viewed with some suspicion for much the same reasons, particularly if it is from an unrecognised software vendor.

There are potential problems with accessing websites that use Java applets, even though Java has been made secure by not allowing applets to write to the user's hard disk without permission. Many users give permission to store configuration information for the applet on the disk though because they are unaware of the consequences or they trust the site they are downloading from. These downloads can result in virus-related problems.

A policy on Internet access should be developed and disseminated within the organisation. It should clearly explain the potential problems associated with Internet use. This, in addition to an effective firewall system, should safeguard the organisation.

Authentication

Authentication deals with proving the identity of a person. Passwords, hardware tokens or smart cards, or biometric properties, such as fingerprints or retinal patterns, are all forms of authentication. Passwords are the most commonly used — although also probably the most abused — form of security measure. Users predictably choose names and favourite words as their passwords and sometimes write them down, and before long a system that could be effective becomes quite ineffective. The system should force users to develop passwords that are:

> longer than five characters
> a combination of characters and digits
> changed regularly.

Biometrics can be used as an alternative or supplement to passwords in authentication systems. These are the technologies for measuring and analysing body characteristics, such as fingerprints, retinal patterns and voice patterns, so that they can be checked automatically. Factors to be considered in the choice of a particular characteristic include public acceptability, ease of use and accuracy levels.

Fingerprints are the most widely used biometric today. Iris identification is even more accurate than fingerprints; however, a small percentage of people cannot use those systems because of an inability to stabilise their iris. Biometrics can be foiled by a sudden change in a person's body; for example, a cut finger might mean a person cannot log in.

Threats to computer systems come from different categories of people and not all have malicious intent:

> *Employees*. Poorly trained staff can be a threat to the security of systems and can create several problems for maintenance staff. Disconnecting equipment or trying to use systems for which they are not trained can be potentially damaging to the overall effective running of the system. Disgruntled employees may deliberately attempt to delete or alter files, and are difficult to stop because they have authority to use the system.
> *Other users*. Suppliers or customers may have access to systems through the Web.
> *Hackers*. The antics of hackers have been reported for some years now. A distinction is sometimes made between 'hackers' (those who do not damage the system in any way but gain unauthorised access) and 'crackers' (those who gain unauthorised access with the intent of deliberately creating problems such as deleting files).
> *Criminals*. Some people gain access to systems for personal profit, such as accessing credit card details without authorisation.

[**Key concept:** Most security problems arise from not implementing the fundamentals of security effectively.]

> **Reflection question 7:** Would your passwords stand up to scrutiny?

Companies are spending more on trying to keep their systems secure. As a consequence of information systems continuity planning, the information security policy of an organisation is taking on increased significance. Organisations have typically been reactive rather than taking the initiative in relation to security: the information security policy only becomes a hot issue again when there has been a breach of security or the auditors have planned to visit.

High rates of staff turnover in the information systems and IT industry have meant threats are likely to come from a broader range of people. In the days when mainframes were commonly used, people used to stay in one position longer and knew that they would be one of the first suspects if anything happened. When an increasing proportion of an organisation's information systems operations are outsourced and there are temporary workers in information systems support, establishing trust can be made more difficult. Security policies have to consider staff turnover in all sensitive positions (Connolly 2000).

Data privacy

The issue of **data privacy** is related to information security. The increasing amount of personal data stored in computer databases has created a major issue in modern society in terms of protecting the privacy of the individual. Many organisations, including government departments, universities, schools and banks, keep personal details of students, customers and so on. If there is a serious breach of confidentiality and these details fall into the wrong hands, it could result in fraud, unsolicited phone calls from businesses or harassment.

The onus is on the companies that store this personal information to protect the data and act ethically in relation to their use. Many countries have legislation to protect the rights of the individual in this area, and companies that do not adequately protect personal data are fined. Legislation also gives people the right to ask for copies of their personal records to determine whether they are correct, because inaccurate data can have serious consequences, such as being refused credit because of an incorrectly recorded bad debt. Together, data privacy and freedom of information Acts provide some comfort in an increasingly digital world, where data can be rapidly copied, merged and transferred over networks and the Internet.

> **Reflection question 8:** Have you experienced an invasion of your privacy as a result of personal data being used for a purpose other than the one it was intended for?

Managing projects and development teams

Information systems managers spend a great deal of time managing projects and development teams. A US study in 1995 found that a large percentage, as high as 40 per cent, of information systems projects were cancelled before completion, with many others overrunning time and budget. It is worthwhile identifying the critical aspects of project management and the underlying reasons that some projects fail.

Senior executive support

Significant initiatives require senior management support. If the operation has a strategic impact on the organisation, then everyone should know about it and get behind it. Despite new trends in organisational structures, staff still take a lead from senior management.

Projects can easily run into problems if they do not have management backing. Team members may find that people are not so cooperative in providing information or are slow to respond to requests. They may even find that the project is continually being questioned, even though it has been given the go-ahead. Having highly visible senior management backing for an application oils the political machinery within a company and makes the developers' tasks so much easier. Senior people can lend support to the development of information systems by being involved in various ways: in the creation of strategy, by being part of the first tier of the ongoing management structure of the project and by taking a high profile throughout the project and communicating with team members and the rest of the staff regularly about the progress and significance of the initiative.

Assessing the organisation's requirements

The organisation's requirements must be accurately assessed. Information systems projects should have a clearly defined strategy. Some information systems initiatives do not provide the return on investment that the organisation had hoped for because what was expected was never clearly stated. So the developers deliver a system that fulfils the requirements as specified but is not good enough to produce significant returns to the company.

Defining the scope of the project

Developing information systems within a company can take many forms. Consequently, development team members need to be clear on the scope of the initiative they are taking on. To do this will typically involve some form of feasibility assessment, which includes a definition of the scope of the project. Doing this can avoid arguments later on over the success of the delivered system. To clarify the scope of the project early in the proceedings is a worthwhile investment in time and energy, and radically improves the chances of a successful application being delivered.

Assessing the most worthwhile projects

Many projects are undertaken without paying due regard to return on investment. Focusing on the applications that maximise the returns means that the benefits are quickly brought back to the company and the perceived success of the system acts as an impetus to develop other applications.

Being wary of changing requirements

The scope of the project can change along the way. This happening without a conscious decision being made is known as 'scope creep'. It arises because enthusiastic managers begin to see the beneficial implications of the applications being developed, so they suggest further applications or requirements be considered. The team leaders must assess how critical these suggestions are to the overall success of the system. If they are outside the scope of the current development and are not critical, then they should be logged but not tackled immediately. If they are critical and are within the scope of the system, then they should be built into the requirements and planning adjustments made accordingly. The major difficulty with scope creep is that the resources for the project are stretched so far that the success of the project overall comes into question.

Blending team-member skills

Team members must have the right blend of skills to tackle the project. Often, this must be considered well in advance because some skills and knowledge take a long time to acquire. Besides technical skills, team members need to develop their communication skills continually. Project management skills need to be developed through training and on-the-job guidance and experience.

Setting realistic targets

Many managers set unrealistic project deliverables and targets in the hope that they will be given the go-ahead with the project. In other words, the project is often doomed from the start because the deadlines and returns are not possible to achieve. Managers and team members must be wary of falling into this trap: they should not commit to unrealistic targets or present inaccurate progress reports.

Project Management Institute

The Project Management Institute (PMI) is a global organisation that represents 200 000 professionals from 125 countries. PMI professionals work across many industry sectors including aerospace, automotive, business management, construction, engineering, financial services, IT, pharmaceuticals, healthcare and telecommunications. The institute provides training and certification as well as seminars and networking opportunities for professionals. In addition, PMI is a global leader in the development of standards for the practice of project management. Its standards document, *A guide to the Project Management body of knowledge* (*PMBOK guide*), is widely recognised as an excellent framework for managing projects.

Assessing project risks

Every project has a certain amount of risk associated with it. It is not possible to eradicate risk altogether but it can be managed. Managing risk involves four basic steps: identification, assessment, response and reassessment.

Risk identification

Each project should be assessed in terms of the sources of risk. In information systems projects, the main risks are related to a failure to identify the main requirements; poor project planning and resource allocation; the technology; and external contractors and the management of relationships.

Risk assessment

Risks should be assessed according to the probability of occurrence and the severity of their impact if they do occur. This can be presented in a risk severity matrix (see figure 8.2).

Probability					
5					
4		Increase in cost of software licence		User resistance	
3					
2					
1					Hardware problems
	1	2	3	4	5

Impact

Major risk	Moderate risk	Minor risk

Figure 8.2 Risk severity matrix

Risk response

When a risk is identified, a strategy to reduce the damage caused by the risk needs to be developed. There are five responses to risks.

Mitigating risk

This involves reducing the probability that the event will occur or minimising the impact of the risk if it does occur. For example, user resistance may be a real threat but if appropriate steps are taken in the development process, the risk of it happening can be reduced.

Avoiding risk

Risk avoidance can be used to avoid or eliminate the risk. For example, developers could choose technology that is tried and tested to avoid technology failures.

Transferring risk

Risk can be transferred to another party. For example, an organisation can negotiate a fixed price with an external company for an information system being developed. However, this means that the external company is absorbing risk. It is likely that the company will take this into account when costing the project.

Sharing risk

Risk can be shared by different parties. For example, in a strategic alliance between companies, the risks and costs associated with developing a new software system can be shared by both companies.

Retaining risk

A company may be prepared to live with the consequences of a risk event happening. The project owner assumes the risk because the probability of the event happening is considered low or the consequences are not severe. This could happen in relation to software upgrades. If a company decides to adopt a particular software system, there is a chance that a new version could be released within a couple of years. If this does happen, the company can retain its current version of the software and not have the latest features of the software at its disposal or take on the additional expense of the upgrade.

In addition to the risk responses, contingency plans need to be made. This typically involves setting aside funds to draw upon if an event takes place. For example, if a software development team falls behind schedule, some funds will be required to cover the cost of the developers.

Risk reassessment

The risks have to be managed throughout the life of a project. The risk plan has to be monitored and adjustments made when new risks are detected. Effective management processes are needed to deal with changes affecting the project.

Monitoring project progress

Monitoring the development refers to gathering information about the status of the project and comparing it with the initial plans and targets. Monitoring can be undertaken on three levels: tasks completed (including time), expenditure and quality.

P & A Construction (New Zealand) tracks projects wirelessly with Orb Communications

Keeping tabs on a mobile workforce used to be a headache for P & A Construction. Then the company turned to Orb Communications and an award-winning solution which harnessed the power of mobile broadband.

Like many building firms, Wellington-based P & A Construction has been busy in the last couple of years. The company has 25 staff and takes a wide variety of commercial and residential projects. On a typical weekday day all but two or three of its employees will be working away from the office on sites.

In the past, having such a mobile staff used to cause management headaches according to P & A director Phil Stewart. The hours worked on various projects and the materials used were all recorded on paper forms which then had to be collated in a laborious and time consuming process.

'Everything was done manually – from timesheets to purchase orders – it just took a hell of a lot of time,' Stewart says.

Then Stewart made contact with Orb Communications, and a web development company, Webspeed, with its award-winning mobile data service called dbonair. This service is designed to gather information and to make it available on mobile devices as simply as possible. Once data has been uploaded to Webspeed's server it can be searched and presented a variety of ways.

'Timesheets are now entered into software on PDAs [personal digital assistants] using drop-down boxes,' says Stewart. 'All of the information is then transferred wirelessly over the Mobile Broadband network to the dbonair website and it's consolidated into reports. We can check each person's hours to make sure that no one has been over-allocated and we can get a break down of the costs associated with any area of a project.'

Orb Communications were able to supply and support the necessary mobile hardware to make it possible. Because the dbonair service is web-based it is device independent, so P & A can use anything from simple WAP-capable mobile phones to advanced PDAs. Stewart says the company started out using mobile phones but has since progressed to using PDAs which are connected via mobile broadband.

Stewart says he is very satisfied with the level of advice and service he has received from Orb for all of these products. Most of P & A's projects are in the Wellington area but the company can also call upon any of Orb Communication's 43 branches, located from Kaitaia to Invercargill, if necessary. 'They are good, there's been no dramas at all,' says Stewart.

Thanks to the mobile solution Stewart says he now has a much better and up-to-date picture of how any project is progressing, and whether it is within budget and on track to meet its deadline. 'We still get ups and downs in the business — but at least we know where we are at. It's a bit scary sometimes because you see what you didn't see before — but it's better that you know.'

Source: This article appeared at www.istart.co.nz.

Tasks not completed on time, budgets blowing out, communication problems and high levels of stress are all signs of poor project management. A project can be monitored by checking the tasks that have been completed against those that should have been completed according to the project plan. This is helped by identifying 'deliverables' throughout using strategy reports or reports detailing requirements, designs and prototypes. Each module or phase of the project can be summarised in a report. For project management purposes, meetings are held to determine what has been accomplished and what should be accomplished in relation to the overall goals of the initiative, to identify new problems and to revise the project plan for the remainder of the project.

If monitoring highlights project problems, team leaders must take corrective action. However, if there is no hope of achieving any of the deliverables, the project may have to be cancelled.

Corrective action

Problem projects may require different types of corrective action. A new project plan, which is realistic and achievable, must be created to reschedule events. There may be scope for running two tasks in parallel when more is known about the project and the team members.

The priorities of individual team members can be reviewed. It may be that some members have not been assigning priorities correctly, and consequently are not working on the most critical tasks. This is a chance to review workloads and assess time and project management skills.

People may at times lack the necessary motivation to do sustained high-quality work. This problem may be fixed in the short term with additional rewards. If there is conflict among team members, this might be resolved by the sensitive reshuffling of personalities across teams. However, in the longer term, motivation problems can be resolved only by new attitudes within the organisation. In some cases, this may involve retrenchments and acquiring more motivated staff. Motivated staff still require careful management and usually need a constant stream of achievable targets and challenges to remain motivated. Staff may require on-the-job training, especially junior staff. If staff lack specialist skills, a short intensive training course may be appropriate to rectify, or at least improve, skill levels.

Additional staffing for a project may at first glance seem the easiest way to get the project back on track, but several potential problems are associated with this option. Good help is hard to find, especially at short notice. People who are new to a project that has been under way for some time have a steep learning curve to overcome. They will not be aware of the key issues and problems and may therefore need considerable help and information before they can be fully productive. Providing help may take people away from their tasks and consequently slow the project down overall.

Using charts in project management

Explaining project schedules and monitoring project progress can be enhanced with the aid of various charts, tables and diagrams. Two of the most commonly used techniques in project management are Gantt and program evaluation and review technique (PERT) charts, which can both be developed and maintained using software such as Microsoft Project.

A **Gantt chart** is a form of bar chart, showing the activities of a project and the amount of time each task will take (see figure 8.3). The time required for each task is estimated. Once this is done, the tasks are listed on the left-hand side of the chart in their intended order of completion. The period for the project is defined along the top of the chart from left to right. A bar is drawn on the chart for each task, with the left of the bar identifying the start date for the task and the right of the bar indicating the completion date for the task. If there is no bar for a task, this means there is no activity associated with the task during that period.

The charts can be presented at several levels. A top-level chart can show the main stages of the project with other levels breaking down the main stages into more detail. A Gantt charts' main benefit is as an aid in monitoring project progress. Given a certain date, it is easy to see what activities should be in progress. Of course, these charts are continually revised and updated, so project management software has become indispensable to project managers.

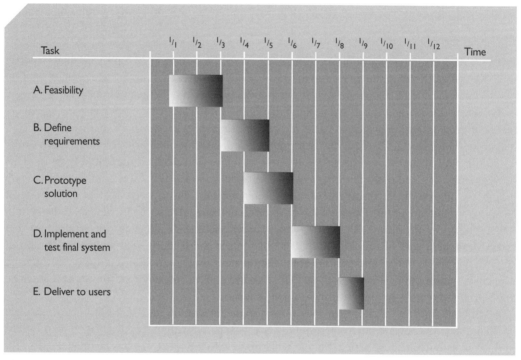

Figure 8.3 Gantt chart

A more sophisticated diagrammatic tool for specifying the complexity of a project (including software development) is **program evaluation and review technique (PERT)** (see figure 8.4). The tasks of a project are often interdependent; that is, one task cannot start until another has been completed. The problem with Gantt charts is that they do not show these interdependencies and do not highlight the critical tasks, which are the tasks that have to be completed before other work can be done.

A project consists of events and tasks. A task (or activity) is a piece of work that is clearly defined and can be assigned to a person or team, such as 'gather requirements for a system' or 'install software'. An event is the stage that marks the beginning or end of a task and is represented by a node (i.e. a circle in figure 8.4). A predecessor task is a task that precedes another task (obviously, the first task in the chart does not have a predecessor task). A successor task is a task that follows a task (the last task in the network does not have a successor task).

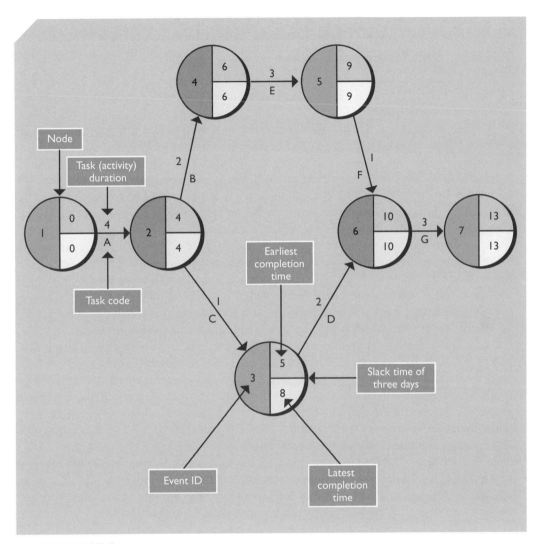

Figure 8.4 PERT chart

Typically, in PERT charts, each node includes the earliest and the latest completion time for the event. The earliest completion time for a task is calculated by taking the earliest completion time for the preceding event and adding the expected duration for the task in hand. (For example, in figure 8.4, the earliest completion time for event 3 is day 5, because the earliest completion time for event 2 is day 4 and the duration time for task C is one day.) The latest completion time for an event is found by taking the latest completion time for the following event and deducting the estimated duration time for the task leading to that event. (For example, for event 3, the latest completion time is calculated from event 6, which follows it — there, the latest completion time is day 10, and because task D takes two days, event 3 must be completed by day 8. Note that this means that event 3 has a 'slack time' of three days, that is, there are three days between the earliest completion time and the time the event must be finished by. Slack time is significant if tasks on that path fall behind schedule a little.)

Turning project failure into success

AG Edwards, a St Louis-based retail brokerage firm had a terrible IT project management history. Project costs were typically over budget, many projects dragged on for years and some were never finished.

The chief technology officer, John Parker, was appointed to turn this poor project management history around. In addition, Parker had to manage migration of a mission-critical mainframe system.

Several years later, things have changed dramatically. The company's project success rate (defined by the number of projects that arrive on time and within budget and deliver the expected business value) has increased from 54 per cent to 88 per cent. Improved project management has had a dramatic impact on the company's financial situation.

This turnaround was achieved by transforming how IT operated. Parker knew that successful project management involves more than a methodology and software. Successful projects depend on sound leadership and constructive relationships between IT managers and the business. With this in mind, Parker started to work with the company's top executives to identify the most important projects and also provided leadership training for his IT managers, with the aim of improving their credibility within the business.

According to Parker, 'If you try to fix project management without fixing the top first, you're not going to have much success' (Levinson 2006). He argues that the IT leaders need to take responsibility and manage projects effectively, rather than depending solely on project management procedures and tools. A project management expert was also brought in to oversee changes. Instead of adopting a rigid project management methodology, he introduced a standard framework for measuring, monitoring and reporting on a project's progress that encourages transparency and accountability.

AG Edwards also changed its project management office. Project managers used to report into a centralised office; now they report into different functional groups within IT, such as application development, network engineering and quality assurance. This has increased commitment to project success and feels less bureaucratic.

Source: Information from Levinson, M 2006, 'When failure is not an option', *CIO Magazine,* 1 June, www.cio.com.

The capability maturity model for software

The information systems function should be striving to become more effective and professional in all aspects of its operations and planning. The capability maturity model for software is a useful framework for checking the progress of an information systems department in becoming more proficient in software development (see figure 8.5). The basic idea, although designed for software development, can be useful for examining other aspects of a department's operations.

The capability maturity model for software was developed by the software community in association with the Software Engineering Institute at Carnegie Mellon University in the United States. It is a model that can be used for judging the sophistication or maturity of the software processes of an organisation and for identifying the key practices that are required to increase the maturity of these processes (SEI 2000). It is useful to note that a second, more complex version of the model known as the capability maturity model integration has also been developed, although the capability maturity model remains a valuable framework for the purposes of this text.

The stages in the model are:

> *Initial*. Ad hoc processes and success depend on individual effort.
> *Repeatable*. Basic project management processes are in place to track costs, schedules and functionality. Thus earlier successes on projects with similar applications can be repeated.
> *Defined*. The software processes are standardised and documented.
> *Managed*. Detailed measures of the software process and product quality are collected. Statistics on the software quality process are gathered.
> *Optimising*. The process is continually improved using quantitative feedback and innovative ideas are piloted.

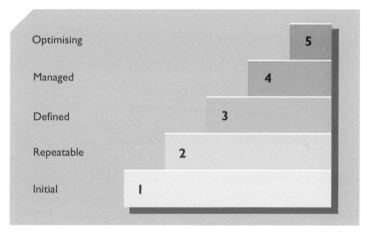

Figure 8.5 The capability maturity model
Source: This figure appeared in an article by the Software Engineering Institute.

Summary

Managing the information systems function requires breadth of knowledge and a wide range of skills. The information systems manager should have one eye on the internal machinations of the organisation and the other on developments in the business world. The key points in this chapter are:

> Information systems management must develop good working relationships with information systems professionals, users, senior management and external partners, customer groups and suppliers.
> Managing staff effectively is perhaps the greatest challenge facing the information systems manager. Staff require challenges, flexibility and consideration of their personal and family responsibilities.
> Creativity is as much a part of the information systems profession as is problem solving.

> The day-to-day performance and effectiveness of the information systems function, including the network, software and database systems, have to be monitored.
> Risks associated with projects need to be effectively managed.
> Information security is mostly about getting the basics right day in and day out.
> Techniques such as Gantt and PERT charts can help monitor project performance.

Questions

1. Explain the main groups of people with whom information systems management should develop good relationships.

2. What are the typical operational activities that the information systems manager is responsible for?

3. Do organisational politics always have negative implications for information systems developers?

4. What are some examples of physical security measures?

5. When an information systems project is running over its projected time, what are the likely causes and potential remedies?

6. How can Gantt and PERT charts help in managing information systems projects?

7. In relation to the stages of technology adoption, what are the advantages and disadvantages of being in the innovator group?

Exercises

1. Develop a risk severity matrix for common risks associated with IT projects. Even though a lot depends on the context, you should be able to identify common risks and place them roughly in the matrix.

2. Using the Internet, gather information on biometrics for system authentication. Assess which are most likely to be widely used and explain why.

3. Think of several organisations with which you are familiar and assess whether they are innovators, early adopters, early majority, late majority or laggards in relation to IT. Explain the reasons behind their approach to adoption.

CASE STUDY: A nightmare project

Actel is a large telecommunications company with a significant customer base. To improve its relationships with customers, it decided to implement a customer relationship management (CRM) system. All the senior staff agreed that retaining customers in a competitive telecommunications environment is essential and they knew that it was a matter of time before more of their customers would be poached.

However, what seemed an excellent initiative went terribly wrong and almost led to the downfall of the company. Within 12 months, the company lost many customers and significant revenue. In addition, the company's image took a battering.

The situation was probably at its worst when the CRM system crashed and new accounts could not be established. The phone systems ended up being overloaded and customers could not get through to Actel. What follows is an account of how the situation got to this point.

The CRM system upgrade had run into difficulties. The IT staff had heard a rumour about the possible outsourcing of the CRM project and even possible redundancies. These rumours had an impact on their morale.

The CEO of the company had announced in the press that the system would be upgraded by the end of the year. He said that his reputation as CEO was on the line because past project problems had damaged the company. This created problems for the IT staff because it was a tough deadline to meet. The CRM system interfaced with 15 other systems in the company and the complexity of the project had been underestimated. The telephone sales force wanted to have all the necessary information on the screen at the same time. Before the project started, the sales force had to access six screens of information from a range of database systems. This meant that it could not be effective in signing up new customers over the phone.

The software development teams responsible for customising the CRM system were badly coordinated. A team might write some code but could not test it properly because other teams had not completed their modules. The management of the project was given to an external company called ProMan, which should have coordinated all of this but was not responsive to the criticisms that were made.

On top of these problems, some IT development staff were actively looking for other jobs because they felt they did not have a future at Actel. This partly undermined the motivation of the development unit.

A critical point came in the CRM upgrade when the chief information officer (CIO) left the company. The new person appointed was thought to be a person who would retrench staff and outsource the IT development. The situation was not helped by the first address the new CIO gave to the staff. He said, 'Come in to work as though you could be the next person to leave the company'. Somehow, he thought that this would motivate staff but it had the opposite effect.

The expected disaster finally happened. An attempt was made to bring up the new CRM system but it crashed almost immediately. The team worked for the three days solid but with no success because the system was very unstable. The project management company had cut back on the time for testing modules in its efforts to get the system working on time. As more and more modules were added, the number of errors grew and they became impossible to trace.

At this point, an announcement was made that Actel would reduce the workforce by 1000 people. It did not mention where the staff cuts would be made but the IT staff thought the worst.

Actel did not really have a plan B. Contingency plans had not been put in place. For example, there was no plan in place to fall back to the old CRM system that had been stable for several years.

Source: Information from Koch, C 2004, 'AT&T Wireless self-destructs', *CIO Magazine*, 14 April, www.cio.com.

Questions

1. What were the main project management problems at Actel?
2. Could anything have been done to improve morale?
3. What should have been considered as the major risks of the project?
4. What lessons should be learnt from a project management perspective from this case study?

References

Bartol, KM, Martin, DC, Tein, MH & Matthews, GW 1998, *Management: a Pacific Rim focus*, 2nd edn, McGraw-Hill, Sydney.

Connolly, PJ 2000, 'Security starts from within', *Information Age*, October/November, pp. 12–15.

Grover, V, Lederer, AL & Sabherwal, R 1988, 'Recognising the politics of MIS', *Information and Management*, vol. 14, pp. 145–56.

Hirschheim, R & Newman, M 1991, 'Symbolism and information systems development: myth, metaphor and magic', *Information Systems Research*, vol. 2, no. 1, pp. 29–62.

Hofstede, G 1991, *Culture and organisations: software of the mind*, McGraw-Hill, London.

Jasperson, J, Carte, TA, Saunders, CS, Butler, BS, Croes, HJP & Zheng, W 2002, 'Power and information technology research: a metatriangulation review', *MIS Quarterly*, vol. 26, no. 4, pp. 397–459.

Levinson, M, 2006, 'When failure is not an option', *CIO Magazine*, 1 June, www.cio.com.

Limerick, D, Cunnington, B & Crowther, F 1998, *Managing the new organisation*, Business and Professional Publishing, Sydney.

McKenna, R 1999, *New management*, Irwin/McGraw-Hill, Sydney.

Myers, MD, & Tan, F 2002, 'Beyond models of national culture in information systems research', *Journal of Global Information Management*, vol. 10, no. 1, pp. 24–32.

Pfeffer, J 1981, *Power in organisations*, Pitman, London.

Software Engineering Institute (SEI) 2000, 'Capability maturity model for software', Carnegie Mellon University, August, www.sei.cmu.edu.

Thompson, P & McHugh, D 1995, *Work organizations: a critical introduction*, Macmillan, New York.

Vecchio, R, Hearn, G & Southey, G 1997, *Organisational behaviour*, Harcourt Brace, Sydney.

Walsham, G 2002, 'Cross-cultural software production and use: a structurational analysis', *MIS Quarterly*, vol. 26, no. 4, pp. 359–80.

CHAPTER 9
E-business

LEARNING OBJECTIVES

After reading this chapter, you should be able to:

» explain the features of the Internet that have created so many business opportunities

» explain the different forms of systems in e-business

» understand the role of strategy in e-business and how an opportunistic approach to e-business can be effective

» understand the components of business models and where e-business can be used effectively

» explain how e-marketplaces are changing supply chains

» describe and explain a range of e-business concepts relating to planning and strategy.

Introduction

The growth of e-business has had a profound influence on many aspects of business. As a consequence, this chapter examines e-business strategies and techniques to take advantage of the opportunities provided by the Internet effectively.

E-business is the use of the Internet and related technologies and services in business. It encompasses e-commerce, which is generally viewed in a narrower sense as the marketing, selling and buying of products and services through the Internet or proprietary networks. E-business therefore is a term that includes such things as relationship building between suppliers and consumers, information provision and after-sales service. If organisations explore the broader dimensions of e-business, they are more likely to tap into a greater amount of the potential provided by the Internet. This chapter examines the world of e-business. It discusses its evolution, effective e-business models and the development of e-strategies. Web development and design issues are covered in chapter 10.

E-business opportunities

The Internet has had and continues to have a profound effect on the business world for many reasons.

> It is very accessible. A website can sell goods and services around the clock, 365 days of the year. (This is sometimes shortened to 24/7/52, meaning 24 hours a day, seven days a week, 52 weeks a year.)

> It is convenient. People can access the Internet from home, from work or even while they are on the move by using their mobile phone or a palmtop or laptop computer. Accessing the Internet from a mobile phone or personal digital assistant to engage in business is known as m-commerce (mobile e-commerce).

> The number of people worldwide with access to the Internet is increasing. Although trying to estimate the number of Internet users accurately is difficult, it is clear that it is a very large market, which will increase in size. A large market provides companies with a great opportunity to sell their products or services.

> The global reach of the Internet provides an opportunity for companies to market their products and services internationally. Many companies that once thought only about servicing local customers are now selling products and services to customers from other countries. The Internet has contributed greatly to the trend of globalisation. This means that companies have to think in terms of global markets rather than national boundaries. The Internet has created a type of global marketplace, where buyers and sellers can be matched irrespective of national boundaries.

> Businesses can make significant cost savings by providing information, products and services over the Internet. Something as simple as putting the company's annual report online can create substantial savings on the costs of printing and mailing.

> Consumers can do some comparison shopping on the Internet because it is relatively easy and quick to visit comparable websites to check prices and models.

> The Internet has increased the level of choice for consumers. Your local bookshop cannot stock every title and is unlikely to hold very many specialist books. However, consumers are more likely to be able to find what they want on the Web.

> The Internet can link buyers directly with sellers. This factor can change entire industry supply chains by cutting out companies which act as intermediaries. For example, a wholesaler may bypass retailers and sell directly to consumers over the Internet.

The impact of the Internet on business is radical and far reaching. To be effective, however, companies cannot simply transfer their current business operations to the Web; they need to redefine their business model and strategy, reinvent business processes, change corporate culture and improve relationships with customers and suppliers.

The Internet has the potential to change the nature of work in organisations. Employees can:

> work from home and access and input company data and information through the Internet

> cooperate in virtual teams and use the Internet and email to communicate and share information

> be part of decentralised organisations, since the Internet provides a rich medium for communicating and sharing knowledge.

[**Key concept:** Some technologies, albeit rarely, create a business revolution.]

infobyte

The next big thing on the Internet?

Industry practitioners are always interested to know the next big thing about to happen in the information technology (IT) sector, especially related to the Internet. If they know what is going to happen over the next couple of years, they can prepare themselves personally and professionally and perhaps make recommendations at work to take advantage of the changes. Some would say the next big thing is that there is not one major change about to happen but rather a continuation of the changes of the past few years. Supported by information and communication technologies, these changes are having a major impact on how we work. For example, the Internet is enabling more people to work from home because they can access the corporate intranet to obtain information and process data. A few companies encourage people to work at home if they want to. They have found that if they shift their thinking to evaluating employees based on the amount of work completed rather than the hours they have worked, productivity increases and employees are happier. Another example is answering emails and phone calls on a mobile phone while going to work on the train. Is that being at work? The major trends that these examples illustrate are the blurring of work and personal time, the move away from the 'in office = at work' mentality.

Consumers are changing in that they are more educated and discerning. Increasingly, they require a high level of customisation in products and services, many of which become obsolete very quickly. Two key trends are influencing consumer, employee and employer expectations. One is globalisation. This is the trend fuelled by a range of information and communication technologies breaking down the barriers of distance and national boundaries. The second is the blurring of work, leisure and personal time, also influenced by information and communication technologies. Ever more people do part of their paid work from home or on the way to work aided by mobile devices and laptop computers. Companies should take into account the changing profile of consumers and global trends if they are to be effective in their marketing.

E-business has a number of advantages to offer organisations, such as:
> reducing costs by streamlining processes
> increasing income by adding revenue sources
> improving customer service by providing more and better quality information and greater convenience
> increasing innovation by sharing ideas
> improving information and knowledge management through the use of intranets.

Although few organisations would dispute that e-business provides real opportunities for businesses, the opportunities can be realised only by developing and implementing effective strategies.

[**Key concept:** Business and information technology are merging to the extent that in many cases you cannot do business without the technology.]

Types of systems

Web-based systems can be classified according to whether they are intended for customers, citizens, suppliers or business partners, or for employees of the company (see figure 9.1). These are briefly explained in this section and are elaborated on later in the chapter.

Business-to-consumer e-business

Web systems developed for individual customers are used for business-to-consumer (B2C) e-business. There are various aspects of B2C e-business that can be exploited by companies:
> *Product or service information.* The Internet can be used to help a potential customer make a purchasing decision by providing information on products and services.

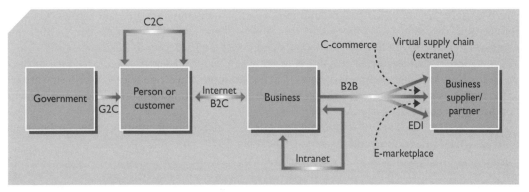

Figure 9.1 Types of e-business

> *Purchasing facility.* A website can be developed to include a transaction facility for purchasing and paying for products and services.

> *Aftersales service.* Aftersales service relates to all the forms of service that can be provided once the customer has made a purchase. It can include answering enquiries about faulty products and information on how best to use the product.

> *Marketing data.* Information can be gathered from customers and potential customers to create customer profiles, which can be used in marketing and product development.

> *Business partnerships.* Companies can provide links to other websites and so recommend particular products or services that are complementary to their own. For example, a hotel may include a link to a taxi service, which, in turn, includes a link back to the hotel.

> *Brand image and public relations.* The Internet can be used to promote the brand image of a company and thus increase awareness among consumers of their products or services. Some companies provide more general information about the organisation to keep the public informed about their strategies and values. For example, a mining company can inform the public about its environmental policies or a fast-food company may explain how it is involved in community projects.

> *Investor information.* Providing information on the company's financial performance is of interest to investors and may include the facility to download annual reports and company press releases.

Consumer-to-consumer e-business

A company can act as an intermediary and set up an electronic marketplace to allow consumers to sell to other consumers. An example is eBay (www.ebay.com). The intermediary can make money through advertising, commission on the sales or subscriptions to the site.

Business-to-business e-business

Business-to-business (B2B) e-business can be developed to link companies for purchasing and selling products and services. The term 'extranet' is often used to describe web systems linking a company with its suppliers. Through the system, the supplier can access a company's stock levels and product information and automatically send more products when an item is below its specified reorder level. Web-based systems that integrate suppliers down the supply chain are known as 'virtual supply chain systems'.

E-marketplaces are web-based environments in which suppliers are matched with buyers for the sale of products, services and specialised equipment. They are exchanges that are challenging many of the fixed virtual supply chain systems (see later in this chapter).

Electronic data interchange (EDI) is the sale of goods and services and exchange of data and information through proprietary networks. For example, travel agencies subscribe to various reservation systems that allow the booking of airline seats and hotel rooms. These systems are not directly available to customers.

Collaborative commerce (c-commerce) refers to online collaboration between business partners. Data, information and ideas may be exchanged as part of the collaboration.

IS in action

Hospital intranet leads the way

A major hospital in Manila called Medical City houses 500 patients and is expected to grow to 1500 in the future. The development of a leading edge intranet is seen as key way of improving efficiency and patient service in the hospital. Not only is the new Medical City the largest hospital in the country, it is also the only institution to use what Dr Bengzon (a senior hospital administrator) calls 'filmless imaging systems' — meaning all of its X-rays, like MRIs and CT scans, will be digitised. 'We needed a full networking solution capable of carrying information services such as patients' records and X-rays, thus reliability was extremely important,' he added. 'We are also holding very sensitive information such as laboratory results and other medical information, that is why security was another crucial component of our requirement.'

A Web-based hospital information system will be used in the new hospital complex to provide optimum connectivity — and meeting this prerequisite was another key consideration. Developed in-house, SHAMAN (Strategic Hospital and Medication Automation Network) is a fully integrated hospital information system that automates the entire business process of The Medical City from patient admission to discharge. The system also includes pharmacy, laboratory, radiology, nuclear medicines and a mini-ERP (enterprise resource planning) system to take care of logistics, human resources and finance. Evolved from an earlier ASCII-based system to a GUI (graphical user interface)-based application, SHAMAN is now a fully Web-based application. Consulting with Trends & Technologies, a local Nortel Networks channel partner, Dr Bengzon settled on a Gigabit Ethernet LAN solution from Nortel Networks.

One of the major benefits of the Nortel solution to The Medical City, according to Dr. Bengzon, is making 'telemedicine' a reality. 'Major medical procedures, such as, MRIs, CT scans, X-rays and nuclear medicine are critical services that our hospital offers the public, and the Nortel network infrastructure is right smack in the middle of this. We can shoot a digitised X-ray or scan from one floor to another if a doctor needs it, or we can push an MRI to a specialist at the ICU (intensive case unit),' he explained.

Looking ahead, Dr Bengzon and The Medical City have ambitious plans for a telemedicine initiative that will make patient information and digitised imaging available to doctors outside the hospital premises — allowing local physicians and surgeons to leverage the hospital's network to enable medical teleconferences with colleagues not only across the Philippines but also in other parts of the world.

Source: This case is reproduced with permission of Nortel Networks www.nortel.com. 'Supporting healthcare to make telemedicine a reality', Copyright © 2005 Nortel Networks. All rights reserved.

Intranets

Hypertext systems designed for the employees of a company are known as intranets. Intranets have evolved from basic information repositories, through to document management systems, to data processing applications and knowledge management systems.

E-business as a strategic driver

Chapter 7 covered information systems strategic approaches and the importance of strategic thinking overall was stressed. It was mentioned that information systems and IT can be, in certain situations, strategic drivers of the business. The e-business area has many examples of this in practice. However, this approach does have dangers. Traditional information systems planning emphasises a top-down approach. In this model, the corporate strategy defines the business goals and these determine which technologies should or should not be chosen (see figure 9.2 overleaf). These methods are well documented (see chapter 7).

A criticism of the 'traditional' approach is that it is not opportunistic enough. Because the business environment is rapidly changing, it is difficult to predict long in advance. Strategic approaches generally take at least a medium-term perspective. However, the more detailed the strategy, the less scope there is to take advantage of new opportunities if and when they arise.

Many technological or information systems innovations can have such an impact on businesses that companies that adopt a technology or technique early are able to gain a competitive advantage. This can, with careful management, become a sustainable advantage. Therefore, scanning the technological environment and adopting new, appropriate technology can be seen as a strategy in its own right. This can be described as an information systems and IT-driven approach (see figure 9.3 overleaf).

The Web is an example of a technology for which other uses have evolved *after* it has been initially adopted in organisations. There are many other cases of this happening in the information systems field. It seems to go completely against the grain as far as previous information systems and IT strategies are concerned, because it can be seen as a bottom-up rather than a

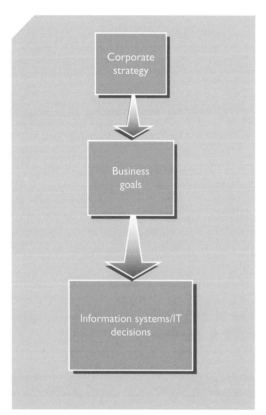

Figure 9.2 Strategy-driver information systems and IT planning

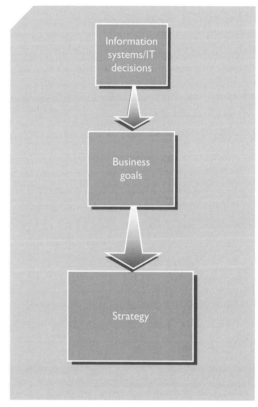

Figure 9.3 Information systems and IT as strategic drivers

top-down approach; that is, the technology is adopted, uses are found for it and then this affects the business goals and strategy, which change accordingly. The approach is more opportunistic and flexible than previous approaches and realises the profound impact IT can have.

Of course, there are several dangers with this approach. Some might argue that it is high risk and hence likely to have high failure rates. For example, what happens if a technology is adopted but is never properly made use of? Dotcom businesses make use of the Web (a form of technology) as their main business advantage, yet many commentators suggest this explains their high failure rates. Although it is higher risk, for those who do succeed there are phenomenal advantages. As a whole, the approach is certainly more experimental but if the outlays are minimised, then risk is also minimised, while still allowing for many benefits.

An IT-driven approach does not abandon planning and strategic thinking altogether. Rather, there is a shift in emphasis from strategic to opportunistic approaches (see table 9.1). This may be considered a more effective way to operate in a rapidly changing environment, and relevant for the digital world, in which new business concepts and technologies are emerging all the time.

> **Reflection question 1:** How do the strategic and opportunistic approaches discussed apply to your personal use of information systems and technology?

TABLE 9.1 Strategy-driven versus technology-driven approaches

Characteristics	Strategy driven	Technology driven
Key feature	Planned	Opportunistic
Role of technology	Support system emphasis	Business driver
Risk	Low to medium	Medium to high
Rationality approach	Highly rational	Live with uncertainty
Gains (period)	Medium to long term	Short to medium term
Technology adoption (see figure 9.1)	Early majority	Innovators, early adopters

[**Key concept:** The business environment is changing constantly and planning methods should adapt to new conditions.]

E-business models

The growth of electronic business has generated many references to the concept of business models. In particular, researchers and practitioners have proposed that e-business has made a massive impact on the business world.

Some definitions of a 'business model' emphasise the economic basis of the idea. Others take a broader view according to three main features, which are as follows:

› *Business configuration.* This covers how the business works. It describes which activities the business performs and whether they are outsourced.

› *Value proposition.* This defines how the business benefits customers. The business must have a competitive advantage in relation to its services or products.

› *Revenue model.* This explains how the business generates revenue.

The following is an analysis of Internet business models.

Website functionality

Some researchers have tried to classify e-business models by examining website functionality. These classifications and 'models' abound in the literature and typically include such types as the advertising model, the online brochure and transaction-based systems.

Classifications of website functionality provide descriptions of systems that vary in complexity. The simplest ones, such as the poster or brochure model, provide general basic information about the product or service in an online brochure. In relation to e-business models, the question often asked is 'Where is the revenue stream?' The revenue may come from selling products, from commission in a brokerage system or from selling advertising space. Of course, not all e-business systems create a revenue stream; but they can still affect the bottom line by attracting new customers to the offline channel, or by keeping customers informed, thus improving customer retention rates offline.

Organisational structure

Organisational structure is a component of a business model. The structure should allow the implementation of the business objectives. Flatter network organisational structures are put forward as being able to respond more quickly to change than more hierarchical structures. Communication technologies can be instrumental in promoting newer organisational forms.

Organisational management

Management approaches are another aspect of business models. They range from cautious, bureaucratic approaches, whose emphasis is on accountability and procedures, to highly innovative and entrepreneurial environments, which require a style that is more encouraging and tolerant of risk. Management styles are certainly influenced by the culture of the organisation. In network organisations, for example, executives guide ideas through the network, most of the routine functions are outsourced and power is seen as an attribute of value-adding capability rather than position. Management is seen as key in getting new initiatives off the ground and encouraging innovation. Companies wishing to engage in e-business need to consider how they can incorporate an effective management culture.

Other business model components

Other relevant components of business models include:

> *Distribution channel*. This considers how the product or service is distributed to customers. For example, software can be distributed through retail outlets on CDs or can be downloaded from a website.
> *Partnerships and alliances*. An organisation could be totally independent or engage in partnerships or alliances with other organisations.
> *Marketing approach*. The marketing function can be viewed as a separate component of the business model.
> *Revenue stream*. A company may have single or multiple revenue streams.

The human resources model and the information systems and IT function can also be viewed as significant components of a business model.

Effective e-business models

For a business model to be effective it must consider most, if not all, components (see figure 9.4). Considering just one aspect of the model, such as marketing or organisational structure, will not create an effective e-business model.

E-business strategies

The Internet can be used to implement a range of business strategies. The last section looked at various business model components and how they can be tailored to the e-business paradigm. In this section, e-business strategies are examined in detail.

Marketing and advertising on the Internet

The Web can be used for brand-name marketing, and for providing sales information, product catalogues and product or service announcements. Marketing systems, just as retailing systems do, require considerable planning and support. Many strategies and techniques can be used

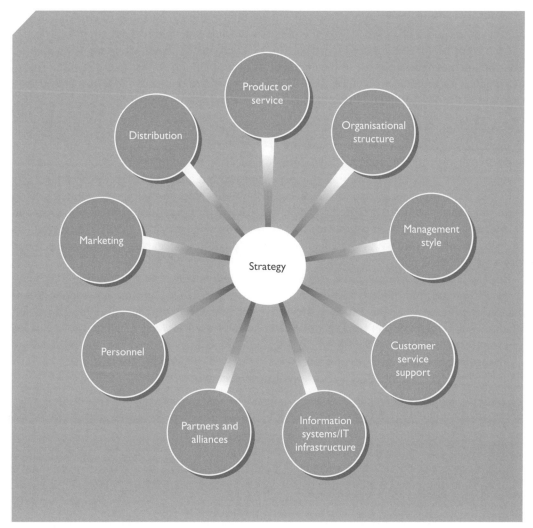

Figure 9.4 Key components of a business model

to market over the Internet and many are unique to the Web in that they have no offline equivalent. The Web has unique attributes: all customers can be accessed and informed at once; large amounts of information can be communicated cheaply; users can interact with the system and information can be personalised very easily. Personalisation of information involves taking into account what a customer has accessed or bought previously and then changing what is presented on the web pages to be more relevant. This is different from customisation, which is the process in which a user sets preferences at a site, such as selecting categories of information to be displayed on a search engine.

The Web can be used strategically to capture an increased share of a particular market segment. Some companies are aggressively marketing on the Web, with advertisements at leading Internet sites. For example, some credit card companies have chosen to advertise at sites that attract young people in the hope that they can tap into new markets.

Email marketing is now an important technique in marketing. Databases of email addresses are set up but to be effective among the plethora of emails people receive, the email header and the content of the email need to grab people's attention. The better examples of marketing over the Internet make good use of the interactivity of the medium and the facility to allow users to exchange information with other users. The development of online communities provides an example of the real potential of the Internet for marketing (see chapter 10).

Retailing on the Web

Transaction-based online shopping systems, which allow customers to buy various products and services over the Internet, are now commonplace. Many companies use this approach to supplement their traditional retailing channels. It provides a convenient service for consumers who can order products at a time and place of their choosing. For companies, this model is not as straightforward as it might first seem because the web application should be preceded by a strategic plan and be accompanied by a transaction support infrastructure. These systems need to deal effectively with payments, ideally link to corporate database systems and provide customer service support.

Beyond a basic retail model, the Web can be used in innovative ways to retail products and services. For instance, Internet auctions can provide an alternative to offline approaches. Retail auction sites generally require many visitors to generate the level of competition needed to sell products and services cost effectively. The method can be used as a way of selling slow-moving stock and attracting general interest in the website. Online auctions have been used for selling airline seats, cars and even cases of wine. Reverse auctions occur when the customer makes an offer for a product and the seller decides whether to accept it.

IS in action

eBay

eBay (www.ebay.com) is the world's largest online trading community and is a great example of consumer-to-consumer e-commerce. eBay started as a company in 1995, and has grown to be a well-known marketplace for the sale of both goods and services, mainly for individuals and small businesses.

The eBay site (see figure 9.5) is the Web's most popular e-marketplace by user numbers and, when measured by total user minutes spent at the site, is the most popular shopping destination on the Internet.

eBay's mission is basically to help people trade anything they wish. These people include collectors, hobbyists, dealers, unique-item seekers, bargain hunters, opportunistic sellers and browsers. Items that are sold include cars, jewellery, musical instruments, photographic equipment, computers, furniture and sporting goods. The total value of goods sold per year runs into billions of dollars. Sales can be conducted on a local, national and international basis.

eBay's site now combines traditional auction-style trading and fixed-price trading. To put in a bid for an item, the prospective buyer must first register at the site, then put in a maximum bid for the item and wait to see if the bid is accepted. The seller faces two basic charges: an insertion fee for putting an item up for sale through eBay and a final-value fee at the end of the auction, which is generally in the range of 1.25 per cent to 5 per cent of the final sale price.

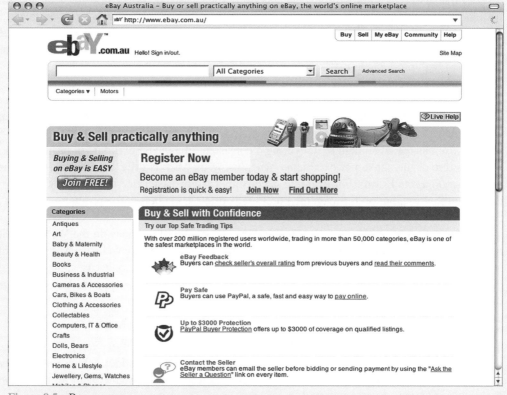

Figure 9.5 eBay

A particularly successful form of web retailing has been seen in the area of digital goods. Software, for example, is easy to download from the Internet, and downloadable music is a major issue in the music industry. Similarly, research reports and magazines can easily be sent to subscribers over the Internet. Even providing access to the Web in different ways from different situations can be a strategy, and, of course, this is where m-commerce makes an impact.

Although highly innovative websites gain media attention, more traditional products and services can use the Internet just as effectively. Many business owners thought that the Internet was suited only to businesses with certain characteristics, yet selling groceries over the Web has caught on in some parts of the world. This provides an interesting retail case, because there has been a common assumption that high-value, low-weight goods are better suited to retailing online because of their cost-effective distribution and high returns. However, many supermarket chains have had success with online sales.

> **Reflection question 2:** What do you think are some of the problems associated with selling groceries online?

Selling services on the Web

Some argue that all Internet-based marketing, even the marketing of products, can be seen as part of broader services marketing. This is because data, convenience, empowerment and time savings are largely intangible and services in general are viewed as being more intangible than physical products. On the Web, it is more difficult to distinguish between products and services because e-business is about service or a retailing event. Services can be stand-alone or they can be bundled with products to make them seem more tangible.

The Web has strengths in relation to service delivery. For example, on the Web, time dependency is reduced because the service receiver and the service deliverer do not need to meet physically. Services can be consistently delivered over the Web, compared with retail outlets, where much can depend on the knowledge or approach used by staff providing the service. The website also has the advantage of delivering a consistent image and brand to all customers.

The nature of the consumer experience when using the Web is different from the consumer experience in a retail store. For example, a consumer buying a service in a store can ask for a demonstration first, but on the Web the purchase is often made before the product or service is fully evaluated.

There are still issues in relation to the marketing and sale of services on the Web. It is difficult to replicate the personal touch of a shop assistant, although some websites have assistants answering questions online. Customer care is difficult to replicate. In some cases, the consumer has more control on the Web and typically might not feel the same pressure to buy that might be felt in a store with a shop assistant.

Customer service and support on the Web

The Web can be used to improve customer service and support cost effectively. The consumer goes through several stages of decision making before buying a product, which may involve one or several enquiries. The process typically involves researching product features and prices. Once the product has been purchased, the customer may experience difficulties that need to be sorted out. It makes sense therefore for many organisations to use the Web where possible for these functions. Web-based customer service enquiry and support systems typically reduce the cost per enquiry to 20 per cent or less from that of traditional telephone enquiries. For the customers, the main benefit is the convenience of being able to get support and service at a time and place of their own choosing.

The Web can be used for providing aftersales support in the form of extra information on how to use or care for a product. Software patches or updates can be downloaded cheaply and efficiently, so that the Web acts as a distribution channel for customer support. Online chat systems can be used if the customer base is large enough, so that customers can help one another.

Customers or potential customers can make enquiries over the Web and receive personalised replies. Airlines, for example, can have systems for frequent flier points, which the user can query easily, rather than telephoning a customer service centre.

A company can provide information and interactive applications to improve customer relationships and service. The Australian Tax Office, for example, can provide information on completing tax returns, or a bank can provide information on the types of accounts it offers. Collaborative e-business has emerged to meet the growing demand for real-time customer care. Other terms that are used to cover the same area include 'customer interaction software', 'one-to-one consumer intimacy' and 'web-based call centres'. Some people argue that the Web is very impersonal, which is a barrier to attracting more buying customers, but online chat, for example, can be used to provide a real-time, personal interaction.

The Internet is ideal for public relations campaigns. Information can be presented in different ways and will have a longer life than advertisements in newspapers and on television. However, in a cluttered environment such as the Web, effort must be made to stand out from the crowd. It is important to target the desired audience. Tactics have to be used to attract interest in the website or the email. This may require using keywords, catchy titles or, on occasion, even outrageousness.

Environmental scanning

The Web can be used for environmental scanning. This concept uses the Internet to gain information on market trends and the strategies of competitors. Companies have performed environmental scanning, either formally or informally, for many years. In some cases, specialist staff are employed to investigate trends in the marketplace and to check what competitors are doing, so that this information can be fed back into product or service development. In other cases, environmental scanning is outsourced to market research companies. The Web is a cost-effective tool for environmental scanning in that it provides access to a wealth of information on trends and the competitive environment (see table 9.2).

TABLE 9.2 Environmental scanning on the Web

Advantages	Disadvantages
Cost effective	The Web being unstructured
Can be done internally within the organisation	Content not always reliable
Most competitors have websites	Can be very time consuming

> **Reflection question 3:** What are other advantages and disadvantages of environmental scanning via the Web?

B2B e-business

Many organisations are moving into using B2B e-commerce in their supply and purchasing chains. As the drive towards a unified e-business effort continues, it is expected that significant changes will take place within these organisations. The changes will affect organisational structure, management approaches, business models, staff levels and responsibilities and relationships with customers and suppliers.

The nature of business with suppliers and customers is changing, with the increasing use of supply chain software linked with Internet technology, with the goal of virtual end-to-end supply chain management or virtual supply chain management. For example, Solectron, a manufacturer in the electronics industry, has reduced the time taken to produce a prototype from 10 days to 24 hours through its Internet-based supply chain system, mainly as a result of the improved exchange of data between suppliers and customers. For many suppliers, e-business projects are externally driven because their major buyer may demand they take part in an e-marketplace. Although there is no disputing the technical difficulties for suppliers involved in integrating back-end transaction systems, data warehouses, manufacturing and inventory tracking systems with web applications, some believe that the *organisational issues* are more difficult to overcome. These issues include changing management and organisational culture, and increasing trust among companies. Companies must be confident in their suppliers, so as to allow supply chains to open up to partners, and thereby providing increased visibility into the company.

E-marketplaces

Many of the virtual supply chains that have been implemented are relatively fixed because companies are fully integrated with their suppliers (see figure 9.6). Other developments on the Web are creating opportunities for marketplace relationships between companies. Some are suggesting that the Web will be increasingly used for transient supplier relationships between traders with little or no pre-established relationship in e-marketplace arrangements (see figure 9.7).

Indeed, e-marketplace trading is likely to threaten the more fixed forms of virtual supply chains. These types of opportunities bring not only potential benefits but also difficult issues relating to trust and risk. The rapid emergence of e-marketplaces is creating trading hubs, at which suppliers are matched with buyers for specialised equipment, products and services. Some companies want to be the owner of the dominant trading hub for their industry but know that if they become too dominant, they will deter many other companies from becoming involved.

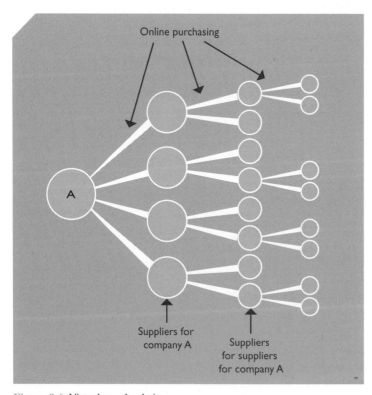

Figure 9.6 Virtual supply chain

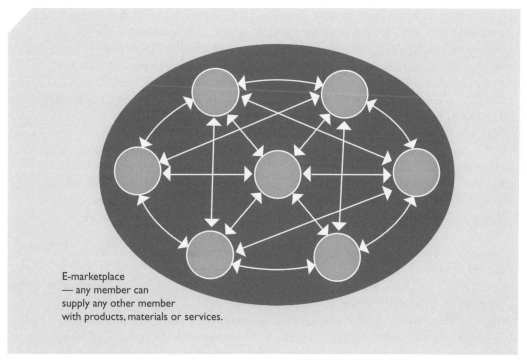

E-marketplace
— any member can
supply any other member
with products, materials or services.

Figure 9.7 E-marketplaces

E-marketplaces can be classified in many ways. The vertical (sector based) and horizontal (across sectors) classification is widely referred to, but there are other factors used to classify them:

> *vertical/horizontal:* according to industry sector
> *geographic coverage:* whether the market is national, regional or global
> *size of companies involved:* whether used by large or small companies (e-marketplaces are thought of as being the preserve of large companies but small companies can also create them)
> *operating model:*
  – catalogue model, providing information from the seller for the buyer but possibly not supporting negotiation between buyer and seller
  – the mediated operating model, making the marketplace an active intermediary between buyers and sellers, supporting transactions through the marketplace
> *private versus public:* whether users and accessibility are restricted by private e-marketplaces or, in the case of public marketplaces, they are not.

There are many examples of e-marketplaces. Quadrem.com is a major e-marketplace for mining, minerals and metals, operating globally with most of the major mining companies involved. Covisint.com is the e-marketplace for the automotive industry, operating globally.

Many factors influence success in the development and sustainability of an e-marketplace:

> *Technology infrastructure.* This includes the compatibility of the software with other software systems and its reliability and performance with many members.

> *Transaction administration system.* E-marketplace software should handle payments and contracts effectively, as well as the general management of membership services.
> *Income stream.* Several models describe how the e-marketplace makes money. These include membership subscriptions and commission on trades or other marketplace services.
> *Participants.* A major issue for e-marketplaces is whether they have sufficient members for viability. It is generally thought that it is better to draw existing customers and suppliers in than to rely on new participants.
> *Fulfilment of participant needs.* An e-marketplace that fulfils the needs of the participants will be successful. Therefore, it should be tailored to participant requirements and add value to the process.
> *Competitive advantage.* In this type of arrangement, gaining a competitive advantage by becoming the leader of the marketplace gives rise to a sustainable advantage.
> *Relationship management.* The issue of relationships, in particular, developing and maintaining trust among the participants in the marketplace, is important.
> *Security.* Security in relation to financial transactions and in the confidentiality of information must be achieved.
> *Level of independence.* Many consider it important for the e-marketplace to be neutral, in that the owners of the marketplace are not participants.

Perhaps the most critical factor for success is the minimum number of participants required by an e-marketplace to make it effective. This is an important issue because in some industry sectors, e-marketplaces have struggled to obtain a critical mass of participants. Many independent B2B e-marketplaces have found it difficult to generate sufficient and sustainable revenue, with many ceasing to exist. However, what has resulted from the decline in the numbers are many effective and sustainable e-marketplaces.

Problems associated with e-marketplaces

Several problems have been highlighted in relation to e-marketplaces:
> there being too many, so some suffer from a lack of participants
> lack of revenue because of a lack of participants or viable income streams
> security in relation to payments and confidentiality of information
> technical and administrative performance of e-marketplaces
> legal issues relating to contract handling.

Benefits associated with e-marketplaces

The main benefits reported in the literature on e-marketplaces relate to savings for both buyers and sellers and exposure to new customers:
> cost savings in selling
> savings in purchasing
> speed selling/purchasing
> exposure to new customers (global reach)
> convenience for users
> transparency to users, since a marketplace (by definition) is an open environment
> better quality of product or service (global reach)
> greater choice of products and services for buyers
> better-quality information on products and services.

E-procurement in the government of Andhra Pradesh, India

The Government of Andhra Pradesh (GoAP) has implemented many statewide e-Government applications since the year 2000, when the Central Government of India enacted the IT Act of 2000 to provide legal recognition to electronic transactions. As a part of these initiatives, GoAP has set up an E-Procurement Marketplace, linking government departments, agencies and local bodies with their vendors. The main objectives of the e-Procurement initiative are to: *reduce* the time and cost of doing business for both vendors and government; *realize* better value for money spent through increased competition and the prevention of cartel formation; *standardize* the procurement processes across government departments/agencies; *increase* buying power through demand aggregation; *provide* a single-stop shop for all procurements; *allow* equal opportunity to all vendors; *bring* transparency and ultimately reduce corruption.

The GoAP procures goods, services, works and turnkey contracts worth $2.0 billion every year. This procurement is done centrally through a single unit, as well through individual Government agencies who manage their own procurement needs. Procurement processes are governed by the guidelines of the GoAP and sometimes of external agencies like the World Bank, which may be funding a project.

Prior to the introduction of an e-Procurement platform, procurement in Government departments was carried out through a manual tendering process. The complete process required a long chain of internal authorizations and scrutiny (at times involving several departments), several visits by suppliers to departments, and the generation of reams of paper-based statements and evaluations.

Source: This article appeared on http://web.worldbank.org.

Digital content is a national priority

Digitising content has become highly political and is a key goal of many countries. For example, New Zealand has developed a digital content strategy, which is a substrategy of the nation's digital strategy. It is a five-year vision to provide New Zealanders with seamless, easy access to the information that is important to their lives, businesses and cultural identity.

Digital content is seen as one of the strategic enablers of the New Zealand digital strategy. Access to and creation of content, including the applications that are vital for creating, using and sharing content, are driving reasons to provide digital connectivity, skills and security. The availability of unique New Zealand content will help drive demand for broadband, improve the return on investment in capability and create opportunities for commercial use.

Source: Information from The Digital Strategy, www.digitalstrategy.govt.nz.

Intra-organisational systems

Intranets are being used for a range of organisational applications that are revolutionising internal communication and information processing. As document management systems, intranets provide a cost-effective method of presenting documents that incorporate policies, procedures and organisational initiatives. Transaction and query systems can be developed for many internal functions, such as IT support systems, internal purchasing, raising orders and matters related to payroll and leave entitlements.

Intranets can be used for sharing information. People can post documents for others to read, and bulletin boards can be used to share ideas or raise questions. Intranets are being viewed as knowledge management tools. Many are simply designed to capture and present data and information, but for effective knowledge management, more than this is required. Techniques for capturing and sharing information and knowledge that provide an environment conducive to knowledge transfer need to be explored.

Some of the uses of intranets include:

> accessing information in databases
> accessing company manuals and documents
> providing information on the latest company initiatives
> processing internal data and information through software applications
> internal sales and purchasing
> communicating company guidelines and policies
> advertising employment opportunities within the organisation
> promoting activities and events internally
> keeping contact details of employees including email addresses and telephone numbers.

Intranets have become an essential part of the most medium and large companies. They have replaced the mass of paper that used to be circulated to keep people informed. Most employees in organisations where intranets are used find that their work is severely hampered if they cannot access the intranet for an hour. However, the design of intranets is still an evolving science (or art!), with many lacking an effective structure to help people find what they need. Many intranets store a lot of content that is out of date and frequently misleading. A more advanced stage for intranets is to allow connection to them from external partner organisations, so that data, information and knowledge can be effectively processed and shared. The intranet then becomes an extranet.

Virtual organisations

Several characteristics are commonly used to define the term virtual organisation. A key feature of virtual corporations is that they form structures made up of different companies or individuals that come together to complete certain tasks and therefore appear as one organisation to the customer or client. They communicate, cooperate and coordinate with the use of IT.

Virtual organisations or teams must share data, information and knowledge. This type of organisational structure is typically formed to share knowledge explicitly. Organisational websites, whether Internet or intranet, can play a strategic role in providing a rich medium for knowledge communication.

Despite the many articles written about virtual organisations, there is still some ambiguity over their definition. It is argued, for example, that there are degrees of virtuality. Some organisations may interact totally through information and communications technology, whereas others also include face-to-face communication. It is assumed in the literature that virtual organisations need to be flexible to cope with a variety of tasks and locations. However, flexibility has varying degrees and it is a relative concept. Trust is often viewed as an important characteristic of virtual organisations but some studies conclude that it is no more significant in virtual organisations than it is in nonvirtual ones (Staples & Ratnasingham 1998).

A commonly proposed characteristic of virtual enterprises is that they operate with some informality and with a flatter management structure than the traditional hierarchies found in many bureaucratic organisations. Some suggest that this is an oversimplification of the management approaches required in virtual environments. They argue that the management approach (hierarchical/centralised or flatter/decentralised) should depend on the task or the project being undertaken.

The Internet or intranet applications of a virtual enterprise require careful thought and consideration, just as they do for nonvirtual organisations. Indeed, because of virtual organisations' heavy emphasis on the use of information and communication technology and their geographically distributed nature, it could be assumed that their websites would be even more strategically significant.

Virtual organisations are often confused with **dotcom** companies. A dotcom is usually taken to mean a company that exists entirely on the Web and has no real offline equivalent. It does not have to be an amalgamation of independent entities that come together to deliver a product or service. In practice, though, many dotcoms rely on other companies for functions such as distribution of the product.

E-government

Web-based systems have the potential to change how governments interact with citizens radically. Although some may argue e-government is not part of e-business, it has developed as a major trend. For many government agencies, the problems of introducing new approaches are not technical but organisational. Traditionally, government agencies have been slow to change, so cultural changes are required to adopt e-business effectively. Governments adopt the Internet and the Web for several purposes. A primary reason is to improve access to information. Brochures, leaflets and documents can be published online. Many governments have introduced portals to provide a central entry point to government-related information. Services can also be made available online, and citizens can have the convenience of paying bills from home. Some local governments have introduced community-based portals that are developed and maintained by the citizens themselves to keep one another informed about activities and events.

[**Key concept:** For many technologies, their uses developed over time, sometimes long after their initial introduction. The same can be said for the Web: many uses for this technology are still evolving.]

Strategic concepts related to e-business

Some concepts related to e-business are worth exploring. In this section creative destruction, channel conflict, disintermediation and global markets are discussed.

Creative destruction

It is argued that radical transformation sometimes cannot take place without the replacement of certain parts of the business. Traditionally, in the business world, the emphasis has been placed on adding new business directions to current operations. However, in today's competitive environment, it may be impossible to develop a radically transformed business without destroying some aspects of the existing business. This process has been termed creative destruction. For example, a company's Web strategy and existing business goals may be in conflict or be competing and therefore difficult to maintain. For example, a chain of travel agencies may abandon opening further retail outlets or even sell off some outlets to develop their online offerings.

[**Key concept:** In times of change and opportunities, a business may not be able to do everything but should identify the opportunities with the greatest potential.]

Channel conflict

There are many accounts of retail companies across business sectors experiencing some form of e-channel conflict and competition. Channel conflict arises when the competition among channels has an adverse effect on the cooperation among channel members.

Some strategies have been observed and classified to deal with channel conflict. These are considered, on the whole, quite defensive:
> limitation of electronic sales to those customers who are not served through conventional channels
> electronic sales of products not offered through conventional channels
> electronic sales of a limited product selection
> maintaining prices at least equal to conventional retail prices
> selling through hybrid intermediaries
> promoting and supporting conventional retailers.

However, complementary factors are at work in the relationship between offline and online business components:
> increased customer awareness of a product type
> increased brand awareness built up over years
> improved trust because of offline presence
> customers viewing a transaction as less risky because the company is established offline
> supplementary support from offline operations for online operations
> coverage of diverse customer preferences.

An example of channel conflict in education would occur if a university offered online courses to local students who would otherwise attend classes on campus. Basically, the university is taking on additional expense but does not gain any greater market share.

Disintermediation

Besides performing a competitive analysis, organisations should assess the threat of disintermediation. Because of the ease with which suppliers of products and services can market and sell directly to consumers, those companies that act as intermediaries in the distribution chain risk being bypassed. This has disastrous consequences for the intermediaries and is termed disintermediation. The businesses that are most at risk of disintermediation are those that do not significantly add value to the products and services they are distributing.

Intermediaries add value to the sales chain by creating a space where the parties to the business transaction can meet and where the search costs are reduced. For example, an online broker provides insurance quotes from several insurance companies for potential consumers. The website provides convenience for the consumer because a range of quotes can be obtained in one visit to the site. Reintermediation, as the term suggests, is all about intermediaries repositioning themselves on the Web. For example, many insurance brokers found that insurance companies could target consumers directly on the Web, lessening demand for their services. However, as more insurance companies went online, the consumer spent a lot of time comparing quotes from different sites. This led to online intermediaries springing up that compared different insurance offerings at one convenient website.

[**Key concept:** Some technologies actually cause a restructuring of industry sectors.]

Global strategy

The growth of the Internet has created a large global market. Some companies are able to take advantage of the global opportunities provided by the Internet. National borders, timezone differences and the cost of advertising in remote areas become less of a problem. The flexibility provided by the Web means that a one-person operation can develop a global strategy and implement it cost effectively. A global strategy needs to consider the differences in culture, language and distribution mechanisms. The Web can be used to gather information or find products and services from suppliers to cut costs or provide a stimulus for improvement. A small environmental protection consultancy, for example, could use the Web to find suitable projects and research grants. Its expertise may be in demand worldwide, but it may have been applying for projects within a restricted geographic domain only, because the print publications it uses to advertise with are locally or nationally oriented. Through the Web, however, the company can apply for projects around the globe.

Although many companies are considered global entities, there is no generally accepted understanding of what makes a business successful globally. Companies that have managed to sustain a competitive advantage globally have certain characteristics. The following six areas can be applied when developing a global Internet commerce strategy.

> *Governance and responsibility.* The directors need to be knowledgeable about the regions they are to market to. The company should disclose data and information, so that it is readily accessible to other countries, and the ethical standards of the organisation need to be understood by employees worldwide.

> *Strategy and planning.* Projects need to be given the go-ahead according to their potential to create value for shareholders, customers and employees. The company should have the ability to develop alliances with other companies in foreign regions and the world should be seen as a single economic and operating entity.

> *Marketing and service.* Marketing should be global and should attempt to develop a global brand, but it should take into account local needs.

> *Operations and technology.* The company should source materials from the most cost-effective supplier. Core processes should be standardised, yet allow for specialisation at the local level. The Web can play a leading a role in the technological infrastructure by improving the supply chain management systems and in the marketing and retailing of services and products.

> *Research and development.* Researchers require information about global markets, and knowledge sharing should be encouraged. This again can be facilitated by Web technology, which can also be used to develop strategic partnerships across the world.

> *Organisation and human resource management.* Staff should be moved to geographical locations where they can both disseminate knowledge and absorb it.

Summary

E-business has made a huge impact on the business world. Although many of the rules of business are the same, many new lessons need to be learned when doing business on the Internet. The key points in this chapter are:

> The Internet is available 24/7/52, has created a global marketplace and provides companies with many opportunities to increase revenue and reduce costs.

> Although strategy is still important in e-business, opportunistic IT-driven approaches can provide a competitive advantage.

> E-business can be used to market and sell products, support customers and deal with suppliers.

> E-marketplaces are revolutionising the way companies acquire products and services from suppliers.

> The Web may create the threat of disintermediation for some companies that add little value to the product or service, but it also provides opportunities for reintermediation, where convenience or choice, for example, are provided for the customer.

Questions

1. Provide three examples of how a website can reduce costs for a company.
2. What role is the Internet playing in the trend towards globalisation?
3. What are the likely problems associated with a badly designed intranet?
4. What is meant by B2B e-commerce?
5. What are the advantages of trading on an e-marketplace?
6. What is meant by the term 'business model' and what are its components?
7. Explain with the aid of examples how local government can use the Internet for the benefit of citizens.
8. What is a virtual organisation?
9. How can the Web be used for conducting environmental scanning?
10. What does a company need to consider when developing a global e-business strategy?

Exercises

1. A pearl retailer in Broome, Western Australia, wants to have a website developed so that he can promote his business, and make extra sales if possible. Provide guidance on how to develop a Web strategy for his pearl business.

2. Visit the website of a major company. Strategically analyse the website and the strategy behind it. Do you think it has scope for improvement?

3. Examine a local government website. Assess the types of services it provides. Do you think it has scope for improvement? Visit a second local government website and carry out a comparative analysis with the first website.

Westsea Airport hosts about 1.5 million passengers a year, and is one of the UK's fastest-growing regional airports. The customers are mainly recreational travellers on scheduled and charter airlines and a small percentage of business travellers on trips to Ireland.

The airport had a website but not a clearly defined Web strategy. The airport saw the potential of the Internet for implementing a simple document-publishing system and for the development of a major customer-focused Web presence, and to integrate partners' systems to provide services to customers.

In essence, the airport wanted to develop online services that would generate income and ultimately increase profitability. In addition, it was thought that the website should offer local residents information on how the airport might affect them as one way to maintain and improve community relations.

The airport was aware that it did not have internal expertise in web development, so it would need to seek an outside partner to design, develop and maintain its Web presence.

Because the airport has complex relationships with the companies that operate within its boundaries, it was clear that the business objectives of the airport would need to be handled sensitively to maintain the high level of rapport enjoyed among all parties.

The airport considered the website to be fundamentally important, so it decided it should host the system. The website had to integrate with existing systems, such as the CRM database and messaging systems, along with the platforms used by partners and suppliers. The preferred approach was to have a fully integrated system under the Westsea Airport brand.

An underlying principle was to make use of existing technology as much as possible. Also, the solution had to fit wherever possible with existing skill sets in the organisation. The airport decided to pick the technical infrastructure requirements, leaving the supplier to design and build the solution.

The airport required a solution developer with the technical expertise to design and develop a fully functional website that was integrated with backend systems. The web developer also had to be qualified to act as a one-stop-shop partner, which would assume full responsibility for the design, building and installation of the website and be able to provide 24/7/52 operational support, capable of understanding the airport's business and to communicate with and work with all airport staff.

The shortlist of web designers and developers included the following:

> A-to-Z Web Design, based locally, specialised in web design and had an impressive list of clients. However, it did not develop sophisticated websites, preferring to outsource this to one of several companies.

> I-Design was a major web design and development company, based 400 km south of Westsea in London. It had a great track record. The initial discussion with I-Design had proved problematic since they had many big projects in progress. Several discussions with technical developers had resulted in little progress.

> One-Web was a small web development company based locally. Although the staff were very approachable, they had not developed such a large website before.

> SmartWeb was based about 10 km from the airport, met all of the airport's selection criteria and was very comfortable working closely with nontechnical staff. They had tackled projects of a similar size and complexity before and were very interested and helpful in initial discussions with the airport staff.

(continued)

SmartWeb was the company chosen to develop the airport's website. After gathering requirements over several months, SmartWeb decided to break the project into stages. The first stage of the website development provided up-to-the-minute details of arrivals and departures, similar to those shown in the passenger lounges at the airport. This reduced the number of phone calls enquiring about the timing of flights. The website provided the facility to book scheduled flights and hotel accommodation. Rather than develop a new system, it was decided to integrate with the already available Telme.com online travel booking service. This integration was designed to be seamless.

To use many of the services supplied on the site, users must register online. These data are then used whenever a service is requested. If the customer wishes to book a flight through Telme.com, the airport's own CRM system feeds information into the Telme system, receives data in response and then passes it to the user as appropriate. A significant amount of effort was expended to ensure that the functioning of the website met the real-world requirements of users by involving them in the testing process.

The second phase of the operation was targeted to exploit the new Web presence and the online Westsea Airport brand. The second-phase offerings included the ability for customers to:

> preorder duty-free products online
> reserve airport car parking spaces
> book charter flights and package holidays
> preorder foreign currency.

The website receives up to 10 000 hits per day. The benefits of the e-business systems are many. Passengers are feeling more comfortable with the airport as a result of the website because they can understand the layout, parking, shopping and currency exchange facilities before they leave home. Local-community residents can be informed of developments at the airport, which helps community relations. Through the online shopping and ordering systems, income and profits are increasing. Finally, the airport has received substantially increased revenue from car parking. Before the new website, an outside company had sole control of the parking, and the airport received only 5 per cent of revenue. With online booking, 90 per cent of the revenue now comes to the airport.

Overall, the main lessons learned from their experiences are: exploit the experience of employees; work closely with the real end-users and work with suppliers in a partnership fashion.

From an e-business perspective, the system is successful because it provides what the users want conveniently. Travellers require timely and accurate data, and the new web applications provide them.

Questions

1. Identify the key business objectives related to the airport's e-business initiatives.

2. Draw up a list of factors to evaluate the four web development companies.

3. Classify the main benefits of the new website.

4. Visit an airport of your choice's website and write a 250-word review of the site. Take note that Westsea does not exist!

Reference

Staples, DS & Ratnasingham, P 1998, 'Trust: the panacea of virtual management', *Proceedings of the International Conference on Information Systems*, pp. 128–46.

CHAPTER 10
Web commerce development

LEARNING OBJECTIVES

After reading this chapter, you should be able to:

» describe the characteristics of web applications

» describe how the Internet developed

» understand the various web technologies and web-authoring tools

» assess the feasibility of adopting web commerce

» explain how the scope and complexity of web projects affect development

» understand the types of users of web systems

» understand the implications of working with an international outlook

» describe the critical issues in website design

» understand how to attract visitors to websites

» explain how to measure the effectiveness of websites.

Introduction

Website development is an area of information systems in its own right. It incorporates the analysis of requirements, design, implementation and, of course, the issue of evolution and updating. Website projects can vary significantly in scope and complexity. There is a lot of pressure to design and implement a website well the first time because a problematic website is likely to lose customers. Chapter 9 examines the strategies behind e-business. This chapter looks in some detail at the issues surrounding the development of websites.

Characteristics of web applications

Web applications are systems developed for the web environment. Although web applications have some similar characteristics to other types of information systems, they also have certain unique characteristics. This is largely because of the demands put on web applications by being directly accessible by customers and suppliers. Some of the main characteristics of web applications are described below.

Websites often evolve from simple beginnings to become multifunctional. Common functions include providing information to users or customers, developing relationships with customers, enabling customers to perform transactions and documenting management systems for internal users (intranet). The multifunctionality of many systems forces organisations to work across traditional departmental boundaries. A customer focus epitomised by the question 'how do we meet the customer's needs?' requires an integrated effort from sales, marketing, customer service and information systems. This requires a high degree of collaboration, which means that traditional organisational boundaries are de-emphasised.

Teams made up of different business representatives may not be adequate for developing web applications, especially if they are led by an information systems person. The problems associated with representative teams are that members do not speak the same language and have different goals and expectations. The teams that are required for web applications development need to have a business focus and be led by a 'producer' figure, who has expertise in the technical, marketing and business aspects of the organisation. The analogy of a film production team is useful, because such teams have one goal in mind but manage diverse skills and tasks in the process. Large web project teams can include:

> a project leader, who coordinates the team and project
> systems analysts, who gather requirements for the website
> web designers
> graphic designers, who do detailed designs of logos and icons
> content providers, who provide the information content for the site
> technical developers
> web editors, who ensure that the content is correct and that links work
> web marketing specialists, who build the marketing techniques into the site
> representative users or customers, who make sure the system is acceptable and fulfils the requirements.

> **Reflection question 1:** Which role do you think has the greatest influence on the project?

Because of the multifunctionality of many websites, there are often diverse groups of stakeholders. These can include people both within and outside the organisation. Internal stakeholders may be specialised categories of employees, and external stakeholders may be current customers or key suppliers. These stakeholder groups can live locally, in another state or overseas. Overseas users may have a different cultural and linguistic background, which may have to be considered in web application development. As a result, responsibility for the website within the organisation can be ambiguous, and the overall management of the web strategy may be given little consideration.

The content and functionality of websites change. Because of this, the notion of project completion is inappropriate. Even the standard six-monthly update reviews used with traditional information systems applications may be unsuitable for managing the rapid amount of change required. Websites can be viewed as organic systems that are continually adapting to their environment. Some components of sites flourish under certain conditions, but other components become redundant and wither away. Systems can start off as intranets and go on to develop an Internet or extranet component, and others start off as websites for external use and develop an intranet component.

[**Key concept:** Evolutionary development approaches dominate in e-commerce.]

History of the Internet

The Internet developed in the mid-1960s as a US Defense Department network called ARPAnet. It was an experimental network, designed specifically to withstand various forms of attack on communications lines. In the ARPAnet model, communication always occurred between source and destination computers. To send a message, the data was put into a packet of data called an 'Internet protocol packet' and addressed. The computers, not the network, were given the responsibility of ensuring that the communication was completed. The approach worked on the premise that the network itself was unreliable and open to attack. In the early 1980s, universities began to use the Internet as an inexpensive and convenient method for communicating. The Internet expanded rapidly with improvements in the telecommunications infrastructure and its use by commercial organisations.

The World Wide Web (also referred to as the Web and WWW) is a network of information sites. The sites are created using hypertext, which is the method of linking information and screens, which allows simple navigation and linking together of sources of information. Even though the Web is expanding rapidly, it is largely an unorganised and unstructured web of information available on servers throughout the world.

The idea of the Web was first developed in 1989 by Tim Berners-Lee at the European Laboratory for Particle Physics (CERN) in Geneva and has grown to be a huge number of information repositories today. The success of the Web owes much to the simplicity of hypertext, a type of 'point and click' interface that was used earlier in Apple Computer's hypercard system.

Web technologies

You need to have some understanding of various web technologies, including browsers, search engines, hypertext, web addresses, and communication protocols. This section briefly introduces these concepts.

Browsers

The World Wide Web can be accessed by software applications known as browsers, such as Mozilla Firefox and Microsoft Internet Explorer. The browser allows the user to input a uniform resource locator (URL), that is, the website address. A connection is made to the remote computer (using that URL) and the hypertext markup language (HTML) code is returned to the client and formatted as a page within the browser. Browsers make temporary copies of the page in an area of memory called the 'cache'. These pages are used when the user clicks the 'back' button or otherwise accesses the same page in the same session, which saves accessing the pages over the Internet again. Web browsers are becoming more sophisticated in terms of the operations they support. Some typical facilities supported by web browsers are:

> retrieving web pages
> navigating through web pages
> searches based on keywords
> accessing web pages by inputting the URL
> retrieving previously viewed web pages
> saving web pages
> printing web pages.

Search engines

The browser does not do the searching on the Internet but uses search engines. These are software systems located at websites, which collect and order information from the Internet. Examples of search engines are Google, AltaVista, Yahoo! and Excite. Different search engines work on different principles and will often retrieve different 'finds'. However, most tend to list keywords and headings on the screen with the information's location in a hypertext link that can be selected to take the user to that site. Some search engines are general, and others are more specialised, either geographically (focusing on a country) or in terms of subject matter. Meta-search engines are systems that use more than one search engine in the search process. Accessing six or ten search engines within one search is clearly an effective way of searching.

> **Reflection question 2:** Which search engine do you use? Why?

Hypertext and hyperlinks

Web pages can be linked using hyperlinks. These are a method of navigating the Web. The hyperlink can be a word or words or a picture or area within a page. Words that are hyperlinks are typically highlighted in some way and, once clicked, take the user to another page. HTML is a language for developing hypertext documents that can be viewed in a browser. The transmission of documents on the Web is handled by the hypertext transfer protocol (HTTP).

HTTP

Hypertext transfer protocol (HTTP) is the web communications protocol, which handles the transfer of data over the Internet. When a client opens a connection to a web server, an HTTP header is sent, which contains a command to, for example, get or input data. The server transmits a message back to the client, which includes the format of the data being returned. This allows the browser to display different types of data such as text, images and HTML.

Websites

Related web pages located together on a computer or the Internet are known as a website. Universities typically have websites that run into thousands of pages. (For example, check out Edith Cowan University's website at www.ecu.edu.au.) Of course, the organisation and management of these large sites are complex and time consuming. The management of content on large websites has developed into a specialised area known as content management.

Web addresses

Websites must have a unique address to avoid clashes and ambiguity for those accessing the data. The address is composed of several pieces of information and known as the uniform resource locator (URL). The URL is composed of the protocol, the server and the path of the file or web page, for example, http://www.looksmart.com.au. In this example, the letters 'http' stand for hypertext transfer protocol, and 'www.looksmart.com.au' is the server address, which includes the domain name, the type of organisation (in this case, 'com' stands for *commercial*) and the country where it is located (in this example, 'au' denotes Australia).

Examples of Internet address codes are:

biz   businesses

com   commercial institutions

edu   educational institutions

gov   government organisations

net   networks

uk   United Kingdom

nz   New Zealand

jp   Japan

ca   Canada

The United States does not have a country abbreviation, for example, http://www.ibm.com/.

Mobile commerce

Mobile commerce (m-commerce) has become a key feature of the e-commerce landscape. The term is used to describe activity involving transactions with monetary value conducted by a mobile phone or a personal digital assistant that connects with or includes phone technology. The transaction could be for intangible goods, such as information in digital format sent to the mobile device, or it could involve physical goods. A further distinction in mobile transactions is between remote transactions and point-of-sale transactions.

A significant amount of m-commerce involves the purchase of different types of digital content for the mobile phone itself. These include ringtones, screensavers, wallpapers, games, music and video clips.

M-commerce is convenient and easy to use. Therefore, new applications that are too difficult to use are unlikely to be successful. They should build on existing ways of working and then add mobile value. The benefits of m-commerce are immediate access and delivery of service, flexibility, personalisation, location awareness or better customer service (see, for example, www.forum.nokia.com).

Dude for a day

SPEED is a cable network dedicated to motor sports. It is available to 70 million homes in North America. SPEED used a company called MindComet to develop its online presence. MindComet developed the idea of 'Dude for a Day' as an integrated promotion to raise awareness and increase viewers of SPEED's *2 wheel Tuesday*; increase the number of people accessing its website and expand its database of viewers.

A competition through the TV program provided a chance to win a motorbike. A unique code was given out each week on the TV show and this had to be input at the website along with personal details. Ads ran online before the official start of the competition and were designed to get people to watch *2 wheel Tuesday*. They also employed email marketing with a series of HTML emails to drive users to the site. TV advertisements were also used to promote the TV program and the competition.

The strategy was very effective and it attracted many people to the website, allowing their details to be captured in a database, which could be used in the future to send emails about new TV programs.

Source: Information from MindComet n.d, 'Dude for a day', www.mindcomet.com.

[**Key concept:** The trend for systems is to provide greater flexibility of access.]

infobyte

Plinking

Ever heard of plinking? Imagine you are watching a video online and see a pair of jeans but you do not know where to buy them. Plinking allows you to find out. Users can pause the video and then click on tagged items. Clicking on the article of clothing (or anything for that matter) will take the user to a web page of the retailer. Viewers will also be able to contribute in the future as they will be able to add links to existing videos and get some share of the revenue!

Design issues are very important in m-commerce. It is important to pick applications that will provide immediate value to customers. For example, mobile phones have a restricted display area and small keypad, so it is important to focus content. Loyalty can be built up with customers with personalised services.

> **Reflection question 3:** What uses would you make of a mobile phone that could access the Web?

Web authoring tools

An organisation developing a website or intranet needs to consider which web authoring tool or tools to use. It is a good idea to decide on one as a standard for the organisation for three main reasons: training in the web authoring package can be focused; supporting one package is easier from a help and advice perspective; and licensing arrangements will be eased and may even be more cost effective.

Hypertext markup language (HTML) has become the language of the Internet and is used for describing web pages to web browsers. A text editor can be used to develop HTML files in the HTML command language. However, most people developing websites use software packages such as Macromedia Dreamweaver or Microsoft's Frontpage. These packages provide a graphical environment for page development, which is a better option for people without programming skills because they have a WYSIWYG ('what you see is what you get') interface. HTML is based on standard generalised markup language (SGML). SGML is a system of rules for describing the treatment and use of documents. HTML is a specialised application of SGML. However, professional developers often use a variety of scripting and programming languages to add extra functionality to the systems. Some of the main scripting and programming languages used on the Internet are described in the following sections.

XML

HTML is not sophisticated enough to deal with all the demands of e-business today. XML, which stands for extensible markup language, is a simplified version of SGML. XML allows the display of text and data in a browser as HTML does, but it is also a flexible way of creating common information formats and sharing *both* the format and the data on the Web, intranets and elsewhere. In other words, where HTML describes the content of a web page only in terms of how it is to be displayed and interacted with, XML describes the content in terms of what data are being described, so it provides metadata and a way of structuring data. XML documents are associated with their own information contexts. This means document tags can be defined that have meanings within that context. This provides a powerful environment for document management because XML could define the document type, its use and other features that would be helpful in structuring the information space. A benefit of XML is that it allows data to be shared among different applications because the tags relate to the function and identity of the data rather than anything application specific.

Web client programming languages

Web pages can have scripts (VBScript, JScript or JavaScript) or Java applets embedded in them, which are then executed on the client machine once the page has downloaded. These scripts and applets add interactivity to the web pages and perform specialised functions such as data validation on data input into forms. In addition, they take some of the processing burden off the web server.

The importance of Java

Java is a programming language that can be used to develop programs that can be embedded in web pages to add extra functionality such as animation and forms. Much media attention has surrounded the Java programming language, because Sun Microsystems (the company that developed Java) has to compete in the same environment as Microsoft, so to get noticed there has to be a concerted promotion of the product; and Java is a sound language that has innovative features.

Sun Microsystems developed a language called Oak, which was used for consumer electronic devices. This language was small, reliable and architecture independent. The developers realised that, with the rise of the Internet, an architecture-neutral language was needed, so Java was developed from Oak.

Java is described as 'a simple, object-oriented, distributed, interpreted, robust, secure, architecture-neutral, portable, high-performance, multi-threaded and dynamic language' (Sun Microsystems 2004). Although this description might seem too good to be true, Java does have excellent attributes for being used on the Internet. Java is an interpreted language but is also compiled first into byte code. This means that a Java program can be downloaded and interpreted by a browser whatever the operating system or hardware (as long as the Java interpreter is available). This is possible because the device-dependent features of the program are loaded in at runtime. This makes Java programs or **Java applets** (graphical Java programs) very portable between machines, hence the phrase 'write once, run anywhere', often used with Java.

[**Key concept:** Technical programming is just as important as ever.]

Assessing the feasibility of adopting web commerce

Feasibility is about assessing whether the proposed project is viable. Viability is normally assessed in terms of the costs and benefits attached to the development of the application. Generally, the benefits, which are quantified financially, should outweigh the costs of developing and running the system. A time scale of three-to-five years can be used to examine the feasibility, because much of the cost of a system is incurred early in its life, whereas the benefits are more evenly spread throughout the life of the system.

The costs are typically such things as staff time, hired expertise, equipment and programmer time. The benefits are increased orders, less cost per transaction processed, more and better-quality information and increased staff and customer satisfaction.

It is difficult to develop a cost–benefit analysis until full details of the system are ascertained. Consequently, a relatively fast feasibility assessment should be conducted at the start of the planning and strategy development stage, and further assessment should be made periodically. A feasibility study should also be carried out for each component of the web development.

Some organisations view their web commerce initiatives as an investment in the future. Rather than taking a typical cost–benefit analysis perspective, in which future benefits are estimated, the main benefit is seen as providing scope and choice for future business directions. This perspective assumes that a company that has stepped into the web commerce arena is in a better position to take advantage of new opportunities that arise in the area than a company that is watching from the sidelines.

[**Key concept:** Feasibility is a moving target.]

Project complexity and scope

A web development project can vary in scope from setting up an entire website for a large organisation, to developing a component of a large website, to developing a small website of limited functionality. These are very different types of projects, which vary greatly in complexity, depending on several factors:
> *The scope of the project.* This usually refers to the functionality of a system. A system could have a narrow, well-defined scope, in that it might deal only with customer enquiries, or it may be broader in scope, covering a wider range of customer service options.

> *The size of the project.* This can be measured in many ways, such as the number of functions, the number of sites and the volume of information.

> *The number of users and range of users.* As the number of users increases, so too can the complexity of the system. A larger number of users often means more time spent consulting them to determine requirements for the system. The organisational dynamics of workgroups often increase the complexity of systems. Workgroups form social and political entities that cannot be ignored when developing information systems.

> *The geographic distribution of users.* This has an effect in several ways. The communications hardware and software infrastructure becomes more complex as data are sent across several sites. If users are internationally dispersed, linguistic and cultural differences may affect the design process.

> *The type (complexity) of functionality required in the system.* This can be characterised by general functionality and applies equally to an intranet and the Internet:
>   – *Static document publishing systems.* These are often used for intranet applications to put company manuals and documentation on the Web and to provide information to customers. They are relatively simple systems because they are not connected to databases, although they can be multimedia systems that include text, graphics, video and animations.
>   – *Dynamic web applications.* These are more sophisticated interactive systems. They include forms for input of customer details, which are then stored in a simple database or file. Querying facilities, for example, to find staff telephone extension numbers, may also be present.
>   – *Complex web applications.* These types of systems provide a fully interactive interface, which connects to one or several databases. They can complete transactions such as adding, amending or deleting. Examples include allowing suppliers access to inventory control systems, and allowing customers to make purchases that automatically update the order-entry and stock-control systems.

> *The stage of evolution of the overall website.* If there are no web applications in the organisation, the project will involve work at a strategic level to define the goals of the system. On the other hand, if the site is relatively mature and working well, then later projects will be additions that will not usually require the same broad planning phases, although some strategic planning will still be required.

> *The amount of expertise within the organisation.* The less expertise there is for any information systems project within an organisation, the higher the risk associated with the project. Expertise can save a great amount of time as it improves the chances of completing tasks correctly, working appropriately, using suitable tools, estimating better and so on. If expertise does not exist within the organisation, the expertise has to be brought into the organisation from outside. This can alleviate some of the problems but adds complexity because the organisation has to source suitable consultants or vendors and assess their performance.

> *The number of interfaces with other systems.* The more connections with other systems, the more complex the development and testing process.

> *The strategic or critical nature of the project.* If the project is critical to the organisation, for example, if it is costing a large amount of money or the system it connects to is part of

the core business system or systems, then the consequences of failure will be significant. In these cases, the project could influence corporate profits or relationships with customers and suppliers.

A company can use several strategies when developing a new website. It is unlikely, unless the site is small, that the whole site will be designed and implemented in one project cycle. A major issue in website development is defining responsibility for both the development and maintenance of sections of the website. A team working centrally may take responsibility for development of the website. In other situations, each organisational unit may have its own team. An issue that needs to be resolved, therefore, is the overall development strategy and the level of responsibility given to organisational units. The key website development alternatives are:

> plan the entire site and strictly regulate its distributed development
> plan the core of the site (outsourcing or in house) and make no further changes
> plan the core of the site and let user departments develop their own neighbourhoods
> plan the core of the site and loosely regulate the development of the rest of the site
> allow unregulated development of the entire site (not recommended)
> plan the entire site, develop the core and then incrementally develop the rest of the site.

Defining the users

Many different groups of people interact with websites. Understanding their characteristics and the roles these groups play helps define the requirements for a web application. The more detail that can be added to the development of user profiles, the more likely the completed system will be of use. For example, many types of customers may interact with a business. Understanding how they differ should go a long way to understanding how their needs can be served.

Surfers

The Web is an environment in which people stumble on a website without any intention of making a purchase. They may simply be browsing, which is similar to window shopping in a shopping centre. This type of user will just pass through quickly if the site is not appealing or easy to navigate. If the site is memorable, they may return at a later date to look again or even make a purchase. Increasingly, people are more focused in their use of the Web. They are less likely to surf and are more likely to be using the Web with a specific objective in mind.

Buyers

These people come to the site to make a purchase. They have some knowledge about the item required. A clear, well-designed system will help the customer complete the transaction.

Member and nonmember customers

In some organisations, customers must be members. This may give them special privileges or discounts that are not open to nonmembers. Nonmembers must complete an application form and apply for membership.

Dissatisfied customers

There should be some way for customers to make a complaint. This can be done by providing customer service contact details on the website.

Recipients

The person who buys the goods may not be the same who receives the goods. This must be taken into account in the information system.

Suppliers

Suppliers may access an extranet to determine which products require supplying.

Internal users

Many people within an organisation interact with the website:

> systems developers such as the analyst who defines the requirements of the system

> designers, who decide on the layout and design features of the system

> content specialists, who provide the text for the system

> those who have the technical expertise to implement the system

> the database administrator if the system is connected to corporate databases

> customer service representatives and marketing and sales staff.

Senior management will be involved more in developing the website strategy. If there is an intranet available, then anyone in the company may use the system.

[Key concept: Know your users. **]**

> **Reflection question 4:** Which type or types of user are you?

Working with different cultures and languages

If the product or service is to be promoted to people of different linguistic backgrounds, then translations of web content should be provided. Tourism-related sites, in particular those intended to appeal to overseas tourists, should provide at least translations into the languages of the targeted nationalities. For example, the Australian National Tourism Site, a site aimed at tourists visiting Australia (www.australia.com), has translations into several languages, including Japanese. The developers may also have to consider alternative languages for local residents who cannot read the national language, and currency exchange rates or links to a currency exchange site.

Although the Internet may appear to be making the world a 'global village', there are still many cultural differences among people of different nationalities. Religious, economic, political, legislative and social differences dictate what is appropriate web content.

Muslim countries usually have certain expectations in terms of how women are portrayed in advertisements. For many years, the French restricted travel advertising, believing it had a negative impact on their domestic tourism revenue. There can be restrictions on advertising with an overt or covert political message. Some countries restrict the advertising of tobacco.

World Wide Web Consortium

The World Wide Web Consortium (W3C) was created in 1994 and now has more than 400 member organisations from around the world. The mission of W3C is to promote inter-operability and an open forum discussion on issues related to the Web's development. In particular, W3C has three long-term goals:

> *universal access:* to work towards the Web being accessible to all sections of the community by taking into account differences in culture, education, ability, material resources and physical limitations

> *semantic Web:* to work towards a software environment that helps users to make the best use of the resources available on the Web

> *Web of trust:* to play a role in guiding the Web's development from a legal, commercial and social perspective.

W3C activities are organised into groups:

> working groups for technical developments

> interest groups for more general work

> coordination groups for communication among related groups.

The work of the consortium breaks down into four main areas:

> *architecture domain:* for examining issues related to the underlying technologies of the web

> *interaction domain:* specialises in improving user interaction with the web

> *technology and society domain:* focuses on developing the web infrastructure to solve social, legal and public policy concerns

> *Web accessibility initiative:* examines accessibility (for people with disabilities) of the Web through five main areas of work: technology, guidelines, tools, education and outreach, and research and development.

Source: Information from www.w3.org.

Design issues for web commerce

Designing a web commerce system involves more than just developing web pages with appropriate content. Today, organisations are using the Web as a unifying portal to tie their disparate corporate systems together. In a sense, the organisational expectations in relation to information technology (IT) have not changed. They should be flexible systems that help the organisation by improving productivity. Consequently, the development of web systems is an opportunity to examine the entire information systems and IT infrastructure to determine how and where improvements can be made.

Developing a website in an organisation involves decisions related to the hardware and software for the client machines and web server. If the system is to perform transactions that access the corporate databases, then an applications server and database server will be needed. The design of the site's pages requires making decisions on the design framework, the navigation mechanism and the detailed layout of pages.

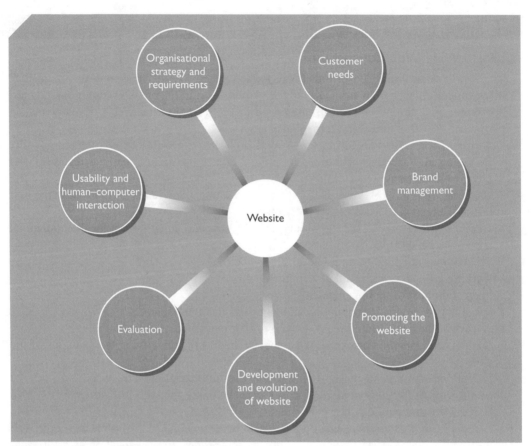

Figure 10.1 Issues related to website design

Web accessibility issues

Web accessibility design issues have been highlighted in relation to people with disabilities (Sellitto & Wenn 2000). The general perception was that the Web was accessible by all. This is not strictly true because some high-profile websites have been identified as not catering to people with various disabilities, such as physical, visual, hearing and cognitive or neurological disabilities.

A range of design features can be built into websites to help people with disabilities, such as:
> captioned (transcripts) audio files for people with hearing impairment
> voice output of all text for people with vision impairment, and descriptions of graphics files so they too can be voice output; the layout of text is very important, because the text reader must follow a logical flow; tables are especially problematic in relation to this feature
> control of colour settings and styles for people who are colour blind
> keyboard equivalents for mouse-driven commands, to avoid repetitive stress injury from constantly clicking a mouse
> magnification tools to aid readability, and avoidance of scrolling text
> use of clear and simple language for people with cognitive disabilities, and consistent design and navigation options.

Many national governments have disability discrimination acts, which cover issues related to the design of websites, and the W3C is keen to promote the design of accessible websites for the people with disabilities.

Evolution of website designs

The conventions used in the design of websites have undergone considerable evolution over the Web's brief history. Early website designs were characterised by a simplistic functionality. They tended to have text across the full width of the screen and in continuous paragraphs on one page. Often, they had been constructed by technical people, with the main aim of conveying a simple message.

Later design approaches took advantage of extensions to HTML. Images and graphics replaced some of the text and the pages were organised in simple hierarchies. (If you surf the Web, you will find many of these so-called first- and second-generation sites.)

Effective design

Design is a multifaceted concept, with harmony and balance at its core. Design of websites has evolved to ensure better usability and functionality. Technical features are not the overriding factors. Design is evident in the structure of a website, in the navigation mechanisms, in the metaphors used and in the detailed layout of each page.

Designing effective web interfaces is both an art and a science. It is an art because a certain amount of creativity is required to develop web systems that are functional yet aesthetically pleasing to look at and work with. This aspect of website design is influential in developing the brand image of a company. Sometimes fashion and fun play a vital role in the design; a scientific, engineered or more purely rational approach would not achieve the same level of success. However, people process and interpret information according to cognitive principles, and adhering to these helps a designer to develop systems that communicate effectively. So a more scientific or engineered approach provides a strong underlying set of principles, which can serve as a framework for design.

Human–computer interaction is an important field within the information systems and IT disciplines. It involves the theory and practice of how users interact with computer systems and the usability of systems. It draws on cognitive psychology for principles of how people interpret information. Designing systems according to these principles generally leads to systems with a higher level of usability.

Research in cognitive psychology tells us that in most situations people are easily cognitively overloaded. For example, people find it difficult to remember much more than seven, plus or minus two, chunks of information. These could be instructions or digits or keywords. Therefore, designers should not expect users to remember a great deal of information or data from one web page to another, but should have this information repeated on each screen if it is important. The brain processes information serially. This means that developing systems with competing features is likely to distract the user from acquiring necessary information. Generally speaking, therefore, simplicity of design and layout is desirable for improving the degree of information communicated.

The designer works with web pages that are displayed in a browser. Each web page provides a design space in which text, graphics, animations and images can be arranged to maximum effect.

Layout

Space can be used on a web page to separate features, whether text or graphics, and thereby communicate meaning and relevance without using lines or borders that would add to the cognitive load on the user (see figure 10.2). The techniques of using space and position in design are evident, of course, in newspapers, magazines and books. Using space wisely creates a design that is both simple and effective.

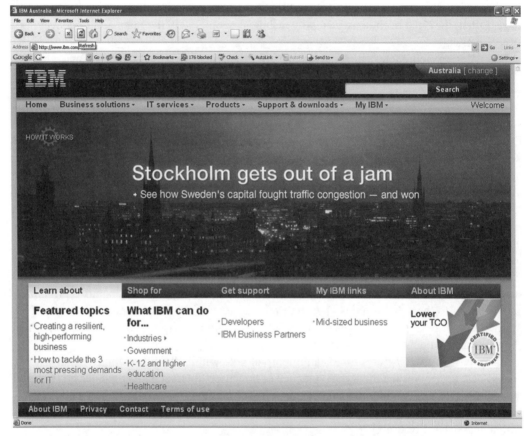

Figure 10.2 IBM's Australian home page showing clear and simple web page design
Source: IBM, www.ibm.com.au.

Consistency

Consistency is an easy principle to understand but one which is often forgotten. Consistency relates to the uniform application of terms or keywords, the use of icons and graphics, the position of web page features such as menu items, the use of colour and so on. The designer should work out a design strategy, along with the details, and stick to it. Users will then find it easier to navigate around the website.

Flow of content

People are used to reading from top to bottom and from left to right. What does this mean for web designers? It is important to know how text should be arranged on the web page for ease of reading. For example, examine the two sets of sentences in figure 10.3. The text on the right is definitely quicker and easier to read with its top-to-bottom and left-to-right orientation.

It should also read from left to right. Ideally, it should read from top to bottom. Text should be laid out in a certain way.	Text should be laid out in a certain way. Ideally, it should read from top to bottom. It should also read from left to right.

Figure 10.3 Text top-to-bottom and left-to-right principles

The desire to create distinctive websites has led many developers to ignore cognitive principles. The resulting applications are then often distinctive for the wrong reasons.

Zoning

Browser windows or screens can be divided up into zones. These are areas of the screen which are used for certain functions. For example, figure 10.2 shows zones for the menu, advertisements and title, and the bulk of the screen area for displaying other information. There are many different zone layouts that can be used to great effect. The main advantage of zoning is that all pages will have a similar structure and consequently provide a consistent framework for the designer and the user.

Grouping

Logically related items should be grouped together. In this respect, proximity conveys meaning. This applies to links, icons and menu items, for example.

Text

The size of the text denotes its significance. For example, the heading for a web page is usually larger than the other text on the page. A problem for designers is that HTML is so limited in terms of text sizes and fonts. An additional problem associated with headings in HTML is that they leave too much space underneath. Therefore, many designers use a text heading that has been created in a graphics package and saved as a GIF file. Headings can then be developed along the lines of a logo and their effect can contribute to the image branding of the site.

Subheadings can also be developed as GIFs or can be left in bold with no space following. Two levels of headings are usually enough for most designs — if you need another level, you should go to another page.

Horizontal lines in any form to separate areas of the web page should be avoided because they simply add to the cognitive load without conveying useful information. A blank line-space is preferable in most cases.

Margins are effective for making the text stand out on the page.

One of the main design problems with many websites is that the text is difficult to read. This is because it is either too small or in the wrong font. Long lines of text on a screen make reading difficult for the user. Few words per line should be a general aim, although much of the control, in terms of window size and font size, is down to the user's browser. It is also best not to use multiple columns of text: it is a great deal of work for little reward because the user must scroll back up the window to see the next column.

Alternative text sizes can be used to capture the user's attention (see figure 10.4). Highlighting in bold or the use of a bright colour can have the same effect.

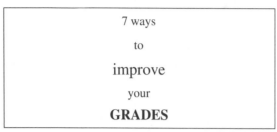

Figure 10.4 Varying text size and font to attract attention

Colour

Inexperienced designers often make the mistake of designing web pages using many different colours. It results in what is known as the 'Christmas-tree effect'. Good design does not rely primarily on the use of different colours. Usually, it is better to design originally in black and white to focus on layout and other features — the colour can be built in where needed afterwards. When more than four or five colours are used in any web page, the cognitive load on the user tends to increase. A colour scheme should be chosen that adds value to the design but that does not become the overriding feature.

Certain combinations of colours go well together; others contrast and are not aesthetically pleasing to the eye. Blue and dull white go together well but purple and blue do not. Background and foreground colours need to be carefully chosen so that the text is easy to read. The background should not be too bright, such as a bright white, because it can strain the eye, but a dull white is a common background because black text shows up well against it. Readability is the key to good presentation.

> **Reflection question 5:** What are some considerations for designing for people with some form of colour blindness?

Graphics and use of icons

Icons are used extensively in webpage design because they can incorporate and convey a lot of information. The designer can use location (on the screen), colour, space between icons, and size, interior and shape to convey information to the user.

Some problems and challenges have been documented with iconic systems. Not all tasks can easily be represented by an icon. Ideally, the purpose of an icon should be obvious from its graphics. Searching, for example, is an action that is somewhat difficult to design an icon for — some software packages use a torch for this function. When many functions are represented in iconic form, users may find it difficult to differentiate among the icons.

Metaphors

Metaphors have played a significant role in software design. They help people understand and experience a concept in terms of another. In the software world, the desktop metaphor has been the most notable. Metaphors can be used at various levels of the interface. They can be a unifying model for the entire design or used at the icon level. Some people liken a website to visiting a library or an art gallery — or a restaurant: think about the equivalents of smelling the aromas, waiting for a table, looking at a menu, paying for the meal and so on.

Navigation

A website is an information space divided into pages. The designer must provide a mechanism for navigating around the web space. Hyperlinks are used to move from one page to another; they are normally placed as menu items or on icons. Keywords in the text can also be hyperlinks to connect to a page somewhere in the system. In a large website with many pages, these links form a complex network of paths.

infobyte

According to an article published by eMarketer.com, by 2010, advertising spending on social networking sites is expected to increase by more than 600 per cent. These sites (for example MySpace) only accounted for a little more than 2 per cent of the US$16 billion spent on online advertising in the United States in 2006 but the prediction is that by 2010, social networking sites will account for 10 per cent of online advertising sales. In particular, reaching Generation Y through advertising will be a top priority for many companies.

| Generation X | 1961 to 1981 |
| Generation Y | 1982 onwards (no fixed date) |

Source: Information from www.genyvoodoo.com.

[**Key concept:** Systems are for people; design them accordingly.]

Form design

A form consists of questions or prompts and text input boxes (see figure 10.5 overleaf). Designing an effective form involves:
> logically sequencing questions and input boxes
> using meaningful prompts or questions
> avoiding jargon and abbreviations
> aligning prompts and input boxes for ease of data entry
> providing the facility to make corrections and cancellations
> providing access to help facilities to provide information to complete the form
> having correctly sized input boxes to view data
> minimising keyboard input as much as possible
> using dropdown lists for restricted options
> providing validation of input
> providing informative error messages
> grouping related input boxes.

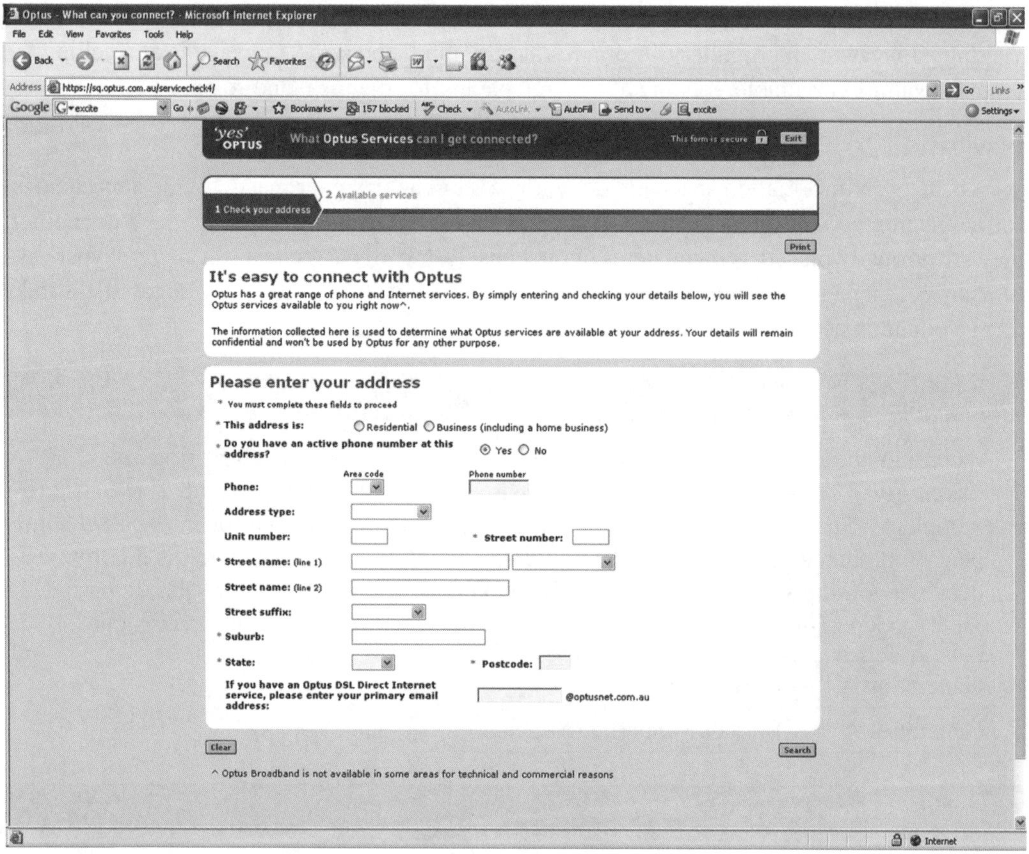

Figure 10.5 A form
Source: Optus, www.optus.com.au.

Input boxes should be left aligned, and text can be displayed above the text input box or to the left and aligned right (preferably) or left. (If text prompts are aligned left, however, there may be large gaps between the text prompt and the input box.)

IS in action

Jakob Nielsen

Jakob Nielsen is considered, by many, a guru of usability. Here's what he had to say in a recent interview:

> An even newer trend in advertising is the contextual text link. In this format, certain key-words are associated with, and hotlinked to, specific sponsors. What's the average user's perception of those ads, and should advertisers be buying into this new format?

> 'Disgusting' is the only appropriate term for these ads.

> They are undermining the most central element of the Web's user experience, which is the understanding of what a blue underlined word stands for. Hint: it doesn't stand for

an ad. Luckily these ads are found on very few websites, so they haven't confused users that much yet. But if the ads were to become prominent, users would become much more reluctant to click on links, which again would drastically reduce the usability of the entire Web.

When visitors do finally arrive on a web page, you've noted a huge disjoint in the number of users who will scroll on a content page (42%) or a Search Engine Results Page (SERP) (47%) vs. the homepage (23%). Why do you think this is?

In the studies we describe in the book, homepages were scrolled much less than other pages for two reasons.

First, many websites actually do a pretty good job at putting the most important features or biggest news items at the top of the page. Thus, users often don't *need* to scroll.

Second, users don't want to engage with a homepage. They're on a website for a reason, and that reason doesn't include finding out about all the site's offerings. People are very fast at moving off the homepage because they want to get to the part of the site that addresses their current concern. Content pages and SERPs get scrolled more because they tend to be focused on a problem that's specific to the user rather than providing a generic overview of twenty different things.

Source: This interview appeared on www.sitepoint.com.

Techniques for marketing and attracting visitors to sites

There are many ways to attract visitors to a website. The site should:
> have a clear strategy and aim
> have a clear and easy-to-use design
> contain creative and memorable features
> be relevant, with recent content
> be registered with search engines
> be promoted offline
> have a relevant and easy-to-remember domain name
> have online events, such as chatting with a celebrity
> give something away, such as a gift or simply useful information.

To make the experience of visiting the website more personal, other techniques include developing an online community and moving to interactive functionality.

Online communities

Online communities are real-time online forums where people can communicate and exchange information. They use online chat, publishing tools to gather and share information, message boards and email, and generally emphasise a high level of interactivity. The interactions may be among the users themselves or between the company and the users. Online communities form a business model in their own right. They provide a framework for integrating content, communication and business and usually fulfil social and business objectives. Communities can be based around any common interest, such as geography, age, providing support (e.g. Cancer Society) or activities (e.g. professional activities and sports).

Five key attributes distinguish an Internet community from other online ventures:

> *Community members*. These are the people who visit the site and feel part of the community. People choose to be members and are not compelled to take part. The members have something in common but membership may be shortlived. Members of the community feel a sense of ownership and contribute in various ways to the community by providing information, and chatting and posting to discussion groups. In this way, the members create the community.

> *Community organisers*. The community requires an organiser who is responsible for the virtual space in terms of growth and maintenance. The owner needs a sponsor who will invest in the community for a reasonable time span.

> *Guiding principles*. Rules and guidelines must be used to make sure that the purpose or purposes of the community are upheld in the running of the community. Some examples of guiding principles are tolerance of alternative opinions, a clear statement of moral expectations and what is considered to be the focus of the community.

> *Institutional benefits*. There should be clear institutional benefits in building the community. Intranets can be developed to build a sense of community and sharing or internets can be used to create a loyal customer base.

> *Interactivity*. The richer the media space, the more scope there is for developing a vibrant community. The easier the system is to use, the lower the barrier to entry to the community.

Community building is not suited to every company and product. For example, a soccer club with a large supporter base may find it worthwhile to develop an online community, because through it, it could improve its image, and advertise merchandise, club games and so on. But a consulting company is not likely to want its clients to chat to one another: they may swap information on fees paid and what they got (or did not get) for their money.

> **Reflection question 6:** Are you part of any online community? What is its purpose?

Online customer interaction and involvement

The impersonality of many websites is proving a barrier to more customers purchasing over the Web. Customers get confused by website options, and frequently have questions about a product or service. Frequently asked questions on web pages are helpful to a point but are still impersonal. Bulletin boards can provide a more customer-focused perspective, but can be a rambling mess of comments unless moderated properly by the company. Of course, potential customers can always email their enquiry, but by the time a reply is sent, potential customers may have changed their mind.

With online sales in particular, some websites have tried to create a more personal experience with the use of specialist software to manage the interaction between a sales assistant and a customer. This includes the management of email enquiries so that customers get a response within a reasonable time, the one-to-one chat sessions with customers and, with some packages, a web video link with the customer.

Companies have gone a stage further than just interacting with consumers, by getting them to generate content for their websites and in some cases advertising material. These usually take the form of video clips developed by consumers. This is sometimes referred to as consumer-generated media. Content developed by consumers has many benefits in developing the brand image of a company. Consumers become active participants in promoting a product and they are likely to communicate their efforts to many people. This is a form of viral marketing, in which the advertisements (video files or image files) are emailed from person to person without much intervention from the company that develops the product.

Many websites provide podcasts to inform consumers. These are audio files which can be listened to online or downloaded to portable devices and listened to at a later time. Although podcasting is generally understood to refer to audio files that can be played on mp3 players it also extends to video podcasting.

infobyte

Customer carewords

According to Gerry McGovern (www.gerrymcgovern.com), customers typically want to complete a few tasks out of the many that can be performed on a website. In a survey of a tourism website, he found that 5 per cent of the tasks got 35 per cent of the votes. The top seven tasks got more votes than the bottom 120 tasks. To identify the key tasks from a customer or user perspective, McGovern has created a unique method called 'Customer Carewords'. Within this approach, he emphasises keywords that users relate to. The importance of getting certain words right is illustrated by the following:

> Microsoft changed one word in a heading and found a 300 per cent increase in the number of people who clicked on the heading.

> A client changed three words on a particular Webpage and obtained a 30 per cent increase in sales inquiries.

> Changing the text in a button from 'Click to qualify — it's free' to 'Am I eligible? Find out instantly' resulted in a 40 per cent increase in people clicking the button.

Source: Information from www.gerrymcgovern.com.

Building trust online

In e-commerce, transactions frequently take place between parties that have never physically met. Trust has always been a significant factor in doing business and is regarded as just as important in online business. Although trust is a complex concept to define, three sources of trust have been identified as being important in business (Ba & Pavlou 2002). The first is familiarity, which relates to repeated interaction between parties. The second is calculativeness, which is based on an assessment of the costs and benefits to the other party of cheating. The third is values, which are related to aspects of the organisational culture that convey trustworthiness and goodwill. There are two types of trust: benevolence and credibility. The former relates to a genuine interest in the other party, even under adverse conditions. The latter relates to a belief in a party's honesty, reliability and competence. The credibility type of trust is generally viewed as being more applicable to online business (Ba & Pavlou 2002).

How can trust be improved through website design? Some ideas have been proposed to try to improve the perception of the trustworthiness of e-business sites:

> Refer to the offline business if there is one because this adds credibility to the online business. It will reassure the customer that the business is established.

> Develop a level of quality in the website that conveys commitment. Mistakes in content or out-of-date content will dent confidence and trust.
> Develop a strong brand design that will increase the level of trust.
> Try to include recommendations from high-profile customers and satisfied customers because they will add to the credibility of the website and help develop trust.
> Make sure offline deliveries are carried out effectively.
> Include statements about the company's commitment to quality.

IS in action

Measuring the quality of a website

An instrument for ascertaining the perception of website quality by customers has been developed by Barnes and Vidgen (2005). It is called eQual. It assesses e-business website quality on a seven-point scale. It assesses the site in relation to usability, information quality and service interaction quality. The eQual questionnaire follows:

Category	Questions
Usability	1. I find the site easy to learn to operate?
	2. My interactions with the site are clear and understandable?
	3. I find the site easy to navigate?
	4. I find the site easy to use?
	5. The site has an attractive appearance?
	6. The design is appropriate to the type of site?
	7. The site conveys a sense of competency?
	8. The site creates a positive experience for me?
Information quality	9. Provides accurate information?
	10. Provides believable information?
	11. Provides timely information?
	12. Provides relevant information?
	13. Provides easy to understand information?
	14. Provides information at the right level of detail?
	15. Presents the information in an appropriate format?
Service interaction	16. Has a good reputation?
	17. It feels safe to complete transactions?
	18. My personal information feels secure?
	19. Creates a sense of personalisation?
	20. Conveys a sense of community?
	21. Makes it easy to communicate with the organisation?
	22. I feel confident that goods/services will be delivered as promised?
Overall	23. Overall view of the Web site?

Figure 10.6 The eQual questionnaire

Source: The questionnaire appeared in an article in *Proceedings of the 13th European Conference of Information Systems.*

Measuring the effectiveness of the website

Measuring the effectiveness of a website is often overlooked, because so much effort has gone into the analysis and development of the site that little energy or enthusiasm may be left, once it is up and running, to evaluate its effectiveness properly. In addition, the evaluation may be postponed because of the argument that the site is quickly evolving, so there is little point in evaluating now. Of course, there is never an ideal point to evaluate the effectiveness of the system but it should still be done.

The site's effectiveness should be evaluated because it is an investment of organisational resources and should not be treated differently from any other resource. Evaluations should be completed periodically as the site develops and matures. Useful information should be fed back into the development and evolution process. Good times to perform a review of the effectiveness of the site are three months and six months after it has gone online: this should be enough time to identify any immediate problems with the system. Further reviews can be conducted six-monthly or as necessary.

Senior management should be involved in the reviews to determine whether the requirements that were detailed early in the project are being met by the website. It is quite possible that the requirements may change over several months of development. These need to be discussed and, if viewed as critical, should be built into the system as early as it is feasible to do so.

Web efficiency variables that can be used in determining the overall efficiency of the website include:

> number of hits on the site (visitors)
> number of active visitors (visitors who interact with the site)
> number of purchases
> number of repurchases (people who purchase repeatedly).

If only a small number of users access the site, then it may not be the site in particular that is at fault but rather how it is being advertised and promoted. This may be rectified by registering the site URL with all the major search engines, by advertising on other sites and by promoting the site by more traditional methods such as putting the URL on company stationery and business cards.

Using basic statistics such as the number of hits is a very limited way of evaluating a site. A more business-centric approach is needed rather than a technical one that relies on hits and views. For example, Northwest Airlines in the United States aims to sell as many tickets online as possible. The advantage of selling tickets online is that they are 50 per cent cheaper for each transaction to process than through traditional methods. So the most important measurement for Northwest Airlines is the number of bookings made through the Web. A second important statistic is the number of enquiries handled through the site, because every enquiry handled in this way is cheaper to deal with compared with telephone calls made to a call centre. Northwest is mostly concerned with increasing revenue and reducing costs, so its measurement statistics reflect this.

Another variable is the percentage of visitors to a site who actually make a purchase. Simply attracting visitors may not actually do a business much good in the long run. The site needs to be improved to handle large numbers of visitors, but there is a cost for that, and unless there is a payback, it may be a poor business investment. The site has to be designed to attract the right type of person, ideally one who is likely to make a purchase or interact with the site in some cost-saving way for the organisation.

Some organisations that have nothing to sell directly through the Web, such as those involved in publishing, can monitor how long people stay at the site. They can try to measure whether the person is actively engaged with the content and whether they return to the site. Employment recruitment sites can monitor the number of enquiries made through the site and the number of applications for jobs that are made. Companies can review the effectiveness of the site from the perspective of how much revenue is generated from advertising, if that is part of their objectives.

Interviews and questionnaires can be used to obtain feedback from internal and external users of the site. The results can provide information on the problems users face, what they like about the site and whether the design features are easy to use.

Some of the benefits of a website may be very difficult to quantify, such as improved public relations. Surveys can be conducted to determine what effect the site is having in such areas. This may mean that external research companies are used if the expertise to conduct professional surveys does not exist within the organisation. A company's site can also be compared with other companies' sites for functionality, design effectiveness and level of innovation. Therefore, considerably more work has to be put into obtaining information on intangible benefits, compared with finding out how many new orders have come in online.

Summary

Designing effective websites is a complex task that requires a range of skills. Attracting visitors to a site requires the site to be easy to navigate, to be aesthetically appealing and to engage the user as much as possible. The key points in this chapter are:

> The external focus of many web applications has created a whole new set of issues for systems developers.

> The complexity of website development depends on factors such as the amount of functionality required and the level of integration with other corporate systems.

> Effective website design requires structure, and good use of space, text, colour and graphics.

> Website designers need to consider how they can develop trust with their customers.

> Online communities, chat and voice over Internet protocol are ways of attracting visitors to a website.

> Measuring the effectiveness of a website relies on a number of methods beyond a simple 'hit rate'.

Questions

1. Explain the various roles involved in a large web project development team.

2. What general rules should be applied to the use of text on web pages?

3. What factors affect the scope and complexity of web-development projects?

4. How should Web pages be designed to consider the visually impaired?

5. What is viral marketing?

6. What is meant by the term m-commerce? Provide some examples.

7. Why is it important for organisations to integrate their web applications with other corporate applications?

8. What techniques can be used to attract visitors to a website?

9. How can online community members be encouraged to feel a sense of ownership and belonging?

10. How can trust be developed through the design of a website?

Exercises

1. Google is a very popular search engine. Are there any problems or issues related to its popularity? Discuss this question in small groups.

2. Develop ten key design guidelines for website design. Evaluate three websites using your guidelines.

3. What are social networking websites? Discuss whether these types of site have business implications.

CASE STUDY: Colours of Spain

Colours of Spain is using the web to successfully tap into a market gap — that of broker between owners of holiday villas and people searching for holiday rental properties.

Objectives

Increasingly, British holidaymakers are moving away from package holidays towards arranging their own foreign breaks, from flights through to accommodation. The Spanish holiday property market is a prime business opportunity because of the country's enduring popularity with Britons and the increasing number of British people who are buying Spanish properties to rent out for at least part of the year.

Catalogues have been the traditional medium for advertising such properties. However they suffer from the obvious disadvantages of high cost of production combined with the fact that they are static and date quickly. Colours of Spain decided to exploit a website's ability to show a high level of detail while permitting rapid and frequent changes of content, all at a relatively low cost. It also wanted to be able to allow its customers to search across a variety of criteria — such as house characteristics, location, and proximity to leisure activities and airports.

It wasn't just British owners of Spanish properties who were targeted by Colours of Spain. Because the Spanish tend to take holidays at different times of the year to the British, it provided an opportunity to offer Spanish owners a chance to broaden their client base.

'Essentially, it would be an enhanced matchmaking service between holidaymakers who want to rent in Spain and property owners who want to rent out,' says Karen Spiller, Director of Colours of Spain Ltd. And, of course, it would have to cater for owners and renters who did not necessarily speak the same language.

(continued)

Karen made a decision to generate the revenue stream from the property owners themselves, asking them to pay an annual subscription for advertising their property. The site would also have to handle the business with as little administrative input as possible and the system would need to provide financial and other reporting.

Solution

A decision was made to develop the site using open source software, to minimise costs, and four main areas of functionality were developed. Firstly, property owners are able to set up an account and fill in templates, principally tickboxes and numbers, to create an advert for their property with online payments processed through a third party provider. A second area allows holidaymakers to search for properties and create a preferred shortlist. They are then able to contact the relevant owners with further questions if necessary. To provide added value, a third area acts as a travel guide, providing a matrix of information covering a range of topics such as food, climate and sites of interest. Users can select topics that interest them and that are relevant to the area they want to visit. The output can be saved (complete with a full table of contents), printed or emailed as a PDF document. Finally, a secure area allows Colours of Spain staff to manage and administer the site.

A key design element has been the linking of parallel language files to a single database file. The advert-upload templates are two separate language files (Spanish and English) that both feed into a single file in the database that is used for the front end (what the holidaymaker sees). The user can upload in English, tick 'house' or upload in Spanish and tick 'casa', the advert will only ever display in English and the holidaymaker will see 'house'. The only exception to these preconfigured templates is the free text description. It's important for owners to be able to express what makes their property interesting and different and this can't be achieved through pre-prepared templates! This text is translated manually by Colours of Spain to avoid all the incomprehensible texts generated by automatic translation. This allows parts of the site to be truly bilingual. In order to keep costs low, the system has been designed to minimise administrative functions. Terms and conditions are viewed and accepted online, management information and VAT invoices are all generated automatically and contacts between holidaymakers and advertisers are carried out electronically.

As a further attention to detail, the site allows renters and owners to identify common languages to help them communicate. If they don't have a language in common, it offers a bilingual e-mail tool which works by matching a list of English phrases against Spanish phrases to construct a logically-phrased message. The phrase list is constantly updated, using the site's own content management tools.

Results

Compared to a paper-based system using catalogues, Colours of Spain can achieve huge cost savings. Over a three year period, it calculated that catalogue printing cost would be around £383 000. However, website costs for the same period are only around £29 000 — an overall saving of almost £354 000. And of course, the site also offers much greater flexibility than a catalogue format. 'It wouldn't be possible to offer something like the online travel guide through print — the costs would be prohibitive and hard to control. In fact in print, the more successful the travel guide became, the greater the cost, yet because it doesn't correlate directly with the expenditure on a holiday, its 'success' would not necessarily benefit our bottom line,' comments Karen. Managing the company is also much simpler using online rather than traditional methods. 'It's simple to update and correct information, and financial information, is generated automatically,' says Karen. 'The content management system also allows rapid, highly-targeted mailings to advertisers.'

Soon after its launch to Spanish owners, the site had more than 100 properties with 350 more in the pipeline through a contract with the Avila region's Associations of Rural Houses which is spending a significant part of its annual advertising budget to promote its members' properties through the Colours of Spain website. The numbers show the success as the site now has 540 properties with another 500 in the pipeline.

Challenges

Colours of Spain had to overcome one common problem any start-up faces: persuading existing property owners to begin to use it. 'At the beginning, nobody wants to advertise on a website that doesn't have any advertisers,' says Karen. 'We overcame this problem by offering free advertising for a year to owners in the province of Granada.' This had the benefit of letting the website team test the system before a general launch and also meant that when it did launch the company already had some properties in place to attract clients.' 'The wide variety of IT systems used by customers is also a problem. Finding ways to let property owners upload information to the site simply has proved difficult,' says Karen. 'Some of it requires a browser with Javascript enabled, but not everyone does that,' she explains. 'We have tried to minimise this problem by making the technical requirements explicit in the upload demo.'

Because of its comprehensive coverage, the site's information requirements are broader than some competitors. A number of property owners find supplying sufficient information rather time-consuming. 'However owners have told us it's worth it,' says Karen. Another potential problem is that because the site only acts as an advertiser, and bookings are made directly with owners, data about properties' availability may be out-of-date. 'We encourage owners to keep the site's calendar updated by providing a direct link from their account and we reinforce that message wherever possible in the owners' area of the site.' Finally, the bilingual booking phrasebook cannot anticipate every question that holidaymakers will want to ask — although 'it will become more complete over time as we add to it in response to both sides' requests,' Karen explains.

Top tips:

> Going online in a traditional print-based business offers immediate annual and ongoing savings.

> Start-up businesses online may need to offer incentives to persuade potential clients to work with them.

> Some clients may not have the Internet products or skills that you need in order to work with them effectively.

Last Word

Karen sees the possibility of extending the services that Colours of Spain provides: 'We view the content on the site as one of our main assets,' she says. 'There are opportunities to work in partnership with restaurant guides, general travel guides and so on.'

Website: http://www.coloursofspain.com/

Source: Department of Trade and Industry (UK), 'Colours of Spain', www.ecommerce-awards.co.uk/_files/cscoloursspain.pdf.

Questions

1. Summarise the aims of the website.
2. What are the key design features of the Colours of Spain website?
3. How are language problems tackled in the website?
4. Describe a way to measure the effectiveness of the website.
5. Why do you think it is such a successful business idea?

References

Ba, S & Pavlou, DA 2002, 'Evidence of the effect of trust-building technology in electronic markets: price premiums and buyer behaviour', *MIS Quarterly*, vol. 26, no. 3, pp. 243–68.

Barnes, S & Vidgen, R 2005, 'Data triangulation in action: using comment analysis to refine web quality metrics', *Proceedings of the 13th European Conference on Information Systems*, Regensburg, Germany, 26–28 May.

Sellitto, C & Wenn, A 2000, 'Business websites: simple guidelines and practice for checking if a site conforms to emerging standards', *Proceedings of the First International Web Conference*, Fremantle, Australia (CD-ROM).

Sun Microsystems 2004, 'The Java language: an overview', http://java.sun.com.

CHAPTER 11
Information systems infrastructure

LEARNING OBJECTIVES

After reading this chapter, you should be able to:

» define the term 'infrastructure' as it applies to information systems and technology

» recall basic information technology (IT) terminology for memory capacity and processor speeds

» have a working knowledge of basic computer history and the four generations of computer, appreciating the impact that each generation had

» identify the main types of computer and understand their uses

» be aware of the major trends in microprocessor development

» be able to make intelligent purchasing decisions when acquiring a computer for personal use

» understand the acquisition process as it applies to larger organisations

» appreciate the importance of hardware standards from a management and business perspective

» understand the basic principles of IT governance.

Introduction

I t is not realistic to study information systems without some consideration of the technology that forms the basis of the discipline. However, this text restricts coverage of the purely technical to a minimum, because you should always have access to people and resources for technical support and advice. The main focus is on the business issues and implications that arise from technological developments. Information systems is about deploying technology for tactical and strategic advantage in business. Remember, the work is not the business. Previous editions of this text attempted to cover hardware principles in some depth but the authors no longer believe this appropriate. Hardware has long since been 'commoditised'. If you were to buy a blender, you would not expect to endure a long lecture on the history of domestic appliances before you plugged it in and used it. Information systems does require some understanding of technology trends both past and present to be able to appreciate where technology is headed and how we can make best use of it for business. This chapter presents four generations of hardware. It is important to note that these generations overlap in space and time, so that, for example, generations two and three coexisted for as long as eight years. The development of computers and, consequently, information systems changed the pattern of competition within business and within the computer industry itself. An appreciation of this competition is vital to an understanding of contemporary information systems. This text has already considered software, networking and enterprise resource planning (ERP) issues, and this chapter will cover the essentials of hardware, procurement and information systems governance.

What is infrastructure?

A s the term implies, infrastructure supports a 'structure' (a business, an organisation, an ERP system are all 'structures' which need to be supported). Any hardware and software purchasing should be informed by cost–benefit analysis and referred back to the strategic plan to ensure conformance to organisational needs and goals. An infrastructure-based approach is a little more forgiving. In it a wider perspective is taken, with a focus on creating an environment that meets the present and predicted needs of the organisation. The aim is to find a general-purpose hardware and software solution that allows people to use the systems to handle their problems without worrying about the underlying technical details. (The term information systems and IT infrastructure is analogous to everyday infrastructures such as road, rail, electricity and utilities, which businesses use but do not really control. A business may pay licence fees for ERP software and this is infrastructure. It is used by the business but developed and owned by the software vendor.) Information systems infrastructure comprises software, hardware, networking, support and management staff, policies and procedures. If the infrastructure is properly developed, this leads to business agility. (By contrast 'strategic information systems' are highly focused.) Once the infrastructure is established, development effort is incremental (as new functions and subsystems are added) and directed to the maintenance and upgrading of the infrastructure. Infrastructure is not merely hardware and software, but also comprises policies, procedures, procurement and governance. The chapter begins by considering the development of the modern computer.

A brief history of the computer

There have been four generations of computer technology, and each generation brought about large-scale change in a different way. The end of a generation is defined in this book as the point at which replacement technology started to be used. Many computers were made and used after the end of their generation, so there was and is a great deal of coexistence of technologies. Try to appreciate the significant contribution each generation of computer made to modern business methods.

Generation one: valves (1946–59) — transforming business processes

Although mechanical and electromechanical computation devices have existed for many years, most people accept that the birth of the modern computer age occurred in the late 1940s, when a research team at the University of Manchester in the UK produced the first electrically stored-program computer. Although primitive by today's standards, it extended people's mental abilities in the same way that pulleys and levers had extended the lifting capacity of their ancestors. The essence of modern digital computing is to reduce complex operations to a series of binary operations. Operation at its lowest level really consists of switching. By the end of the 1950s, vacuum tubes (valves) were the main switching devices in computers, and by 1960, valve-based computers were in use in many sectors of industry and government in the developed world.

The programs that these machines ran were specific to particular makes and models of computer and were in no way 'portable', as modern software is. Nor were they particularly sophisticated or flexible. However, even with their inherent unreliabilities, they were faster and more accurate than humans. A single computer, or mainframe, served an entire organisation.

The business environment at that time was fairly stable, and the rate at which information and markets changed was fairly modest by modern standards. Businesses tended to be fairly hierarchical in structure: a pyramid with senior management at the top. People's work patterns were changed as to maximise the return on the investment in computers. Work tended to be well ordered and structured in larger corporations. The competitive advantage gained by deploying computer technology was to shorten the timelines of monotonous processes; that is, the processes were automated. However, the organisation and management remained pretty much as they had been in previous decades. Valve-based computers usually had no more than 2 KB of memory and operating speeds of 1000–10000 instructions per second. (Vacuum tubes are more robust than transistors and resist heat, power surges and so on much better. Consequently, they are still used for specialised communications systems and satellites. Current research is directed at producing microscopic vacuum tubes.)

> **Reflection question 1:** It is sometimes said that the old highly centralised mainframe systems were more reliable than modern distributed systems. Are people justified in saying this?

Generation two: transistors (1959–64) — transforming organisations

The development of the transistor in 1947 by William Shockley, Walter Brattain and John Bardeen in the Bell laboratories opened up a new era in electronics and computer science.

Vacuum tubes were large and slow, consumed lots of power and needed replacing fairly regularly. Large computer installations of the late 1950s and early 1960s filled large rooms and sometimes entire floors of buildings. Transistors could do the same job but required a fraction of the size and power to operate. They were also more reliable. Circuit boards could be prefabricated and mass-produced, simplifying production and maintenance. Computer costs plummeted and the takeup rate in business increased dramatically. Profit margins for manufacturers were excellent.

To allow the technology to be more widely used, high-level portable computer languages were needed. Up to this time, computer programs were inextricably entwined with a single make and model of computer. Languages such as COBOL, FORTRAN, BASIC and LISP allowed programmers to write programs that could run on any machine. The trick was to have a translator program called a compiler, which could translate the high-level code into a form that the local computer could handle. The software and the hardware were now independent of each other, and development of each would proceed at a much higher rate. The development of high-level languages allowed organisations to produce specialised, in-house software much more easily than before and to buy in software from specialised software developers at reduced cost. This simple step was to transform business irrevocably. The use of single transistors on circuit boards allowed memory to be extended to 32 KB processing speeds about 300 000 instructions per second.

The first generation of computers merely transformed individual business processes. This second generation allowed a higher degree of intelligence in the software and programs, which in turn allowed business to restructure. Software was now capable of rendering complex analyses and forecasts on the basis of stored data, with much greater speed than a human analyst could. Many routine management functions could also be computerised. The result was

infobyte

The hard sell on soft cell

Most of the world's communication devices are implemented in hardware with specialised microchips performing dedicated tasks. Problems arise when this dedicated technology is asked to perform outside its comfort zone. As an example, consider mobile communications. There are four major standards for mobile phones, plus several emerging ones for mobile voice over Internet protocol or VOIP. Police and emergency services tend to use different systems but sometimes (as was the case with the 11 September attacks) they need to be seen as a single system. Mobile phone, personal digital assistant (PDA) and satellite navigation system makers need to know which standards will prevail because cancelling manufacture of a particular line is expensive and bad for customer relations. The solution is to produce a general-purpose system in which all the signal processing can be handled using software. The main advantage is that devices can be reprogrammed easily for any prevailing standard and are truly portable across international boundaries. Upgrades and conversions can be requested and downloaded in real time, with power consumption and size being reduced. Systems like these are already in use in the United States, courtesy of Vanu Inc. It is merely a matter of time before they become mainstream technology.

Source: Information from www.vanu.com.

that businesses were able to shed several layers of middle management. They moved away from the older hierarchical structures and became flatter, leaner and more efficient. By shortening the lines of communication and the chains of command, businesses were able to respond to situations and opportunities much more quickly and so enjoy advantages over businesses that did not have the benefit of technology. Workflows revolved around the computer's processes because the advantages of the new age demanded sacrifices in terms of job satisfaction and true flexibility.

Generation three: integrated circuits (1965–71) — transforming markets

The trend towards smaller, faster and cheaper machines established in the second generation of computers was continued in the third generation at an exponential rate. These machines relied heavily on integrated circuits (ICs): chips with many thousands of transistors printed onto a very small piece of silicon. The technology favoured mass production and although performance increased, prices continued to plummet and the technology penetrated many aspects of business. This proliferation also had implications for the development of software and, in particular, system software. Average memory sizes were in the order of 2 MB and processing speeds increased to five million instructions per second (MIPS). Perhaps the most significant thing to arise from this time was that computers became capable of running several programs concurrently. Previously, computer systems tended to operate as batch systems, with little or no direct interaction with users. Improvements in technology in the early part of this computer generation provided real-time operation and interaction on a much larger scale. Applications software also became more sophisticated during this time. The demand for computing power outstripped the supply of skilled software developers, so software had to become easier to use.

Generation four: very large scale integration (1971–present) — transforming society

The very large scale integration period began with the invention of the microchip by Marcian (Ted) Hoff in 1971, codenamed the Intel 4004. For the first time, it was theoretically possible to place millions of transistors on the same piece of silicon. This revolutionised the design of mainframes and led to the development of the 8080 chip. The 8080 was used to produce the world's first PC, the 1974 Altair (named after a planet in the TV series *Star trek*), and its successor, the 8088, powered the first IBM PC. For the first time, mass-produced computers became affordable to small businesses and the general public. The advances in hardware were accompanied by advances in software, which became much easier to use and to develop. Current performance figures vary from ten MIPS to three MIPS, and computer memory can be anything from 128 MB to 8000 MB or more, depending on the type of computer.

> **Reflection question 2:** Will computers ever be fast enough?

Types of computers in current use

The following is intended as a 'field guide' only. The distinctions between the types of computers tend to be a little indistinct; for example, when does a high-end mainframe computer qualify as a supercomputer? You should also appreciate that these classifications are subject to change as technology continues to improve. Today's mainframe is tomorrow's desktop. Earlier editions of this text took pains to provide example configurations, cost and performance data. These examples were almost outdated by the time of publication. Therefore, you are encouraged to carry out your own research in this area.

Supercomputers

Supercomputers are the most powerful, most expensive and rarest of the computers in use today. Their main uses have been in military and scientific work for such diverse applications as weather modelling, nuclear explosion simulations and aircraft design. They have also been used by the film industry to create graphic-intensive special effects. They are usually five to ten times faster than mainframes, with some being hundreds of times faster. Supercomputers are about the same size as a family car and have highly specialised environmental needs in terms of power, cooling and airconditioning. The supercomputer market is small and most software is highly specialised.

Mainframes

Mainframe computers were the first type of modern computer. Highly centralised, they provide services for a large community of users. With the centralisation of function comes a centralisation of power and control. With the increasing power of smaller computers and the availability of networks, the mainframe market has diminished and consolidated in recent years. Because there are relatively few mainframes, mainframe software is very expensive and limited in choice compared with PC software. Mainframes are about the size of a large fridge, and many information systems professionals refer to their mainframe as the 'big iron'. Mainframes usually require specially controlled environments in dust-free rooms.

Minicomputers

Minicomputers are almost cut-down versions of mainframes. Although much cheaper than mainframes, they are still relatively expensive. They provide services to a small–medium community of users. Because there are many more minis than mainframes, there is a much greater variety of software to choose from. This larger market attracts more software developers than the relatively restricted supercomputer and mainframe market. Minicomputers are filing cabinet size. As do mainframes, they have the benefit of being centralised, which makes applying physical and logical security controls simpler.

Workstations

A workstation is really a cut-down minicomputer catering to the needs of a single user. Although the distinction between a high-end PC and a workstation has become blurred recently, most professionals regard a workstation as having much greater performance and functionality than a PC: a Silicon Graphics workstation, used to produce special effects for films, is a good example. Workstations frequently make use of a special type of microchip, which has a reduced instruction-set computer (RISC) architecture.

Microcomputers or PCs

Microcomputers or PCs are desktop or portable computers for single users. Most of the software processing is localised, although communications software and hardware allow PCs to access other computers and services. PCs transformed business operations and structures by allowing many activities to be decentralised. The advent of the PC contributed to the contraction and consolidation of the mainframe market.

Technology moves very quickly, and technical specifications for desktop machines change every few months. However, it is possible to generalise to some extent. Physical sizes vary, and it is assumed that you are familiar with basic desktop, tower, minitower and laptop configurations. The increasing use of PCs as multimedia suites and gaming machines has been a major factor in increasing disk and memory capacity in PCs. It should be noted that a fast clock speed does not translate directly into high performance because some computers do more in one 'tick of the clock' than others. Workstations might have a slower clock speed than PCs but usually perform more instructions per second. The term 'PC' is generally taken to mean devices derived from IBM's original PC architecture; however, strictly speaking the term also includes other kinds of desktop computer, such as Apple Macintosh.

'Specialised' PCs are often configured as servers (shared computers on a network, which are dedicated to particular tasks such as email or web services). Although their architecture is PC based, they usually have much higher performance and storage specification (mainframes, minicomputers and supercomputers often operate as servers). Desktop machines that are networked and access servers are referred to as clients; hence the terms 'client–server applications' and 'networks'.

Handheld and wearable computers

Handheld and wearable computers are the smallest computing devices. They include personal organisers and products such as Palm Pilots. The trend towards miniaturisation has led to the development of computer wristwatches, incorporating video-conferencing hardware, and other wearable devices. Handheld and wearable devices are already used by warehousing and distribution operations, but the development trend seems to be towards wearable and hands-free operation. When combined with mobile communications, these have the potential to transform business processes. Sometimes these devices are mere extensions of and access points to a larger system. More usually, they are for use as **personal digital assistants (PDAs)** and organisers. It is not certain whether PDAs will survive in their own right or be subsumed into mobile telephone technologies. Cost, performance and communications coverage are the limiting factors in the takeup rates for PDAs.

IS in action

Fat or thin?

By increasing server power and network capacity, businesses can make use of 'thin' clients (desktop PCs that are stripped-down versions of ordinary PCs). These have a longer service life and are cheaper to buy and to manage than ordinary PCs. However, this comes at the cost of reduced processing power at the desktop. The break-even point for thin-client installations is 10-to-12 users. However, for intensive applications such as design work or publishing, a desktop machine needs its own processing power. With thin clients, upgrades are carried out to the server and can often be managed without stopping any applications. Servers often have many processors and are designed with upgrading in mind. In addition to saving on initial purchase costs by 30 per cent to 40 per cent, thin clients reduce management costs substantially. Many organisations have both thick and thin clients, depending on the needs of users. The terms 'network computer' and 'thin client' are used interchangeably. Thin clients are well suited to 'front end' banking and travel systems because the main data and processing facilities are highly centralised, and because thin clients have limited processing power and autonomy, they are much easier to make secure. It should be noted that it is possible to manage a fat client as though it was a thin client and enjoy the benefits of increased processing power and cost savings.

Blade servers

Chapter 4 covers the concepts of client–server systems. Applications are hosted on servers, which may then be accessed by a community of users. For simplicity, servers are usually dedicated to a particular task, such as a web or mail server. For security, ease of operations and utilities management, servers are usually located together in a single room, and the network handles server-to-server and client-to-server connections. Most servers in common use are not dissimilar in principle to a PC. They are much faster in terms of processing speed and networking speeds and tend to be fault tolerant to some extent. Each server has its own systems software, which might be Linux, Unix or a Windows variant.

Generally, organisations have a commitment to a particular philosophy, which could be open systems or a proprietary system such as Microsoft. The overall aim is to reduce diversity and complexity and, consequently, management costs. The downside is that the choice of application software may become limited as a result, so that companies are forced to compromise on functionality and ease of use. This in turn can limit productivity and the ability to react quickly when new business opportunities arise. When a dedicated server fails, a backup is needed. While large businesses can afford to duplicate expensive resources, smaller businesses do not have the necessary resources. They can outsource the problem but this is not without its problems. If it becomes necessary to move to a new applications platform, then it may be necessary to change the underlying systems software. The choice is to do nothing and suffer, or make huge changes and spend significant amounts of money.

Problems arise as businesses grow; the demand for processing power means that servers and networks must be upgraded and additional servers added to the array. Because many organisations are not using purpose-built facilities, the limits to growth are soon reached. To save floor space, the servers are mounted in racks. From the front, it looks as though someone has built a wall using system units from PCs. From the rear, the most striking thing is the number and complexity of cables that snake around the servers; every wire represents a potential source of failure. Chapter 4 discusses the use of proxy servers for load balancing in client–server networks, but it is apparent that many businesses need smaller units and greater flexibility, which is where blade servers come into their own.

These are a special kind of server. First, they are much thinner than a conventional server, perhaps 25 per cent of the thickness. Second, the server incorporates a special 'backplane', which links to the rack chassis to provide interconnection between the blade servers and fibre-channel switches, networked resources and so on. This means that the blades can be removed and inserted very quickly and that the cabling requirements are much reduced (perhaps down to 20 per cent of the cabling costs for traditional server racks). Third and most importantly, they offer 'virtualisation'.

Virtualisation means that a single server could appear to be several different servers each running different systems software, or many servers as a single server to support a single application. It is not uncommon to find a high-powered server that was purchased for a single application spending much of its time ticking over but the surplus processing power cannot be diverted to other applications, resulting in overcapitalisation and underuse. Virtualisation allows for easier server management because managers work with simple logical views of very complicated storage and networked systems, allowing them to focus on what needs to be achieved without having to involve themselves in the exacting details of how it is to be done.

It is difficult to obtain exact figures but estimates of a 40 per cent reduction in the total cost of ownership by moving to blade servers are not unrealistic. The cost savings are achieved by simplifying management, and reducing the cost of software licences. It is predicted that the market for blade servers will increase by 42.7 per cent a year until 2010, with a predicted market value then of A$12 billion (IDC, in Warren 2006).

A downside of blade servers is the amount of power they consume and heat they generate. In the early 1990s, most server farms generated about 2.7 kW per square metre, but the modern equivalent generates more than 43 kW per square metre, so the demands for electricity and cooling are considerable.

The architecture of the modern computer

To use computers effectively and make good purchasing decisions, it is necessary to have an understanding of the basic architecture and operation of the modern (classical) computer. With the possible exception of the supercomputer group, most computers use the same architecture and operate in the same manner. This architecture is called the **von Neumann machine**. What made the von Neumann architecture special was that it advanced the idea of storing the program in the computer instead of relying on punched tape. This gave a huge increase in performance over other architectures because accessing memory is many times faster than accessing an external storage device.

It is very easy to be impressed by technical terms but it does not hurt to remember that the most complex computer system still performs the same basic functions: input, processing, output, communication and storage. This should help to keep things in perspective when talking to technical specialists and consultants. Input, processing, output and storage devices are covered in detail later. For now, it would be useful to introduce a few IT basics.

Measuring memory capacity and processor speeds

Computers store and manipulate data in binary form, and an executable program code needs to be in memory before it can be run. Therefore, memory capacity is an indicator of computer performance. The more memory it has, the faster things tend to run, because accessing things in memory is much faster than accessing them on a hard drive. Table 11.1 gives the names of commonly used computer memory capacities and real examples.

TABLE 11.1 Computer memory capacity

Memory capacity and name	Amount of data
One **bit** (binary digit)	A '0' or a '1'
One **byte** (8 binary digits)	One alphanumeric character
One **kilobyte** (KB), 1024 bytes (2^{10})	Half a double-spaced page of A4
One **megabyte** (MB), 1 048 576 bytes (2^{20})	500 pages of A4
One **gigabyte** (GB), 1 073 741 824 (2^{30})	Half a million pages of A4
One **terabyte** (TB), 1 099 511 627 776	More than 100 movies

Note: Most people in the industry think about capacity in powers of 10, so a kilobyte is usually approximated to 1000 bytes, a megabyte to 1 000 000 bytes etc.

Computer speeds are defined in two ways: the speed of the system clock, usually quoted in gigahertz (billions of cycles per second), and the number of machine instructions processed in a second (a more meaningful measure). Modern computer speeds demand that speeds are quoted in millions of instructions per second (MIPS). The problem is that clock speed does not necessarily equate to instruction process rate. To give an idea of the number-crunching ability of a processor, a third speed — floating point operations per second — is used. Dual-core processors (discussed later) are a special case, and crude clock speed does not give a true indication of performance.

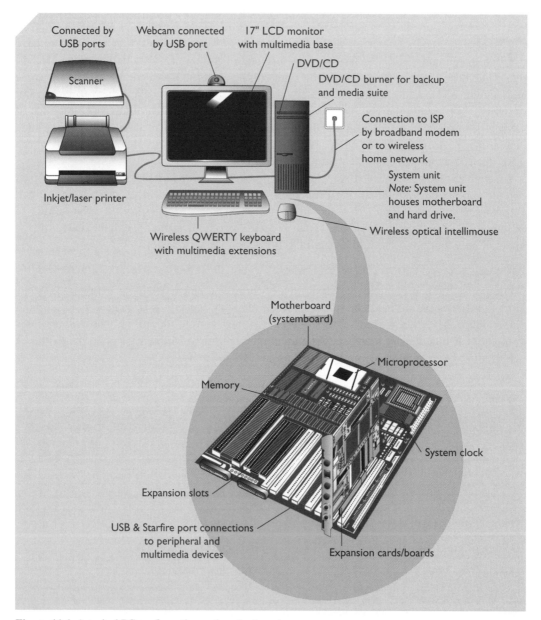

Figure 11.1 A typical PC configuration and motherboard

Figure 11.1 (opposite) shows a typical PC configuration and **motherboard** (also known as **systemboard**). This chapter is PC focused because it is the architecture you are most likely to encounter and the operating principles are no different from those of most mainframe computers and workstations.

It is important to note the distinction between the main 'box', or **system unit**, and the attached devices, which are referred to as peripherals. Figure 11.2 shows a conceptual view of the motherboard, processor, random access memory (RAM), bus, expansion slots and cards. The next sections show how these basic components operate, interact and run programs.

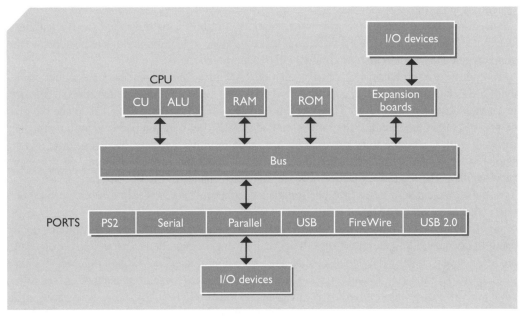

Figure 11.2 A conceptual view of the system unit

An overview of the system unit

At the heart of the computer is the processor or **central processing unit**, which consists of two parts: the **arithmetic and logic unit**, which handles all the mathematical and logical processing, and the **control unit**, which coordinates the processor's activities, overseeing input, output and execution of program instructions. The faster the processor, the better the system will perform. There are different kinds of processors, which are discussed a little later.

The memory of the computer is also divided into two parts: **read-only memory (ROM)**, which is not directly accessible to user programs and holds basic systems software that the computer needs to operate; and **random access memory (RAM)**, which is used to hold programs and data so that they can be accessed by the processor. RAM is often referred to as primary storage. Because it is electrical in nature, if power to RAM is lost, all the data in it will also be lost. Accessing primary storage is many thousands of times faster than accessing secondary storage devices such as hard disks and floppy disks. Generally speaking, the more RAM, the better the computer will perform.

The computer also has a variety of secondary storage media, such as hard drives, CD/DVD drives and possibly an ancient floppy drive for backward compatibility. Whereas primary storage is volatile (i.e. its contents are lost if the power is turned off), secondary storage is more permanent. This permanency comes at a cost — if accessing a hard drive is many thousands of times slower than accessing RAM, then accessing peripheral storage devices will be even slower. Programs and data are stored on the hard drive when the computer is turned off. These devices may be internal or accessed through one of the computer's ports. Secondary storage is discussed in detail later in this chapter.

The **bus** is like an electronic highway connecting all the components on the main circuit board (motherboard). There are various industry standards for buses, and you need to check which is appropriate for your needs.

The motherboard houses the processor, memory and bus, plus dedicated device handlers. The motherboard has **expansion slots**, which allow various special functions to be added to the computer, such as soundcards, fax/modem cards and video cards.

To improve performance, PCs have an area of RAM set aside as a **cache**. Because accessing the RAM is much faster than accessing a hard drive, the system preloads data related to the first lot of data accessed into RAM. The next time a disk access is required, the first place the processor looks is in the cache. If the information is already there, then it needs to look no further; if not, it will access the hard drive as before, with minimal increase in access time. Cache statistics are quoted as hit rates (i.e. the number of times the processor looked in the cache successfully). The bigger the cache, the better the performance of the PC. Microprocessors also have their own caches to improve performance. Accessing memory in the processor is much faster than accessing RAM.

Input usually takes place by keyboard and mouse and output by monitor. Although many cathode-ray tube (CRT) monitors are still in use, they may be regarded as becoming obsolete and are being superseded by flat panel screens. These are not affected by glare and flicker, and have a much smaller footprint. Communication with peripheral devices takes place through the ports, which are affixed to the motherboard or expansion cards. Historically, these were slow serial and parallel ports, which have now all but given way to faster **universal serial bus (USB 2.0)** ports, which operate at 480 Mbps (USB 1.0 ports operated at 12 Mbps). These have the advantage of being able to connect up to 127 devices via the same port and are used for web cameras, flash memory and networked devices. USB ports in their turn are giving way to even faster **FireWire** ports, which support the higher data transfer speeds that modern multimedia applications require. Current FireWire ports operate at 800 Mbps, but versions running at twice this speed will soon be available. As do USB ports, FireWire ports allow 'hot swapping' (connecting and disconnecting devices while the computer is switched on). It is common practice to use a USB- or FireWire-powered external hard drive to make data and applications easily portable.

How programs run

Although you do not need to know processor-specific information regarding the fine details of program execution, you do need to know the basic principles if you are to make informed purchasing decisions and configure systems that perform well. Figure 11.3 shows the simplified processor operating cycle.

The machine cycle consists of two subcycles, the I cycle for instruction and the E cycle for execution. Instructions and data are retrieved from RAM and loaded into registers on the processor. Things are a little more complicated than the simple cycle implies; to ensure that the processor does not sit idle, instructions are preloaded. However, the basic principle remains unaltered.

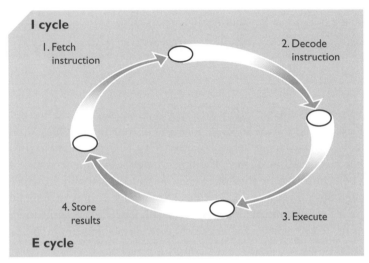

I cycle

1. Fetch instruction

2. Decode instruction

4. Store results

3. Execute

E cycle

Figure 11.3 The simplified processor cycle

Problems with the von Neumann architecture

As you will appreciate from this brief discussion, all the data and every program instruction have to pass through the processor. Although modern processors are very fast compared with their predecessors, the processor imposes a physical bottleneck on computer performance. Equally significant is that software developers need to consider the 'fetch, next, execute' cycle as they produce programs. In other words, the programs are not truly independent of the underlying hardware, and the von Neumann architecture represents a mental as well as physical bottleneck.

> **Reflection question 3:** The processing speed of human consciousness is estimated to be 16 bits per second, and supercomputers are 50 billion times faster than this. Why are humans regarded as being superior to computers in terms of processing ability?

More on PC system components

The preceding coverage is intended to help you understand how the basic components work together to run programs. This section considers the operating principles and underlying technology of the system unit and peripheral devices.

Input devices

In addition to the usual mouse and keyboard, a few specialised input devices exist. Bar code and magnetic code readers may be used in conjunction with a PC, provided that the necessary interfaces are in place. These are sometimes termed 'direct entry devices' because no human input is needed. Many handheld computers use a stylus for input rather than a keyboard because they are small. Most PCs can interface with peripheral input devices such as web cameras and scanners through ports. The standard QWERTY keyboard was developed in the days of mechanical typewriters and was intended to prevent key jamming by placing the most frequently used keys as far apart as possible. There are several more efficient keyboard layouts, but these are under-represented in the marketplace. Because it is very difficult to migrate from one keyboard layout to another, it is hard to imagine the traditional keyboard being superseded.

> **Reflection question 4:** How useful do you think that handwriting recognition technology really is?

Processors

Processors come in two main varieties. The most widely used type is a **complex instruction-set computer (CISC)**, named that because there are literally hundreds of instructions that the chip is capable of carrying out; in other words, the chip is general purpose. CISC chips are used in IBM PC standard systems and Apple Macintosh machines. The other variety of chip is a **reduced instruction-set computer (RISC)** chip, which is able to replace complicated instructions with a few simple instructions. Although this may seem wasteful, the design of the chip is such that it is fully optimised when running the smaller instructions set; that is, although it is running more instructions, it usually outperforms CISC processors. RISC chips tend to be used in high-end workstations and specialised computers.

Faster computers

Making the computer go faster has always been an obsession, and attention has usually focused on the processor. However, performance can be achieved in various ways, for example, by reducing the distance between components on the same chip or simply fitting more components into the same space.

Many people believe that the limits of silicon-based technology have now been reached and that the speed of light and the physical wavelength of light used to etch the chips are the limiting factors in technology development. Therefore, using materials for chip manufacture that will conduct electricity more quickly would be a good move. Gallium arsenide is faster than silicon but the technology is taking a long time to develop.

Alternatively, manufacturers are exploring new computer architectures that use more than one microprocessor, so-called parallel architectures. Multiprocessor systems have been around for some time (although their main applications area was in fault-tolerant computing), but highly specialised, massively parallel architectures have been finding their way into supercomputers. Here, the difficulty is to divide a task up into subtasks that may be executed simultaneously. Another approach is to put more than one processor onto a chip. One of the problems that faster, more powerful single chips cause is unwanted heat. Dual-core and quad-core processors are intended to deliver high performance for lower energy consumption and heat generation. The idea is very simple; take the cores of two processors and place them onto a single piece of silicon wafer to form a new chip that has a dual core (a quad-core chip comprises two dual cores). These chips run at a lower speed but because they work independently (although sharing some resources such as memory), they are faster overall and need less energy and cooling. A dual-core system would allow you to record a high-definition TV program, surf the Web and edit video footage all at the same time, smoothly. For computer gamers, dual-core chips are ideal, and in laptops, dual-core processors extend battery life. Special low-level software is a needed to take full advantage of the extra processing power, but this is rapidly finding its way onto dual-core desktops.

Although contemporary computer performance may seem blisteringly fast, the quest for speed is unlikely to diminish. Computer gaming and demanding media applications are the main drivers of this trend.

infobyte

Face-to-face interface

Say what you will, computers are not that easy to deal with. Interacting with the underlying system requires technical skills, (usually) knowledge of a computer language and the ability to manipulate things using a clumsy mouse. Mark Lucente at IBM's Thomas J Watson Research Centre wants to dispense with keyboards and mice entirely and have computers respond to voice and body movements. At a major computer expo, a ceiling-mounted camera and a pocket microphone monitored Lucente as he commanded the system 'Give me the world' and summoned a globe to appear on a large screen, 'Make it spin,' he said, and the globe began to rotate. 'Move it over here,' and the globe followed the line of his pointing finger and dutifully moved to the lower right-hand corner of the screen. Lucente's view is that we move objects around with our hands in the real world and that computers should interact with users as naturally as possible. The aim is to make computing more intuitive and less learned. Microsoft Vista already includes speech recognition, so Lucente's views are not isolated.

Source: Information from Benedek, E 2007, 'Computers come to their senses', http://domino.watson.ibm.com.

Output devices

Output devices are hardcopy or softcopy. Hardcopy involves a printing process. Softcopy devices are display screens and monitors.

Hardcopy

Laser printers are now the preferred option for most organisations, and good-quality colour options are available for a few thousand dollars. Although laser printers cost more initially, their operating costs are significantly less than those of inkjet printers, which are better suited to low-volume, personal-use systems. Older dot-matrix and daisy-wheel printers relied on impact methods to make an inked impression on the paper. These printers are now of historical interest and cannot match the high throughput rates of modern laser printers. There are one or two exceptions, where business are using three- and four-part carbon invoices, a dot-matrix printer is able to print these, whereas an inkjet or laser printer cannot.

When low-volume printers are used with personal systems, the PC does most of the printer control, that is, the service is dedicated. With networked printers, the printer normally has a significant amount of RAM to enable it to store files. Additionally, files for printing are saved on the disk of a print server whose job it is to ensure that documents are printed and that users are informed of the success (or otherwise) of the operation.

Full of sound and fury

According to futurologists, we may expect to see many things in the next 50 years, including three-dimensional TV, video 'tattoos' and electronic life. But not every prediction comes to fruition. A promising technology is Holosonic's audio spotlight. This creates sound in a very narrow beam, so that it can be heard only where it is wanted. DaimlerChrysler has already used the technology for its new Mercedes, allowing passengers to listen to different radio stations. High-frequency waves are used to create and contain the sounds in the 'spotlight'. The technology is already being used in museums and art galleries, and as computers become more interactive and responsive to voices, it promises to make open-plan offices and factories more comfortable environments in which to work.

Source: Information from Holosonic Research Labs, www.holosonics.com.

Softcopy

Softcopy devices are basically computer screens. These use either CRT technology, as is the case with most desktop machines, or **liquid crystal displays (LCDs)**, which are used in portable computers. CRTs use more power than LCDs but usually come at only a quarter of the cost of an LCD screen of the same size. However, CRTs are virtually obsolete, and in 2006, the sales of flat-panel TVs exceeded CRT sales. LCD panels are better ergonomically because they do not emit radiation or flicker in the same way that CRTs do. LCD screens may have a passive matrix, which has less speed and brightness than the active-matrix variety. If you intend to watch video or play games then a high refresh rate is essential. A recent variation is **organic light-emitting diode** (OLED) displays. These have a very bright display and consume much less power than conventional displays; currently, their use is restricted to smaller handheld devices

Screen clarity, **resolution** and **refresh** rates are very important. The points on the screen that make up the display are called **pixels**. The more pixels the screen has, the better its resolution (clarity). The distance between the pixels also matters: the greater the pixel density, the better the picture. The refresh rate is the number of times per second the display is updated: the higher the refresh rate, the less the image appears to flicker. (A combination of fluorescent lighting and CRT displays can result in a stroboscopic effect, in which displays with high refresh rates appear to flicker. This is very tiring for users.)

The entire display is generated by the PC, so it is important to have a large-capacity video card installed to ensure good performance when running graphic-intensive applications. Many flat-panel widescreen TVs also come with VGA and multimedia ports, so that you can use your computer as an entertainment centre. Consequently, you should make sure that your graphics card supports widescreen formats. Informed opinion is that plasma screens are yielding market share to LCD panels. Ergonomically, a 17-inch (43-cm) screen in a 4:3 aspect ratio comes close to being optimum at eye height about an arm's length from the user, as would a 20-inch (51 cm) 16:9 aspect ratio screen. However, these figures are based on standard definition. High definition increases pixel density and clarity, so larger screens are feasible if you are prepared to increase the distance between eye and screen. High-definition TV tuners are becoming standard and if buying a flat-panel screen, you would be well advised to make sure that it is true high definition and that your computer's graphics card is capable of providing high-definition output to take advantage of the technology. A final point: check the noise rating for your computer. The cooling fans can be very distracting while watching movies or just trying to work, so dual-core processors and water-cooled PCs are worth thinking about.

Primary storage

The von Neumann architecture revolves around the stored-program concept. Put simply, this means that the program (or as many parts of it as are required for now) has to be in the computer's **primary storage** (memory). Memory is divided into ROM and RAM.

ROM

ROM chips are nonerasable hardware modules that usually come with the programs installed. As their name implies, ROM chips can be read but not altered by the user and programs. These chips hold their contents even when the power is cut off, that is, they are nonvolatile. In mobile telephones, ROM chips contain all the software the device requires to operate. In computers, ROM chips are not big enough to hold all the software the system needs to run; instead, ROM chips hold the basic instructions for starting the PC, carrying out basic diagnostic tests and loading the operating system into RAM.

ROM chips are called **firmware**. Additionally, there are **programmable ROM (PROM)** chips, without any software installed, for which the buyer then writes the program to be installed. These require special equipment ('**PROM blasters**'). **Eraseable PROM (EPROM)** chips work in the same way as PROM chips but the programs can be erased. PROMs and EPROMs can be used to add functionality to a computer or to enforce strict licensing conditions for certain software products.

RAM

RAM is referred to as main memory because it stores the data and programs on which the computer is working. Unlike ROM, it is volatile in that its contents are lost if power to the chip is cut. ROM chips are mounted on to boards and then packaged as **single inline memory modules**, which can be plugged into the motherboard. Hardware designers place RAM as close to the processor as possible to guarantee good performance. Because accessing RAM is many times faster than accessing any secondary storage device, a PC with RAM to spare will run programs quickly. As processors have become more powerful, the performance of RAM becomes a key factor in computer performance. RAM chips used to come in two main flavours — SDRAM and DDR — but both of these are giving way to DDR2 and products such as RamBus (RDRAM). It seems likely that RDRAM will become the dominant (if more expensive) standard, at least until something faster comes along.

Secondary storage devices and media

Secondary storage media operate using three basic types of technology: magnetic, using tapes and disks; optical, using writeable CDs and DVDs and electronic, using microchips. The information may be stored for use in two modes: serial access (e.g. tapes, which are slow) and random access (e.g. disks, which are much faster).

Magnetic tape

Magnetic tape provides serial access; you cannot just access the data you want directly, you need to start at the beginning of the tape and wait until the data are located. Although the technology is very old, it is extremely cost effective to store large data archives in this way. Older systems use large tape reels and smaller contemporary ones sometimes use digital audio tape or larger cassette formats. Magnetic tape is still used for older transaction processing systems that operate on a batch basis (i.e. the transactions are stored on tape for later processing) and for very large systems. It is not possible to jump directly to a record on the tape in a short time, so the operating speed of serial media make them useless for modern, real-time interactive systems, apart from data backups. Most modern backup systems have moved to DVD media and some organisations are ignoring traditional backup media altogether and are duplicating disk drives and servers so that data can never be lost.

Magnetic disks

In contrast, random access media allow records to be accessed very quickly by jumping to their location on the storage medium. Random access systems normally use disks or diskettes, but drums are still used in parts of the industry. Floppy drives are intended to store small amounts of information and access speeds are very slow. A few PCs still have them for backward compatibility. Internal hard drives are much faster than peripheral devices but are still many times slower than accessing RAM. However, there is a fundamental tradeoff here between performance and reliability. Secondary storage is nonvolatile, so that if there is a system crash, the hard drive should hold enough information to allow transactions to be completed or properly abandoned. Companies such as Amazon.com ensure that access to the online catalogue is rapid by putting the entire information set into RAM, but will revert to using slower and more reliable methods when processing transactions.

Because all disk drives have mechanical as well as electrical components, they are subject to wear and tear, and accordingly it is very important to make sure that all data are safely backed up. One method used by many companies is to have several disk drives on the same machine or scattered over a network, often with uninterruptible power supplies. This allows data to be replicated and minimises the impact of disk failure. It also allows for swift retrieval of archived data. This strategy is referred to as redundant arrays of inexpensive disks. In many cases, the performance of database products such as Oracle may be improved substantially by using several disks.

Increasingly, online or network-based storage such as Apple's iDisk is employed. Generally, the retrieval speeds are too slow for demanding applications, but they allow important files and directories to be mirrored automatically, giving readily accessible backups in the event of systems problems.

The overwhelming trends for hard drives (and flash memory) are that they are becoming faster and cheaper with much greater storage capacities.

Optical disks

Optical storage media such as CDs and DVDs are significantly slower than their magnetic counterparts when it comes to data retrieval and very much slower when it comes to writing data. Many PC owners use CDs to back up their data; they cost about $0.30 and can hold a lot of data (650+ MB). For single-user systems, performance is adequate. CDs and DVDs have revolutionised the software industry, enabling large software suites to be sent anywhere in the world for a few dollars. Although DVDs are around the same price as CDs and hold many times more data (4.5 GB on a single side), many people continue to use CDs for backward compatibility with computers and music systems. There is little difference in the cost of DVD and CD burners now and both come in rewriteable formats. Modern optical disks offer super-dense storage and consume less power and take up less space than tape or conventional DVDs. Their large capacity and long operating life (50 years plus) make them ideal for backups.

Protecting your data

If your data matter to you, make sure that you have another copy or backup. All magnetic media are badly affected by lightning strikes or magnetism from motors, and just about every storage medium in existence will be wiped out by fire. Backups should be stored in a different place from the live system, so that both are not lost in the same accident. As the performance and affordability of hardware continue to improve, many larger organisations simply duplicate entire databases and systems on the same site and on different sites, so triple redundant backup systems are far from unusual. Although significant investment and duplication of hardware resources are needed to do this, the process is automatic and costs savings in management and the guarantee of business continuity may more than compensate for the expenditure.

Flash memory

Flash memory provides random access and is a sort of hybrid of primary and secondary storage. This technology uses microchips to store data in a stable format. A flash memory card is a little thicker than a credit card and is designed to fit a computer's PCMCIA slot or a USB port with a suitable adapter. (PCMCIA stands for Personal Computer Memory Card International Association, a standard for expansion slots in laptop computers, PDAs and other small devices.) At the time of writing, flash memory cards offer 1 GB capacity for about $80 and some also double as MP3 players. That they have no mechanical components makes them potentially faster than a hard drive but generally performance is a little slower. Advances in chip-circuit density may allow CDs, DVDs and disks to be replaced by flash technology. Certainly, most digital cameras use flash cards in preference to disks and flash memory is widely used in handheld and portable computing devices. Although the cost is much higher than for conventional disk storage, they use only 10 per cent of the power, so they prolong time between battery recharges.

infobyte

Hard limits?

The paramagnetic limit (data storage capacity) of hard drives will be reached any time now. Hard drives do not use energy efficiently and because data are stored in serial format, the maximum transfer speed of disks is 320 Mbps. There are products such as Blu-Ray that could be faster but their basic format is still two-dimensional serial data storage. Some regard these as mere stepping stones on the way to three-dimensional holographic storage. Colossal Storage Corporation aims to have a 100-TB disk, 3.5 inches (about 9 cm) in diameter, using three-dimensional holographic storage on the market in the near future, Plasmon already markets a 29-TB optical disk, which is used by the Ordnance Survey in the UK. The disks will rely on atomic switching, using new nanotechnologies, and will have more than 2000 times the capacity of a Blu-Ray disk: that is enough to store more than 300 000 years of music or 10 000 movies.

Source: Information from transcript of interview with Greg Schmergel, co-founder, president and CEO of Nantero, www.nanotech-now.com; *Byte and Switch* 2006, 'Users open up on optical', 8 November, www.byteandswitch.com.

Moore's law

In 1965, Gordon Moore, one of the cofounders of Intel, noted that the amount of information storable on a square inch of silicon would double about every 18 months. This is called Moore's law (Kanellos 2003). In general terms, this means that the processing power effectively doubles every three to four years, although the actual figure is nearer a 20 per cent increase a year for mainframes and roughly 25 per cent a year for PCs. Although the cost of processors does not seem to change on the same scale, the real cost of one MIPS has decreased by approximately 20 per cent a year. In short, people are buying more sophisticated and proportionately cheaper hardware each year. To appreciate the scale of the improvement, consider the following: if a $1000 investment made in 1977 had shown the same improvement as microchip technology, it would now be worth $4.2 million. If the same improvement rate applied to a car purchased in 1977 with a top speed of 150 km/h, it would now be capable of 320 000 km/h. Moore's law is likely to hold true until 2018, when physical limitations on manufacturing will cause it to fail.

Accordingly, if you are working on the design and implementation of a large system, it is advisable to delay purchasing hardware until it is actually needed.

> **Reflection question 5:** Extending the car analogy, are there things that are routinely tolerated in a computer that would not be acceptable in a car?

[**Key concept:** ABC: assume nothing, believe nothing, check everything.]

How to buy a PC

You will make some very important purchases in life, such as a house and a car. It is suggested that you treat buying a PC in the same vein; it is a serious affair. The following points will hopefully be helpful:

> Analyse your needs. What do you need the computer to do for you?
> Choose software that will support your needs. Which applications do you require?
> Identify potential hardware configurations that will support your software.
> Produce a shortlist (about five) of possible computers. This will normally entail visiting retail outlets. Do not be pressured into buying. If the sales staff cannot answer your questions adequately, do not waste your time there. Do not be afraid of getting advice from different sources.
> Decide on your preferred platform: at the PC level, this will normally mean choosing between an Apple Macintosh and a standard PC. Apple machines are generally better appointed but tend to be more expensive. Because they now use the same chipset as the PC, software compatibility is no longer an issue.
> Now decide whether you need portability, that is, do you need a laptop or a desktop? Laptops are more expensive and more difficult to upgrade than an equivalent desktop machine.
> Review your options. Will the computer meet your needs? Check the processor and memory requirements for the software that you need to run. Remember that processor speed and memory size requirements quoted in software tend to be minimal. Technology changes very quickly, so get the fastest machine you can afford and ensure that it has more RAM and a

larger, faster hard drive than you need now — you will need it later. If you are a computer gamer or intend to use your PC as an entertainment centre, then invest in the best graphics card you can get. Be careful of systems that are cheap and use the main processor to carry out graphics processing. They have performance problems and are very difficult to upgrade.

› Select manufacturers or suppliers and obtain quotations for your chosen platform. Try to avoid little-known companies. Adherence to widely adopted standards reduces risk and increases upgradeability. Most information systems professionals change their PCs every 18–24 months or 36–42 months with an upgrade.

› Narrow your options to one or two suppliers and negotiate the price. Under no circumstances believe that the marked price or package is the best deal that they can offer. Remember that you have the option of buying from well-established companies such as Dell and Gateway online. Online companies tend to offer better prices but are almost impossible to negotiate with, and user support can be an issue too. Online purchasing requires good technical knowledge since you will have to provide input to the configuration of the finished product.

› In making your final decision, remember to take into account warranties and user support.

› Do not be influenced by 'bundling' (the practice of putting together a total package of hardware, software, games, desk, printer and scanner). Often much of the 'bundle' is of limited use to the buyer and serves only to increase the overall price.

› Be aware of consumer law, and do not sign any document that asks you to relinquish any rights.

› Beware of dealer-arranged financing: this comes at a cost. Flexirent-type schemes *may* be useful for a business because the entire cost is tax deductible but do your sums carefully.

› In some countries, the law makes a distinction between hire purchase and a credit sale. In these countries, the credit provider may be jointly responsible for the condition and suitability of the goods. It may pay you to use your credit card (if only for the frequent flier points).

Certain employees, such as company directors, may be reimbursed for the purchase of one laptop computer a year, avoiding fringe benefits tax and maximising personal tax advantages (this does not apply to ordinary desktop machines). This can make a laptop a more cost-effective option despite the more expensive upgrade path. However, the rules are complex, and it is sensible to seek professional guidance.

[**Key concept:** Almost everything is negotiable.]

IS in action

Burbank sharpens IT with blades

Burbank in California is regarded as the media capital of the world. Although Hollywood is more famous in the film industry, most of the actual production takes place in Burbank where many TV and film companies have their headquarters. Its permanent population is more than 100 000 and the city has an extensive information systems and IT infrastructure. In 2004, IT staff were struggling to maintain a complex, heterogeneous data centre, which made use of four different operating systems. The storage limit on the Sun servers had been

(continued)

reached and no more disks could be added to the array. To compound the problems, the city needed to upgrade its flagship Oracle ERP systems as well as other important Oracle-based systems.

What the city needed was a technical solution that was both modular and scalable, and it was decided to move to a Linux-based solution, which provided openness and cost effectiveness. The actual migration would take some time and the city decided on IBM's BladeCenter technology as its platform of choice. Blade servers have certain advantages for a multivendor organisation, in particular, the ability to run virtual instances of any operating system. As the migrated legacy systems reach the end of their service life, they too will be replaced by a Linux solution. Two ten-unit BladeCenters were installed, one in the primary data centre and the other shared with the city's police department to provide disaster recovery capability. The city's entire Oracle application suite now runs on four blades, which simplifies administration and reduces software licensing costs because only one production server version is needed. Technology consolidation has also been a feature of the move. The blade chassis reduces cabling and rack requirements, so now only two racks are needed instead of the previous five. When all legacy systems have been fully migrated, only one rack will be needed. Power, cooling and management costs have all been substantially reduced and there is a lot more free space in the operations room. It is not all about money. Performance has also improved and future upgrades will be incremental rather than quantum, so future planning is also simplified.

Source: Information from IBM, 'The city of Burbank brings Oracle ERP home on IBM BladeCenter', www-306.ibm.com.

infobyte

More and Moore

The components for which Moore's law holds true may make up only 10 per cent of a system. The remaining 90 per cent is mainly passive components, which may be spread over several circuit boards. The Microsystems Packaging Research Centre is working on system on package technologies, which will embed everything a system needs onto a single chip. The size reduction is so great that handhelds will cease being multifunctional and become megafunctional. The technology will make theoretical medical and dental applications a reality, for example, producing capsules that can be introduced into the human body and monitor vital signs and enzymes for diagnostic purposes. It could even deliver precise amounts of drugs exactly where they are needed. This research has the potential to overturn Moore's law and deliver more than Moore.

Source: Information from Tummala, R, 'Moore's Law meets its match', *Spectrum Online*, www.spectrum.ieee.org.

Buying hardware for business systems

The basic principles outlined for PCs apply here. But because the consequences of making mistakes are much greater, care must be exercised in the selection process. All procurement begins with a careful analysis of business needs, then software and communications requirements, and these in turn will strongly influence hardware selection. Management has responsibilities to companies, shareholders and, in the case of government, taxpayers. The decision makers need to choose whether to buy the equipment and build the system themselves or organise supply and installation from a third party. For a small quantity, of course, the process of evaluating bids for supply and negotiating contracts would probably exceed the value of the contract. Assuming that hardware and software needs have been carefully analysed and there is a commitment to proceed, then proceed as for PC selection, with the addition of the following.

Expression of interest

When working for public institutions, it is important to make the tendering process as open as possible, to avoid accusations of favouritism and corruption. Advertisements can be placed in newspapers asking for expressions of interest in tendering for the supply of goods and services, or companies may apply to join the list of government-approved suppliers. In industry, management can either advertise or simply write to potential suppliers with a tender or offer document, also known as a **request for proposal (RFP)**.

Potential suppliers need to be briefed on your exact needs. Usually, this involves preparing an information pack, which gives background information on your organisation, its plans and needs, the timeline required for the project and some indication of the funding available. For large projects, it is often a good idea to engage a consultant, especially if the area is outside your field of expertise. The RFP often forms the basis of a legal contract, so it is very important to ensure that all the technical details are correct. It is also advisable to involve your legal team in the preparation of the RFP. The more work that you put into this document, the more likely it is that unsuitable suppliers will not respond. A business would normally give some indication of the type of company that it is prepared to deal with; for example, it must meet quality standard ISO 9002; it must have been trading for five years; it must have a track record for supply in this area. This reduces risk and the amount of work involved in the evaluation and validation of bids. The information pack must give the criteria for assessment: although price is important, user support and warranties could be very significant. The exact format, content and timing of the bids and tenders are also specified, to make the resulting bids easier to compare. It also makes it much easier to eliminate unsuitable suppliers, because if they cannot deliver a document in the required format, they are unlikely to deliver a system as required.

When all the responses have been received, unacceptable bids and tenders should be eliminated from the process. This means anything that is late or in the wrong format, does not cover the criteria or contains errors of spelling and grammar. Write to these companies to inform them that their bids have been unsuccessful. Acceptable bids and tenders can now be ranked.

From this point, the highest-ranked bids should be selected and validated. Validation means that every claim that the company makes for itself, its products and services is checked. This can be a lengthy, painstaking procedure, so the of bids that are validated should be kept to a minimum: five or fewer is a rough guideline. It is not ethical to change the terms of reference but it may be appropriate to seek clarification from suppliers on certain points.

From childhood experience, you may have memories of Christmas mornings spent with non-functioning toys because optimistic parents assumed that the toys came with batteries included. The information systems industry is not exactly a toy shop but the onus is on you to check the precise wording and specifications that companies give. Several companies have had their business affected by server failures or have failed to notice that the standard manufacturer's warranty did not include a time frame for response — they assumed that engineers would turn up as soon as the fault was reported. Same-day service or on-site replacement is a requirement for mission-critical systems. Suppliers do not usually have time to educate potential clients, so it is taken for granted that you actually want what you ask for. This is one area in which being a member of a professional body is very useful. Many professional bodies publish technology reviews and hold breakfast meetings with industry speakers. If you network within the organisation effectively, it is usually possible to find someone who has detailed knowledge of a particular topic.

[**Key concept:** If you use technical terms, make sure that you understand what they mean and that others do too.]

When the process of validation is complete, it is usually easy to select the final supplier. Remember that the solution should reduce complexity and diversity. Single-supplier solutions do this, and also eliminate many of the compatibility problems that are often found in multi-vendor systems. Next comes the process of negotiating and overseeing the contract. If the RFP has been well prepared, the contract is virtually written, subject to minor clarifications.

For simpler systems, it is possible to obtain quotations from online suppliers. These provide either online catalogues, pricing and shipping information or a confidential guaranteed response to a written request. The assumption here is that you know exactly what you want and that it can be met from a standard package; that is, unless it is a large contract, there is little room for negotiation.

infobyte

No room at the inn

It's a perennial problem for hotels: guests check in and proceed to ignore the rules; they smoke where they should not, they damage or steal things, behave in an antisocial way or try to intimidate staff. The hotel is left to pick up the tab and try to manage aggrieved staff as best they can. Owners of short-stay holiday accommodation face similar issues. An Australian company has a solution. Businesses can register with www.guestsbehavingbadly.com.au for a small fee and offensive guests can be reported. Businesses can check a guest's track record before accepting a booking, and potential guests can look for the GBB logo when making reservations.

Source: Information from www.guestsbehavingbadly.com.au.

Offloading problems

An important aspect of management is how problems are handled. The manager's survival guide says, 'Don't take ownership of any problem that is not rightfully yours'. This can be extended to read, 'Don't take ownership of any problem that you do not need to'. When preparing RFPs and negotiating contracts, think ahead. If PCs are to be supplied with general-purpose software ready installed, have the supplier install your own software, configure the machines to be network ready and even let them do the final installation and configuration on your premises. This can save time, money and effort.

> **Reflection question 6:** Would you trust a supplier to deliver everything on time and according to specification? What precautions would you put into place and how would you handle the situation so as not to cause any unnecessary offence?

[**Key concept:** Let other people do the extra work.]

The importance of hardware standards

To manage effectively, we need to understand what we are trying to manage. So the more diverse and complex things are, the harder they are to manage. One way to reduce complexity and diversity is to standardise on hardware platforms (the hardware forms part of a standard operating environment or SOE). This also gives us better bargaining power because we are buying more machines of the same type, which means that we have a high degree of interchangeability at a component level. In an ideal world, a single hardware standard for desktop machines would be feasible, and indeed that is possible for many small or simple businesses. However, it is important to remember that the hardware is there to support business needs; in practice, this means supporting business software. Many organisations use PCs, Unix workstation and Macintosh computers in their everyday business and use the 'most appropriate tool for the job'. This does not mean that they have abandoned the notion of standards. Each type of hardware platform will be clearly defined. Other businesses have a variety of hardware platforms simply because they do not have the cash to replace older technology. Most information systems and IT managers have a migration plan to reduce hardware diversity to a few manageable standards and consequently simplify the task of management.

[**Key concept:** 'Business needs dictate the choice of software. Software dictates the choice of hardware. Everything else is about making it work efficiently and effectively.' Jane Barton-Grieg, senior information systems consultant.]

> **Reflection question 7:** If you developed a totally new computing concept, something that was a tenth the size and cost, yet gave 100 times the power of a normal PC, would you make it PC compatible? Why?

Information systems and IT governance

Rules and regulations serve as a guiding framework for organisations in terms of legalities, fiscal responsibilities, socio-ethical obligations and environmental practices. The same rules and regulations also extend to the behaviour of executives and directors, and emphasise conformance of individuals and organisations to ensure 'correct' behaviour. This framework has been insufficient to prevent corporate misconduct on a massive scale and (in part) corporate governance has evolved to restore public confidence and improve accountability. Corporate governance is about improving the effectiveness of a business while seeking to align the interests of society, individuals and corporations. Although information systems and IT infrastructures are intended to support business activities and specific projects are intended to support strategic initiatives, it cannot be denied that many projects fail to deliver as promised in terms of time, cost and functionality.

> An estimated 68% of corporate IT projects are neither on time nor on budget, and they don't deliver the originally stated business goals (Jeffrey & Leliveld 2004).

The FBI's virtual case file system had consumed more than $1 billion by the start of 2006 and has failed to meet most of its original requirements (Goldstein 2005) and there are many other examples of spectacular failure (Charette 2005).

Just as corporate governance sought to provide better alignment with social goals, so information systems and IT governance seeks to provide better alignment between information and IT and business objectives. Intrinsic to this alignment is the prioritisation of information systems and IT projects with respect to return on investment and real benefit; rationalising project expenditure to avoid duplication and unnecessary cost; better tracking and management of projects and reducing the total cost of ownership of information systems and IT. Effective information systems and IT governance is grounded in an understanding of business requirements and processes, which makes quality control simpler. However, business processes must be considered in a wider context. Validation of the component parts should never be taken to imply validation of the whole. It may help to think of this in terms of Ps and Cs; the developers and users of systems, *people*, are guided by *policies* and *procedures* as they carry out business *processes* in an environment that focuses on *compliance*, *control*, *consolidation* and *continuity*. This could be simplified to embrace two key concepts: *alignment* with corporate objectives and *accountability* of individuals and departments. Perhaps the best-known approach to information systems and IT governance is COBIT (Control Objectives for Information and related Technology). In its present incarnation it has 34 high-level objectives, covering 215 control objectives operating in the following four domains: planning and organising; acquisition and implementation, delivery and support; monitoring; and evaluation. It serves the combined interest of three constituencies, namely managers, auditors and IT users. COBIT was devised in 1992 as a set of best practices by the Information Systems Audit and Control Association and the IT Governance Institute. Risk analysis and security are intrinsic to COBIT's approach.

Information systems and IT governance and help desks

Information systems and IT governance is also concerned with cost-effective use of resources and budgets. The main area of expenditure for most organisations is not hardware or software. It is user support and configuration management. Anything up to 70 per cent of information systems and IT budgets is devoted to these areas. Once good acceptable use and security policies have been put into place, the day-to-day activity of most people is defined by their interaction and information systems managers can turn their attention to providing high-quality user support. Because users create the wealth of companies, it makes sense to ensure that their time is not wasted by hardware or software problems. If the corporate goals are cost effectiveness and service focus, then the help desk should align with these goals. The help desk is the public face of the information systems and IT infrastructure and the aim is to resolve problems as quickly as possible in a friendly manner. To this end, escalation procedures need to be considered. If possible problems cannot be resolved at the first point of contact over the telephone, then a technician will be dispatched. Good help desk systems will often link into groupware for scheduling purposes, so that the work can be carried out at a mutually convenient time. No matter how the call is resolved, information is recorded and stored for future use. This information is used to track problems and ensure that they are resolved promptly. It is also used to improve diagnostic and service times by creating an information base, which allows data mining on faults by hardware or software or user groups, signature patterns of known hacking and viruses, and effectiveness of information systems and IT staff. In turn, this allows better use of staff, more targeted staff development and better-informed purchasing decisions. Information systems and IT governance is as much concerned with philosophies of information systems and IT as it is with specific methodologies.

Summary

This chapter summarised the history of computers, explained the types of computers and peripheral devices in current use, and speculated on future developmental trends. The key points in this chapter are:

> There have been four main generations of computer, each more sophisticated than its predecessor. Each generation brought about a substantial amount of change.

> The four main types of computers in use today are supercomputer, mainframe, workstation and PC. The boundaries among these devices are sometimes indistinct.

> A typical PC configuration includes keyboard, mouse, monitor, webcam, hard drive, fax/modem, printer and system unit with ports for peripheral devices. Standard PC architecture has expansion slots to allow extra functionality to be added.

> The computer architecture that is most commonly used today is the von Neumann architecture, which imposes physical and mental bottlenecks on system development.

> Processors come in two main types: general-purpose CISC, used on most desktop computers, and RISC, used in high-performance workstations.

> There are two types of computer storage: primary, which is onboard memory that loses its contents when the power is turned off, and secondary, which is semipermanent, cheaper and much slower. Primary storage may be subdivided into RAM for user programs and ROM for specialised system programs. It seems likely that optical storage in one form or another will be more important as time goes by.

> When making any computer purchase, take care to perform needs analysis, product evaluation and price negotiation. For larger systems, it is advisable to employ a consultant and lawyer to help in this process.

> Information systems and IT governance is increasingly important as organisations seek to align information systems and IT goals with corporate goals and to introduce greater accountability of information systems and IT professionals. A major focus of this is to improve communication between business and information systems and IT people.

Questions

1. Most organisations have procurement policies that specify hardware standards. This is seen as part of information systems and IT governance. What are the pros and cons of standardising hardware?

2. Do you think that CDs and DVDs have a long-term future? Explain your answer.

3. Over the past 20 years, the PC market has grown while the mainframe market has shrunk. Do you think that mainframe computers will all but vanish? Explain your answer.

4. How do you see people interacting with computers in five and ten years from now? What changes do you expect to see in interface technologies?

5. Identify the main markets for PCs. What do you think the growth areas are and why? What developmental trends do you see for PCs in the markets that you have identified?

6. Apple has always maintained that its machines make users more productive because they are easier to use, so Apple computers are more cost effective. How valid do you think this view is, and why?

7. Organisations rely on their data to function. As an information systems manager, what precautions should you take with corporate data to ensure business continuity and security?

8. Blade servers allow several 'virtual operating systems' to be run at the same time to support different applications. Does this mean that a business could let its staff use any kind of desktop or laptop computer? Explain why.

9. Why would you carry out needs analysis and software selection before deciding on your hardware platform?

10. Apple now uses the same chipset as that in ordinary PCs. Do you think it would be worthwhile for it to produce and license a version of their operating system to run on a standard PC platform? Explain your answer.

Exercises

1. You have recently assumed the position of manager of a large company. One of your first acts has been to specify SOEs and purchasing requirements. Unfortunately, the system of budgeting is decentralised and each business unit has control of its own purchasing. All the managers have been cooperative, with the exception of the head of marketing. He refuses to adopt your standards because he has a friend who builds PC clones and he gets a 'good deal'. You cannot afford to upset people so soon after joining the company, but equally you cannot afford to be undermined so soon in your career. How would you set about resolving the situation?

2. Working in a small group or individually, consider how wearable computers could transform the way we do business. In your view, how prepared should managers be and what would you suggest that they do to be prepared for the advent of wearable computers?

3. Working in a small group or individually, consider how you would protect your company's PCs from theft and vandalism.

4. Use the Internet to research help desk support software. Identify at least five important features that it should have.

5. Use the Internet to research information systems and IT governance (COBIT would be a good thing to look at). Make a list of reasons a company should consider adopting information systems and IT governance.

'We insure anything' is the marketing mantra of Westralian Insurance Brokers (WIB). Established in 1950 by a Perth businessman who was upset by the cost of motor vehicle insurance, the business has grown into a large organisation with branches in every state in Australia and considerable overseas holdings.

There are seven major insurance areas: motor vehicle; marine; employer's liability; landlord's liability; life; home; and contents. Additionally, WIB's underwriters may accept special policies with the approval of senior managers. Each office is responsible for maintaining its own client information, including data security and backups, and communication among branches is very much on a 'need to know basis', such as when a client has interstate operations. The way that the company grew is a little unusual: as each branch office opened, it became a 'clone' of the Perth branch and the IT infrastructure and business practices were duplicated at the new location. This has been a good strategy in some respects because the skills needed to run the operation were guaranteed to be in house. Major purchasing has also been centrally coordinated, which has helped to reduce costs. On the downside, resources and staff have been considerably duplicated, although as Alan (general manager at Perth) says, 'It may cost a little more but everything works'.

WIB's venture into customer relationship management (CRM) has not proved to be the winning strategy that it was supposed to be. The host mainframe, which resides in Perth, is five years old, and the main CRM package runs under a proprietary operating system. The problem does not seem to reside with the mainframe per se but seems to relate to data capture from the other offices. Additionally, WIB makes extensive use of its intranet and extranet to locate and purchase insurance products for resale. Two years ago, an Internet-based service was launched, allowing WIB's customers to buy insurance directly. The service was aimed at rural communities. This has improved overall turnover and profitability but the service is also being used by suburban customers and the number of telephone and direct sales has dropped by 8 per cent or so. The mainframe will reach the end of its useful life a little more than a year from now and the problem of what to do next is causing some friction. Senior executives have engaged Helen (an independent consultant) to identify possible strategies and make recommendations. Alan is not entirely impressed.

'So, why should we place our trust in you? The larger consulting houses have a better reputation and more resources to call on ... you are just a one-person operation.'

'I have been doing this for more than 20 years; I have a broad portfolio of clients, a long list of references and a pattern of repeat business. Projects like yours are pretty much all I do,' Helen responded calmly. 'I have contacts in the industry that can deliver discounted solutions quickly. The simple fact of the matter is that you paying way too much for your information systems and IT and it is not delivering what you want, when you want it. The CRM system is supposed to be updated in real time, so that you can use it for data mining and promotional marketing. All you are using it for is market analysis. Having each branch handle its affairs independently means that you are losing strategic information. Being organised around PC clients and a mainframe limits your options in terms of applications software.

(continued)

As an example, risk management software has been developed for Linux, which you cannot use under the current conditions. The need to have a technical support person at each branch is also expensive at $800 000 a year alone and your mainframe is underused. My recommendation is that you centralise your information systems operations as much as possible.'

Helen pushed the spacebar on her laptop and moved to the next slide in her presentation.

'As you can see, this is the proposed solution. A blade server array comprising eight blades with dual-core processors linked to a storage area network. The server array is both modular and scalable and allows for an easy upgrade path and can support any operating system you care to name. So you will be able to use any software solution. The storage area network is also easily scalable, so you can add new storage units as they are needed. The mainframe is costing the better part of $2 million a year but its usage rate is less than 20 per cent. The server array will replace it. You will need to change your CRM software but because the data will still be available, this will not be a major concern provided we train people in its use. Your IT manager, Mahendra, has just maintained the status quo. He has not been allowed to make any substantial changes. He has made some very helpful suggestions, which I have incorporated into my proposals.'

'What happens about user support?' asked Alan.

'There are two options: we centralise it or we outsource it. Centralising it means that there will be no local IT support; users will call the central facility in Perth. Because the core systems are located there, user problems can only relate to PC clients, communications and local Internet service. We can outsource that to local companies with the right service-level agreements. This will mean increasing the level of service available in Perth but overall you should be saving a lot of cash and your business operations should improve. You might even be able to use a CRM system for what it was originally intended. You will need to find a site in the Perth area to store your backup data — it is not good practice to do that from your main site. The only other alternative that seems halfway reasonable would be to outsource everything and I would not feel happy about that.'

'I need some time to think,' Alan responded. 'A lot of this is outside my comfort zone. Mahendra, what do you think?'

Questions

1. Is Alan right to be concerned about Helen's status as a one-person company? What precautions would you have taken in his position?

2. Alan is clearly unhappy about making a decision. What should he do to avoid making a bad decision?

3. Why do you think that Mahendra has not been able to make any changes despite being in charge of IT operations?

4. Helen's solution means that every transaction and all the client data are stored at Perth and WIB is 100 per cent dependent on the Internet. What would you suggest that the company should do to mitigate the effects of an Internet outage?

5. Explain how and where Helen's solution offers potential cost savings.

6. How does Helen's solution compare with outsourcing in the medium-to-long term? Which option would you advise Alan to take and why?

7. Would you say that this approach is infrastructure based or strategic in nature? Explain your answer.

8. Why would Helen recommend using an alternative site for backups? Are there any other precautions that you would recommend?

9. If you were making the presentation, what three things would you emphasise as being the main strengths of Helen's solution and why?

10. Is outsourcing the local IT support a shrewd move? What could go wrong and how would you try to prevent it?

11. Is the channel cannibalisation caused by local clients dealing with WIB through the Internet a real cause for concern? Would you change the situation and, if so, how?

12. Helen's solution requires building up a help desk operation at the Perth branch to service all WIB offices. Outline the main tasks that you would need to perform to do this. What obvious logistical problems would you have to overcome?

References

Charette, RN 2005, 'Why software fails', www.spectrum.ieee.org.

Goldstein, H 2005, 'Who killed the virtual case file?', www.spectrum.ieee.org.

Jeffery, M & Leliveld, I 2004, 'Best practices in IT portfolio management', *MIT Sloan Management Review*, 2004, vol. 45, no. 3, pp. 41–9.

Kanellos, M 2003, 'Intel scientists find wall for Moore's law', *ZDNET News*, 1 December, http://news.zdnet.com.

Warren, S 2006, 'Why virtualise?', www.serverwatch.com.

CHAPTER 12
Personal productivity with information systems

LEARNING OBJECTIVES

After reading this chapter, you should be able to:

» describe the skills required to be a knowledge worker in the knowledge economy

» understand the mindsets related to using personal information systems and technology

» explain what is meant by 'information overload', and discuss methods and techniques for coping with it

» explain the effective use of email

» discuss the ethical issues related to using information systems

» understand the concept of ergonomic design in relation to information systems.

Introduction

Most of this book has looked at the impact of information systems and information technology (IT) at the organisational level, which has been very significant. Interestingly, at the individual level, information systems do not seem to have been as widely adopted as personal productivity approaches. Certainly, many people use word processors, spreadsheets and databases as a daily part of work and study. These are part of the personal productivity toolset but are not in themselves an integrated personal information system. Many people say that they are suffering from information overload but use only very rudimentary methods and techniques for coping with personal information daily. The aim of this chapter is to examine where and how information systems and IT can be used to improve personal productivity and how to engage in a lifelong association with information systems effectively.

Many of the methods and techniques discussed earlier in the book can be used to some extent on a personal level.

Skills needed in the knowledge economy

The agricultural age was characterised by most people working in some capacity related to the land. The industrial age saw a large percentage of people move to the cities to work in factories. The postindustrial age is characterised by a large percentage of people working in service industries such as the financial sector, hospitality and tourism, and professions such as accounting and information systems. The postindustrial age can also be termed the **information age** because many people work in office environments and to a large extent buy, process and sell information of one kind or another. This is frequently referred to as the knowledge economy.

Certain skills are essential for operating effectively in the knowledge economy. These skills must be developed to an acceptable standard according to:

> an employer's expectations: these can be seen in job advertisements
> a school or tertiary institution's requirements: these are tested by assignments and examinations
> the standards expected by professional bodies: these are stipulated in the various membership grades.

In the past, the emphasis in education was on memorising many facts. Today, we have access to a vast amount of data and information, too much to spend time memorising it all. Information can become out of date so rapidly that it seems pointless memorising a mass of facts regularly. A certain body of knowledge and facts is required for people to operate as professionals, but a range of general transferable skills is much more significant today, because we can access facts as and when they are needed.

It is worthwhile examining these knowledge economy skills and how information systems are involved. Note that they are basically transferable skills, which can be applied to any profession or discipline.

Research and information gathering

Research skills involve the ability to find relevant information for decision-making purposes. The data or information may come from a variety of sources.

> *The Internet.* The Internet provides an increasing wealth of information sources. There are online magazines, journals and newspapers. In addition, most of the large IT companies provide information about their products and often have case studies that can be downloaded. Reliable sources of information on the Web are professional organisations, which have an image and reputation to maintain and therefore something to lose if they provide unreliable or incorrect information that would tarnish their reputation. However, remember that companies use the Web to promote their products, so the weaknesses or limitations of their products or services are unlikely to be presented in any detail.

> *Libraries.* Libraries provide information in books, magazines and journals, in paper or digital format. Libraries use information systems to provide search and query facilities to their catalogues. Many libraries now have remote access by modems and subscribe to online databases of journals and magazines, which can be downloaded to your own local machine. This means, of course, that you can do your research or information gathering without leaving home or your office.

> *Friends and work colleagues.* A less formal way of gathering information and conducting research is to use a network of people. This may involve face-to-face meetings or communication by telephone, email or chat group. This type of information gathering through networks may not be objective but it is often useful for highlighting strategic or important issues.

> *Associations and societies.* Professional organisations such as computer societies provide information through magazines, journals and meetings of special-interest groups such as computer security and e-commerce.

> **Reflection question 1:** Where do you get most of your information from for assignments?

Planning

Planning is a skill that can be greatly improved with information systems and IT. Planning is the ability to break a task down into components and estimate the time needed for each one. It also requires an understanding of the resources required to complete the task and how these can be effectively applied to the project. Planning requires the ability to take a high-level view of matters, to see the 'big picture'.

Processing information

It is hard to imagine processing data and information these days without the aid of computer technology. There is no shortage of information and data available in the information age and a major factor determining success is how we filter, process and analyse that data. Processing data and information involves:

> extracting and filtering relevant data
> defining relationships between datasets
> analysing data, both numerical and text
> summarising data and information
> adding, updating and amending data and information.

The ability to use information systems greatly affects the ability to process information. Unfortunately, many people receive little or no formal training in the use of information systems for personal productivity.

Presenting information and data has become an important part of most knowledge economy occupations. IT is essential for preparing high-quality reports and presentations that use graphics and charts to summarise data.

Creativity and problem solving

With the range of business opportunities available in a rapidly changing world, the ability to produce innovative ideas and solutions is now very important. New technologies provide opportunities for innovation in organisations. However, it is not just the ability to foresee the implications of a technology's impact on a business sector that is important but also how to instil it in the organisation effectively.

Many problems in organisations are a result of lacking, poor-quality, irrelevant or too much information. Information systems can be used in various ways to solve these problems.

Communication

Communication skills are always rated as important in surveys of employers' expectations and requirements. In some ways, communication has become a more complex skill because there are more channels to use to communicate in business in the information age:

> telephone
> telephone conference
> mail
> fax
> face-to-face meeting
> presentation to a group
> email
> bulletin boards
> web pages
> video conference
> reports
> memorandums.

Teamwork skills

The ability to work as part of a team is a valuable skill. Knowing how to reach a consensus, when to lead the group and when and how to listen are all part of team skills. The communication among group members in today's business world relies heavily on communication technologies.

[**Key concept:** People with excellent transferable skills will always be in demand.]

Using personal information systems and IT

Do you view information systems and IT in a positive or negative light? When was the last time you adopted a new information system or new piece of IT on a personal level?

As a professional in the knowledge economy, you will need to develop a lifelong association with information systems. To a large extent, the success of this relationship depends on your mental attitude or mindset. Consider the following attitudes to information systems and IT.

> *It is just not me*. This view is held by people who feel that they are not 'technical', and is a particular mindset that acts as a barrier to adoption. Information systems are not necessarily technical systems, as have been discussed throughout this book, but rather social systems, of which there is a technical component.

> *I will adopt it when it gets more reliable*. The problem with this attitude is that someone somewhere will always point out a weakness with a certain technology, no matter how long it has been in use. The lesson to learn from this is not to wait for the systems to be perfect before using them.

> *Computer rage syndrome*. Some people get very frustrated when using systems because they expect to be highly productive straight away. In this respect, they have unrealistic expectations and may become very frustrated. Even experienced users often work on the basis that the system will run perfectly all the time and are frustrated when it does not. Always remember that throwing your computer out of the window will set you back in several ways!

> *I will use it when I have to*. Rather than being a laggard, be a leader and get the benefit of the systems and technology from the start.

> *I am developing a lifelong association with information systems and IT*. This attitude takes the view that information systems and IT are integral to the information age.

Although the last perspective is perhaps a more helpful one in terms of using information systems and IT day to day, it lacks a certain energy. It is interesting to reassess regularly how you can work more productively with information systems and IT on a personal level. There are two sides to using computer systems productively. The first is using systems creatively and the second is using systems as a problem-solving tool. These two rely on using both the left and right sides of the brain.

Left-brain thinking is related more to verbal and deductive thinking (logic) skills. Right-brain thinking is related more to visual and inductive thinking (intuition) (Edwards 1979). You may associate computer systems with the more rational and logical side of the brain required for problem solving in organisations. However, to use information systems creatively on a personal level, you need a certain amount of creativity and you need to draw on the right side of the brain. The following discusses some ways to improve your use of information systems and IT.

Go digital early

Try to capture as much work as possible early in digital format. In other words, do not spend hours creating detailed plans or writing out material on paper first. Transfer your thoughts and ideas as early as possible to the computer. Once the ideas are in digital format you will be able to improve them and see them evolve. It also means that you become more skilled with the technology by using it as a planning and thinking tool. Handheld computers are especially useful for this way of working because you can capture ideas as they arise. Palmtop computers boot up almost immediately because the operating system is held in read-only memory (ROM). The boot-up time therefore does not act as a barrier to capturing thoughts digitally.

Cognitive maps or mindmaps can be used to map your information space (see figure 12.1). One author's information space includes the following:

> university administration
> *Journal of Systems and Information Technology (JoSIT)*
> personal stuff

> search engines
> research
> conferences
> journals
> teaching.

These have been incorporated into a series of web pages, which map the author's information space. Each feature is a hyperlink. Bookmarks in your browser can be used in a similar way but they lack the spatial and media richness that can be built up by developing your own information-space website.

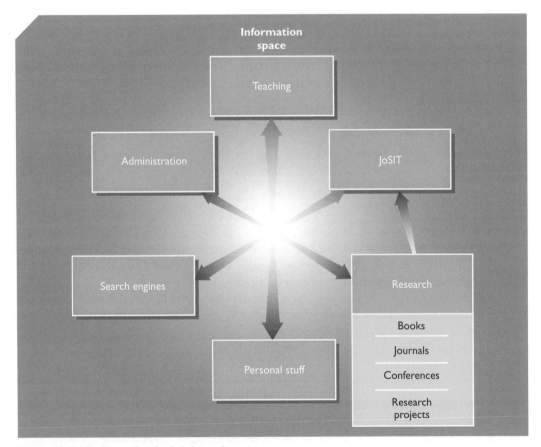

Figure 12.1 Mindmap of author's information space

Think multimedia

Do not think only about text when thinking about information systems — think multimedia. Look for ways to build an information- and media-rich approach in whatever you are doing. Start or expand your database of graphics and photographs and PowerPoint designs, for example. Work as though you expect to be using the same tools, albeit improved ones, in five years. You will change your perspective on whether it is worthwhile creating the information infrastructure for yourself.

Learn from the environment

How do professionals keep up to date these days in such a rapidly changing environment? One way is to learn from the environment itself. IT programs on television, the IT section in the newspaper and certain websites all provide relevant information. The cost of IT is no longer prohibitive, so now you can adopt a technology and learn on the job, rather than thinking that you need to be an expert in that tool before you adopt it. This is rather like getting a new computer game and playing until you are an expert, never having read the instructions.

Set goals and experiment

At some point, you have to experiment with certain technologies. You need to set a goal of using some technology and becoming proficient with it. Voice recognition software, for example, allows your computer to understand your speech patterns and pronunciations, saving you the trouble of typing text into documents. The software, especially inexpensive versions, is not faultless but it has potential when you train it properly. Your short-term goal could be to investigate and try this type of software for its potential for personal productivity gains.

[**Key concept:** You do not need to take a course for everything; most information systems professionals gain much of their knowledge from the environment.]

infobyte

Valuing mobile services

Mobile services (m-services) have become an important part of the e-commerce landscape. Although research has been conducted on which services people use and the benefits they attach to those services, the values associated with the adoption and use of m-services at the individual level is less clear. Research by Patricia Mcmanus and Craig Standing of Edith Cowan University in Western Australia aims to remedy this.

Most research in the area suggests that people use m-services to save time and money and because they are convenient. However, these are intermediate benefits and not the real drivers of adoption. In a study involving more than one hundred interviews, Standing et al. (2006) found that m-services often fulfil such basic needs as self-esteem, achievement, individuality, belonging and wellbeing.

Information overload and personal information systems

Information overload is a real problem for many information economy workers. Few people have an effective personal information system; indeed, it seems that organisational information systems are way ahead of personal information systems in quality and levels of adoption.

The problem in most organisations is not lack of information but too much. Email is one of the main culprits, together with the plethora of reports, meetings, telephone messages and professional journals.

Think how easy it is to contribute to information overload for other people. You have attended a seminar that captured your imagination. Back at your desk you build a website related to the materials and themes of the seminar. You then email everyone in your organisation with a review of the seminar and the URL for your website. You are creating the information equivalent of landfill.

What can be done about information overload? The major problem is the inability of organisations to admit that it is a problem. When a manager's time is spent in meetings every day of every week, there is little time to reflect, organise or just be productive. The same is true of answering a couple of hundred emails each day: if each email takes, on average, a minute or two to answer, then there is little time left to do any work. Most occupations are not meant to have internal messaging as their main feature. In many organisations, this is now out of hand, but admitting that it is a problem signals disorganisation on a personal level. However, a professional must recognise that there may be a problem, decide what the critical success factors are and determine the role that internal messaging plays.

[**Key concept:** Information access has improved significantly in recent years — most people in professional occupations receive too much irrelevant information.]

IS in action

Useless information

Results of a recent survey of more than 1000 middle managers in large companies suggest that the way many organisations gather, use and analyse information is hindering rather than helping employees' productivity.

More than half of those surveyed said they miss pertinent information almost daily as a result of an inadequate information distribution system within their company. Perhaps even more alarming was the discovery that almost as many respondents believed they accidentally used incorrect information at least once a week as a result.

Given that middle managers are estimated to spend in excess of a quarter of their time searching for necessary information, the time wasted searching numerous information sources can add up to an extremely expensive — not to mention frustrating — exercise.

Although survey results suggest many companies fail to provide appropriate channels for disseminating necessary information, part of the problem lies in how managers choose to store their information. In general, there seems to be a lack of collaboration among managers. Most of those surveyed admitted to storing their most important job-related information on their computers or in email accounts. Only a minority said they went to the effort of making such information available to colleagues through a collaborative workplace tool such as a company intranet portal.

'Information is becoming a burden on knowledge workers and will remain so until companies consolidate and streamline the stores and sources of intelligence,' said one senior executive. 'Doing so will enable them to give back part of the working day to staff, helped by better governance, delivery, integration and the archiving and retention of information.'

Source: Information from *Accenture News* 2007, 'Managers say the majority of information obtained for their work is useless, Accenture survey finds', January, http://accenture.tekgroup.com.

Reflection question 2: Can you think of any other contributors to information overload?

Partly because of the concept of customer service, including the notion of treating staff as internal customers, many employees have become victims of the 'do it now syndrome'. Therefore, every enquiry, whether by email, phone or letter, must be dealt with immediately. In this approach, the technology is used to make the employee accessible at all times, in many cases even when at home. The trouble with this approach, however, is that the interruption created by breaking off one task to attend to the enquiry or email has a major impact on productivity. It is not simply the time involved in doing the task; it is also the time taken to get one's thought processes back to where they were before the interruption.

To be effective with information on a personal level requires the adoption of procedures that become a habit. Consider the following suggestions:

> *Batch.* A general principle is to batch (group together) the enquiries and use the technology to advantage rather than be controlled by the technology. For example, you may decide to answer email messages at the start and end of the day, rather than throughout the day. The same can be done with voicemail messages.

> *Use email wisely.* If possible, check your email once or twice a day, rather than continually breaking off work when emails arrive. If you subscribe to mail group lists that are no longer of interest, then unsubscribe. (It is always wise to save the instructions on how to do so.) The fewer emails you have, the more you will feel you are in control of the situation and able to respond to them. File emails in folders rather than keeping them in your inbox. Systems are available to filter unwanted email messages. These work by specifying certain keywords.

> *Use meetings efficiently.* Make a careful note of each meeting you have attended in the last month. Ask yourself whether every meeting was relevant or someone else could have attended in your place. Was the meeting carefully planned and chaired to keep within time constraints? If not, then suggest that this be done in future. Meetings incur expenses for any organisation, including time for the actual meeting, preparation time, travel to and from, food and drinks and opportunity costs (what could have been accomplished if people had not been at the meeting).

> *Become outcome focused.* Identify what is really important in your work and focus on it. Make any communication related to this issue a priority and leave the other things until later.

> *Develop support structures.* There is only so much work one person can get through. Develop a support structure that can share the workload.

> *Know what to keep.* In deciding whether to file a piece of paper or throw it away, ask yourself the following questions:
  - Does it require any action? If not, throw it away.
  - Does it exist elsewhere? If it does, throw it away.
  - Is it recent enough to be useful? If not, throw it away.
  - Do I understand the contents? If not, throw it away.

If you are still seriously in doubt, ask yourself what is the worst possible thing that could happen if you did not have this information. If you can live with the answer, then throw the information away.

> *Develop personal information systems.* A key feature of a support structure should be your personal information system.

Developing a personal information system

Examine how you accomplish the regular tasks you are faced with. Decide whether there is a pattern to how you work or solve problems. If you spend time reinventing processes related to completing tasks, invest some time in documenting how they are completed. In this respect, you are defining your own methodologies for getting things done. As well as being a reference point for you each time you complete a similar task, you can pass on the methodology to others and so delegate or share the workload.

The innovation cycle explained in chapter 8 (see figure 8.1 on page 236) can be used on a personal level. Be more creative and innovative with information systems and IT, rather than one of the last to adopt new methods and approaches. In doing so, you will become skilled in the technology, and early adoption will become a habit.

Consider using personal productivity tools. A personal digital assistant (PDA) is a handheld computer that allows you to store, access and organise information (see figure 12.2). Most PDAs are either Windows based or work on a Palm operating system. PDAs can be screen based or keyboard based, or both.

Basic PDAs allow you to store and retrieve addresses and phone numbers, maintain a calendar, and create to-do lists and notes. More sophisticated PDAs can run word processing, spreadsheet, money manager and electronic book-reading programs, and also provide email and Internet access.

Figure 12.2 Palmtop computer

Some PDAs come with all these programs included. Most PDAs can exchange information with a desktop or laptop computer, although you may need additional accessories. Their advantages include:

> *Convenience and portability*. The small size and light weight of a palmtop mean that it is not difficult to carry. Notebook or laptop computers are comparatively heavy and a burden to carry around. Palmtops or handheld computers can be used for accessing email and the Internet. Because they are small, compact systems, the batteries last for a relatively long time before they need recharging.

> *Speed of boot-up*. The operating system is stored in ROM, which means that a palmtop is very quick to boot up. The delay in booting up a notebook computer can become a barrier if all you want to do is add a name and address to a database of contacts.

> *Software compatibility*. On the more sophisticated palmtop computers, the software is often a cut-down version of the software used on desktop machines. This means that you do not have to learn new instructions and operating procedures.

> *Transferring data*. You can transfer files between your palmtop and desktop machines and set options to synchronise mail messages, contacts, appointments and tasks with your other machine. This allows you to update data in one place only — your other systems will be updated from that location.

[**Key concept:** Take many of the principles used in organisational information systems and apply them at the individual level.]

Email

Email has been fully embraced by the business world in just a few short years. Email is such a part of our lives that it is difficult to imagine living without it. The benefits of email are pretty obvious to everyone who has used it. It is relatively cheap to send, fast and easy to link in to other applications such as word processors. However, even though it has many benefits, there are still issues surrounding its use. Some people in work situations become overloaded by incoming emails. If a manager receives 100 emails a day then a considerable part of the day may be given over to responses. If someone is overloaded by emails, it is difficult to determine which are the most important and which need answering as a priority. Emails can be sent high priority. Priority emails are rapidly increasing because people want their emails to stand out from the crowded inbox! At an extreme, some people spend time late at nights answering emails or work through their backlog of emails at the weekend. Email addiction may seem a joke but some people are so tied to their email systems that they feel they cannot go for more than an hour or two without checking their email. Despite the profound influence email has had so far on our lives, there has been little research conducted on the topic (Weber 2004).

Speed

In evaluating speed, it is important to consider the time it takes to transmit and deliver the communication and the delay time before it is read. The communication process can be broken down into compose, transmit, receive and read. For example, a letter takes time to write, is posted, received and then read. There could be a considerable delay before the letter is read, even though the letter was efficiently delivered.

In terms of speed, telephone and fax messages are quick to send, although there may be several aborted attempts with the telephone to speak to the intended person. Face-to-face communication has the added problem of getting two or more people together at the same time, which can be time consuming and expensive. Mail, sometimes referred to as snail mail, is slow but reasonably inexpensive. Email is fast to transmit but may involve some delay before it is read, especially if the recipient is away or does not regularly check his or her email. If people check their email at specific regular times, the more effective it is as a form of communication and in some cases it can be more effective than the telephone because the message can be read, reread and thought about before a response is made.

One of the main problems with telephone communication is that the people involved must be synchronised; that is, both people must be on the telephone at the same time. Email and traditional mail are asynchronous; that is, the recipient does not need to be present when the communication is sent or delivered. This is especially useful where large distances and different timezones are involved.

Cost

The cost of sending email is so low that the cost factor is probably not considered in organisations. This, coupled with the lack of guidelines on email, has meant that it has added to the information overload many people experience. Other forms of communication generally have a much higher and more obvious cost associated with them.

[**Key concept:** The low cost and other benefits associated with email have meant that it has created email overload in some organisations.]

Accountability

Accountability may be an important issue in communications, especially in business, where the expectation is usually one of formality and accountability, although there are occasions when people are more casual. Consequently, formality and accountability are closely related. Because written (typed) letters have been the accepted form of business communication for many years, other forms of communication may seem less formal and, as a result, hold the senders and recipients less accountable as a consequence. Some people may prefer face-to-face contact with a formal handshake as part of a business deal but it might be legally difficult to prove. Although email may appear to be a very informal form of communication, it could be used as evidence in a court of law. Therefore, people must not underestimate the accountability associated with the content of email.

Conferencing

Sometimes, group communication is needed. The telephone is effective for group conferencing but only for small groups. Fax and mail are poor for conferencing, and face-to-face conferencing is more expensive. Email is fast and effective when dealing with groups of people because the same message can be posted to a large group simultaneously.

Security

Security, as is accountability, is an important issue in business. On many occasions, the communication is private and confidential. Letters can be lost in the mail or opened by others, so they are poor in terms of security. Telephone conversations can be overheard or tapped, but on the whole are moderately secure. Face-to-face communication has number of security problems but is moderately secure as long as basic precautions are taken and people are trustworthy. The problem with faxes is that they are frequently left by the fax machine for other people to read. Email is relatively secure and private as long as basic security measures are adhered to, such as using a good password system and not leaving a computer with the email package open and unattended.

Personal and professional ethics

Ethics in relation to the workplace is now a major issue for most professions, including information systems. Defining what is ethical is not always so easy. To put it simply, ethics involves beliefs about what is right or wrong and is used to guide behaviour. It is linked to morality, which is concerned with the personal beliefs of individuals. Ethical behaviour is decent, fair, good, honest or moral behaviour. Ethical standards are framed by the society in which a person lives and works. But professionals are bound also by legal standards. For example, an information systems professional may send an email criticising someone without being aware of all the facts. This email may be printed out and left in a tray next to the printer for all to see. This is not only unethical behaviour but it could be considered an act of defamation, and the email may be used as evidence in court.

IS in action

IT governance

IT governance has gained more importance as technology has become a critical part of business success. There has been a tendency to think of IT as a way to align business processes without considering how to include it in the corporate governance of the business. This has led to each department, manager or individual developing their own objectives without considering the corporate governance strategy. Ethical improprieties have led to calls for more stringent corporate governance and, because technology pervades most areas of a business, IT governance should be a top priority.

IT governance is described by the IT Governance Institute as 'an integral part of enterprise governance and consists of the leadership and organisational structures and processes that ensure that the organisation's IT sustains and extends the organisation's strategies and objectives' (ITGI 2003, p. 10). Getting every area of the business to work together requires communication between individuals and departments and requires frequent contact with, and from, the IT department. Executives from all departments should be involved in corporate governance committees and support IT governance activities within business units. This will get everyone involved in IT issues and ensure the development of an effective IT governance structure.

There are several corporate governance models that can be used to incorporate IT, such as COBIT. These can form the basis for developing the IT governance policy within an enterprise.

Management issues associated with IT governance are:

> *strategic alignment:* requiring planned and purposeful management processes to align business with collaborative solutions

> *value delivery:* supporting the organisation by optimising expenses and proving the value of IT

> *risk management:* managing operational and system risks, which means safeguarding IT assets and disaster recovery

> *resource management:* optimising knowledge and infrastructure including people, applications, data, technology and facilities

> *performance measurement:* tracking IT projects and monitoring services by using the balanced scorecard approach.

IT governance is a complex area but it must be included in the corporate governance of any entity that uses IT, not left to each department or business unit.

Source: Information from Exler, R 2007, 'IT governance frameworks', *CIO Magazine*, www2.cio.com.

Nobody is above the law, so any illegal act should be reported by an information systems professional. However, many acts on a personal or organisational level may be legal but are still considered unethical. For example, you are concerned about a system that you have been involved in developing. Although you are not aware of any immediate bugs in the system, you feel that standards and testing have been underplayed but your boss, the project leader, wants to deliver the project on time. What do you do? You feel you should comply with your boss's wishes but at the same time, you know that best practice tells you that systems should be tested thoroughly. This is an ethical dilemma in a professional context. Fortunately, professional associations such as computer societies provide ethical codes to guide their members on issues such as this.

Certain values underpin these professional codes of ethical conduct, such as:

> *Integrity.* Professionals must act at all times with integrity and maintain high ethical standards.

> *Honesty.* Professionals must be honest in their dealings with colleagues and in the presentation of their advice.

> *Respect.* Professionals must respect the rights of individuals and treat colleagues with personal respect.

> *Justice or fairness.* This can relate to such things as the inclusion of stakeholders in decisions and balancing differences of opinion in fair and considered manner.

A professional code of ethics has benefits:

> It can help in defining the responsibilities of the profession and professionals.

> It can act in regulatory capacity to protect members, clients and other stakeholders.

> It can raise the profile of the profession.

> It can raise the profile of certain problematic issues within the profession.

[**Key concept:** Ethical behaviour never goes out of fashion!]

Hong Kong Computer Society code of ethics and conduct

This is an extract from the Hong Kong Computer Society Code of Ethics and Conduct. The first two points have been included for each section of the code to give you a flavour of the code. There are many more in the full code, which is available at its website.

Overview

All members have responsibilities: to clients, to users and to the society at large. Those members who are employees also have responsibilities to their employers and employers' customers and, often, to a Trade Union. In the event of apparent clash in responsibilities, obligations or prescribed practice, the Society's Director of Professional Development should be consulted at the earliest opportunity.

A. Professional Competence and Integrity

As a Member of Hong Kong Computer Society (HKCS), I will

1. Be honest and trustworthy, and will not knowingly engage in or associate with dishonest or fraudulent practices.

2. Continue to upgrade my professional knowledge and skills, and shall maintain awareness of technological developments, procedures and standards, which are relevant to my field.

B. Social Implications

As a Member of HKCS, I will

1. Increase my awareness of issues affecting the IT profession and its relationship with the community.

2. Ensure that within my chosen fields, I have knowledge and understanding of relevant legislation, regulations and standards and that I comply with such requirements.

C. Organisation and Leadership

As a Member of HKCS, I will

1. Keep myself and subordinates informed of such new technologies, practices, legal requirements and standards as are relevant to my duties, and seek to conform to recognised good practice including quality standards, which are in my judgment relevant, and encourage my subordinates to do likewise.

2. Encourage my colleagues, employees and students to continue their own professional development, and ensure that subordinates are trained in order to be effective in their duties and to qualify for increased responsibilities.

D. Duty to Profession

As a Member of HKCS, I will

1. Uphold the reputation of the Profession and I will seek to improve professional standards through participation in their development, use and enforcement, and shall avoid any action that will adversely affect the good standing of the Profession.

2. Seek to advance public knowledge and understanding of computing and information systems and technology and to counter false or misleading statements that are detrimental to the Profession.

Source: This code appeared on www.hkcs.org.hk.

Ergonomics

M ost people have heard of the word ergonomics. It is used in many situations including advertisements for kitchens, computers and many other everyday objects.

According to the UK Ergonomics Society (www.ergonomics.org.uk), a definition of the term is:

> Ergonomics is about fit: the fit between people, the things they do, the objects they use and the environments they work, travel and play in. If good fit is achieved, the stresses on people are reduced. They are more comfortable, they can do things more quickly and easily, and they make fewer mistakes.

The 'fit' takes into account not just the physical factors but also psychological and other factors. In some countries, ergonomics is referred to as 'human factors'.

Poor ergonomic design can result in increased error rates and physical fatigue and, in the long term, physical problems. Ergonomics is especially relevant to the office environment and to using computers. One aspect of ergonomics is inclusive design, in which products are designed with, for example, older and disabled users in mind.

Information design or how we use information is another important area of human factors. The design of signs, symbols and instructions is part of information design. This includes the design of computer software interfaces to make them easier and more effective to use.

Reflection question 3: Does your current working situation rate highly ergonomically?

Physical and psychological issues are key areas of concern related to ergonomics and information systems.

Physical issues

Repetitive strain injury (RSI) is caused by the inflammation of muscles, nerves or tendons. In extreme cases the problem can lead to permanent tissue damage. RSI is caused by many repetitions of the same activity, maintaining a static posture for too long, and failing to take short breaks. Use of the keyboard over prolonged periods is a reported cause of RSI.

Arm and neck problems can be a result of badly designed workstations where the user has to reach too far or twist awkwardly in the process of working. These problems can be alleviated by relaxing while working, taking breaks and changing tasks frequently. It is best to have the keyboard positioned right under your hands, with your elbows bent at 90 degrees. The backrest of your chair should support the hollow of your back.

Eyestrain can be caused by focusing on the screen for prolonged periods without taking breaks. The user should also look away from the screen from time to time and focus on distant objects briefly.

Psychological issues

Badly designed systems can lead to poor productivity and as a consequence dissatisfaction in general. In extreme cases, this can cause stress and lead to periods off work. The safety and welfare of staff is an important issue: the work environment should be conducive to high-quality work.

A poorly designed interface can lead to an increase in errors being input into the systems, increased search time when looking for information on the screen and wasted time working through poor software navigation systems.

[**Key concept:** Ergonomic design pays in the long run.]

infobyte

Workplace layout

Symptoms of musculoskeletal disorders are common among workers in office environments. These symptoms most commonly occur in the neck, lower arms, wrists and shoulders. To alleviate these problems, workstation design and layout should be considered. In particular, the placement of the keyboard and mouse and posture while sitting at the workstation should be reviewed.

Some questions that could help you find the best layout of your work area include:
> Is my seat at the right height?
> Where is the best place to position my work?
> Do I need a footrest?
> How high should my bench be?
> What should be the angle of my seat?
> How far should I reach?

The physical layout of your workplace can lead to increased stress levels, especially if you work near noisy equipment or use hazardous materials. Workplace design also includes such things as air temperature, lighting and ventilation.

Summary

Organisational information systems are flourishing but many people are drowning in a sea of information. This chapter has discussed some issues related to being more effective on a personal level with information systems.

The key points in this chapter are:
> The main transferable skills required to be a knowledge worker in the knowledge economy are related to gathering information, processing and organising information and communicating information.
> It is important to have the right mindset to take advantage of digital technology: be in it for the long term.
> Using digital technology requires new approaches to working including getting data into digital format as soon as possible.
> Information overload results from having access to too much information, especially at an individual level. It can be dealt with by having strategies to manage email and by developing a personal information system.
> Computer societies have developed codes of conduct to guide their members in the ethical use of information systems.

> An ergonomically designed system can reduce the potential of physical and psychological problems directly attributed to working with computer systems.

Questions

1. What generic skills (e.g. communication) are required by workers in the knowledge economy?
2. Why do some people dislike using computer systems?
3. Is information overload likely to lead to stress? Why?
4. List and explain five ways to reduce information overload.
5. When should emails be sent with high priority?
6. What techniques and methods can be used as part of a personal information system?
7. What steps can be taken to prevent eyestrain when using computer systems?
8. Explain why ethical behaviour is an important issue for information systems professionals.

Exercises

1. Develop a short questionnaire for use in your class to find out how big a problem information overload is. From where do the problems arise: email, telephone, meetings, paper handouts, computer files? Determine how seriously the issue affects people's lives and their effectiveness as students or employees. Analyse the data obtained and use charts to illustrate your findings.
2. Examine the following ethical issues in relation to using computer systems and discuss appropriate forms of action.
   a. A colleague regularly criticises the work done by others. You feel that this is not justified or based on facts.
   b. You are asked to develop an information system and told not to involve users in the design of the system because they will only create problems.
   c. Your boss tells you that for the next two years there will be no training and development allowance for information systems staff because she wants to build up a financial reserve for the future.
3. Compare the codes of conduct or codes of ethics of two computer societies (e.g. the British Computer Society and the Australian Computer Society). These are typically available on the Web.

CASE STUDY: Mandy's information overload

Mandy recently graduated from university with an accounting degree and landed what seemed to be a great job with a major accounting company. This is her first permanent job, because all her other jobs as a student involved working as a casual in supermarkets or fast-food outlets. After Mandy's first few months in the job, she feels overwhelmed by the sheer volume of information that she has to deal with and feels that if it does not get any better she might have to quit the job.

(continued)

Mandy receives a lot of emails from colleagues. There are some days when she gets 50 or so emails, and she cannot read them all and still get on with her work. Many of the emails have attachments that could be of use some time in the future. Mandy usually tries to be efficient by answering the emails as soon as they arrive. However, this causes an interruption to her work and stops her getting on with the task in hand. Overall, she is very frustrated by the feeling of being overwhelmed. A few weeks earlier, Mandy started to take more work home with her because there were fewer interruptions in the evening and at weekends. This has meant she now has more time for answering emails during the day. In addition, Mandy gave her work email address to friends and relatives, and she thinks this might have been a mistake.

The files on Mandy's office computer are not well organised, and she frequently spends a lot of time trying to find documents. She would like to know the best way for organising files on her hard disk.

Mandy has a computer at home connected to the Internet. It was bought when she was a first-year student to help with her studies. It is now three years old, and it is a bit slow to work on. Mandy is not sure whether she should buy another computer. Maybe a scanner would be useful also.

When Mandy takes work home in the evenings and at weekends she will often work on the computer. On many occasions she has forgotten to take a copy of the computer files back to work with her, and so the additional effort the evening before has been in vain.

Last weekend, she saw a Palmtop computer advertised in a magazine. She wonders whether it would be a worthwhile investment. Maybe she could use her mobile phone to access her emails.

While at work Mandy is passed a lot of forms and paperwork. They are now piling up on her desk and are adding to the feeling of being overwhelmed. Mandy has examined how her colleagues work in an attempt to find a role model. John started work at the same time as Mandy, and he too looks very disorganised. He has even been reprimanded for missing a couple of recent meetings. He said that he completely forgot about them. He looks very stressed most of the time. Margaret on the other hand is completely organised. There is not a paper on her desk, and she never looks stressed at all. Mandy asked her for advice. Margaret replied that the following things are important:

> Refuse as much work as you can get away with. Always tell the boss that you have too much work to do, in the hope he does not give you any more.

> Keep everything computerised. Throw away most paper copies of documents.

> Never take work home — this is fatal!

> Send more emails than you receive. There is a politics to communication, and it makes it look as if you are always thinking about work even if you are not.

Mandy thinks that she has little to learn from either John or Margaret.

Mandy is not finding her new job enjoyable because now there is no time to socialise with friends or even go to the gym. Maybe working in a shop would be better; at least she could have a social life.

Questions

1. What are the main problem areas that Mandy is faced with?
2. What can Mandy do to manage more effectively the information she is getting? Explain your answer in relation to the techniques, methods and IT tools that can be used.
3. Does Mandy have the right attitude towards information systems and IT? Why?
4. Explain what skills Mandy needs to develop to become more efficient in her handling of information.
5. Have you experienced anything in common with Mandy? Did you manage to overcome it? How?

References

Edwards, B 1979, *Drawing on the right side of the brain*, JP Tarcher, Los Angeles.

IT Governance Institute (ITGI) 2003, 'Board briefing on IT governance', 2nd edn, www.itgi.org.

Standing, C, Mcmanus, P, Standing, S & Karjaluoto, H 2006, 'Values and m-services adoption', *Proceedings of the 17th Australasian Conference on Information Systems*, Adelaide.

Weber, R 2004, 'Editor's comments. The Grim Reaper: the curse of email', *MIS Quarterly*, vol. 28, no. 3, pp. iii–xiii.

allocated cost centre
a situation in which information systems costs are allocated to internal clients, which entails internal accounting and budget transfers

alternative solutions phase
a phase in the systems development lifecycle when alternative solutions to the problem or potential systems are defined

application program interface
the toolbars and menus that are used to access software application functions. Ideally, APIs should be obvious and easy to use and standardised over a range of software.

application service provider (ASP)
a third party that provides developmental expertise in, and access to, large customisable software packages for businesses (usually small–medium entities). In some instances, the software manufacturer may assume the ASP role.

applications software
software that performs specific, non-systems related functions for users

arithmetic and logic unit
that part of a microprocessor that carries out arithmetic and logical functions

artificial intelligence (AI)
a system that mimics human expertise, either generally or more usually in a specific field of endeavour such as fault diagnosis

assembly language
second-generation, low-level programming language, which uses mnemonic instructions

authentication
deals with proving the identity of a person

backbone network
a network that connects everything on the same site including other networks. Its main purpose is to provide interconnection.

backups
copies of data and software

bandwidth
the difference in cycles per second (Hz) between the highest and lowest frequencies on a channel. It is the measure of a channel's ability to carry information. The bandwidth of the telephone system is about 3.3 kHz.

baseband
transmission of a signal in its original form, that is, unaltered by modulation. Baseband transmission is digital, most often using direct current.

batch
a style of system operation in which transactions are grouped together (batched) for later processing

batch systems
systems that store up transaction data for processing at a later time

Bluetooth
a mobile wireless communication standard for low-cost, short-range wireless communications between static and mobile PCs, mobile telephones and peripheral devices. Bluetooth was developed by a consortium that includes IBM and Intel, and allows the development of personal area networks.

broadband
an alternative name for analog transmission

browser
software used to display web pages

bus
the part of the system or motherboard that performs interconnection between the onboard components

business-to-business e-business
e-business that deals with procurement between businesses

business-to-consumer e-business
e-business that deals with supplying information, products or services to customers

business engineering
a term that is more inclusive than business process re-engineering because it adopts a 'big picture' perspective on business activities

business-level strategy
plans developed at a business level within an organisation in which the business operates independently

business model
the features and characteristics of a business that describe how a business operates

business process re-engineering (BPR)
redesigning business processes to achieve improvements in performance measures

cache

part of random access memory (RAM) set aside to be accessed as though it was disk, increasing performance. Data related to previous accesses are fetched into the cache on the off-chance that they might be needed. Some processors also have an internal cache to speed access to RAM.

cellular digital packet data (CDPD)

a specification for wireless access to the Internet and other public packet-switched networks. Usage may be point to point or multicast, and is usually offered at 19.2 Kbps.

central processing unit

the microprocessor installed on a motherboard

channel conflict

the issues and problems that arise from having multiple sales channels

Chief executive officer (CEO)

the most senior manager in an organisation; responsible for all decisions made by the board of directors

chief information officer (CIO)

the manager responsible for the information systems and strategy of an organisation

chief technology officer (CTO)

the person responsible for keeping abreast of technology and the market, briefing other staff and outlining plans with which the business could take advantage of the new technology within its existing information systems framework in a cost-effective manner

class

a template from which to create objects defining the data values and methods or functions that can be performed on the data

collaborative commerce

the online exchange of ideas, data and information among business partners

competitive strategic analysis

examination of the competition in the business environment to gain an advantage or advantages

compiler

a program that translates the source code of a high-level language into a form that the processor can execute. Compilers are large programs that translate all of the program in one go. A compiler is only resident in random access memory during the translation process and is specific to a particular hardware platform.

complex instruction-set computer (CISC)

the type of processor most often used in PCs. It has an extensive and versatile instruction set.

componentisation

a trend in many software systems in which a large package is divided into functional modules that can be implemented or ignored as required

computer-aided software engineering (CASE)

software tools to help in the development of systems through providing diagrammatic facilities for modelling the system and managing the process

consumer-generated media

media, usually video clips, that are created by consumers for use on websites

consumer-to-consumer e-business

business in which consumers interact over the Web through an intermediary organisation

control unit

that part of a processor responsible for coordinating and managing the execution of instructions

corporate-level strategy

the highest level of strategy, which is developed by the most senior people in the business, concerning long-term goals and objectives for the entire organisation

creative destruction

closing or discontinuing part of a business to make way for more productive ventures

custom software

software developed to meet a person or organisation's specific needs, as opposed to buying packaged software

customer relationship management (CRM)

the practice of using information systems such as enterprise resource planning (ERP) and extended ERP to manage all aspects of dealings with clients and customers

customisable software

a software package that can be adapted to meet specific needs. This work is often carried out by integrators and value-added resellers.

database

a single central repository for corporate data together with a management system that allows data organisation, retrieval, update and analysis to be performed

database administrator (DBA)

person who exercises control over the use of the database, manages the data and metadata and is responsible for the day-to-day running of the database and its security

database management system (DBMS)
software that allows users to store, retrieve and update data in a database. It also allows the database adminstrator to control accounts, and structure and organise the data.

data-flow diagrams (DFDs)
a diagrammatic technique that models the processes in an organisation

datamart
a smaller and more specialised version of a data warehouse in which archived and organised data may be analysed for relationships and trends

data mining
the process of trawling through archived and processed data for useful information

data modelling
a method of organising and documenting a system's data. Used in the early stages of database design

data (or project) dictionary
a database of data and information gathered during the systems development process

data privacy
concerned mainly with protecting the rights of the individual in terms of privacy

data warehouse
a large collection of data categorised by information type rather than application origin. Data warehouses are equipped with online analytical processing tools for multidimensional analysis.

decision support system
software that helps managers make decisions by modelling various scenarios. The data used can come from many sources, including a data warehouse.

decision table
a technique to explain complex process logic in a tabular format

denial of service (DOS)
a malicious program or use of a server that renders part of a system unusable

dense wave division multiplexing
a type of frequency division multiplexing for optical fibre. Currently, up to 40 10-Gbps channels can be obtained on the same fibre and it is predicted that speeds will rise to a total of 25 terabits (trillion bits) without the need for new fibre.

digital audio tape
serial access format used for data archival

disintermediation
process in which intermediaries are bypassed in the sales chain

divisional information officer (DIO)
similar to a chief information officer but with responsibility for a specific business area rather than the entire enterprise. DIOs are found in distributed information systems organisations.

dotcom
a company that exists entirely on the Web and has no real offline equivalent

e-business
use of the Internet and related technologies and services in business

E cycle
part of the machine cycle concerned with the execution of instructions

electronic data interchange (EDI)
sale of goods and services online, typically on proprietary networks

e-marketplaces
web-based environments in which suppliers are matched with buyers for the sale of products, services and specialised equipment

encryption
a method of changing the text in a file by using a coding system. It can be used when a file is transmitted over the Internet.

enterprise application integration
a method of working that ignores lower-level compatibility problems caused by hardware and data formats and focuses instead on achieving integration at the application level

enterprise resource planning (ERP)
applying materials requirements planning concepts to almost every facet of business operation, including finance, accounting, marketing and human resources management. ERP is usually the province of large companies using large modular software suites, which allow the business to be fully integrated.

entity relationship diagram (ERD)
a diagrammatic style of data modelling that shows the relationships between the data in a business

environmental scanning
gathering data on trends and competitors from various sources

eraseable programmable read-only memory (EPROM)
ROM chips that can be programmed, erased and reprogrammed

ergonomics
the study of the engineering aspects of the relationship between human workers and their working environment

ethical behaviour
decent, fair, good, honest or moral behaviour

executive information system
a very high-level business information system to support management and decision making. Data may come from inside or outside the organisation. EISs may be linked to data warehouses.

expansion slots
spaces left on the motherboard to allow expansion cards to be fitted to add extra functionality to the system, for example, a fax/modem card

expert system
a system that mimics human expertise in a well-defined application area

extended enterprise resource planning (EERP)
an ERP system that incorporates elements of electronic (often web-based) commerce in addition to supply chain management and customer relationship management

failsoft
ability of a system to detect component failures and temporarily modify its processing to prevent irretrievable loss of data or equipment

fast circuit switching
a hybrid scheme that combines the best of circuit and packet switch systems. The access time is very low and dependable and transmission is synchronous. It is more complicated than other methods but gives excellent performance.

fat client
a PC in a client–server network that stores and runs most of its own applications software. Fat clients are more expensive and difficult to manage than thin clients.

feasibility phase
phase in the systems development lifecycle that seeks to determine if a project is worthwhile, that is, if the benefits outweigh the costs.

FireWire
newer standard high-speed PC port

firmware
ROM chips (a chip with software already installed)

flash memory
semistable storage eraseable programmable read-only memory on a card, faster but more expensive than a hard drive and of much lower capacity. Widely used in handhelds, mobile telephones and digital cameras

flexible manufacturing system (FMS)
computer-operated manufacturing tools, that can carry out a wide range of processes instead of the older, highly specialised dedicated machinery. FMSs can be set up economically for short production runs, reducing product-cycle times.

floating point operations per second
measure of processor performance or, more specifically, the ability of the processor to perform mathematical functions

forward engineering
the process of deriving a new system after requirements analysis, specification and design

fourth-generation language
a nonprocedural language. A user formulating a request does not need to specify exactly how that request is to be carried out by the computer. Fourth-generation languages are easier to use than procedural languages and are often found in applications such as databases.

frequency division multiplexing
a method for sharing the use of a communication medium by allocating different frequency bands to different users, thus creating multiple simultaneous channels. Used in analog transmission systems

functional-level strategy
deals with plans at the functional level of a business, such as marketing, information systems and finance

Gantt chart
a form of bar chart that shows the activities of a project and the amount of time each activity will take

general ledger system
a transaction processing system for recording basic financial data. Most of an organisation's transaction processing systems would be tied into a general ledger system somehow.

geosynchronous earth orbit (GEO)
the so-called Clarke orbit in which satellites orbit the Earth at a height of 35 680 km above the equator

gigabyte
approximately 1 billion bytes

gigahertz
a measure of system clock speed, one billion cycles per second

government-to-citizen e-business
governments interacting with citizens via the Web

graphical user interface (GUI)
an interface that allows the user to interact with the system without the need to resort to inputting commands in text format. Windows provides a GUI.

group decision support system
networked hardware and software that allows workgroups to collaborate on brainstorming and decision-making processes. Eliminating human interaction and allowing anonymity sometimes improve the quality and speed of outcomes.

groupware
hardware and software that support document creation, management and communications for work groups. Combined with intelligent agents, groupware improves productivity and facilitates systems integration.

guard band
gaps (wasted bandwidth) between the frequencies allocated to users in radio and microwave analog systems to prevent transmissions interfering with each other. In digital systems, the need for guard bands is minimal, making more effective use of bandwidth.

hierarchical database
a system of database organisation in which data are shown as a logical hierarchy, a series of parent and child nodes. Hierarchical views can model one-to-many relationships very well and deliver excellent performance when used as intended. However, for ad hoc or complex queries, performance is poor due to vastly increased search space.

high-level language
a third-generation procedural language. Third-generation languages are closer to natural language than machine code or assembly languages, and usually incorporate some elements of structure that allow subprogram units to be reused in other programs. Third-generation languages allow programs to be moved from one computer to another and recompiled for use on that machine.

horizontal software
software that is general purpose and widely used throughout business, such as word processing and spreadsheet software

hub
junction boxes that connect computers with the network. These are usually broadcast devices and may also be called concentrators, multistation access units or transceivers. Hubs simplify the process of cabling and make it easier to relocate and add computers to the network.

human–computer interaction
the theory and practice of how users interact with computer systems

hyperlinks
a method of navigating through the Web. They are clickable text, icons or graphics that link to other web pages or other parts of the same web page.

hypertext markup language (HTML)
the language of the Internet used for describing web pages to web browsers

hypertext transfer protocol (HTTP)
the Web communications protocol; handles the transfer of data over the Internet

I cycle
instruction cycle, the half of the machine cycle in which instructions are fetched and translated

implementation
stage in the systems development lifecycle when the system is physically built and put in place

information age
period and societies characterised by a large percentage of people working with information and information systems

information architecture
defines the data, processes, information, organisational network and stakeholders in information systems; explains information technology trends and opportunities; defines the technology needed to support the aims of the organisation

information overload
a syndrome related to receiving too much information to process

information systems methodology
a collection of philosophies, phases, procedures, rules, techniques, tools, documentation, management and training for developers of information systems

infrastructure
software, hardware, networking, support and management staff, policies and procedures that support information systems

integrated circuits
system of electronic manufacture in which
previously separate components are reduced in
size and integrated into a modular subassembly

integrated package
a single software package that performs several
functions, for example, database, spreadsheet and
word processing. Integrated packages are more
limited in functionality than software suites.

integrators
third parties that provide systems solutions by
combining hardware and software from different
sources and adapting them to meet the client's
needs

intelligent agent (IA)
a software entity that carries out tasks for users in
an intelligent and autonomous way, for example,
an IA might search the Web for the cheapest air
fares for a particular journey

interpreter
a translation program similar to a compiler except
that it translates a program line by line and is
permanently in random access memeory at
run-time. Interpreter programs run more slowly
than compiled code.

informations systems planning
the development of medium- and long-
range plans for information technology and
information systems in an organisation

Java
an object-oriented programming language that
can be embedded in web pages to add extra
functionality, such as animation

Java applet
small graphical Java program

joint application design (JAD)
intensive workshops with key personnel and a
skilled facilitator with the aim of capturing the
essential requirements for a system in as short a
time frame as possible

just-in-time (JIT) delivery
the practice of reducing stock on hand by having
suppliers deliver materials as they are required.
This makes available capital that would have
been tied up in stock on hand and reduces direct
overheads.

kilobyte
approximately 1000 bytes

knowledge economy
characterised by the buying and selling of
knowledge, information and data

knowledge management
the process of creating, storing, managing,
accessing and sharing tactic and explicit
knowledge within the organisation

legacy systems
older information systems that need to be
incorporated into the present information systems
environment because it is uneconomical to
redevelop them

light-emitting diode (LED)
used in computer displays, as warning lights or as
signalling devices for multimode optical fibres

Linux
a PC version of Unix developed in 1991 by
Linus Torvalds; the source code was made freely
available, encouraging software developers to
produce applications for it. It has the potential to
be a serious competitor to Microsoft Windows.

liquid crystal displays (LCDs)
devices used to display screen output in laptops
and handheld devices

low earth orbit (LEO)
for satellites at a height of 640–1600 km. Launch
costs are much lower than for other orbits and
because the distances involved are much less,
both satellites and users can use less powerful
signals. However, because of the frequently
changing position of the satellites, more satellites
are needed for global communications.

**lower computer-aided software engineering
(CASE) tools**
concentrate on the later stages of the systems
development lifecycle (implementation and
maintenance)

machine code
first-generation procedural code in binary form.
Has no structure and the code produced is specific
to a particular processor

machine cycle
the cycle that a processor goes through in the
execution of instructions

mainframe
large, centralised computer for corporate use

maintenance
stage in a system's lifecycle when the system
requires amendments and updating

materials as needed (MAN)
a system similar to just-in-time delivery, but
it delivers supplies when and where they are
actually needed

materials requirements planning

a precursor to enterprise resource planning in which the manufacture supply chain is intelligently managed to yield greater efficiencies and cost-effectiveness

m-commerce

mobile e-commerce, that is, accessing the Web for business from a mobile phone

medium earth orbit (MEO)

for satellites used for communications and earth resource mapping. MEOs are inclined to the equator at a height of about 9600 km. The overcrowded geosynchronous earth orbit, shorter delay time and cheaper costs make MEO an attractive option for many applications.

megabyte

approximately 1 million bytes

metadata

data about data; data structures, relationships, methods of data organisation and access are defined. Usually used in a database context

methodology

an approach to solving a problem

metropolitan area network (MAN)

a network that interconnects local area networks and provides gateway services to wide area networks over a citywide area

millions of instructions per second (MIPS)

measure of processor performance

mission statement

expands the vision statement to state the broad objectives of the business

mobile agent

an intelligent agent that 'moves' around in a network to carry out its tasks. By carrying out work at source, it reduces the load on networks. Mobile agents are slow to catch on because of security and portability problems.

modulation

the process in which an electromagnetic wave's amplitude, frequency or phase is changed in order to transmit information. The characteristics of a carrier wave are changed by another 'modulating' waveform.

Moore's law

the rule of thumb that notes that the cost-effectiveness of microprocessor devices increases by a factor of two every 18 months or so

motherboard

also known as systemboard, the main circuit board in a PC holding the central processing unit, random access memory, read only memory, and so on

multimedia interfaces

interfaces that include graphics, text, audio and video

network administrator or manager

person with responsibility for the day-to-day running of all corporate networks, overseeing accounts and so on

network database

system of database organisation that expresses relationships between data nodes by making connections between them. This can be fairly flexible but link management limits its use in complex databases.

network interface card

a PC card that handles the interface between the computer and the network. It converts the computer's parallel logic into network serial logic and vice versa, and carries out signalling.

nonprocedural languages

languages in which users input a request without needing to specify how that request is to be met. For example, when retrieving records from a database, a user might request the names and contact details of all employees earning more than $70 000. The user would not need to specify file names and precise locations, or how the the search should be carried out.

object modelling

defining objects, along with their relationships to other objects, for the system being developed

object-oriented development

systems development methodology that focuses on the use of objects and their reuse as a fundamental design feature

object-oriented programming (OOP)

a system of programming in which data and executable code are packaged together to form an object. These objects can be used as templates to develop new objects, and objects can be copied and reused as needed. Object-oriented programming favours rapid applications development.

online analytical processing

set of multidimensional analytical tools for use in datamarts and data warehouses. They allow hidden trends and relationships to be discovered.

online auction
where an online company, often a broker, takes the highest bid for a product or service

online communities
real-time online forums where people who have something in common can communicate and exchange information

open systems
systems that use software that is not proprietary but that is in the public domain. Often used to refer to products that are proprietary but are available for any industry-standard platform

operational management
management of daily activities in an organisation

optical fibre
hair-thin glass strands used to carry information at high speed. Most fibres are multimode but the fastest fibres are monomode.

order-entry system
a transaction processing system that can accept data from a variety of sources and produce the required billing information

organic light-emitting diodes
newer technology for lightweight, high-definition screen displays that may replace liquid crystal displays

organisational structure
the administrative and decision-making mechanisms within an organisation

outsourcing
transferring responsibility for some area of a business to an outside source

paradigm
the basic framework of a discipline, language or jargon, protocols, systems of thinking and so on. Hence paradigm shift caused by new technology

personal area network (PAN)
a small (one room) network of a PC and associated devices or a one-person network providing mobile network services over a short range. PANs usually (though not exclusively) make use of mobile communications.

personal digital assistant (PDA)
small palmtop or handheld PC or smart organiser for individual use

pervasive networking
communications and networking that are virtually everywhere. As communications continue to improve, it is possible to offload the burden of computing from desktop and handheld machines to the network; in short, the network becomes the computer.

pixel
the smallest addressable point on a display screen

podcasts
longer media, usually audio files but sometimes videos, that can be downloaded and listened to or watched whenever the user wants

point of sales (POS) system
a transaction processing system that gathers transaction data at the point of sale, often using direct data entry through bar codes. Frequently seen in supermarkets

Porter's competitive forces model
emphasises five competitive forces to analyse the competition within an industry

primary storage
on-board memory that may be subdivided into random access memory and read-only memory

procedural language
a third-generation high-level programming language, close to natural language, in which users must specify exactly what must be done and how it must be done

process models
models of the systems that define the processes or actions within an organisation

profit centre
a method of charging out for information systems services that makes no distinction between internal and external clients. This tends to increase prices and increase the likelihood of outsourcing parts of the information systems function.

program evaluation and review technique (PERT)
a sophisticated diagrammatic tool for specifying the complexity of a project

programmable read-only memory (PROM)
ROM chip that can be programmed

programmer
a person who produces software according to a given specification

project architect/applications development manager
monitors and helps coordinate all software development activity with an emphasis on reducing duplication and enforcing standards

project dictionary
see data dictionary

project manager
a person assigned to a particular project to lead it for its duration

PROM blaster
device used to embed software into chips

proprietary systems

systems in which the hardware or software both are specific to their suppliers, making flexibility and adaptability difficult

protocol

the rules that govern the exchange of information within a network. They say how communication is to be established, what to do in case of an error and so on.

prototype

a system that is part of a solution developed to obtain feedback from users and make for a more interactive development cycle

random access memory (RAM)

chips on the motherboard that store programs and data so that the central processing unit can access them

rapid application development (RAD)

combines prototyping, computer-aided software engineering and joint application design in an iterative cycle until the users and developers are satisfied with the system designs

read-only memory (ROM)

chips on the motherboard that have instructions embedded in them, for example, for starting the system, carrying out diagnostics

real-time systems

systems that process transactions as soon as they are received

reduced instruction-set computer (RISC)

a type of chip that is optimised for a number of instructions. Complex instructions are rendered by combining simple instructions. RISC technology is used in workstations and Apple computers and is usually faster than complex instruction-set computer technology.

redundant arrays of inexpensive disks

method of improving system reliability and disk access speeds by distributing and sometimes replicating data over several disks instead of one

refresh

when a screen display changes, it is said to be refreshed. The higher the refresh rate the less the screen seems to flicker.

reintermediation

process in which intermediaries reposition themselves on the Web

relational database

system of database organsiation that groups data into relations or tables. Data are accessed using relationships among and within tables.

request for proposal (RFP)

an invitation to a vendor to prepare a bid for the supply of goods or services

reservation system

a transaction processing system that allows users to reserve hotel rooms, book air travel and so on

resolution

the clarity of a monitor determined by the total number of pixels and the density of pixels on the screen

return on investment (ROI)

a measure of cost effectiveness; more formally, the ratio of generated income divided by outgoing costs

reverse auction

where the customer makes an offer for a product stating how much they are prepared to pay, and the seller decides whether to accept it

reverse engineering

the practice of deriving specifications for software (and often firmware) from an existing, frequently undocumented, system

router

a device that can interconnect similar and dissimilar local area networks and similar wide area networks. Routers have a high degree of software intelligence and can choose the best route for communication when there are multiple paths. They can also handle several message streams, enabling (for example) several simultaneous Internet connections to be managed.

search engines

software systems located at websites that collect and order information from the Internet

single inline memory modules

subassembly of memory chips affixed to the motherboard

small-to-medium entity (SME)

most businesses are assumed to be small if they employ 19 or fewer people; the number required for a medium-sized enterprise is widely accepted to be fewer than 650. Changes in technology and economics have led to an increase in the number of SMEs worldwide.

social networking

websites that create links among users by encouraging participation

soft systems methodology (SSM)

a people-centred methodology for defining the problem and requirements of a system

software crisis

a term used in the 1970s when it was realised that the demand for software was increasing exponentially while the supply of software developers was increasing only linearly. This shortfall limited the amount of software that could be supplied.

software suite

a set of separate programs that may be purchased individually or as a bundle and that can work together and share information. Microsoft Office is a well-known example.

solutions architect

a person who elicits information and knowledge requirements throughout the organisation, consolidates and rationalises those needs and then provides infrastructure-based solutions. Solutions architects are especially useful in enterprise resource planning.

strategic driver

a force that enables the business to improve in relation to competitors

strategic plan

a map of actions to be taken that has been developed from the strategy

strategy

the planning and directing of actions to achieve overall objectives

structured English

a restricted English technique to clearly explain an organisational procedure

supply chain management

the practice of linking one's suppliers into core business processes. This usually involves the use of information systems to improve linkages between supplier and customer to facilitate ordering, payment and delivery.

switch

connects two or more network segments that use the same protocol, or individual users within the same network segment. Because switches provide synchronous communication and allow all ports to be in use at the same time, they make much more efficient use of bandwidth than hubs and allow applications such as video conferencing.

SWOT analysis

an assessment of the strengths and weaknesses, environmental opportunities of and threats to an organisation

system unit

the main box of a PC containing the motherboard, hard drive, DVD drive and so on; does not include the monitor, mouse, keyboard or peripheral devices

systemboard

another term for motherboard

systems analyst or **business analyst**

often the graduate entry position into the information systems industry. Involved with every aspect of the systems development lifecycle with the exception of programming

systems conversion

phase in the systems development lifecycle when the system is handed over to the users

systems design

phase in the systems development lifecycle when the features of the proposed system are defined in detail

systems development

the process of developing or building information systems

systems development lifecycle (SDLC)

a framework for developing information systems. Consists of the classical phases of analysis, design, implementation and maintenance; provides a logical and structured approach for building systems

systems manager/operations manager

the person responsible for the entire day-to-day running of the information systems division from an operational perspective

systems software

software that controls the underlying resources of the computer, manages file systems, drives devices and so on. and that provides a convenient interface between the user and the hardware. Microsoft Windows is a well-known example.

telecommuter

a person who works away from the company, at home or on the road, and who uses communications technology to access corporate systems

testing

the stage in developing systems when components, such as software, are checked for correctness and reliability

thin client

a PC in a client–server network that downloads most of its application software from a server as required. Thin clients are cheaper and easier to manage than fat clients.

time division multiplexing
a system of 'turn taking' to control the use of a communication medium. Transmitting parties are given a time slot during which they have exclusive use of the medium. It is most common in (but not exclusive to) digital transmission systems.

transaction
a group of instructions that are grouped together for atomic execution, that is, the entire group of instructions either executes or does not — there are no half measures

transaction processing system
a system that executes transactions in a reliable manner and records their details

turnkey system
an off-the-shelf ready-to-roll system for a particular industry segment, such as the restaurant trade

unallocated cost centre
a system of accounting in which the information systems function is considered to be an organisational cost. The information systems manager often receives a one-line budget for the financial year and no further budget transfers or charges are made.

uniform resource locator (URL)
a website address

universal serial bus (USB 2.0)
a newer PC port standard, that is much faster than older serial and parallel ports. It is used for webcams, flash memory, scanners and other applications that require a high transfer rate.

Unix
an older example of system software that is well established and available for most computer platforms. Its PC derivative, Linux, is much less demanding in terms of hardware requirements than products such as Windows. Unix is an open system in which the source code is available to anyone who wishes to develop programs for the Unix (or Linux) platform, in contrast to systems such as Windows that are proprietary.

upper computer-aided software engineering (CASE) tools
CASE tools that focus on the early stages of the systems development lifecycle, especially the analysis and design phases

usability
a measure of how readily a user can interact with a system

value-added reseller
a person or company that takes an existing software product and adds extra functionality to it in order to increase its value to a client. Many software companies have a list of approved value-added resellers.

value-chain analysis
examination of the business as an input–output chain

vertical software
software that is targeted to a particular function or narrow market sector in business, that is, software that could not be widely used, as word processing software is

very large scale integration (VLSI)
refers to microchips having millions of components on the same piece of silicon, a vast improvement on the previous integrated circuit technology

viral marketing
a form of marketing in which advertisements are emailed from person to person without intervention from the company that created the product they advertise

virtual organisations
structures that are made up of different companies or individuals that come together to complete certain tasks

virtual private networks (VPNs)
include both public and private resources. A company can lease a bundle of circuits and configure the VPN on a needs basis so that some traffic flows over the public carrier and some on the private network. As can a virtual local area network, it may be thought of as a network within a network.

virtuoso programmer
a specialist and highly talented programmer. For example, these people may rewrite critical portions of software to improve the performance of a system.

virus infection
in this context it means a software program designed to damage or infect other files or consume system resources

vision statement
a definition of the main purpose of the business

voice over IP (VOIP)
a way to converse over an Internet connection, even while browsing web pages

Von Neumann machine
> the architecture used by most modern computers; relies on a single processor and data and programs being stored in random access memory

web manager/administrator
> person who manages websites. Often controls the company intranet and performs web site design.

wrapper engineering
> 'wrapping' old systems in newer, more friendly systems, providing a more convenient interface to users and other systems

XML (extensible markup language)
> allows the display of text and data in a browser like hypertext markup language but also provides a context and a structure for creating a knowledge structure

Index

A

Accenture, Bargain Finder   58
acceptable use policies   124–5
accountability (email content)   351
accountancy, and information systems   23–4
ad hoc reports   81
Adobe Acrobat   46, 60
ADSL *see* asymmetric digital subscriber line
adversarial testing   142
advertising, on the Internet   262–4
AG Edwards (company)
    project management   248
agile software development   200
AI *see* artificial intelligence
alliance profiles   218
allocated cost centre model   139
alternative solutions phase
    systems development   174
AM *see* amplitude modulation
amplitude modulation (AM)   100
analog communication   101–3
analog information   99–100
analog signalling   100–1
analysis phase
    systems development   171–2
analytical skills
    systems analysts   168–9
Andhra Pradesh
    e-procurement   271
AP Consulting Group   226–7
Apple   49–50
Apple Macintosh   49
application-level firewalls   124
application program interfaces   150
application service providers (ASPs)   154–6
applications development managers   142
applications software   40–4, 51–3
    defined   39
    related to systems software and hardware   56
arithmetic and logic unit   319
ARPAnet   282
artificial intelligence (AI)   57
ASPs *see* application service providers
assembly languages   35
associations, as information sources   342
asymmetric digital subscriber line (ADSL)   103
asynchronous communication   88, 103
auctions on the Internet   264

audio spotlight   324
authentication   239–40

B

Babbage, Charles   33
backbone networks   108
backing up   144, 238
bandwidth   102
Bargain Finder *see* Accenture, Bargain Finder
baseband   100
BASIC   312
batch systems   70, 326
batching enquiries   348
behavioural methodologies   195
benevolent testing   142
BigDog   112
biometric authentication   239
blade servers   316–17
    Burbank   330
Bluetooth   110–11
boundary roles   229
BPR *see* business process re-engineering
BQI (company), ERP system   83
brand image
    in website design   293
broadband   101
    Internet access   119
    usage   25
Brown-Forman Corporation
    enterprise resource planning (ERP)   220
browsers   52, 283
Burbank (California)   329–30
buses (computers)   320
business
    pressures and responses   20–1
    trends   11–12
business analysts   142–3
business engineering   151–2
business-level strategy   211
business models   261
business process re-engineering (BPR)   14, 99, 212, 218–19
business-to-business (B2B) e-business   257–8, 267–8
business-to-consumer (B2C) e-business   256–7
buyers, website users   289
bytes   74, 317
    calculating time   73

C

c-commerce *see* collaborative commerce
cabling, LANs   114
caches   320
capability maturity model, software   248–9
car parking facilities
  automation, case study   28–9
CASE *see* computer-aided software engineering
catalogue knowledge   69
cathode ray tubes (CRTs)   324
CDMA *see* code division multiple access
CDPD *see* cellular digital packet data
Ceedo   79
cellular communication systems   109–10
cellular digital packet data (CDPD)   109
censorware applications   124–5
central processing unit (CPU)   319
centralised organisation
  information systems   136–7
CGI proxies   125
channel conflict   274
charts
  use in project management   245–7
cheathouse.com   13
chief information officers (CIOs)   137
  job description   140–1
  strategic role   208
  see also information systems, management
chief technology officers, (CTOs)   143–4
Christmas-tree effect   296
CIOs *see* chief information officers
circuit switching   104
CISCs *see* complex instruction-set computers
classes
  object-oriented methodology   196
client–server architecture   121–2
  enterprisewide   151–2
CMS *see* content management systems
coaxial cables   114
COBIT   334, 352
COBOL   35, 312
code division multiple access (CDMA)   109
code of ethics and conduct
  Hong Kong Computer Society   354
cognitive maps   344–5
collaborative commerce (c-commerce)   258
collaborative e-business   266
colleagues, as information sources   342
colour, in website design   296
Colours of Spain   305–7

communication
  categories   88
  proliferation   19
  skills   343
communication modes   104
communication skills
  systems analysts   168
communications media   105–7
  comparisons   107
communications networks   107–13
  defined   107
  future developments   127
  security   123–6, 238
communications software   47
  and step-lock cycle   50–1
competitive forces   15–18
competitive forces model (Porter)   15–16, 212, 213
competitive strategic analysis   213–16
  value-chain analysis   219–20
compilers   35
complex instruction-set computer (CISC)   322
complex web applications   288
componentisation   150
computer-aided software engineering (CASE)   143
  role in systems development   173
computer rage syndrome   344
computers
  architecture   317–21
  in current use   313–17
  history   311–13
conferencing   351
consistency, in website design   294
consumer-generated media   301
consumer-to-consumer e-business   257
content management systems (CMS), Kromann
     Reumart   203–4
context diagrams   191
continuity planning   236–40
Control Objectives for Information and related
     Technologies   334, 352
control unit   319
convergence   17–18, 118
Coordinated Universal Time (UTC)   72–3
Corel   42
corporate goals
  alignment of information systems   217–18, 334
corporate-level strategy   211
corporate strategy   209–12
  components   210
  levels   211

cost centre models   138–9
CPU *see* central processing unit
creative destruction   274
creativity   233, 343
CRM *see* customer relationship management
CRT Group, systems integration   176
CRTs (cathode ray tubes)   324
CTOs *see* chief technology officers
culture
    attributes (Hofstede)   232–3
    see also organisational culture
custom software   40, 54, 55
Customer Carewords   301
customer relationship management (CRM)
    software   156, 158
    systems   207
        case study   250–1
        Westralian Insurance Brokers   337–8
customer service, on the Web   266–7
customers, websites *see* online customers
customisable software   40, 54, 55, 175–6
customised software *see* customisable software

D

data
    analysis   185–8
    compared with information and knowledge   3–4
    defined   3
    entry errors   78–9
    hierarchy   74
    mining   82
    modelling   182
    normalisation   185–8
    organisation   75–9
    protection   327
    related to management levels and tasks   68
data dictionaries   74, 173
    entries   192–3
data entities   183–4
data-flow diagrams (DFDs)   172, 173, 188–92
data privacy   240
data warehouses   75
    and decision support systems   82
database administrators (DBAs)   141
database management systems (DBMSs)   73–5
databases   14, 73–9
    defined   73
    design   174–5
    types   75–9
datamarts   75, 82
DBAs *see* database administrators

DBMSs *see* database management systems
decision support systems   81–2
    and data warehouses   82
decision tables   193
denial of service (DOS) attacks   123
dense wave division multiplexing   107
design phase
    systems development   174–6
design prototyping   199
development teams   240–2
    blending skills   241
    web projects   281
DFDs *see* data flow diagrams
digital audio tape storage   326
digital communication   101–3
digital content   271
digital format, use   344–5
digital information   99–100
digital signalling   100
DIOs *see* divisional information officers
direct conversion   178
disintermediation   274–5
dissatisfied customers, websites   290
distributed organisation
    information systems   137–8
divisional information officers (DIOs)   137
document management software   52
document publishing systems   288
DOS attacks   123
Drucker, Peter, three waves of knowledge   2–3
dual-core processors   318
dynamic web applications   288

E

e-business   18, 254–78
    defined   254
    global strategies   275–6
    models   261–2
    opportunities   254–6
    strategic concepts   273–6
    as strategic driver   259–61
    types of systems   256–9
E cycles   321
e-government   273
e-marketplaces   258, 268–70
    classification   269–70
    problems and benefits   270
e-procurement   271
eBay   264–5
economic feasibility   170–1
EDI *see* electronic data interchange

EERP *see* extended ERP systems
effective design
  websites   293
electrical media   106
electronic data interchange (EDI)   69, 258
email   350–2
  efficient use   348
  software   52
  use of intelligent agents   58
employees
  ethical issues   237
  motivating   235
encryption   112, 118, 126
  extranets   121
  reverse proxies   125
enterprise application integration   151
enterprise architecture
  vs service-oriented architecture   225
enterprise resource planning (ERP)   24–5, 80
  advantages   151–2
  BQI   83
  Brown-Forman Corporation   220
  extended systems   152–3
  and improvements in value chains   220
  introduction   157
  and SMEs   154
  Toy Time   160–1
enterprisewide client-server architecture   151–2
entity relationship diagrams (ERDs)   172, 182–4
environmental scanning   215, 259
  on the Web   267
eraseable PROM (EPROM)   325
ERDs *see* entity relationship diagrams
ergonomics   355–6
ERP *see* enterprise resource planning
Ethernet   111, 114, 115, 116
ethical behaviour, employees   237
ethics   352–5
event-driven reports   81
evolutionary conversion   179
executive information systems   85–6
executive support, for projects   240
expansion slots   320
expert systems   83–5
explicit knowledge   90
expressions of interest
  supply of hardware   331–2
eXtended Copy Protection   44
extended ERP systems (EERP)   152
extensible markup language (XML)   286

external integration   150
extranets   121

F

face-to-face interface   323
failsoft   113
fast circuit switching   105
faster computers   322–3
fat clients   51
feasibility phase
  systems development   170–1
feasibility prototyping   199
feasibility studies   170–1
fifth-generation languages   37
file creation, groupware   89
firewalls   123–4
FireWire ports   320
first-generation computers   311
first-generation languages   35
first normal form   185–6
five competitive forces *see* competitive forces model
flash memory   327
flexible manufacturing systems (FMS)   11, 12
  Toy Time   160–1
floating point operations per second   318
flow of content
  websites   294–5
FM *see* frequency modulation
FMS *see* flexible manufacturing systems
form design, for websites   297–8
FORTRAN   35, 312
forward engineering   149
fourth-generation computers   313
fourth-generation languages   36–7
  and databases   75
freeware   42–3
frequency division multiplexing   101
frequency modulation (FM)   100
friends, as information sources   342
full duplex communication mode   104
functional-level strategy   211–12
funding   138–9

G

GaAs chips   34
Gantt charts   245–6
general ledger systems   71–2
geosynchronous earth orbit (GEO)   116
gigabytes   317
gigahertz   318
global strategies   275–6

Google   86–7
graphical user interface (GUI)   46, 47–8
    Apple Macintosh   49
graphics, in website design   296
group conferencing   351
group decision support systems   82
grouping, website design   295
groupware   87–92
    and knowledge management   90–1
    problems   90
guard bands   102
GUI *see* graphical user interface

H

half duplex communication mode   104
handheld computers   315
hardcopy   323
hardware
    acquisition   176, 330–3
    contrasted with software   37–8
    related to systems and applications software   56
    standards   333
    see also infrastructure
hardwire media
    compared with softwire media   105–6, 107
Harley-Davidson   14
help desks   334–5
hierarchical databases   75, 76
high-definition TV   324–5
high-level languages   35–6
Hofstede, Geert
    attributes of culture   232–3
Hollerith, Hermann   33
Hong Kong Computer Society
    code of ethics and conduct   354
horizontal software   40
    applications   51–3
    evaluation   52–3
    groupware   88
HTML   286
    text sizes and fonts   295
HTTP *see* hypertext transfer protocol
hubs   115
human–computer interaction   293
hybrid organisation
    information systems   138
hyperlinks   283
hypertext   118, 259, 282, 283
hypertext markup language (HTML)   286
hypertext transfer protocol (HTTP)   283, 284

I

I cycles   321
IAs *see* intelligent agents
icons, in website design   296–7
ICs *see* integrated circuits
implementation phase
    systems development   177–9
implementation prototyping   199
individualism/collectivism   233
Industrial Revolution   2
information
    compared with data and knowledge   3–4
    defined   3
    gathering
        systems development   180–1
    management, use of intelligent agents   58
information age   341
information architecture   216–17
information engineering   195
information gathering   341–2
information overload   346–50
    case study   357–8
    groupware   90
information processing skills   342–3
information revolution   6–7
information systems
    as a study   23–4
    alignment with business goals   217–18, 334
    architecture
        defined   136
        see also information architecture
    benefits   21–2
    common problems   172
    defined   6
    functions   8
    history   6–8
    and information technology   9–10
    infrastructure *see* infrastructure
    management   10–11, 229–51
        communication systems   229–30
        development of boundary roles   229
        effective working environment   230
        of information systems professionals   231
        internal and external relationships   231
        of operations   233–6
        responsibilities   229
    methodologies   194–5
        examples   195–8

organisation
  centralised   136–7
  defined   136
  distributed   137–8
  hybrid   138
and other disciplines   9–11
planning   169–70
as strategic driver   208, 259–60
strategic planning   206–25
visions   2
information technology (IT)
  alignment   217–18, 334
  experimentation   346
  governance   333–5, 352–3
  impact on work   14, 255
  and information systems   9–10
  personal use   343–6
  plans   215–16
  as strategic driver   208, 259–60
  see also infrastructure
infrastructure   310–38
  defined   136, 310
  integration   151
infusion profiles   218
innovation   233, 234
input devices   321–2
integrated circuits (ICs)   313
integrated software   41–2, 52
integrators   53
intelligent agents (IAs)   56–9
  applications   58–9
  the future   59
  software development   58–9
intelligent switches   126
intercepting proxies   125
interconnection devices   115
interface cards   114
internal integration   150
internal users, websites   290
Internet   117–18
  access   119–20
    policies   238
  advertising on   262–4
  auctions   264
  browsers   52, 283
  developments   255
  global marketing   275–6
  history   282
  impact on business   254–6
  marketing on   262–4

social networking   256, 297
  as source of information   342
  see also e-business; World Wide Web
interpersonal skills
  systems analysts   168
interpreters   35–6
intranets   120–1, 259, 272
  hospitals   258
Iridium project   117
IT see information technology

J

Jacquard, Joseph Marie   33
JAD see joint application design
Java applets   287
  security risks   238
Java (programming language)   286–7
JIT see just-in-time
job descriptions   139–44
joint application design (JAD)   164, 181
just-in-time (JIT) delivery   11–12

K

knowledge   69
  compared with data and information   3–4
  defined   3, 5
  three waves   2–3
knowledge economy   3, 341
  development   19
knowledge management   85
  and learning organisations   223–4
  related to groupware   90–1
Kromann Reumart, content management
    systems   203–4

L

language, websites   290
LANs see local area networks
laptop computers   38–9
layout, website design   294
LCDs see liquid crystal displays
learning organisations   222–3
  and knowledge management   223–4
LEDs see light-emitting diodes
legacy systems   149–50
LEO see low earth orbit
libraries   342
light-emitting diodes (LEDs)   106
Linux   50, 60
liquid crystal displays (LCDs)   324
LISP   35, 312

local area networks (LANs)   108
   administration   141
   compared with WANs   112
   optical fibres   106
   packet switching   105
   switch technologies   104
   technology   114–16
Lovelace, Ada Byron, Countess   33, 53
low earth orbit (LEO)   117
lower CASE tools   173

M

m-commerce *see* mobile commerce
m-services *see* mobile services
machine code   35
machine cycles   321
macrocells   109
magnetic disk storage   326
magnetic tape storage   325–6
mainframe computers   311, 314
maintenance   179
MAN *see* materials as needed
management
   groupware   89
   and information systems   10–11, 24
management information systems   79–83
   strategic plans   216–17
management levels
   related to data and tasks   68
management reporting systems   80–1
MANs *see* metropolitan area networks
market entry costs   13
marketing
   and information systems   23
   on the Internet   262–4
masculinity/femininity metaphor   232–3
materials as needed (MAN)   121
materials requirements planning   24
medium earth orbit (MEO)   117
meetings, efficient use   348
megabytes   317
member customers   289
memory capacity, measurement   317–19
mentors   230
MEO *see* medium earth orbit
metadata   74
metaphors, in website design   296–7
methodologies   7
   defined   194
   systems development   194–8
metropolitan area networks (MANs)   112–13

microcells   109
microcomputers   314–15
Microsoft   49–50
   integrated software   41–2
   Internet browser   42–3
millions of instructions per second   318
mindmaps   344–5
minicomputers   314
MIPS   318
mission statements   211
   Woodside Petroleum   209, 217
mobile agents   90
mobile commerce (m-commerce)   284–5
mobile services (m-services)   346
modulation   100
monomode fibres   107
Moore's law   328, 330
motherboards   318, 319
motivation, of employees   235
Mozilla   42, 43
multimedia   345
   interfaces   169
multimode fibres   106
multiprocessor systems   322–3
MySQL   53

N

NAT *see* network address translation
national culture   232
navigation, websites   297
Negroponte, Nicholas   38–9
Netscape   42–3, 118
network address translation (NAT)   125
network administrators   141
network computers *see* thin clients
network databases   75, 76
network interface cards (NICs)   114
network managers   141
network operating systems   115–16
networks *see* communications networks
NICs *see* network interface cards
Nielsen, Jakob   298–9
nonmember customers   289
nonprocedural languages *see* fourth-generation
   languages

O

object modelling   197
object-oriented methodology   195–8
object-oriented programming (OOP) 36
offloading problems 332–3

offshore partnering   221
OLEDs *see* organic light-emitting diodes
online analytical processing   82
online auctions   264
online communities   299–300
online customers   289–90, 300–1
OOP *see* object-oriented programming
open source software, vs proprietary software
      59–61
open systems   45–6, 149–50
operational feasibility   170
operational management   235
operations managers   141
optical disk storage   326–7
optical fibres   106
   LAN connections   114
order-entry systems   70, 71
organic light-emitting diodes (OLEDs)   324
organisational culture   232–3
organisational goals *see* corporate goals
organisational learning   223–4
organisational management   262
organisational politics   232
organisational strategy *see* corporate strategy
organisational structure   262
outcome focus   348
output devices   323–5
outsourcing   144–8
   benefits   221
   considerations   146–7
   current practice   148
   defined   144
   as information systems strategy   220–1
   pros and cons   145–6

P

P & A Construction (NZ)
   monitoring projects   244
package-specific intelligent agents   58
packaged software   54, 55
packet-level firewalls   124
packet switching   104–5
pandora.com   150
PANs *see* personal area networks
paradigms   3, 7
   new software   36
parallel conversion   178
paramagnetic limits   327
Parcelhouse   4–5
parking, case study   28–9

PCs   314–15
   buying   328–30
   configuration   318, 319
PDAs *see* personal digital assistants
performance measurement   353
personal area networks (PANs)   108
personal computers   314–15
   buying   328–30
   configuration   318, 319
personal digital assistants (PDAs)   315, 349–50
personal ethics   352–5
personal information systems   343–6
   development   349–50
   related to information overload   346–50
PERT charts   246–7
pervasive networking   111–12
phased conversion   179
physical security   237–8
pilot conversion   179
pixels   324
planning skills   342
plinking   285
plug and play   114
PMI *see* Project Management Institute
podcasts   301
point-of-sales (POS) systems   70–1
politics, in organisations   232
Porter, Michael, competitive forces model   15–16,
      212, 213
POS systems *see* point-of-sales (POS) systems
power distance   232
primary storage   325
problem-solving skills   343
   systems analysts   168–9
procedural languages   36–7
process modelling   188–92
processors   322–3
   power   328
   speeds, measurement   317–19
professional associations
   as information sources   342
professional ethics   352–5
profit centre model   139
Program Evaluation and Review Technique *see*
      PERT charts
programmable ROM   325
programmers   143
programming
   simplification   36
   see also software

programs, running   320–1
project architects   142
project dictionaries *see* data dictionaries
project management   240–2
  AG Edwards (company)   248
  corrective action   245
  and scheduling   52
  use of charts   245–7
Project Management Institute (PMI)   242
project managers   142
projects
  assessment   241
  and organisational requirements   241
  progress monitoring   243–5
   P & A Construction (NZ)   244
  realistic targets   241
  risk assessment   242–3
PROM blasters 325
proprietary software   148
  vs open source software   59–61
proprietary systems   43, 46, 148–9
protocols   105
prototypes   198–9
proxy servers   124–5

R
RAD *see* rapid application development
radio   106
radio frequency identity *see* RFID
RAM (random access memory)   319–20, 325
rapid application development (RAD)   164, 199
read-only memory (ROM)   319, 325
ready-to-roll systems *see* turnkey systems
real-time systems   70
reduced instruction-set computers (RISCs)   322
redundant arrays of inexpensive disks   326
refresh rates   324
reintermediation   275
relational databases   77
Renault   49
requests for proposal (RFPs)   331
requirements phase
  systems development   172–3
requirements prototyping   199
research skills   341–2
reservation systems   71
resolution   324
resource-based strategies   222–4
resource management   353
retailing, on the Web   264–5

return on investment (ROI)
  applications software   40–1
  intranets   120
reverse auctions   264
reverse engineering   149
reverse proxies   125
RFIDs   12
  in admission tickets   22
  in soccer   22
RFPs *see* requests for proposal
RISCs *see* reduced instruction-set computers
risk analysis   237
risk assessment   242
risk management   353
risk response   243
Robotic Parking   28–9
ROI *see* return on investment
ROM *see* read-only memory
routers   115, 126

S
satellites   116–17
scheduled reports   81
scheduling *see* project management, and scheduling
schemas   74
Schriver, Jens   13
scientific management   2–3
SDLC *see* systems development, lifecycle
search engines   86–7, 283
second-generation computers   311–13
second-generation languages   35
Second Life   19–20
second normal form   186–7
secondary storage devices   325–7
security   236–40
  emails   351–2
  networks   123–6
  risk analysis   237
senior executive support
  for projects   240
service-oriented architecture
  enterprise architecture   225
SHAMAN (Strategic Hospital and Medication
  Automation Network)   258
shareware   42–3
simplex communication mode   104
SingHealth
  information systems management   147
single inline memory modules   325
small systems, lifecycle   179–80

small-to-medium entities (SMEs) 11
  enterprise resource planning 154
  market entry costs 13
social networking
  on the Web 256, 297
societies, as information sources 342
soft systems methodology (SSM) 195, 200–1
softcopy 324–5
software
  acquisition 176
  capability maturity model 248–9
  competition 47–8
  contemporary 39–47
  contrasted with hardware 37–8
  generations 34–7
  history 32–4
  reuse 36
  security 238–40
software crisis 36
software engineers 143
software suites 41–2, 52
softwire media
  compared with hardwire media 105–6, 107
solutions architects 141–2
Sony, copyright protection 44
SPEED 285
  email 350–1
  processors 317–19
spreadsheets 214
SQL (Structured Query Language) 37
SSM see soft systems methodology
stand-alone software packages 41
static document publishing systems 288
step-lock cycle 47
  and communications software
    50–1
storage area networks 109
strategic alignment 353
strategic alliances 129
strategic analysis 212–21
  choice of approach 212–13
strategic drivers
  e-business 259–61
  information systems 208, 259–60
  information technology 208, 259–60
Strategic Hospital and Medication Automation
  Network see SHAMAN
strategic planning
  information systems 206–25
  role 209–12

strategic plans 206
strategy
  defined 206
  e-business 262–73
  importance 206–8
strategy-driven approaches
  compared with technology driven
    approaches 261
structured English 193–4
Structured Query Language 37
subschemas 74
subsystem diagrams 191
supercomputers 314
supply chain management 152, 153
surfers 289
Swire 46
switch technologies 104
SWOT analysis 212, 213–14
Symantec 49
synchronous communication 88, 103–4
system units 319–20
systemboards see motherboards
systems, defined 5–6
systems analysts 142–3, 164
  information gathering 180
  skills requirements 168–9
systems conversion 178–9
systems design 174–6
systems development
  lifecycle (SDLC) 164–7
    small systems 179–80
  methodologies 194–5
    examples 195–8
  phases 169–80
  tasks 169–80
systems integration 150
  CRT Group 176
systems managers 141
systems modelling 181–94
systems software 44–6
  defined 39
  related to application software and hardware 56

T
tacit knowledge 90
  and groupware 91
TCP/IP 105, 122–3
teamwork 343
technical feasibility 170
technical skills
  systems analysts 169

technology
  adoption stages 236
  convergence 17–18, 118
  management 25
  proliferation 19
  related to business trends 11–12
  related to competition 21–2
technology-driven approaches
  compared with strategy-driven approaches 261
telecommuters 14
terabytes 317
Tesco
  sale of antivirus software 85
testing 178
text, website design 295–6
thin clients 51, 315
third-generation computers 313
third-generation languages 35–6
  and data definition 75
third normal form 187–8
three waves of knowledge (Drucker) 2–3
time division multiplexing 100
Toy Time 160–1
training officers 144
transaction-processing systems 69
transactions 69–70, 71–2
transmission control/Internet protocol 122–3
transmission control protocol/Internet protocol 105
trust, building online 301–2
Turnitin.com 18
turnkey systems 71
twisted pairs 114

U

ultra-wideband (UWB) 102
umbrella cells 109
UML *see* Unified Modelling Language
unallocated cost centre model 138–9
uncertainty avoidance 232
Unified Modelling Language (UML) 198
uniform resource locators (URLs) *see* websites,
  addresses
universal serial buses (USBs) 320
Unix 45
upper CASE tools 173
URLs *see* websites, addresses
US Patent and Trademark Office
  IT plan 215–16
usability
  computer systems 293
  websites 298–9

USBs *see* universal serial buses
useless information 347
user interfaces
  use of intelligent agents 58
  see also graphical user interface
users, websites 289
UTC *see* Coordinated Universal Time
utility profiles 218
UWB *see* ultra-wideband

V

validation of bids 331–2
value-added resellers 53
value-chain analysis 212, 219–20
value delivery 353
Vaucanson, Jacques de 32–3
vertical software 40
very large scale integration 313
video podcasting 301
viral marketing 301
virtual networks 115, 126
virtual organisations 272–3
virtual private networks (VPNs) 108, 126
virtualisation 316
virtuoso programmers 143
virus infection 238
vision statements 209
VOIP (voice over IP) 127–8
Volkswagen 21–2
von Neumann architecture, problems 321
von Neumann machines 317
VPNs *see* virtual private networks

W

W3C *see* World Wide Web Consortium
WANs *see* wide area networks
waterfall methodology 167
wearable computers 315
Web 118, 282
  accessibility issues 292–3
  customer service 266–7
  retaining on 264–5
  selling services on 266
  technologies 282–7
  use by Colours of Spain 305–7
  see also Internet
web addresses *see* websites, addresses
web administrators 142
web applications 281–2
  feasibility 287
  project development

complexity   287–9
design considerations   291–9
scope   287–8
teams   281
user definition   289–90
web authoring tools   285–7
web browsers   283
web client programming languages   286
web commerce
feasibility   287
project development
complexity   287–9
design considerations   291–9
scope   287–8
teams   281
user definition   289–90
web managers   142
web proxies   124–5
website functionality   261
websites   281, 284
addresses   283, 284
attracting visitors   299–302
cultural considerations   290
customers   289–90, 300–1
design, evolution   293–9
design considerations   291–9
effectiveness, measurement   303–4
language considerations   290

navigation   297
quality measurement   302
users   289
Westralian Insurance brokers (WIB)   337–8
Westsea Airport   277–8
WIB *see* Westralian Insurance brokers
wide area networks (WANs)   108
administration   141
circuit switching   104
compared with LANs   112
wikis   256
wireless networking   111
wisdom   68, 69
Woodside Petroleum
mission statement   209, 217
workplace layout   356
workstations   314
World Wide Web Consortium (W3C)   291
World Wide Web (WWW) *see* Web
wrapper engineering   150
WWW *see* World Wide Web

X

XCP *see* eXtended Copy Protection
XML (extensible markup language)   286

Y

zoning, website design   295